Financial Risk Manager (FRM®) Part I
Foundations of Risk Management

Second Custom Edition for
Global Association of Risk Professionals
2012

Pearson Learning Solutions, 501 Boylston Street, Suite 900, Boston, MA 02116
A Pearson Education Company
www.pearsoned.com

Printed in the United States of America

4 5 6 7 8 9 10 V092 16 15 14 13 12

000200010271268363

RG/JG

ISBN 10: 1-256-40675-9
ISBN 13: 978-1-256-40675-4

Contents

2012 FRM Committee Members

The Need for Risk Management 1

Excerpt is Chapter 1 of Value at Risk: The New Benchmark for Managing Financial Risk, *3rd Edition, by Philippe Jorion.*

Learning Objectives

After completing this reading, FRM Candidates should be able to:

- Define risk and describe some of the major sources of risk.
- Differentiate between business and financial risks and give examples of each.
- Relate significant market events of the past several decades to the growth of the risk management industry.
- Describe the functions and purposes of financial institutions as they relate to financial risk management.
- Define what a derivative contract is and how it differs from a security.

- Define financial risk management.
- Define value-at-risk (VaR) and describe how it is used in risk management.
- Describe the advantages and disadvantages of VaR relative to other risk management tools such as stop-loss limits, notional limits, and exposure limits.
- Compare and contrast valuation and risk management, using VaR as an example.
- Define and describe the four major types of financial risks: market, liquidity, credit, and operational.

All of life is the management of risk, not its elimination.

—Walter Wriston, former chairman of Citicorp

Corporations are in the business of managing risks. The most adept ones succeed; others fail. Whereas some firms accept risks passively, others attempt to create a competitive advantage by judicious exposure to risks. In both cases, however, the risks should be monitored carefully because of their potential for damage.

This chapter motivates the need for careful management of financial risks. The first section describes the types of risks facing corporations and argues that financial risks have increased sharply over the last 30 years. The need to hedge against these risks had led to the exponential growth of derivatives markets, which are described in the second section. Derivatives are very efficient instruments to hedge against, or speculate on, financial risks. Used without proper controls, however, they have the potential for creating large losses. Thus they should be used only with good risk management. The third section explains the evolution of risk management tools, which has led to the widespread use of *value at risk* (VaR) as a summary measure of market risk. Finally, the various types of financial risks are discussed.

FINANCIAL RISKS

What exactly is risk? *Risk* can be defined as the volatility of unexpected outcomes, which can represent the value of assets, equity, or earnings. Firms are exposed to various types of risks, which can be classified broadly into business and financial risks.

Business risks are those which the corporation assumes willingly to create a competitive advantage and add to value for shareholders. Business risk includes the *business decisions* companies make and the *business environment* in which they operate. Business decisions include investment decisions, product-development choices, marketing strategies, and the choice of the company's organizational structure. This includes *strategic risk*, which is broad in nature and reflects decisions made at the level of the company's board or top executives. The business environment includes competition and broad *macroeconomic*

risks. Judicious exposure to business risk is a *core competency* of all business activity.

Other risks usually are classified into *financial risks*, which relate to possible losses owing to financial market activities. For example, losses can occur as a result of interest-rate movements or defaults on financial obligations. For industrial corporations, exposure to financial risks can be optimized carefully so that firms can concentrate on what they do best—manage exposure to business risks.

In contrast, the primary function of financial institutions is to manage financial risks actively. The purpose of financial institutions is to assume, intermediate, or advise on financial risks. These institutions realize that they must measure financial risk as precisely as possible in order to control and price them properly. Understanding risk means that financial managers can consciously plan for the consequences of adverse outcomes and, by so doing, be better prepared for the inevitable uncertainty.

Change: The Only Constant

The recent growth of the risk management industry can be traced directly to the increased volatility of financial markets since the early 1970s. Consider the following developments:

- The fixed exchange rate system broke down in 1971, leading to flexible and volatile exchange rates.
- The oil-price shocks starting in 1973 were accompanied by high inflation and wild swings in interest rates.
- On Black Monday, October 19, 1987, U.S. stocks collapsed by 23 percent, wiping out $1 trillion in capital.
- In the bond debacle of 1994, the Federal Reserve, after having kept interest rates low for three years, started a series of six consecutive interest-rate hikes that erased $1.5 trillion in global capital.
- The Japanese stock-price bubble finally deflated at the end of 1989, sending the Nikkei Index from 39,000 to 17,000 three years later. A total of $2.7 trillion in capital was lost, leading to an unprecedented financial crisis in Japan.
- The Asian turmoil of 1997 wiped out about three-fourths of the dollar capitalization of equities in Indonesia, Korea, Malaysia, and Thailand.
- The Russian default in August 1998 sparked a global financial crisis that culminated in the near failure of a big hedge fund, Long Term Capital Management.

• On September 11, 2001, a terrorist attack destroyed the World Trade Center in New York City, freezing financial markets for six days. In addition to the horrendous human cost, the U.S. stock market lost $1.7 trillion in value.

The only constant across these events is their unpredictability. Each time, market observers were aghast at the rapidity of the changes, which created substantial financial losses. Financial risk management provides a partial protection against such sources of risk.

To illustrate the forces of change in the last 40 years, Figures 1-1 to 1-4 display movements in exchange rates, interest rates, oil prices, and stock prices since 1960. Figure 1-1 displays movements in the U.S. dollar against the Deutsche mark (now the euro), the Japanese yen, and the British pound. Over this period, the dollar has lost about two-thirds of its value against the yen and mark; the yen/dollar rate has slid from 361 to close to 100, and the mark/dollar rate has fallen from 4.2 to 1.5. On the other hand, the dollar has appreciated by more than 50 percent against the pound over the same period. In between, the dollar has reached dizzying heights, just to fall to unprecedented lows, in the process creating wild swings in the competitive advantage of nations—and nightmares for unhedged firms.

Figure 1-2 also shows that bond yields have fluctuated widely in the 1980s, reflecting creeping inflationary pressures spreading throughout national economies. These were created in the 1960s by the United States, trying to finance the Vietnam War, as well as a domestic government-assistance program, and spread to other countries through the rigid mechanism of fixed-exchange-rates. Eventually, the persistently high U.S. inflation led to the breakdown of the fixed exchange rate system and a sharp fall in the value of the dollar. In October 1979, the Federal Reserve forcefully attempted to squash inflation. Interest rates shot up immediately, became more volatile, and led to a sustained appreciation of the dollar. Bond yields increased from 4 percent in the early 1960s

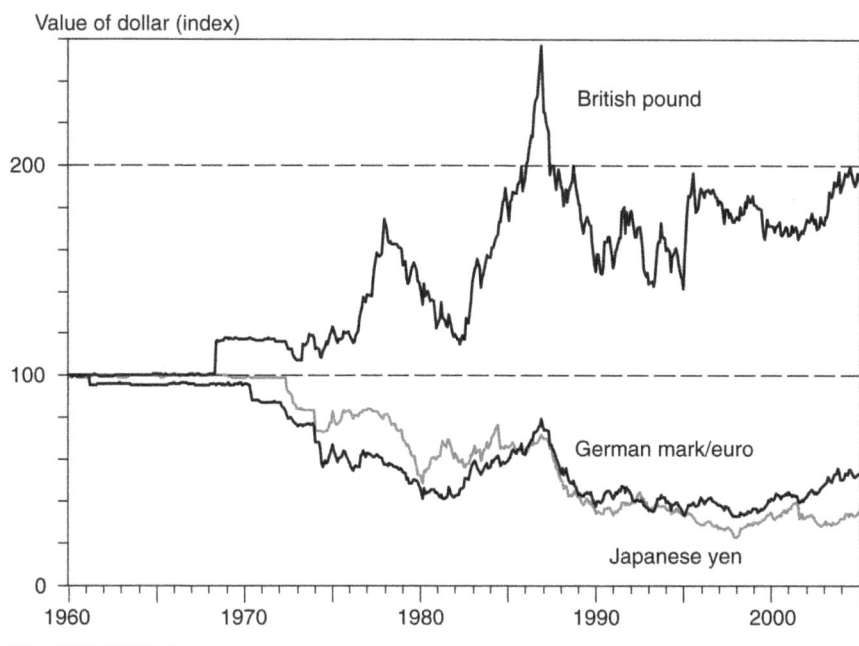

FIGURE 1-1 Movements in the dollar.

FIGURE 1-2 Movements in U.S. interest rates.

to 15 percent at the height of the monetarist squeeze on the money supply, thereby creating havoc in savings and loans that had made long-term loans, primarily for housing, using short-term funding.

Figure 1-3 shows that oil prices also have fluctuated widely. The sharp oil price increases of the 1970s seem

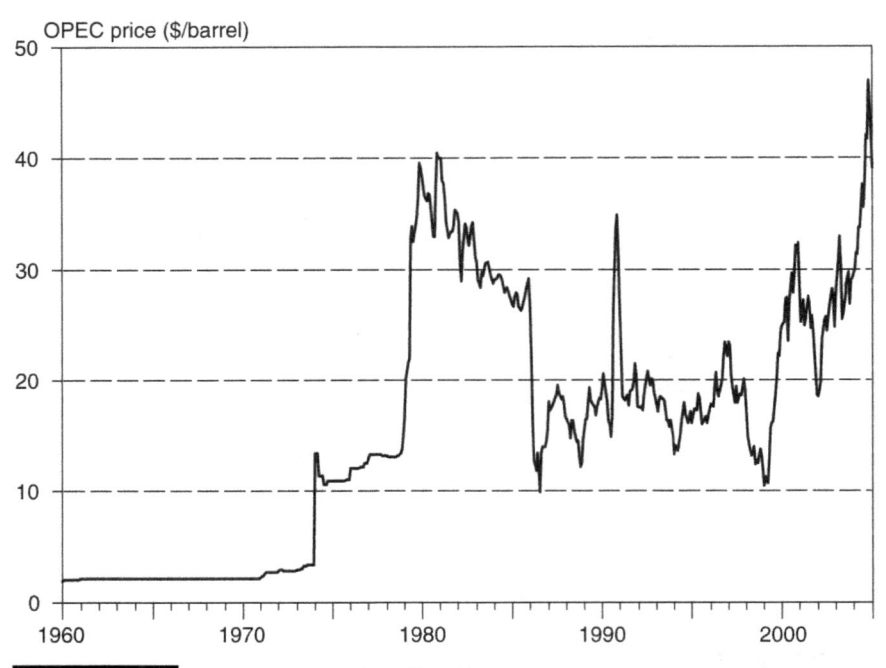

FIGURE 1-3 Movements in oil prices.

FIGURE 1-4 Movements in stock prices.

a good grasp of the underlying economics, as well as the links between major risk categories.

In addition to this unleashed volatility, firms generally have become more sensitive to movements in financial variables. Prior to the 1970s, banks were either heavily regulated or comfortably cartelized in most industrial countries. Regulations such as ceilings on interest-rate deposits effectively insulated bankers from movements in interest rates. Industrial corporations, mainly selling in domestic markets, were not too concerned about exchange rates.

The call to reality came with deregulation and globalization. The 1970s witnessed a worldwide movement to market-oriented policies and deregulation of financial markets. *Deregulation* forced financial institutions to be more competitive and to become acutely aware of the need to address financial risk. Barriers to international trade and investment also were lowered. This *globalization* forced firms to recognize the truly global nature of competition. In the process, firms have become exposed to a greater variety of financial risks.

But Where Is Risk Coming From?

This begs the question of the origins of these risks. Risk comes from many sources. Risk can be human-created, such as business cycles, inflation, changes in government policies, and wars. Risk also occurs as a result of unforeseen natural phenomena, including weather and earthquakes. Risk also arises from the primary source of long-term economic growth, namely, technological innovations, which can render existing technology obsolete and create dislocations in employment. Thus risk and the willingness to take risk are essential to the growth of our economy.

Much of the finance and insurance industry has been devoted to the creation of markets to share these risks. At the most basic level, the accumulation of assets, or savings,

correlated with increases in bond yields. These oil shocks also had an impact on national stock markets, which are displayed in Figure 1-4. Indeed, the great bear market of 1974–1975 was a global occurrence triggered by a three-fold increase in the price of crude oil. This episode shows that it is difficult to understand financial risk without provides a cushion against income risk. The introduction of personal loans, first recorded in ancient Greece, allows smoothing of consumption through borrowing. Insurance contracts, which have been traced to the Babylonian system of robbery insurance for caravans, use diversification principles to protect against accidents and other disasters. Even the modern publicly held corporation can be viewed as an arrangement that allows investors to spread the risk of ownership in a company across many investors.

Financial markets, however, cannot protect against all risks. Broad macroeconomic risks that create fluctuations in income and employment are difficult to hedge. This is why governments have created "safety nets" that the private sector cannot provide. In this sense, the welfare state can be viewed as a risk-sharing institution.

Governments, unfortunately, also can contribute to risks. The Asian crisis of 1997, for instance, has been broadly blamed on unsustainable economic policies that created havoc with a fragile financial sector. Time and again, government interference in the banking system seems to lead to systematic misallocation of credit that ultimately leads to banking crises. Also, countries that fix their exchange rate at an unrealistic level create serious imbalances in their domestic economies. This apparent stability encourages institutions to borrow excessively in foreign currencies, creating the conditions for a disaster out of a simple devaluation. This explains why large economies are now either letting their currency float freely or moving toward complete monetary integration, in the form of dollarization or a monetary union, such as in Europe.

A common currency, though, may not provide more stability because it simply may shift the risk to another location. Giving up fluctuations in currencies in exchange for greater fluctuations in output and employment may not be a bargain.[1]

Going into the debate of the best outlet for these fundamental risks is beyond the scope of this book. These risks manifest themselves in financial risks or macroeconomic risks. What we do know is that fluctuations in market-determined financial prices generally can be hedged in financial markets with derivatives.

---

[1] Much of the discussion of the pros and cons of the European Monetary Union has been devoted to this issue of tradeoffs between various risks in a monetary union. See Paul De Grauwe (1997).

DERIVATIVES

What Are Derivatives?

Derivatives are instruments designed to manage financial risks efficiently. A *derivative contract* can be defined generally as a private contract deriving its value from some *underlying* asset price, reference rate, or index—such as a stock, bond, currency, or commodity. Such a contract also specifies a *notional* amount, defined in terms of currency, shares, bushels, or some other unit. In contrast to *securities*, such as stocks and bonds, which are issued to raise capital, derivatives are *contracts*, or private agreements between two parties.

The simplest example of a derivative is a forward contract on a foreign currency, which is a promise to buy a fixed (notional) amount at a fixed price at some future date. This contract can be used, for instance, by a firm importing foreign products and for which the cost is billed in a foreign currency. The importer could buy the foreign currency forward, thus eliminating the risk of subsequent currency fluctuations.

This derivative is equivalent economically to a position in the cash market, invested in the foreign currency, and financed by a domestic loan. Since there is no upfront cash flow, the instrument is *leveraged*, that is, involves borrowing. Intrinsically, however, it is no more risky than dealing the same notional amount in the underlying cash market.

This is a crucial point. It will be made very clear by the *mapping* process, the first step in risk measurement that will be developed further in this book. Mapping replaces positions in instruments by exposures to fundamental risk factors. A position in a forward contract is equivalent to the same notional amount invested directly in the spot market, leveraged by cash so that there is zero net initial investment.

The leverage, however, is a double-edged sword. It makes the derivative an efficient instrument for hedging and speculation owing to very low transaction costs. On the other hand, the absence of an upfront cash payment makes it more difficult to assess the potential downside risk. Hence derivatives risks have to be monitored carefully.

Derivatives now can be used to hedge a wide array of different risks, as shown in Table 1-1. Sophisticated

TABLE 1-1   The Evolution of Derivatives Markets

1972	Foreign currency futures
1973	Equity options
1975	Treasury bond futures
1981	Currency swaps
	Eurodollar futures
1982	Interest-rate swaps
	Equity index futures
1983	Options on equity index
	Interest-rate caps and floors
1985	Swaptions
1987	Compound options
	Average options
1989	Quanto options
1990	Equity index swaps
1991	Differential swaps
1994	Credit default swaps
1996	Electricity futures
1997	Weather derivatives
2001	Single-stock futures
2004	Volatility index futures

TABLE 1-2   Global Markets for Derivatives— Outstanding Contracts ($ billion)

	Dec. 1986	March 1995	Dec. 2005
Exchange-traded instruments	583	8,838	57,817
Interest rate	516	8,380	52,297
Currency	18	88	174
Stock index	49	370	5,346
OTC instruments	500	47,530	284,819
Interest-rate swaps	400	18,283	163,680
Currency swaps	100	1,957	13,393
Others	—	27,290	107,746
Total	1,083	56,368	342,636

Source: Bank for International Settlements for 1995 and 2005 data; ISDA survey for 1986, which only covers swaps.

of *outstanding positions*, measured in notional amounts, which give some measure of the transfer of risk that occurs between cash and derivatives markets. Since 1986, these markets have grown from $1,083 billion to $343,000 billion in 2005, that is, $343 trillion.

On the surface, these numbers are amazing. The annual gross domestic product (GDP) of the entire United States was only $12 trillion in 2005. The derivatives markets are greater than the value of global stocks and bonds, which total around $85 trillion.

For risk management purposes, however, these numbers are highly misleading. Notional amounts do not describe market risks. The gross market values for all OTC contracts is only 3.7 percent of their notional amounts, which is $9.1 trillion.[2]

Even this number is still inadequate because many of these positions are hedging each other, including cash-market risks. In addition, what matters is not only the current market value but also potential changes in market values. This is precisely what VaR attempts to measure.

Nevertheless, the size of this market is astonishing, especially when one considers that financial derivatives have

instruments have been developed in response to client needs. This has led to a new field of finance, called *financial engineering*, that can be defined as the "development and creative application of financial technology to solve financial problems and exploit financial opportunities."

Derivatives Markets: How Big?

Trading for derivatives occurs on *exchanges,* which provide a centralized market for futures and options, and in *over-the-counter* (OTC) *markets*. These markets are spreading rapidly. As recently as the mid-1980s, the futures industry largely was concentrated in Chicago. Now, futures exchanges can be found all over the world.

Table 1-2 describes the growth of selected derivatives instruments since 1986. The table shows the dollar value

---

[2] This number represents the sum of the absolute values of all positive and negative market values for all outstanding contracts.

existed only for about 30 years. The first financial futures were launched in Chicago on May 16, 1972. This was a propitious time for currency futures because exchange rates were just starting to float. By now, these markets have proved essential to exchange financial risks. Because they allow risks to be transferred to those best able to bear them, one can argue that they actually lower the total amount of risk in the global economy.

On the downside, the technology behind the creation of ever-more complex derivatives instruments seems at times to have advanced faster than our ability to control it. While the 1980s witnessed a proliferation of derivatives, a string of highly publicized derivatives disasters in the early 1990s has led to a much-needed emphasis on risk management, to which we turn next.

RISK MANAGEMENT

The Toolbox of Risk Management

Financial risk management refers to the design and implementation of procedures for identifying, measuring, and managing financial risks. Imagine yourself as a risk manager in charge of controlling the risk of a group of fixed-income traders. How do you limit potential losses while still allowing traders to take views on markets? This is the essence of a risk manager's job.

One possibility is to establish *stop-loss limits*. If the cumulative loss incurred by a trader exceeds some limit, the position has to be cut. This approach is used widely. However, the problem is that the controls are applied ex post, or after the facts. There is no guarantee that the loss will be close to the limit. With bad luck, it could be much larger.

Instead, the risk manager needs to use ex ante, or forward- looking risk controls. A limit could be placed on the *notional amount*. This is not sufficient, however. For the same notional amount, some bonds have extreme risks and others no risk. The risk manager needs to know how the instruments respond to risk factors, as well as the range of potential movements in risk factors.

Figure 1-5 describes the conventional risk measurement approach for a typical 10-year coupon-paying bond. The first step is a *valuation problem*,

which involves solving for the price given the current yield. The second step is a *sensitivity analysis*. This leads to the concept of duration, which measures the linear exposure, or slope, of the bond value to interest-rate risk. Another approach is *scenario analysis*, or *stress tests*, which reprices the portfolio over a range of interest rates.

Limits on notionals and sensitivities are used widely. These linear sensitivities are called *duration* for exposure to interest rates, *beta* for exposure to stock-market movements, and *delta* for exposure of options to the underlying asset price. The risk manager could set a limit of $100 million on the notional amount, or a dollar duration limit of four years times $100 million.

This approach is still incomplete, however. It does not consider the volatility of the risk factors, which could vary across markets, nor their correlations. It cannot be used to set consistent limits across bonds and equities, for example. Because sensitivity measures are not additive, they cannot be used to aggregate risks. They do not translate easily into a dollar loss.

This is where VaR comes in. VaR combines the price-yield relationship with the probability of an adverse market

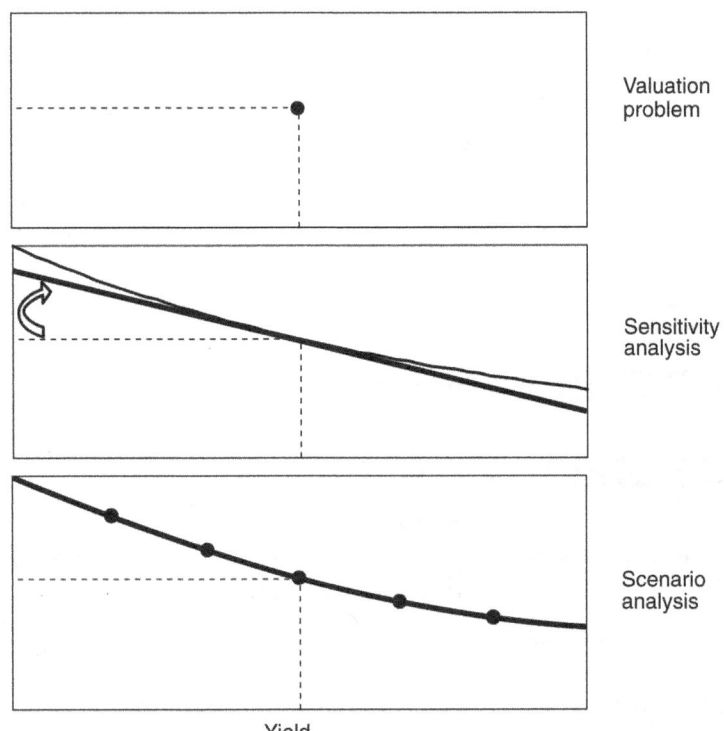

FIGURE 1-5 Conventional risk-measurement methods.

movement. This is shown in Figure 1-6, which describes how the price function is combined with a probability distribution for yields to generate a probability distribution for the bond price. Thus VaR is a *statistical risk measure* of potential losses.

VaR is much broader than this simple example, though. Besides interest rates, it can encompass many other sources of risks, such as foreign currencies, commodities, and equities, in a consistent fashion. VaR accounts for leverage and correlations, which is essential when dealing with large portfolios with derivatives instruments. Table 1-3 summarizes the pros and cons of various risk limits.

Table 1-4 describes the major developments in financial risk management. Early tools were sensitivity measures,

such as duration, beta, and "Greek" sensitivities for options. These were used eventually for setting limits. Then came VaR, which has been applied to market, credit, and operational risk.

The methodology behind VaR is not new, however. It can be traced back to the basic mean-variance framework developed by Markowitz in 1952. What is new is the integration of all risks into a centralized common metric.

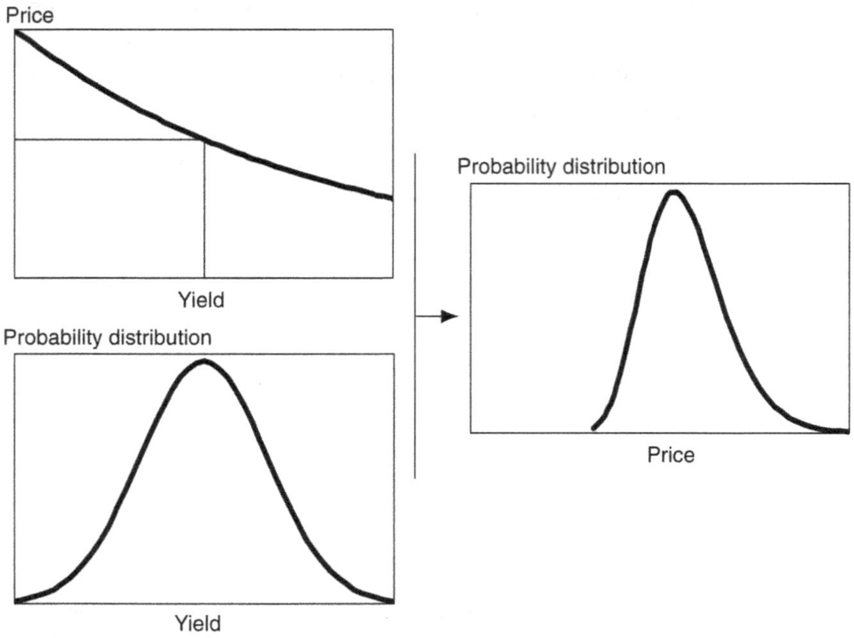

In Brief, What Is VaR?

Every morning, Lesley Daniels Webster, global head of market risk at J.P. Morgan Chase, receives a thick report that summarizes the value at risk (VaR) of the bank. The document is generated during the night by the bank's global risk measurement system.

Today, many banks, brokerage firms, investment funds, and even nonfinancial corporations use similar methods to gauge their financial risk. Bank and securities markets regulators and private-sector groups have widely endorsed statistical-based risk management methods such as VaR. But what is this VaR?

VaR can be given the following intuitive definition:

> VaR summarizes the worst loss over a target horizon that will not be exceeded with a given level of confidence.

More formally, VaR describes the *quantile* of the projected distribution of gains and losses over the target horizon. If c is the selected confidence level, VaR corresponds to the $1 - c$ lower tail level. By convention, this worst loss is expressed as a positive number (see Box 1-1).

Illustration of VaR

To illustrate the computation of VaR, consider, for instance, an investor who holds $100 million (notional) worth of medium-term notes. How much could the position lose over a month?

To answer this question, we simulate the 1-month return on this investment from historical data. Figure 1-7 plots monthly returns on

FIGURE 1-6 Risk measurement with VaR.

TABLE 1-3 Comparison of Risk Limits

Characteristic	Stop Loss	Notional	Exposure	VaR
Type	Ex post	Ex ante	Ex ante	Ex ante
Ease of calculation	Yes	Yes	No	No
Ease of explanation	Yes	Yes	No	Yes
Aggregation	Yes	No	No	Yes

TABLE 1-4   The Evolution of Analytical Risk Management Tools

1938	Bond duration
1952	Markowitz mean-variance framework
1963	Sharpe's single-factor beta model
1966	Multiple-factor models
1973	Black-Scholes option-pricing model, "Greeks"
1983	RAROC, risk-adjusted return
1986	Limits on exposure by duration bucket
1988	Limits on "Greeks"
1992	Stress testing
1993	Value at risk (VaR)
1994	RiskMetrics
1997	CreditMetrics
1998–	Integration of credit and market risk
2000–	Enterprisewide risk management

5-year U.S. Treasury notes since 1953. The sample size is 624 months. The graph shows returns ranging from below 5 percent to above 5 percent.

Now construct regularly spaced "buckets" going from the lowest to the highest numbers, and count how many observations fall into each bucket. For instance, there are two observations below –5 percent. There is another observation between –5 and –4.5 percent. And so on. By so doing, we construct a *frequency distribution* for the monthly returns, which counts how many occurrences have been observed within a particular range. This *histogram*, or probability distribution, is shown in Figure 1-8.

Next, associate with each return a probability of observing a lower value. Pick a confidence level, say, 99 percent. We need to find the loss that will not be exceeded in 99 percent of cases, or such that 1 percent of observations, that is, 6 out of 624 occurrences, are lower. From Figure 1-8, this number is about –3.6 percent.

The choice of the confidence level and horizon will be discussed in greater detail in a later chapter. Here, we picked a 99 percent confidence level, which has become a

BOX 1-1   The Origins of VaR

Till Guldimann can be viewed as the creator of the term *value at risk* while head of global research at J.P. Morgan in the late 1980s. The risk management group had to decide whether *fully hedged* meant investing in long-maturity bonds, thus generating stable *earnings* but fluctuations in market values, or investing in cash, thus keeping the market *value* constant. The bank decided that "value risks" were more important than "earnings risks," paving the way for VaR.

At that time, there was much concern about managing the risks of derivatives properly. The Group of Thirty (G-30), which had a representative from J.P. Morgan, provided a venue for discussing best risk management practices. The term found its way through the G-30 report published in July 1993. Apparently, this was the first widely publicized appearance of the term *value at risk*.

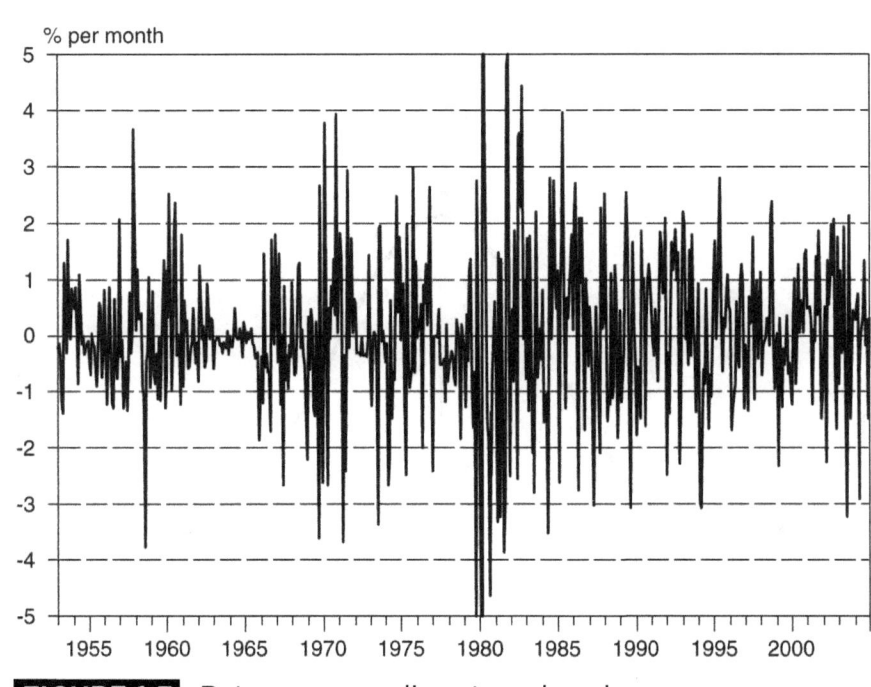

FIGURE 1-7   Returns on medium-term bonds.

standard choice in the industry. A higher confidence level should give fewer cases of losses worse than the VaR but consequently will increase VaR.

The choice of the holding period, for example, 1 month or 1 day, is also relatively subjective. A short horizon typically is selected for bank traders because they have very high turnover and invest in liquid assets that could be sold very quickly. In contrast, investment managers or hedge funds typically have longer horizons, such as 1 month. Ideally, the holding period corresponds to the longest period needed for an orderly portfolio liquidation. Because risk increases with the horizon, a longer horizon will increase VaR.

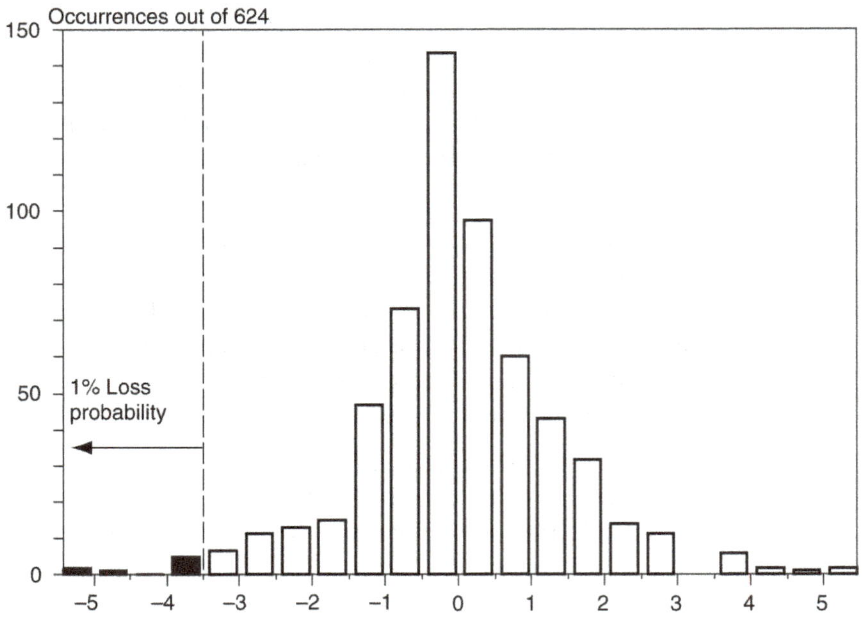

We are now ready to compute the VaR of a $100 million portfolio. Based on the preceding analysis, we are 99 percent confident that the portfolio will fall by no more than $100 million times –3.6 percent, or $3.6 million, over a month. Hence the VaR is about $3.6 million.

The market risk of this portfolio now can be communicated effectively to a nontechnical audience with a statement such as this: *Under normal market conditions, the most the portfolio can lose over a month is about $3.6 million at the 99 percent confidence level.*

VaR and Derivatives

In a broad sense, VaR extends current valuation methods for derivatives instruments. To price options, for instance, we need to make an assumption about the distribution of the driving risk factor. The option then is priced by taking the present value of the *expected* option value at maturity. This is made convenient by the Black-Scholes model, which shows that the pricing can be done as if investors were risk-neutral. If there is no closed-form solution, numerical simulations can be used.

With little modification, this framework can be used as well for risk measurement purposes. For example, the simulations can be used to construct the distribution of the option value at the horizon. VaR then is simply the worst loss in this distribution at the given confidence level.

Figure 1-9 compares the different views of the payoff distribution. Valuation models focus on the *mean* of the distribution. VaR, on the other hand, describes the potential *variation* in the payoffs. At the same time, it seems obvious that VaR measures are not

FIGURE 1-8   Measuring value at risk.

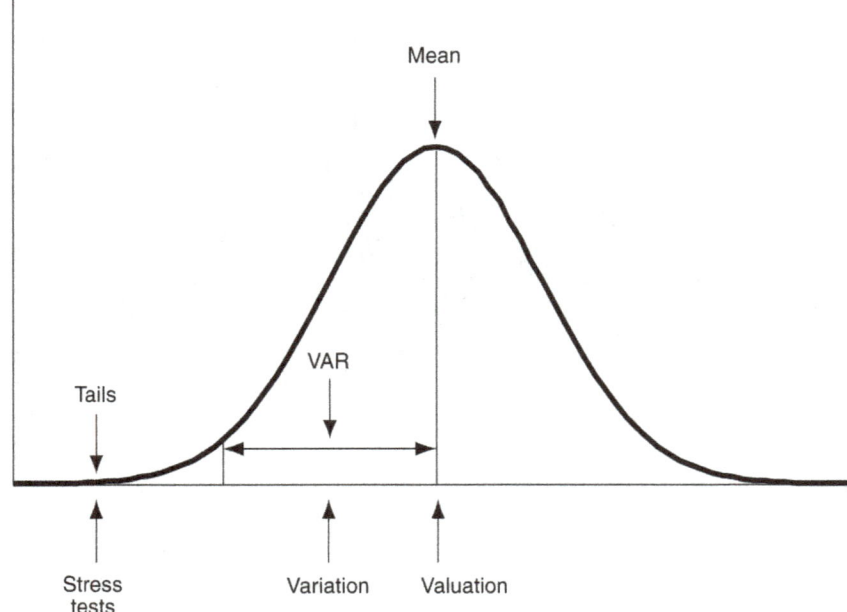

FIGURE 1-9   Different views of the payoff distribution.

meant to give the worst potential loss. The behavior in the *tails* can be analyzed through stress-testing techniques, which must be viewed as an indispensable complement to VaR.

Table 1-5 compares valuation and risk management approaches. While the two approaches have much methodology in common, there are some notable differences. Valuation methods require more precision because accurate prices are needed for trading purposes. This is less so for risk management methods, which simply try to provide a rough measure of downside risk; pricing errors also tend to cancel out. Another difference is that valuation methods operate in a risk-neutral world, whereas risk management methods deal with actual distributions.[3]

The sudden realization that our vast body of knowledge in the field of derivatives could be put to direct use for risk management explains why VaR quickly has become the "standard benchmark" for measuring financial risks.

No doubt this was helped by the effort of J.P. Morgan, which unveiled its RiskMetrics system in October 1994. Available free on the Internet, RiskMetrics provides a data feed for computing market risk. The widespread availability of data, as well as a technical manual, immediately engaged the industry and spurred academic research into risk management.

Since then, VaR methods have been applied to a variety of other risks, which are described next.

TYPES OF FINANCIAL RISKS

Generally, financial risks are classified into the broad categories of market risks, liquidity risks, credit risks, and operational risks. As we will show, these risks may interact with each other.

TABLE 1-5   Valuation and Risk Management

	Derivatives Valuation	**Risk Management**
Principle	Expected discounted value	Distribution of future values
Focus	Center of distribution	Tails of distribution
Horizon	Current value, discounting	Future value
Precision	High precision needed for pricing purposes	Less precision needed, errors cancel out
Distribution	Risk-neutral	Actual (physical)

Market Risk

Market risk is the risk of losses owing to movements in the level or volatility of market prices. Market risk can take two forms: *absolute risk*, measured in dollar terms (or in the relevant currency), and *relative risk*, measured relative to a benchmark index. While the former focuses on the volatility of total returns, the latter measures risk in terms of *tracking error*, or deviation from the index.

Market risk can be classified into directional and nondirectional risks. *Directional risks* involve exposures to the direction of movements in financial variables, such as stock prices, interest rates, exchange rates, and commodity prices. *Nondirectional risks*, then, involve the remaining risks, which consist of nonlinear exposures and exposures to hedged positions or to volatilities. *Basis risk* is created from unanticipated movements in the relative prices of assets in a hedged position, such as cash and futures or interest-rate spreads. Finally, *volatility risk* measures exposure to movements in the actual or implied volatility.

Market risk is controlled by limits on notionals, exposures, VaR measures, and independent supervision by risk managers. Market risk is the main subject of this book.

Liquidity Risk

Liquidity risk is usually treated separately from the other risks discussed here. It takes two forms, asset liquidity risk and funding liquidity risk. *Asset-liquidity risk*, also known as *market/product-liquidity risk*, arises when a transaction cannot be conducted at prevailing market prices owing to the size of the position relative to normal trading lots. This risk varies across categories of assets and across time as a function of prevailing market conditions. Some assets, such as major currencies or Treasury bonds, have

---

[3] For pricing purposes, *risk-neutral* means that expected returns can be set equal to the risk-free rate. For risk management purposes, the trend needs to be set to the actual expected return on the risk factor. We require the *actual* distribution, instead of the *risk-neutral* one. The actual distribution is sometimes called the *physical*, or *objective*, *distribution*. In practice, if the horizon is short, there is little difference between these distributions.

deep markets where most positions can be liquidated easily with very little price impact. In others, such as exotic OTC derivatives contracts or emerging-market equities, any transaction can quickly affect prices. But this is also a function of the size of the position.

Market/product-liquidity risk can be managed by setting limits on certain markets or products and by means of diversification. Liquidity risk can be factored loosely into VaR measures by ensuring that the horizon is at least greater than an orderly liquidation period.

Funding-liquidity risk, also known as *cash-flow risk*, refers to the inability to meet payments obligations, which may force early liquidation, thus transforming "paper" losses into realized losses. This is especially a problem for portfolios that are leveraged and subject to margin calls from the lender. Cash-flow risk interacts with product-liquidity risk if the portfolio contains illiquid assets that must be sold at less than fair market value.

Indeed, if cash reserves are insufficient, we may have a situation where losses in market values create a need for cash payments, which may lead to an involuntary liquidation of the portfolio at depressed prices. This cycle of losses leading to margin calls and further losses is sometimes described as the "death spiral" (see Box 1-2).

Funding-risk can be controlled by proper planning of cash-flow needs, which can be controlled by setting limits on cash-flow gaps, by diversification, and by consideration of how new funds can be raised to meet cash shortfalls.

Credit Risk

Credit risk is the risk of losses owing to the fact that counterparties may be unwilling or unable to fulfill their contractual obligations. Its effect is measured by the cost of replacing cash flows if the other party defaults. This loss encompasses the *exposure*, or amount at risk, and the *recovery rate*, which is the proportion paid back to the lender, usually measured in terms of "cents on the dollar."

Losses owing to credit risk, however, can occur before the actual default. More generally, credit risk should be defined as the potential loss in market-to-market value that may be incurred owing to the occurrence of a credit event. A *credit event* occurs when there is a change in the counterparty's ability to perform its obligations. Thus changes in market prices of debt owing to changes in

---

BOX 1-2   Askin's Failed Market-Neutral Strategy

Some hedge funds lost heavily in the 1994 bond market debacle. David Askin was managing a $600 million fund invested in collateralized mortgage obligations (CMOs). CMOs are securities obtained from splitting up mortgage-backed securities and can be complex to price.

He touted his funds to investors as nondirectional or *market-neutral*, in his words, "With no default risk, high triple-A bonds and zero correlation with other assets." David Askin used his proprietary valuation models to identify, purchase, and hedge underpriced securities, with an objective to return 15 percent and more to investors. The $600 million investment, however, was leveraged into a total of $2 billion, which actually was betting on low interest rates. From February to April 1994, as interest rates were being jacked up by the Fed, Askin's funds had to meet increasingly large collateral call payments that in the end could not be met. After the brokers liquidated their holdings, all that was left of the $600 million hedge fund was $30 million—and a bunch of irate investors.

Investors claimed that they were misled about the condition of the fund. In the 1994 turmoil, the market for CMOs had deteriorated to a point where CMOs were quoted with spreads of 10 percent, which is enormous. As one observer put it, "Dealers may be obliged to make a quote, but not for fair economic value." Instead of using dealer quotes, Askin simply priced his funds according to his own valuation models. The use of model prices to value a portfolio is referred to by practitioners as *marking to model*.

Askin initially was reporting a 2 percent loss in February, but this was later revised to a 28 percent loss. One year later he was sanctioned by the Securities and Exchange Commission for misrepresenting the value of his funds. He also was barred from the investment industry for a minimum of 2 years.

Askin's investors were victims of market, liquidity, and model risk.

---

credit ratings or in the market's perception of default also can be viewed as credit risk, creating some overlap between credit risk and market risk.

Credit risk also includes *sovereign risk*. This occurs, for instance, when countries impose foreign-exchange controls that make it impossible for counterparties to honor their obligations. Whereas default risk generally is company-specific, sovereign risk is country-specific.

> ### BOX 1-3   Herstatt's Settlement Risk
>
> On June 26, 1974, at 15:30 Central European Time, the German authorities closed Bankhaus Herstatt, a troubled midsize bank. The bank was very active in the foreign-exchange markets, however. At the time of closure, some of its U.S. counterparties had irrevocably sent large amounts of Deutsche marks but had not yet received dollars in exchange because U.S. markets had just opened. These U.S. banks became exposed to losses on the full amount they had sent. This created disruptions in financial markets and sent global transaction volumes in a tailspin.
>
> This systemic risk episode led central bankers to realize the need for coordination at a global level. Herstatt was the impetus for the creation of the Basel Committee on Banking Supervision (BCBS), which 15 years later promulgated capital adequacy requirements for the banking system.

> ### BOX 1-4   Credit Risk and Legal Risk
>
> Investors who lose money on a transaction have the nasty habit of turning to courts to invalidate the transaction. One such approach is the *ultra vires* claim used by municipalities to invalidate losing transactions. The legal doctrine underlying this claim is that the investment activity was illegal because it went beyond the municipalities' powers.
>
> The most extreme situation encountered so far is that of interest-rate swaps entered by city councils in Britain. The municipalities of Hammersmith and Fulham had taken large positions in interest-rate swaps that turned out to produce large losses. The swaps were later ruled invalid by the British High Court. The court decreed that the city councils did not have the authority to enter into these transactions and therefore that the cities were not responsible for the losses. As a result, their bank counterparties had to swallow losses amounting to $178 million. Thus the large market losses led to default, which was made possible by legal considerations.

One particular form of credit risk is *settlement risk*, which occurs when two payments are exchanged the same day. This risk arises when the counterparty may default after the institution already made its payment. On settlement day, the exposure to counterparty default equals the full value of the payments due. In contrast, the presettlement exposure is only the netted value of the two payments. Settlement risk is very real for foreign-exchange transactions, which involve exchange of payments in different currencies at different times, as shown in Box 1-3.

Credit risk is controlled by credit limits on notionals, current and potential exposures, and increasingly, credit enhancement features such as requiring collateral or marking to market. The new methods to quantify market risk are now being extended to credit risk.

Operational Risk

Operational risk is the risk of loss resulting from inadequate or failed internal processes, people and systems or from external events.

Inadequate or failed *processes* can cause breakdowns in information, transactions processing, settlement systems, or more generally, problems in *back-office operations,* which deal with the recording of transactions and reconciliation of individual trades. Operational risks also can lead to market or credit risk. For example, an operational problem in a business transaction, such as a settlement

"fail," can create market risk because the cost may depend on movements in market prices.

Model risk is part of inadequate internal processes. This refers to the risk of losses owing to the fact that valuation models may be flawed. Traders using a conventional option pricing model, for instance, could be exposed to model risk if the model is misspecified. Unfortunately, model risk is very insidious. Assessing this risk requires an intimate knowledge of the modeling process. To guard against model risk, models must be subjected to independent evaluation using market prices, when available, or objective out-of-sample evaluations.

People risk includes internal or external *fraud*, such as situations where traders intentionally falsify information. This is also related to market risk. *Rogue traders* typically falsify their positions after they incur a large market loss.

Operational risk also includes *legal risk*, which arises from exposure to fines, penalties, or punitive damages resulting from supervisory actions, as well as private settlements. Legal risk generally is related to credit risk because counterparties that lose money on a transaction may try to find legal grounds for invalidating the transaction (see, for example, Box 1-4).

It also can take the form of shareholder lawsuits against corporations that suffer large losses. After Procter & Gamble announced that it had lost $195 million on complex interest-rate swaps entered with Bankers Trust, for example, a disgruntled shareholder filed suit against company executives.

Legal risks are controlled through policies developed by the institution's legal counsel in consultation with risk managers and senior management. The institution should make sure that agreements with counterparties can be enforced before any deal is consummated. Even so, situations that involve large losses often end up in costly litigation simply because the stakes are so large.

The best protection against operational risks consists of redundancies of systems, clear separation of responsibilities with strong internal controls, and regular contingency planning. The industry is currently making great strides in measuring and controlling operational risk. As with market and credit risk, operational risk is now being quantified increasingly.

SUMMARY

This chapter has shown how financial risks have led to the growth of the derivatives markets and to modern VaR-based risk management methods. By now, risk management has become an essential aspect of financial engineering.

VaR methods have revolutionized the management of financial risks. VaR is a common language to compare the risks of different markets. It is a statistical risk measure of potential losses.

The main idea behind VaR, which goes back to Markowitz, is to consider the *total portfolio risk* at the highest level of the institution. Thus VaR accounts for leverage and diversification effects. Initially applied to market risk, it is now used to measure credit risk, operational risk, and enterprisewide risk.

Lest we forget, VaR is no panacea, however. VaR measures are only useful insofar as users grasp their limitations. As Till Guldimann, then head of J.P. Morgan's global research, described his firm's system, "RiskMetrics isn't a substitute for good management, experience and judgment. It's a toolbox, not a black box." Thus VaR is only an educated estimate of market risk. This does not lessen its value, though. Educated estimates have been used widely in other fields. Likewise, engineering

is sometimes defined as the "art of the approximation" (as opposed to the exact sciences). The same concept applies to risk management systems.

Overall, VaR should be viewed as a necessary but not sufficient procedure for managing risk. It must be supplemented by stress tests, limits, and controls, in addition to an independent risk management function. Indeed, the widespread use of VaR has led to a widespread focus on sound risk management practices. In my view, this development is beneficial.

Questions

1. Assume that General Motors loses money in three scenarios: (a) a depreciation in the value of the euro exchange rate, (b) the cost of recalling and repairing defective automobiles, and (c) missing out on a major automobile segment, which is that of hybrids (cars operating on two sources of energy). Which of these risks can be defined as business, strategic, and financial risk?

2. "Financial risks can be analyzed independently of each other. For instance, a stock analyst does not need to worry about oil prices because these are different markets." Comment.

3. "Financial markets create a lot of risk due to speculation. They can be compared to the Las Vegas casinos." Comment.

4. What is a derivative contract? Give an example. How are derivatives related to risk management?

5. List some derivatives traded on organized exchanges and on OTC markets.

6. What feature makes derivatives particularly effective but also dangerous to use?

7. "The fact that the total of derivatives notional amounts is much greater than cash markets should be a major reason for concern. This could cause systemic risk." Discuss this argument. Are notional amounts the appropriate measure of risk?

8. What is VaR?

9. Is VaR only applicable to derivatives risk?

10. How do we interpret a $2.5 million daily VaR with 95 percent confidence level? Consider what could happen over the next 100 days.

11. Is the following statement related to VaR true? "The confidence level corresponds to the probability of getting a return worse than the VaR."

12. Does risk management need as much precision as derivatives pricing, and why?

13. What are the major categories of financial risks?

14. Explain directional and nondirectional market risks.

15. Do credit losses only occur at the event of default?

16. Explain how settlement risk is a particular category of credit risk.

17. A trader purchases two 10-year corporate bonds issued by Company A and Company B in exchange for cash. Consider now two scenarios: (a) The trader makes the first payment to Bank C, which defaults the next day before delivering Bond A, and (b) the trader receives Bond B from another bank, but Company B defaults after 2 years. Which type of risk is involved in the two scenarios? *- Credit*

18. Discuss whether different categories of risk can be viewed in isolation from each other.

19. Why are VaR limits more advisable than limits based on notional amount, on sensitivity, and on leverage?

Creating Value with Risk Management

2

Excerpt is Chapter 3 of Risk Management and Derivatives *by René Stulz.*

Learning Objectives

After completing this reading, FRM Candidates should be able to:

- Explain how risk management can create value by handling bankruptcy costs.
- Explain how risk management can create value moving income across time and reducing taxes.
- Describe how risk reduction benefiting a large shareholder or stakeholder may increase or decrease firm value.
- Explain the relationship between risk management, managerial incentives, and the structure of management compensation, and its effect on firm value.

- Describe debt overhang, and explain how risk management can increase firm value by reducing the probability of debt overhang.
- Explain how risk management can reduce the problem of information asymmetry and increase firm value.

Mr. Smith is the CFO of Software Inc. He has worked hard to keep up with new developments in finance. He recently attended an advanced executive development program where much time was spent discussing the Modigliani and Miller propositions. Understanding that shareholders can hedge on their own account, he has paid scant attention to risk management. However, looking at his firm's situation, he discovers that it will not be able to make use of a valuable tax shield arising from past losses because exchange rate losses have unexpectedly reduced his firm's net income. The tax shield will be gone forever after this year. Yet, had the firm been profitable this year, the tax shield would have allowed the corporation to reduce its tax bill by $50 million. He realizes that if he had been able to hedge his income against exchange rate fluctuations, Software Inc. would have been richer by $50 million. Instead, because he had not hedged, $50 million of shareholder wealth walked out the door. In this chapter, we show that there are many reasons to hedge.

A risk management program cannot increase firm value when it costs the same to bear a risk within the firm or outside the firm. We established this result, called *the risk management irrelevance proposition*. The irrelevance proposition holds when financial markets are perfect. If the proposition holds, any risk management program that a firm puts in place can be replicated by any investor through "homemade" risk management. The risk management irrelevance proposition is useful because it allows us to find out when homemade risk management is not equivalent to risk management by the firm. This is the case whenever risk management by a firm affects firm value in a way that investors cannot mimic. In this chapter, we identify situations where there is a wedge between the cost of bearing a risk within the firm and the cost of bearing it outside the firm. Such a wedge requires the presence of financial markets imperfections (perfect markets have no frictions—no transactions costs, no taxes, perfect competition, no costs of writing contracts).

We use the example of a gold-producing firm. We continue that example here. Pure Gold Inc. is exposed to gold price risk. It can bear that risk within the firm. This means the firm has lower income if the price of gold is unexpectedly low and higher income if it is unexpectedly high. If the irrelevance proposition holds, the only cost of bearing this risk within the firm is that shares are worth less if gold price risk is systematic risk, because in this

case shareholders require a risk premium to compensate them for gold price risk. Similarly, the only cost to the firm of having gold price risk borne outside the firm is that the firm has to pay a risk premium to induce the capital markets to take that risk. The risk premium the capital markets require is the same the shareholders require. Consequently, it makes no difference for firm value whether the gold price risk is borne by shareholders or by the capital markets, which is what the risk management irrelevance proposition states.

For risk management to increase firm value, it must be more expensive to take a risk within the firm than to pay the capital markets to take it. For Pure Gold, risk management creates value if an unexpectedly low gold price entails costs for the firm that it would not have for the capital markets. Suppose that with an unexpectedly low gold price, the firm does not have funds to invest, and hence has to give up valuable projects because it would be expensive for the current shareholders to raise funds in the capital markets with such a low gold price. Thus, shareholders not only lose income now with unexpected low gold prices, but they also lose future income because the firm cannot take advantage of investment opportunities. Pure Gold bears an extra, indirect, cost or burden from the low gold prices. Indirect costs resulting from financial losses are called **deadweight costs**.

To understand deadweight costs, suppose you asked yourself how Pure Gold could be put back in the situation it would have been in had gold prices not been low. If all it takes is to make up the loss Pure Gold experienced on its sales of gold, then there are no deadweight costs—no additional losses caused by the low gold prices. However, if, in addition, Pure Gold has to be compensated for profits it did not earn because of investments it could not make, there are deadweight costs.

The reason risk management creates value for Pure Gold if there are deadweight costs associated with gold price risk is that risk management reduces or eliminates deadweight costs. If the gold price risk is borne by the capital markets, Pure Gold does not incur additional costs resulting from low gold prices since it makes no losses from low gold prices. In this case, the cost of putting the gold price risk off on the capital markets is less than the cost the firm will pay if it bears the risk within the firm and sacrifices future opportunities by not being able to invest when the gold price is low.

In this chapter, we investigate how a firm can use risk management to increase firm value. We discuss the reasons why a firm might find it more expensive to bear a risk within the firm than pay the capital markets to bear that risk. We thus show the sources of the benefits of risk management.

We gave the example of Homestake as a gold mining firm that had a policy of not hedging its gold price exposure. As you saw, management based its policy on the belief that Homestake's shareholders value gold price exposure. We showed that this belief is wrong because investors can get gold price exposure without Homestake on terms at least as good as those that Homestake offers, and most likely better. So, is Homestake's value lower than it would have been with hedging? Throughout this chapter, for each source of value of hedging we document, we investigate whether this source of value applies to Homestake.

BANKRUPTCY COSTS AND COSTS OF FINANCIAL DISTRESS

In our analysis of the value of risk management, we take the distribution of Pure Gold's cash flow before hedging (the cash flow from operations) as a given. We assume that it sells one million ounces of gold at the end of the year and then liquidates. Pure Gold has no debt. The gold price is assumed to be normally distributed with a mean of $350 per ounce. There are no operating costs for simplicity. All the cash flow accrues to the firm's shareholders. This situation is represented by the straight line in Figure 2-1, where cash flow to Pure Gold is on the horizontal axis and cash flow to the holders of financial claims against it is on the vertical axis. In this case, the only claimholders are the shareholders. In perfect financial markets, all cash flows to the firm accrue to the firm's claimholders, so there is no gain from risk management.

At the end of the year, Pure Gold distributes the cash flow to its owners, the shareholders, and liquidates. If the firm hedges by selling its production at the forward price, the shareholders get the proceeds from selling the firm's gold production at the forward price. Suppose the forward price is $350. If the gold price turns out to be $450, for example, the hedged firm receives $350 per ounce by

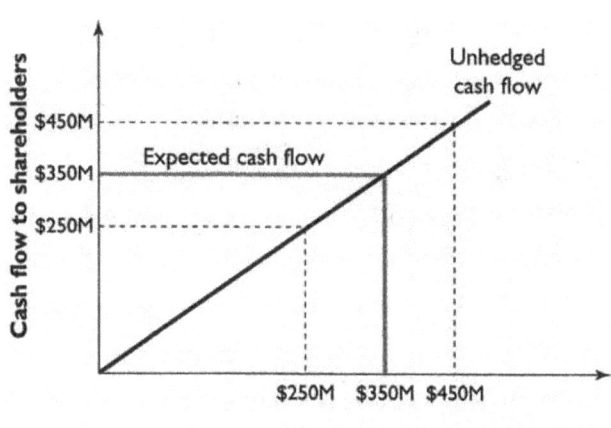

FIGURE 2-1 Cash flow to shareholders and operating cash flow.

The firm sells one million ounces of gold at the end of the year and liquidates. There are no costs. The expected gold price is $350.

delivering on the forward contract, while the unhedged firm would receive $450 per ounce.

The shareholders, however, can obtain for themselves the payoff of the unhedged firm when the firm is hedged and vice versa. This is shown in Figure 2-2. An investor who owns the hedged firm and takes a long forward position on personal account receives $350 per ounce of gold from the hedged firm plus ($450 − $350) per ounce from the forward contract, for a total payoff of $450 per ounce, which is the payoff per ounce for the unhedged firm. Hence, even though the firm is hedged, investors can create for themselves the payoff of the unhedged firm.

Now, suppose Pure Gold has some debt. We still assume that markets are perfect, that the distribution of the cash flow from operations is given, and that there are no taxes. At the end of the year, the cash flow to the firm is used first to pay off the debtholders, and then shareholders receive what is left over. The firm's claimholders still receive all of the firm's cash flow, and the firm's cash flow is not changed by leverage, but there are now two groups of claimholders, debtholders and shareholders. Leverage does not affect firm value. It simply specifies how the pie—the firm's operating cash flow—is divided among its claimants—the debtholders and the shareholders. Since

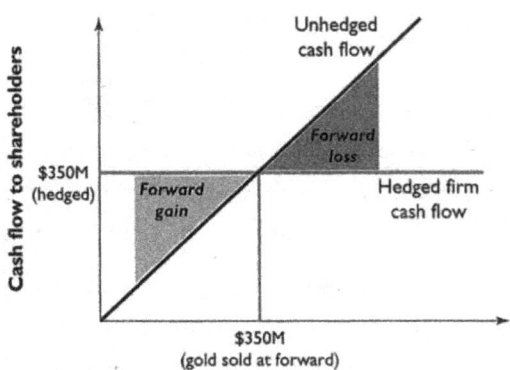

FIGURE 2-2 Creating the unhedged firm out of the hedged firm.

The firm produces one million ounces of gold. It can hedge by selling one million ounces of gold forward. The expected gold price and the forward price are $350 per ounce. If the firm hedges and shareholders do not want the firm to hedge, they can recreate the unhedged firm by taking a long position forward in one million ounces of gold.

the cash flow to claimholders is the firm's entire cash flow, risk management does not affect firm value.

In the real world, it is costly for firms to file for bankruptcy and renegotiate debt. Firms have to hire lawyers, incur court costs, and need to pay for all sorts of financial advice. Costs incurred as a result of a bankruptcy filing are called **bankruptcy costs**. The present value of future bankruptcy costs reduces the value of a firm that has debt relative to one that does not. While there are benefits to leverage, for the time being we ignore them. As shown in Figure 2-3, these bankruptcy costs create a "wedge" between cash flow to the firm and cash flow to the firm's claimholders. This wedge corresponds to the bankruptcy costs incurred by the owners.

The extent to which bankruptcy costs affect firm value depends on their extent and on the probability that the firm will have to file for bankruptcy. The probability that a firm will be bankrupt is the probability that it will not have enough cash flow to repay the debt. We know how to compute this probability for a normally distributed cash flow. Figure 2-4 shows how the distribution of cash flow from operations affects the probability of bankruptcy. If Pure Gold hedges its risk completely, it reduces its cash flow volatility to zero because the claimholders receive the present value of gold sold at the forward

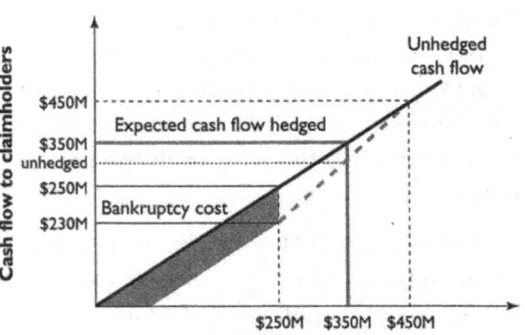

FIGURE 2-3 Cash flow to claimholders and bankruptcy costs.

The firm sells one million ounces of gold at the end of the year and liquidates. There are no transactions costs. The expected gold price is $350. Bankruptcy costs are $20 million if cash flow to the firm is $250 million. Suppose that the firm can have a cash flow of $250 million with probability p or a cash flow of $450 million with probability $1 - p$. Expected cash flow of the unhedged firm is given by the equation $p \times \$230M + (1 - p) \times \$450M$ and is plotted by the dotted line. The case where the forward price of gold is $350 and equal to expected gold price corresponds to $p = 0.5$. With this case, expected cash flow of the hedged firm is $350 million and expected cash flow of the unhedged firm is $340 million.

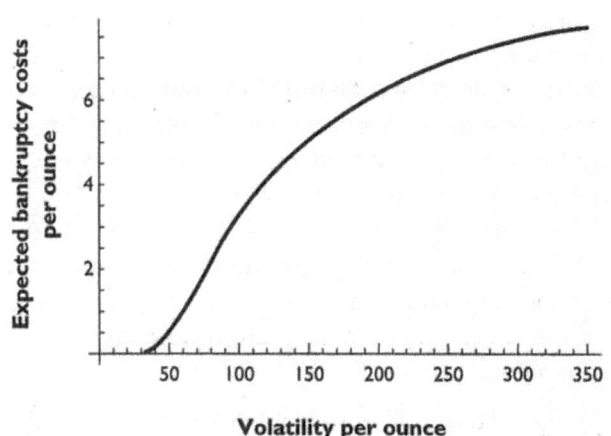

FIGURE 2-4 Expected bankruptcy costs as a function of volatility.

The firm produces one million ounces of gold and then liquidates. It is bankrupt if the price of gold is below $250 per ounce. The bankruptcy costs are $20 per ounce. The gold price is distributed normally with expected value of $350. The volatility is in dollars per ounce.

price. In this case, the probability of bankruptcy is zero and the present value of bankruptcy costs is also zero. As cash flow volatility increases, the present value of bankruptcy costs increases because bankruptcy becomes more likely. This means that the present value of cash flow to Pure Gold's claimholders falls as cash flow volatility increases.

Therefore, by hedging, Pure Gold increases its value; that is, it does not have to pay bankruptcy costs, and hence its claimholders get all of the firm's cash flow. In this case, homemade risk management by the firm's claimholders is not a substitute for the firm's risk management. If the firm does not reduce its risk, its value is lower by the present value of bankruptcy costs. Homemade risk management can do nothing about this deadweight cost of low gold prices.

Bankruptcy Costs and Firm Value

We can use the present value equation to show that risk management increases firm value when the only financial market imperfection is the presence of bankruptcy costs that affect firm value. We therefore assume that markets are perfect for hedging instruments traded in capital markets, so that hedging involves no transaction costs. Remember that in the absence of bankruptcy costs, the firm's claimholders receive the cash flow at the end of the year when the firm is liquidated. Under our new assumptions, the claimholders receive the cash flow only if the firm is not bankrupt. Denote this cash flow by C. If the firm is bankrupt, the claimholders receive C minus the bankruptcy costs. Consequently, the value of the firm is now:

$$\text{Value of firm} = PV(C - \text{Bankruptcy costs})$$

We know that the present value of a sum of cash flows is the sum of the present values of the cash flows. Consequently, the value of the firm is equal to:

$$\text{Value of firm} = PV(C) - PV(\text{Bankruptcy costs})$$
$$= \text{Value of firm without bankruptcy costs}$$
$$- \text{Present value of bankruptcy costs}$$

Let's now consider the impact of risk management on firm value. If the hedge eliminates all risk, then the firm does not incur the bankruptcy costs. Hence, the cash flow to the firm's owner is what the cash flow would be in the absence of bankruptcy costs, which is C. This means that with such a hedge the claimholders get the present value

of C rather than the present value of C minus the present value of bankruptcy costs. Assuming that no market imperfections affect the cost of hedging instruments, the gain from risk management is:

$$\text{Gain from risk management} = \text{Value of firm hedged}$$
$$- \text{Value of firm unhedged}$$
$$= PV(\text{Bankruptcy costs})$$

A simple example of the benefit of hedging is as follows. We assume that the interest rate is 5 percent and that gold price risk is unsystematic risk. The forward price is $350. Because gold price risk is unsystematic risk, the forward price is equal to the expected gold price. As before, Pure Gold produces one million ounces of gold. Consequently, $PV(C)$ is equal to $350M/1.05, or $333.33 million. The present value of the hedged firm is the same (this is because expected cash flow, $E(C)$, is equal to one million times the expected gold price, which is the forward price).

To get the present value of the bankruptcy costs, we must specify the debt payment and the distribution of the cash flow. Let's say that the bankruptcy costs are $20 million, the face value of debt is $250 million, the gold price is normally distributed, and its volatility is 20 percent. The firm is bankrupt if the gold price falls below $250. The probability that the gold price will fall below $250 is 0.077. Consequently, the expected bankruptcy costs are 0.077 × $20M, or $1.54 million. By the use of risk management, Pure Gold ensures that it is never bankrupt, thus increasing its value by the present value of $1.54 M. Since gold price risk is assumed to be unsystematic risk, we discount the expected bankruptcy costs at the risk-free rate of 5 percent to get a present value of bankruptcy costs of $1.47 million ($1.54M/1.05).

In the presence of bankruptcy costs, the risk management irrelevance theorem no longer holds. The cost to Pure Gold of bearing gold price risk is $1.47 million. Because we assume that gold price risk is diversifiable, the cost of having the capital markets bear this risk is zero. The capital markets therefore have a comparative advantage over the firm in bearing gold price risk.

Note that if gold price risk is systematic risk, capital markets will charge a risk premium for bearing the gold price risk—the same risk premium that shareholders charge in the absence of bankruptcy costs. Hence, the capital markets still have a comparative advantage for bearing risk;

it is measured by the bankruptcy costs saved by having the capital markets bear the risk. There is nothing that shareholders can do on their own to avoid the impact of bankruptcy costs on Pure Gold's value, so homemade risk management cannot eliminate these costs.

Bankruptcy Costs, Financial Distress Costs, and the Costs of Risk Management Programs

A study of bankruptcy for 31 firms over the period from 1980 to 1986 by Weiss (1990) finds an average ratio of direct bankruptcy costs to total assets of 2.8 percent, with a high of 7 percent. Other researchers find similar estimates. Bankruptcy also entails large indirect costs. Managers spend much of their time dealing with the firm's bankruptcy proceedings instead of managing operations. Managers of a firm in bankruptcy lose control of some decisions. They might not be allowed to undertake costly new projects, for example.

Many of these indirect costs start accruing as soon as a firm's financial situation becomes unhealthy. The costs firms incur because of a poor financial situation are called **costs of financial distress**. Costs of financial distress can occur even if the firm never files for bankruptcy or never defaults. Managers have to think about finding ways to conserve cash to pay off debtholders. They might cut investment, which means the loss of future profits. Potential customers may become reluctant to deal with the firm, leading to losses in sales.

Our analysis of the benefits of risk management in reducing bankruptcy costs holds for all costs of financial distress also. Any time costs of financial distress divert cash flow away from the firm's claimholders, they reduce firm value. Reducing firm risk by minimizing the present value of costs of financial distress naturally increases firm value.

Reducing the costs of financial distress is one of the most important benefits of risk management. Consequently, we study in more detail how risk management can be used to reduce specific costs of financial distress in later sections in this chapter.

In the example, Pure Gold eliminates all of its bankruptcy costs through risk management. If managers identify other costs of financial distress that occur when the firm's cash flow is low, they could eliminate them as well through risk management. Some risks, however, are too expensive to reduce through risk management. In the absence of risk management costs, though, we would always eliminate all bankruptcy and financial distress risks.

There are transaction costs of taking positions in forward contracts. The transaction costs of risk management increase the cost of paying the capital markets to take the risk. As transaction costs increase, risk management becomes less attractive. If the firm bears a risk internally, it does not pay these transaction costs.

Bankruptcy Costs, Homestake, and Enron

At the end of the 1990 fiscal year, Homestake had cash balances of more than $300 million. Its long-term debt was $72 million, and it had unused credit lines amounting to $245 million. Homestake could have repaid all its long-term debt and still have had large cash balances. Bankruptcy was not likely. Suppose it had more long-term debt, though. Would bankruptcy and financial distress costs then be a serious issue?

Homestake's assets are its mines and its mining equipment. These assets do not lose value if Homestake defaults on its debt. If it makes sense to operate the mines, the mines will be operated, whoever owns them. Neither bankruptcy costs nor financial distress costs in this case provide an important reason for Homestake to practice risk management. Homestake is an example of a firm for which the reduction of financial distress costs is not an important benefit of risk management.

For many financial institutions, the mere appearance of some possibility of financial distress is enough to threaten the firm. In a bank, concerns of financial distress could prompt a run on the bank.

An example of how financial distress can lead to disaster is that of Enron. Enron was the seventh largest firm in the United States. It had a large and profitable online trading business—it traded energy, broadband, credit risks, and other goods. When its management lost credibility and its debt was downgraded from investment grade in November 2001, this started a sequence of events that led Enron to file for bankruptcy within weeks because financial distress removed the underpinnings of its trading business. Who wants to trade with an entity that has a significant probability of default?

TAXES AND RISK MANAGEMENT

Risk management creates value when it is more expensive to take a risk within the firm than to pay the capital markets to bear that risk. Corporate taxes are a good example. These taxes can increase the cost of taking risks within the firm.

We all accept that if a dollar of taxes has to be paid, paying it later is better than paying it sooner. While derivatives are sometimes used to create strategies that move income to later years, for now we focus on how managing risk, as opposed to timing income, can reduce the present value of taxes.

To understand the argument, it is useful to think about one important tax planning practice. If you know that in some future year your tax rate will be lower, you should try to recognize income in that year rather than today or in years your tax rate is higher. Pension plans are the prime example. If you can defer taxation on current income through a pension plan, you do so assuming that your retirement years' tax rate will be lower than the tax rate in your high-earning years.

Risk management, rather than altering in which tax year income is recognized, aims to alter the risks one takes to decrease expected tax payments in a given year. Suppose there are some outcomes—often called states of the world in finance—where this year's income is high and taxed at a high rate, and other outcomes where it is low and taxed at a low rate. For instance, if gold prices are high, gold companies have high income and a high tax rate. If we can rearrange the risks we take so that we have less income when the tax rate is high and more income when the tax rate is low, the present value of taxes paid is reduced.

Let's consider Pure Gold again. A firm generally pays taxes only if its revenue exceeds some level. Let's assume that Pure Gold pays taxes at the rate of 50 percent on the cash flow in excess of $300 million and does not pay taxes if its cash flow is below $300 million. For simplicity, we assume in this section that it is an all-equity firm, so there are no bankruptcy costs.

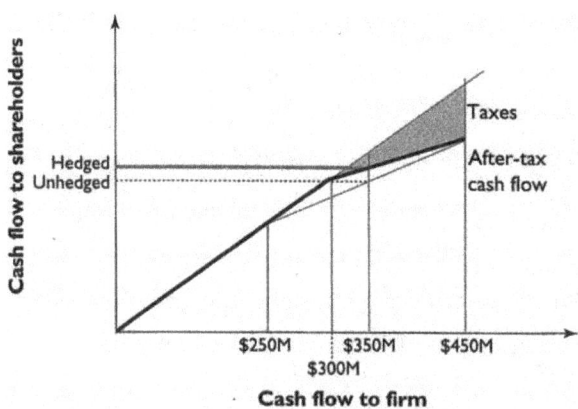

FIGURE 2-5 Taxes and cash flow to the shareholders.

The firm pays taxes at the rate of 50 percent on cash flow in excess of $300 per ounce. For simplicity, the price of gold is either $250 or $450 with equal probability. The forward price is $350.

Figure 2-5 graphs Pure Gold's after-tax cash flow as a function of the pretax cash flow. We see a difference between the firm's operating cash flow and what its shareholders receive, and this is due to taxes. Now, assume further that there is a 50 percent chance the gold price will be $250 per ounce and a 50 percent chance it will be $450, so the expected gold price is $350. Assuming that gold price risk is unsystematic risk, the forward price for gold is the expected gold price of $350. As before, the interest rate is 5 percent.

In the absence of taxes, the value of Pure Gold is the present value of the expected cash flow, $350 million discounted at 5 percent, or $333.33 million. With taxes, the present value of the firm for its shareholders is reduced, because the firm pays taxes when the gold price is $450. In this case, the firm pays taxes of 0.5($450 − $300)1M, or $75 million. With taxes, the value of the firm's equity is:

$$
\begin{aligned}
\text{Value of firm with taxes} &= PV(\text{Gold sales} - \text{Taxes}) \\
&= PV(\text{Gold sales}) - PV(\text{Taxes}) \\
&= PV(\text{Firm without taxes}) - PV(\text{Taxes}) \\
&= \$333.33M - 0.5 \times \$75M/1.05 \\
&= \$333.33M - \$35.71M \\
&= \$297.62M
\end{aligned}
$$

Let's figure what it costs shareholders to have the firm bear gold price risk compared to having the firm lay off the gold price risk by selling gold forward. To do this, we have to compare firm value if gold is sold on the spot market after it is produced with firm value if gold is sold at the forward price. Remember that the gold price can be either $250 or $450. If the gold price is $250, the shareholders get $250 per ounce. If the gold price is $450, they get $375 per ounce ($450 minus taxes at the rate of 50 percent on $150). The expected cash flow to the shareholders is therefore (0.5 × $250) + (0.5 × $375), or $312.5 per ounce. Since the expected cash flow would be $350 absent taxes, expected taxes are $37.5 per ounce. If the gold price is fixed at the forward price instead, so that cash flow is not volatile, shareholders receive $325 per ounce once they pay taxes at the rate of 50 percent on $50. In this case, expected taxes are $25 per ounce. Taking present values, the equity value is $309.52 per ounce if gold is sold at the forward price and $297.62 if gold is sold at the spot market price. Hence, it costs the shareholders $11.90 per ounce for having the firm bear the gold price risk, or $11.90 million for the firm as a whole.

The reason the firm saves taxes through risk management is straightforward. If the firm's income is low, the firm pays no taxes. If the firm's income is high, it pays taxes. If Pure Gold shifts a dollar from when income is high to when income is low, it saves the taxes it would pay on that dollar when the income is high. In our example, shifting income of a dollar from when income is high to when income is low saves $0.50 with probability 0.5.

Homemade risk management cannot work in this case. If the firm does not use risk management to eliminate its cash flow volatility, its expected taxes are higher by $12.5 million. This is money that leaves the firm and does not accrue to shareholders. Through homemade risk management, shareholders can eliminate the volatility in the share price resulting from gold price volatility, but they cannot affect the taxes the firm pays, so that the tax saving from risk management at the firm level cannot be obtained by shareholders through homemade risk management.

Let's figure out how shareholders would practice homemade risk management. Shareholders receive $375 per share or $250 per share from the firm with equal probability. To eliminate the gold price risk resulting from holding a share of Pure Gold, a shareholder can take a forward position so that the hedged payoff is the same whatever the gold price. Let h be the short forward position per ounce. Remember that the forward price is assumed to be $350 per ounce. Therefore, a short forward position of one unit pays $350 − $250 if the gold price is $250 and $350 − $450 if the gold price is $450. To eliminate the impact of gold price risk, the shareholder must choose h so that the income is the same whatever the gold price:

$$\$250 + h(\$350 - \$250) = \$375 + h(\$350 - \$450)$$

Solving for h, we get 0.625. By selling short 0.625 ounces forward, the shareholder guarantees a payoff of $312.5 per ounce at the end of the year. If the gold price is $250 per ounce, the shareholder receives $250 per share from the firm and 0.625 × ($350 − $250), or $62.50, from the forward position. This amounts to $312.50. The shareholder is clearly better off if the firm hedges directly, since in that case she gets $325, or $12.50 more than if the firm does not hedge and she practices homemade risk management.

The Tax Argument for Risk Management

The tax argument for risk management is straightforward: If it moves a dollar away from a possible outcome in which the taxpayer is subject to a high tax rate and shifts it to a possible outcome where the taxpayer incurs a low tax rate, a firm or an investor reduces the present value of taxes to be paid. The tax rationale for risk management applies whenever income is taxed differently at different levels. The tax code introduces complications in the analysis. Some of these complications decrease the value of hedging, whereas others increase it. Some of these complications are discussed next.

1. **Carrybacks and carryforwards.** A firm that has negative taxable income can offset future or past taxable income with a loss in this tax year, subject to limitations. One limitation is that losses can be carried back or carried forward only for a limited number of years. In addition, no allowance is made for the time value of money. To see the importance of the time value of money, suppose a firm makes a gain of $100,000 this year and then a loss of $100,000 in three years. It has no other income. The tax rate is 30 percent. Three years from now, the firm can offset the $100,000 gain of this year with its loss. But it must pay $30,000 in taxes this year, and it gets back only $30,000 in three years, so it loses the use of the money for three years.

2. **Tax shields.** There is a wide variety of tax shields. One is the tax shield on interest paid. Another is the tax shield on depreciation. Firms also have tax credits. All

these complications mean that a firm's marginal tax rate can be quite variable. Further, tax laws change, so at various times firms and investors know that taxes will rise or fall. In such cases, the optimal risk management program is one that increases cash flows when taxes are low and reduces them when they are high.

3. **Personal taxes.** Our discussion ignored taxes paid by investors. Suppose that taxes paid by investors decreased the forward price. In this case, hedging would be less advantageous at the firm level because the forward price would be less attractive. There is no reason to suspect that taxes create biases in the prices of forward contracts—or other derivative contracts—that make hedging at the firm level unattractive.

It is difficult to capture all real-life complications in an analytical model to evaluate the importance of the tax benefits of risk management. To cope with this problem, Graham and Smith (1999) use a simulation approach instead. They do not take into account personal taxes, but otherwise they incorporate all the relevant features of the tax code. They simulate a firm's income, and then evaluate the tax benefit of hedging. For about half the firms, there is a tax benefit from hedging. The typical benefit is that a 1 percent reduction in the volatility of taxable income for a given year reduces the present value of taxes by 1 percent.

The Tax Benefits of Risk Management and Homestake

In 1990, Homestake paid taxes of $5.827 million. It made a loss on continuing operations because it wrote down its investment in North American Metals Corporation. Taxation in extraction industries like minerals and oil and gas companies is notoriously complicated. However, the annual report shows why Homestake's tax rate differs from the statutory tax rate of 34 percent as follows (in thousands of dollars):

Homestake loss: $13,500 at 34% would yield taxes of	$(4,600)
Depletion allowance	(8,398)
State income taxes, net of federal benefit	(224)
Nondeductible foreign losses	18,191
Other, net	858
Total	$5,827

Homestake paid taxes even though it lost money. The exact details of the nondeductible foreign losses are not available from the annual report. Therefore, we cannot say for sure that risk management could have decreased taxes paid by Homestake. However, risk management enables a firm to shift income from states of the world with high tax rates to states of the world with low tax rates. Perhaps risk management could have enabled Homestake to avoid paying taxes while it was making a loss.

Decreases in the price of gold could easily lead to a situation where Homestake would make losses. Avoiding these losses would smooth out taxes over time and hence would increase firm value. Based on the information in the annual report, we cannot quantify this benefit. Petersen and Thiagarajan (2000) compare American Barrick and Homestake in great detail. They find that Homestake has a tendency to time the recognition of expenses when gold prices are high to smooth income. Obviously, in the year discussed here, smoothing income that way did not prevent Homestake from having to pay taxes while it was making a loss.

OPTIMAL CAPITAL STRUCTURE AND RISK MANAGEMENT

Generally, interest paid is deductible from income. A levered firm that pays interest on debt therefore pays less in taxes than one without interest payments for the same operating cash flow. Debt has a tax benefit, which increases the value of the levered firm relative to the value of the unlevered firm. In the presence of costs of financial distress, an increase in the firm's debt has an offsetting cost resulting from the increased likelihood of financial distress. Risk management enables the firm to have a higher debt level, and hence a greater tax shield from debt, for any likelihood of financial distress.

The Tax Shield of Debt, Costs of Financial Distress, and Risk Management

Let's see how risk management enables a firm to increase its tax benefits from debt without increasing its probability of financial distress. Suppose that the costs of financial distress are so high for Pure Gold that it is never worthwhile for Pure Gold to issue an amount of debt so that it defaults when it sells gold for $250. Absent risk management, Pure Gold can issue risk-free debt so that its debt payments at maturity are $250 million. It can use the proceeds of the debt issue to pay a dividend to shareholders. With that debt level, the interest rate on debt is the risk-free rate of 5 percent, so that Pure Gold pays interest of $11.90 million and borrows $239.10 million. The firm's value for its shareholders is the present value of 0.5 × $250M + 0.5 × [$450M − 0.5 × ($450M − $300M − $11.90M)], or $315.475 million.

Using risk management, Pure Gold can issue more risk-free debt and therefore reduce the present value of its tax payments. With risk management, it can lock in pre-tax income of $350 million and therefore can commit to pay $350 million in the form of debt principal, debt interest, and tax payments.

Since the tax shield increases with the debt principal outstanding, Pure Gold wants to issue as much debt as it can without incurring costs of financial distress. Since Pure Gold does not need the cash raised through debt for investment, it pays it out to the shareholders as a dividend. Figure 2-6 plots firm value imposing the constraint that total debt and tax payments cannot exceed $350 million. In this case, Pure Gold can always make its debt payments, so that we assume that there are no costs of

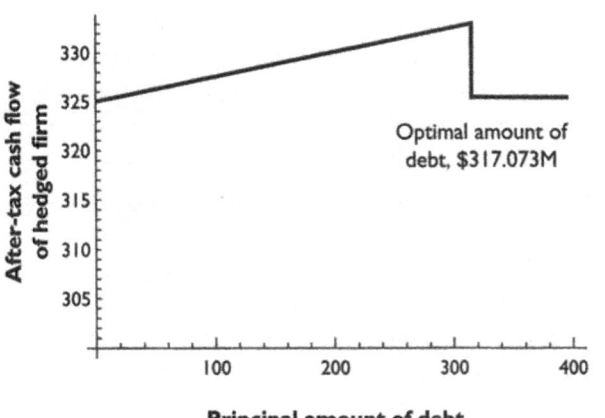

FIGURE 2-6 Firm after-tax cash flow and debt issue.

The firm has an expected pre-tax cash flow of $350 million. The tax rate is 0.5 and the risk-free rate is 5 percent. The figure shows the impact on after-tax cash flow of issuing more debt, assuming that the IRS disallows a deduction for interest of debt when the firm is highly likely to default.

financial distress. If the firm sells more debt, it is bankrupt. Consequently, if F is the principal amount of the debt issued, it must be that:

Debt principal + Debt interest + Taxes = $350M

$F + 0.05\,F + 0.5 × (\$350M − \$300M − 0.05\,F) = \$350M$

Solving for F, we get $317.073 million. To see that this works, note that the firm has to pay taxes on income of $350M − $300M − 0.05 × $317.073M, corresponding to $17.073 million. The debt payments are $317.073M + 0.05 × $317.073, or $332.927 million. The sum of debt payments and taxes is therefore exactly $350 million.

By issuing more debt than F, Pure Gold would always be bankrupt as we have seen already. If it issued less debt instead, it could increase debt and make the shareholders better off. To see this, suppose the firm had $1 million less of debt. Its dividend to shareholders would fall by $1 million and it would have $1.05 million less of debt payments at the end of the year. The decrease in debt payments would reduce the tax shield of debt by $0.25 million, so that the shareholders would receive $1.025 million at the end of the year instead of $1 million today if the firm issued debt instead. The present value of $1.025 million is less than $1 million, so that shareholders are worse off.

In general, firms cannot eliminate all risk, so that debt is risky. By having more debt, firms increase their **tax shield from debt** but increase the present value of costs of financial distress. The **optimal capital structure** of a firm balances the tax benefits of debt against the costs of financial distress. A firm can reduce the present value of the costs of financial distress through risk management by making financial distress less likely. As a result, it can take on more debt. This is the case even if the firm cannot eliminate all risk as in the case of Pure Gold.

One complication we have ignored is that investors pay taxes too. Miller (1978) has emphasized that this complication can change the analysis. Suppose investors pay taxes on bond income but not on capital gains. In this case, they will want a higher return on debt than on equity to offset the high taxes. A higher yield would reduce the tax benefit of debt to the firm. The consensus among financial economists is that personal taxes may limit the corporate benefits from debt but not eliminate them. Whether there are personal taxes or not, the corporation will want to maximize the value of its tax shields.

Does Homestake Have Too Little Debt?

Homestake pays taxes every year. Most years, its tax rate is close to the statutory rate of 34 percent. In 1990, as we saw, Homestake paid taxes at a rate that exceeded the statutory rate. It has almost no debt, and its long-term debt is dwarfed by its cash balances. It surely has too little debt.

By increasing its debt, Homestake takes advantage of the tax shield of debt and reduces its taxes. An increase in debt similarly amplifies the importance of risk management.

SHOULD THE FIRM HEDGE TO REDUCE THE RISK OF LARGE UNDIVERSIFIED SHAREHOLDERS?

Investors who own well-diversified portfolios are relatively unaffected by firm-specific events. On average, their risks balance out, except for the systematic risks of the economy as a whole, which can be controlled by investors through their asset allocation. For other investors who have a large position in a firm, these risks do not balance out. Managers, for example, may have a large stake in the firm for control reasons or because of a compensation plan. Other large investors might value a control position. Investors who cannot diversify firm-specific risk care about the risks that the firm bears. They might want the firm to reduce risk, unless they can reduce it more cheaply through homemade risk management.

Suppose Pure Gold has only one large shareholder who holds 10 percent of the shares and nothing else. This undiversified shareholder cares about the diversifiable risk of the gold mining firm. She wants to reduce the risk of her investment. To do this, she could sell her stake and invest in a diversified portfolio and the risk-free asset. Second, she could keep her stake but use homemade hedging. Third, she could try to convince the firm to hedge.

The firm may have a comparative advantage in hedging and homemade hedging may not be possible for this large investor. Why should the firm expend resources to hedge to please that large investor? If the only benefit of hedging is that this large investor does not have to hedge on her own, the firm uses resources to hedge

without increasing firm value. If the firm gains from having the large shareholder, however, then it can make sense to hedge to make it possible for the large shareholder to keep her investment in the firm.

Large Undiversified Shareholders Can Increase Firm Value

Large shareholders can increase firm value. Smaller and highly diversified shareholders have little reason to pay much attention to what a particular firm is doing. Their smaller stakes give them little benefit from evaluating carefully the actions of managers. A shareholder with a large undiversified stake in a firm will follow the actions of management carefully with an interest in increasing the value of the firm. Evaluating managers and trying to improve what they do is called monitoring management. Larger shareholders get greater financial benefits from monitoring management than smaller ones.

There are two reasons why shareholder monitoring can increase firm value. First, an investor might become a large shareholder because he has some ability in evaluating the actions of management in a particular firm. Such an investor has knowledge and skills that are valuable to the firm. If management chooses to maximize firm value, management welcomes such an investor and listens to him carefully.

Second, managers do not necessarily maximize firm value; they maximize their welfare like all economic agents. Doing so sometimes involves maximizing firm value. What a manager does depends on the incentives. If an action increases firm value but is very risky, a manager on a fixed salary may decide against it because a firm that is bankrupt cannot pay her salary. Monitoring can make it more likely that managers maximize firm value.

A large shareholder who finds that management failed to take an action that maximizes firm value might draw the attention of other shareholders to this fact. In some cases, a large shareholder may even convince another firm to attempt a takeover to remove management and take actions that maximize firm value.

A firm's risk generally makes it unattractive for a shareholder to have a stake large enough to make monitoring worthwhile. If it hedges, a firm may make ownership more attractive to a shareholder who has some advantage in monitoring management. As the large shareholder takes such a larger stake, all other shareholders benefit from the monitoring.

Risk and the Incentives of Managers

One way shareholders can ensure that managers are motivated to maximize the value of the company's shares is through a managerial compensation contract that gives managers a stake in how well the firm does. If managers earn more when the firm does better, this induces them to work harder. Managerial compensation related to the stock price also can have adverse implications for managers. In fact, making managerial compensation depend strongly on any part of the stock return that is not under control of management could be counterproductive. Suppose a firm has large stocks of raw materials that are required for production. In the absence of a risk management program, the value of these raw materials fluctuates over time. Random changes in the value of raw materials may be the main contributors to the volatility of a firm's stock price, yet managers have no control over the price of raw materials. Making managerial compensation depend strongly on the stock price in this case forces management to bear risks, but provides no incentive effects and does not align management's incentives with those of shareholders.

In general, it makes sense to tie managerial compensation to some measure of value created without trying to figure out what is and is not under management's control. If the firm can reduce its risk through hedging, firm value depends on variables that management controls; in this case, relating compensation to firm value does not force managers to bear too much risk and does not induce them to make decisions that are not in the interest of shareholders to eliminate this risk. When managers work hard to increase their compensation, they also work hard to increase shareholder wealth.

Ownership of shares in the firm ties managers' welfare more closely to shareholders' welfare. If they own shares, managers bear risk. Since managers are not diversified shareholders, they care about the firm's total risk. This may lead them to be conservative in their actions. To the degree risk is reduced through risk management, the total risk of the firm falls, and managers become more willing to take risks. Firmwide hedging thereby makes managerial

stock ownership a more effective device to induce managers to maximize firm value.

A risk management program eliminates sources of fluctuation in market value due to forces that are not under management's control. This reduces the risk attached to management's human capital and makes it less likely that managers will undertake risk-reducing activities that diminish firm value. If the risk attached to management's human capital is lower, there may be a willingness to accept a lower compensation. Saving compensation enhances firm value.

Not every form of compensation that depends on firm value motivates management to reduce firm risk. Managerial compensation contracts that include call options on the firm's stock create incentives to take risks. To see how options might induce management not to hedge when hedging would maximize firm value, suppose Pure Gold's management owns a call option on 1,000 shares with exercise price of $350 per share. For simplicity, we assume that management received these options in the past and that exercise of the options does not affect firm value. Assuming a tax advantage to hedging, as we have discussed, firm value is maximized if the firm hedges. Hedging locks in a firm value before managerial compensation of $309.52. Management's options are worthless in this case. If the firm does not hedge, there is a 50 percent chance that the shares will be worth $375, which represents a 50 percent chance that the options will pay off. In this case, management chooses not to hedge even though shareholders would be better off otherwise.

Large Shareholders, Managerial Incentives, and Homestake

The Homestake proxy statement for 1990 shows that the directors own 1.1 percent of the shares. Homestake's CEO, Harry Conger, owns 137,004 shares directly and has the right to acquire 243,542 shares through an option plan. The shares in the option plan have an average exercise price of $14.43, but the share price in 1990 never dropped below $15.30. Managers and directors hold few shares directly and less than is typical for a firm of that size; most of managers' ownership is in the form of options. There is not much incentive for management to protect its stake in the firm through hedging.

A large shareholder who monitors management might be able to increase firm value. To attract such a shareholder, the firm might have to commit to a risk management program. Yet it does not seem that management would want such an outcome. Homestake has one large shareholder, Case, Pomeroy and Co. This company owns 8.2 percent of the shares. Two executives of that company are on the board of directors. Case has been decreasing its stake in Homestake and has a standstill agreement with Homestake that prevents it from buying more shares and gives Homestake rights of first refusal when Case sells shares.

STAKEHOLDERS

Besides large undiversified shareholders, there are individuals and companies whose welfare depends on how well a firm is doing but who cannot diversify the impact of firm risks on their welfare. They can be workers, suppliers, or customers. Such individuals and firms are often called **stakeholders**. Does it make sense to reduce firm-wide risk to reduce the risk borne by these individuals and companies?

When Should Firms Care About Stakeholders?

It is not unusual to hear that a firm should be managed for its stakeholders. In general, though, owners of the firm want the firm to be managed to make them better off, so that maximizing the welfare of stakeholders cannot be a legitimate corporate goal. Yet it is sometimes advantageous for shareholders to reduce the risks that stakeholders bear. Shareholders may want stakeholders to make long-term firm-specific investments. The firm, for instance, might want workers to learn skills that would have minimal value outside the firm. Or it might want a supplier to devote R&D to design parts that only the firm will use. In another case, the value of a product customers buy depends on the firm's implicit warranty. In all these cases, the stakeholders will be reluctant to make firm-specific investments if they question the firm's financial health. If the firm gets in financial trouble, it may not be able to live up to its part of the bargain—that the stakeholders are investing in exchange for benefits from the firm over the long term.

Hedging makes it easier for the firm to honor its bargain with stakeholders. It can hedge at lower cost than the monetary compensation it would have to give to

stakeholders to offset the impact on their welfare of the firm's risk. Without reducing risk, a firm may be able to get the stakeholders to make the requisite investments only by "bribing" them to do so. This means paying workers more so that they will learn the requisite skills, paying the suppliers directly to invest in R&D, and selling products more cheaply to compensate for the risks associated with the warranty. Such economic incentives are more expensive than hedging. Managing risk can therefore help the firm in getting others to make firm-specific investments and lower its costs of doing so.

Stakeholders and Homestake

Are stakeholders important for Homestake? Most likely, no. There is no reason to suspect that workers or suppliers have to make important firm-specific investments whose value would be seriously damaged if Homestake had financial difficulties. The welfare of Homestake's workers and suppliers depends on whether it makes sense to exploit Homestake's mines, not on whether Homestake is financially healthy. Should Homestake fail financially and file for bankruptcy, the new owners of the mine would still want to take advantage of the firm-specific investments made by workers and suppliers if it makes sense to extract gold from Homestake's mines.

A risk management program cannot make it profitable for Homestake to extract gold from its mines when otherwise it would not be. To understand this, suppose the price of gold falls to $150 per ounce, Homestake's extraction cost is $300, and Homestake hedged so that it sold gold forward for $350 per ounce. Rather than extract gold, Homestake is better off buying gold on the spot market to deliver on its forward contracts. It makes a profit of $200 per ounce this way. Producing gold, it only makes a profit of $50 per ounce.

Buyers of gold do not care about its provenance, so Homestake does not have to worry about relationships with customers.

RISK MANAGEMENT, FINANCIAL DISTRESS, AND INVESTMENT

So far, we have paid little attention to the fact that firms are ongoing entities that have opportunities to invest in valuable projects. Suppose Pure Gold has the opportunity to open a profitable new mine a year from now. A large investment must be made first. Without sufficient internal resources, the firm has to borrow or sell equity to finance the opening of the mine. If the costs of external financing are too high, Pure Gold might not be able to open the mine, and shareholders would lose the expected profits.

We investigate the main reasons why firms might not be able to invest in profitable projects because the cost of external financing is too high, and show how risk management can help avoid such situations.

Debt Overhang

Too much debt induces shareholders to take on negative net present value projects and to avoid investing in valuable projects because they require issuing equity that dilutes their stake in the firm. When a firm has so much debt that it leads it to make investment decisions that benefit shareholders but affect its total value adversely, the firm has a **debt overhang**. As long as a firm has debt and risk, there is some possibility it may end up with a debt overhang. The probability that the firm might experience a debt overhang in the future reduces its value today. Consequently, risk management that reduces this probability increases firm value today.

A debt overhang can make shareholders take actions that reduce firm value but increase the value of the firm's equity. To see this, consider a firm, Highly Levered Gold (HLG). HLG never intended to have high leverage, but after successive mining disasters, it became highly levered because losses ate away at its equity. Suppose that the financial situation of HLG is such that if firm value does not increase sharply before the maturity of its debt, shareholders will receive nothing and the creditors will own the firm. Suppose further that if shareholders do nothing, HLG's value cannot increase sufficiently to enable it to repay its creditors. To make it more likely that firm value will increase sufficiently to make their shares valuable, shareholders can increase HLG's risk. If they take projects that have some chance of a large payoff but otherwise lose money, shareholders make money if the projects do well but do not lose money if the projects do poorly since they would have received nothing anyway. In fact, shareholders will be willing to take these long-shot projects even if they have a negative net present value.

When a firm has a large debt overhang, its shareholders may decide against raising funds to finance valuable new projects. Suppose that HLG has a valuable investment opportunity: By investing \$10 million, the firm acquires a project that has a positive net present value of \$5 million. The project is small enough that it will not enable HLG to repay its debt. The firm has no cash. The only way it can invest is by raising funds.

Borrowing is not an option. Consequently, HLG would have to sell equity to raise funds. Consider the impact of having an investor invest one dollar in new equity. The investor will only invest the dollar if she can expect to earn an appropriate return given the risk she takes. If an investor invests one dollar in a new share, that money most likely will end up in the pockets of the creditors since the most likely outcome is that the firm will not have money left after paying the creditors. This extra dollar will be a windfall for the creditors. Since the creditors will receive that dollar without having to pay for it, the old shareholders will have to pay for it through a reduction in the value of their stake brought about by the fact that they have to share the equity payoffs with the new investor. Hence, even though the project would increase firm value, the current shareholders will not want the firm to take it because it will not benefit them. The only way the firm would take the project is for shareholders to renegotiate with creditors so that they get more of the payoff of the project. Such a renegotiation is difficult and costly, and sometimes, no such renegotiation succeeds.

To understand why the debt overhang leads to underinvestment, let's look at a simple example. Suppose HLG can sell one million ounces of gold at either \$450 or \$250 at the end of the year. Each outcome has a probability of 0.5. Gold price risk is not systematic risk. HLG has debt payments of \$400 million. The value of the debt is therefore $[(0.5 \times \$250M) + (0.5 \times \$400M)]/1.05$, or \$309.524 million. The value of equity is $0.5 \times \$50M/1.05$, or \$23.8095 million. Now, HLG receives an investment opportunity that pays \$10 million for sure but costs \$5 million. It has to raise \$5 million to finance the investment opportunity.

Firm value without the investment opportunity is $\$350M/1.05$, or \$333.33 million. With the investment opportunity, it is $\$360M/1.05$, or \$342.857 million. Taking the investment opportunity increases firm value, but who benefits from the investment opportunity? If the gold price is \$250, the bondholders get all the benefit of the funds raised—they get \$10 million more. If the gold price is \$450, the shareholders get all the benefit of the funds raised. The value of equity therefore increases by

0.5 × 10M/1.05, or $4.7619 million. The shareholders raise $5 million, but equity increases by less. Since the new shareholders must receive $5 million worth of claims against the firm, the value of the claims of the old share-holders must fall from $23.8095 million to $23.5714 mil-lion. The share price must fall as the firm takes advantage of the new investment opportunity even though firm value increases. The old shareholders therefore prefer that the firm does not raise funds and does not invest in the investment opportunity. The firm therefore underinvests—it does not invest in a project that is a positive net present value project for the firm.

The value of a firm in the capital markets is lower when there is a probability that it may not enter into valu-able projects because its financial health might be poor. Reducing this probability through risk management increases firm value as long as risk management is cheap enough.

Information Asymmetries and Agency Costs of Managerial Discretion

The key problem management faces in raising funds is that managers know more about the firm's projects than the outsiders they are dealing with. When one party to a deal knows more than the other, we call this an **informa-tion asymmetry**. Suppose that the firm's equity with its current projects is $100 million. Managers believe that by raising $100 million of new equity and investing the pro-ceeds, they can invest in a project with a net present value of $50 million. If they ask you to invest, you have to figure out the return on your investment based on the informa-tion provided to you by management.

Generally, managers benefit from firm growth, so that they have much to gain by undertaking new projects, which can lead to biases. They may tend to minimize problems. Even if they are completely unbiased and reveal all the information they have to potential investors, you as an investor cannot easily tell that. Often, management has enough to gain from undertaking a project that it might want to invest even if the chance of success is low enough that the project is a negative net present value project.

The costs associated with management's opportunity to undertake projects that have a negative net present value when it is advantageous for them to do so are called **agency costs of managerial discretion**. When manag-ers have discretion to take actions, they can pursue their own objectives, which creates agency costs. That is, the agent's interests, or management's interests, are not aligned with the interests of the principals who hire man-agement, namely, the shareholders.

Agency costs of managerial discretion make it harder for a firm to raise funds and increase the cost of funds. If out-siders are not sure that the project is as likely to pay off as management claims, they want more compensation for providing the funds. Even if the project is as described, having to pay a higher expected compensation reduces the profits from the project. The project may not be prof-itable because the cost of capital for the firm is too high.

There is more than one way to reduce the costs of mana-gerial discretion and hence reduce the costs of the funds raised. A firm could entice a large shareholder to come on board. This shareholder would see the company from the inside, and would be better able to assess whether the project is valuable. Or a risk management strategy might preserve ongoing firm value and hence might enable the firm to take the project. A firm whose value is not in doubt may be able to borrow against assets rather than try to borrow against the future project.

A risk management strategy that preserves firm value might help the firm to finance the project for another reason. Investors who look at a firm's history have to fig-ure out what a loss in firm value implies. In general, it will be difficult for outsiders to see exactly what is going on. They will therefore always worry that the true explanation for the losses is incompetent management. There could be many explanations for a loss in firm value. Firm value could fall because a stock of raw materials fell in value, because the economy is in a recession, because a plant burned down, or because management is incompetent. Outsiders cannot be sure. If it reduces risk through risk management, the firm makes it easier for investors to assess the ability of management since it eliminates some sources of unexpected losses.

The Cost of External Funding and Homestake

Is it really the case that external funding can be more expensive than internal funding? The answer is yes. There is much empirical evidence that shows that firms with poor cash flow have to cut back investment. The problem with that evidence is that poor cash flow might signal bad investment opportunities, in which case it would not

BOX 2-1 Warren Buffet and Catastrophe Insurance

Insurance companies hedge some of their exposure to catastrophes such as earthquakes, hurricanes, or tornadoes by insuring themselves with reinsurers. A typical reinsurance contract promises to reimburse an insurance company for claims due to a catastrophe within some range. For example, an insurance company could be reimbursed for up to $1 billion of California earthquake claims in excess of $2 billion. Catastrophe insurance risks are diversifiable risks, so bearing these risks should not earn a risk premium. This means that the price of the insurance should be the expected losses discounted at the risk-free rate. Yet, in practice, the pricing of reinsurance does not work this way.

Let's look at an example. In the fall of 1996, Berkshire Hathaway, Warren Buffett's company, sold reinsurance to the California Earthquake Authority in the amount of $1.05 billion insured for four years. The annual premium was 10.75 percent of the annual limit, or $113 million. The probability that the reinsurance would be triggered was estimated at 1.7 percent at inception by EQE International, a catastrophe risk modeling firm. Ignoring discounting, the annual premium was therefore 530 percent of the expected loss (0.1075 is 530 percent of 0.017). If the capital asset pricing model had been used to price the reinsurance contract, the premium would have been $17.85 million in the absence of discounting and somewhat less with discounting.

How can we make sense of this huge difference between the actual premium and the premium predicted by the capital asset pricing model? A reinsurance contract is useless if there is credit risk; that is, the reinsurer has to have liquid assets that enable it to pay the claims. The problem is that holding liquid assets creates managerial discretion agency costs. It is difficult to ensure that a reinsurer will indeed have the money when needed. Once the catastrophe has occurred, the underinvestment problem would prevent the reinsurer from raising the funds because the benefit from raising the funds would accrue to the policyholders rather than to the investors. The reinsurer therefore has to raise funds when the policy is agreed upon. Hence, in the case of this example, the reinsurer would need, if it did not have the capital, to raise $1.05 billion minus the premium.

The investors have to be convinced that the reinsurer will not take the money and run or take the money and invest it in risky securities. Yet the reinsurer has strong incentives to take risks unless its reputational capital is extremely valuable. In the absence of valuable reputational capital, the reinsurer can gamble with the investors' money. If the reinsurer wins, it makes an additional profit. If it loses, the investors or the insurer's clients lose.

Another problem with reinsurance is due to information asymmetries and agency costs in the investment industry. The reinsurer has to raise money from investors, but the funds provided would be lost if a catastrophe occurs. Most investment takes place through money managers who act as agents for individual investors. In the case of funds raised by reinsurance companies, the money manager is in a difficult position. Suppose that he decides that investing with a reinsurance firm is a superb investment. How can the individual investors who hire the money manager know that he has acted in their interest if a catastrophe occurs? They will have a difficult time deciding whether the money manager was right and they were unlucky or the money manager was wrong. This problem leads the money manager to require ample compensation for investing with the reinsurance firm.

Berkshire Hathaway has reputational capital that makes it unprofitable to gamble with investors' money. Consequently, it does not have to write a complicated contract to ensure that there will not be credit risk. Since it has already large reserves, it does not have to deal with the problems of raising large amounts of funds for reinsurance purpose. Could these advantages be worth as much as it seems in the great difference between the California premium and the theoretical price? There is no evidence that there were credible reinsurers willing to enter cheaper contracts. With perfect markets, such reinsurers would have been too numerous to count.

Source: Kenneth Froot, "The limited financing of catastrophe risk: An overview," *The Financing of Property Casualty Risks*, University of Chicago Press, 1997.

---

be surprising to see that firms with poor cash flow cut investment. However, this is not the whole story. Lamont (1997) shows that drops in oil prices led oil companies to cut back investment in their non-oil activities. An oil company that sees its cash flow drop has no reason to reduce investment in the department stores it owns unless external financing is more costly than internal financing, so

that when the firm has to switch from internal financing to outside financing, the cost of capital increases and some investments are no longer worthwhile.

Box 2-1, Warren Buffett and Catastrophe Insurance, provides an example where an insurance product is priced in a way that can be explained only by the existence of steep costs of external finance because of agency costs. The example also shows that the agency costs and information asymmetries discussed in this section can make risk management products more expensive.

Homestake could repay all its debt with its cash reserves, so that debt overhang is not an immediate issue. The firm also has enough cash that it could finance large investments out of internal resources. Yet if gold prices fell, Homestake's resources would shrink over time. At some point, its ability to undertake new projects might be compromised. When gold prices are low, Homestake might have few good investment opportunities. However, if it expects to have more valuable investment opportunities if gold prices fall, it might want to put in place a risk management program that insures that it will have appropriate financial resources to finance these investment opportunities.

SUMMARY

In this chapter, we have investigated ways that firms without risk management can leave money on the table. They can:

1. Bear more bankruptcy costs and financial distress costs than they should.
2. Pay more taxes than they should.
3. Have less leverage than they should.
4. Have managers provided with poor incentives.
5. Fail to retain valuable large shareholders.
6. Fail to get stakeholders to make firm-specific investments.
7. Find it unprofitable to invest in positive net present value projects.
8. Find it profitable to take bad projects.

We have identified benefits from risk management that can increase firm value. We move on to the question of whether and how such benefits can provide the basis for the design of a risk management program.

Key Concepts

agency costs of managerial discretion, 33
bankruptcy costs, 22
costs of financial distress, 24

deadweight costs, 20
debt overhang, 32
information asymmetry, 33
optimal capital structure, 28
stakeholders, 31
tax shield from debt, 28

Questions

1. How does risk management affect the present value of bankruptcy costs?
2. Why do the tax benefits of risk management depend on the firm having a tax rate that depends on cash flow?
3. How do carrybacks and carryforwards affect the tax benefits of risk management?
4. How does risk management affect the tax shield of debt?
5. Does risk management affect the optimal capital structure of a firm? Why?
6. Does it pay to reduce firm risk because a large shareholder wants the firm to do so?
7. How does the impact of risk management on managerial incentives depend on the nature of management's compensation contract?
8. Is risk management profitable for the shareholders of a firm that has a debt overhang?
9. How do costs of external funding affect the benefits of risk management?

Literature Note

Smith and Stulz (1985) provide an analysis of the determinants of hedging policies that covers the issues of bankruptcy costs, costs of financial distress, stakeholders, and managerial compensation. Diamond (1981) shows how hedging makes it possible for investors to evaluate managerial performance more effectively. DeMarzo and Duffie (1991) and Breeden and Viswanathan (1998) show that hedging is valuable because of information asymmetries between managers and investors. Froot, Scharfstein, and Stein (1993) derive explicit hedging policies when firms would have to invest suboptimally in the absence of hedging because of difficulties in securing funds to finance investment. Stulz (1990, 1996) discusses how hedging can enable firms to have higher leverage. Stulz (1990) focuses on the agency costs of managerial discretion. Hedging makes it less likely that the firm will not be able to invest in valuable projects, so it can support higher leverage. One reason debt is valuable is because it prevents managers from making bad investments. Tufano (1998) makes the point that reducing the need to go to the external capital markets also enables managers to avoid the scrutiny of the market. This will be the case if greater hedging is not accompanied by greater leverage. Myers (1977) was the first one to provide an analysis of debt overhang, showing how it can lead shareholders to be unwilling to raise funds for valuable new projects. The empirical evidence on the positive relation between investment and cash flow is discussed in Hubbard (1998). Bessembinder (1991) and Mayers and Smith (1987) analyze how hedging can reduce the underinvestment problem. Leland (1998) provides a model where hedging increases firm value because (1) it increases the tax benefits from debt and (2) it reduces the probability of default and the probability of incurring distress costs. Ross (1997) also models the tax benefits of hedging. Petersen and Thiagarajan (1998) provide a detailed comparison of how hedging theories apply to Homestake and American Barrick.

Delineating Efficient Portfolios 3

Excerpt is Chapter 5 of Modern Portfolio Theory and Investment Analysis, *8th Edition, by Edwin Elton, Martin Gruber, Stephen Brown and William Goetzmann.*

Learning Objectives

After completing this reading, FRM Candidates should be able to:

- Calculate the expected return and volatility of a portfolio of risky assets.
- Explain how covariance and correlation affect the expected return and volatility of a portfolio of risky assets.
- Describe the shape of the portfolio possibilities curve.

- Define the minimum variance portfolio.
- Define the efficient frontier and describe the impact on it of various assumptions concerning short sales and borrowing.

In this chapter we look at the risk and return characteristics of combinations of securities in more detail. We start off with a reexamination of the attributes of combinations of two risky assets. In doing so, we emphasize a geometric interpretation of asset combinations. It is a short step from the analysis of the combination of two or more risky assets to the analysis of combinations of all possible risky assets. After making this step, we can delineate that subset of portfolios that will be preferred by all investors who exhibit risk avoidance and who prefer more return to less.[1] This set is usually called the efficient set or efficient frontier. Its shape will differ according to the assumptions that are made with respect to the ability of the investor to sell securities short as well as his ability to lend and borrow funds.[2] Alternative assumptions about short sales and lending and borrowing are examined.

COMBINATIONS OF TWO RISKY ASSETS REVISITED: SHORT SALES NOT ALLOWED

Previously, we treated the two assets as if they were individual assets, but nothing in the analysis so constrains them. In fact, when we talk about assets, we could equally well be talking about portfolios of risky assets.

Recall that the expected return on a portfolio of two assets is given by

$$\bar{R}_P = X_A \bar{R}_A + X_B \bar{R}_B \tag{3.1}$$

where

X_A is the fraction of the portfolio held in asset A

X_B is the fraction of the portfolio held in asset B

$\bar{R}_P$ is the expected return on the portfolio

$\bar{R}_A$ is the expected return on asset A

$\bar{R}_B$ is the expected return on asset B

In addition, since we require the investor to be fully invested, the fraction she invests in A plus the fraction she invests in B must equal one, or

$$X_A + X_B = 1$$

---

[1] In this chapter and most of those that follow, we assume that mean variance is the relevant space for portfolio analysis.

[2] Short selling is defined at a later point in this chapter.

We can rewrite this expression as

$$X_B = 1 - X_A \tag{3.2}$$

Substituting Equation (3.2) into Equation (3.1), we can express the expected return on a portfolio of two assets as

$$\bar{R}_P = X_A \bar{R}_A + (1 - X_A)\bar{R}_B$$

Notice that the expected return on the portfolio is a simple-weighted average of the expected returns on the individual securities, and that the weights add to one. The same is not necessarily true of the risk (standard deviation of the return) of the portfolio. The standard deviation of the return on the portfolio was shown to be equal to

$$\sigma_P = (X_A^2 \sigma_A^2 + X_B^2 \sigma_B^2 + 2X_A X_B \sigma_{AB})^{1/2}$$

where

σ_P is the standard deviation of the return on the portfolio

σ_A^2 is the variance of the return on security A

σ_B^2 is the variance of the return on security B

σ_{AB} is the covariance between the returns on security A and security B

If we substitute Equation (3.2) into this expression, we obtain

$$\sigma_P = [X_A^2 \sigma_A^2 + (1 - X_A)^2 \sigma_B^2 + 2X_A(1 - X_A)\sigma_{AB}]^{1/2} \tag{3.3}$$

Recalling that $\sigma_{AB} = \rho_{AB}\sigma_A\sigma_B$ where ρ_{AB} is the correlation coefficient between securities A and B, then Equation (3.3) becomes

$$\sigma_P = [X_A^2 \sigma_A^2 + (1 - X_A)^2 \sigma_B^2 + 2X_A(1 - X_A)\rho_{AB}\sigma_A\sigma_B]^{1/2} \tag{3.4}$$

The standard deviation of the portfolio is not, in general, a simple-weighted average of the standard deviation of each security. Cross-product terms are involved and the weights do not, in general, add to one. In order to learn more about this relationship, we now study some specific cases involving different degrees of co-movement between securities.

We know that a correlation coefficient has maximum value of +1 and minimum value of −1. A value of +1 means that two securities will always move in perfect unison, while a value of −1 means that their movements are exactly opposite to each other. We start with an examination of these extreme cases; then we turn to an examination of some intermediate values for the correlation coefficients. As an aid in interpreting results, we examine a specific example as well as general expressions for risk and return. For the example, we consider two stocks: a large manufacturer of automobiles ("Colonel Motors") and an electric utility company operating in a large eastern city ("Separated Edison"). Assume the stocks have the following characteristics:

	Expected Return	Standard Deviation
Colonel Motors (C)	14%	6%
Separated Edison (S)	8%	3%

As you might suspect, the car manufacturer has a bigger expected return and a bigger risk than the electric utility.

Case 1—Perfect Positive Correlation (ρ = +1)

Let the subscript C stand for Colonel Motors and the subscript S stand for Separated Edison. If the correlation coefficient is +1, then the equation for the risk on the portfolio, Equation (3.4), simplifies to

$$\sigma_P = [X_C^2\sigma_C^2 + (1 - X_C)^2\sigma_S^2 + 2X_C(1 - X_C)\sigma_C\sigma_S]^{1/2} \quad \textbf{(3.5)}$$

Note that the term in square brackets has the form $X^2 + 2XY + Y^2$ and, thus, can be written as

$$[X_C\sigma_C + (1 - X_C)\sigma_S]^2$$

Since the standard deviation of the portfolio is equal to the positive square root of this expression, we know that

$$\sigma_P = X_C\sigma_C + (1 - X_C)\sigma_S$$

while the expected return on the portfolio is

$$\bar{R}_P = X_C\bar{R}_C + (1 - X_C)\bar{R}_S$$

Thus with the correlation coefficient equal to +1, both risk and return of the portfolio are simply linear combinations of the risk and return of each security. In footnote 3 we

show that the form of these two equa… all combinations of two securities that are perfec… related will lie on a straight line in risk and return space.[3] We now illustrate that this is true for the stocks in our example. For the two stocks under study

$$\bar{R}_P = \frac{\sigma_P - \sigma_S}{\sigma_C - \sigma_S}\bar{R}_C + \left(1 - \frac{\sigma_P - \sigma_S}{\sigma_C - \sigma_S}\right)\bar{R}_S$$

Table 3-1 presents the return on a portfolio for selected values of X_C, and Figure 3-1 presents a graph of this relationship. Note that the relationship is a straight line. The equation of the straight line could easily be derived as follows. Utilizing the equation presented above for σ_P to solve for X_C yields

$$X_C = \frac{\sigma_P}{3} - 1$$

Substituting this expression for X_C into the equation for $\bar{R}_P$ and rearranging yields[4]

$$\bar{R}_P = 2 + 2\sigma_P$$

In the case of perfectly correlated assets, the return and risk on the portfolio of the two assets is a weighted average of the return and risk on the individual assets. There is no reduction in risk from purchasing both assets. This can be seen by examining Figure 3-1 and noting that combinations of the two assets lie along a straight line connecting the two assets. Nothing has been gained by diversifying rather than purchasing the individual assets.

---

[3] Solving for X_C in the expression for standard deviation yields

$$X_C = \frac{\sigma_P - \sigma_S}{\sigma_C - \sigma_S}$$

Substituting this into the expression for expected return yields

$$\bar{R}_P = \frac{\sigma_P - \sigma_S}{\sigma_C - \sigma_S}\bar{R}_C + \left(1 - \frac{\sigma_P - \sigma_S}{\sigma_C - \sigma_S}\right)\bar{R}_S$$

$$\bar{R}_P = \left(\bar{R}_S - \frac{\bar{R}_C - \bar{R}_S}{\sigma_C - \sigma_S}\sigma_S\right) + \left(\frac{\bar{R}_C - \bar{R}_S}{\sigma_C - \sigma_S}\right)\sigma_P$$

which is the equation of a straight line connecting security C and security S in expected return standard deviation space.

[4] An alternative way to derive this equation is to substitute the appropriate values for the two firms into the equation derived in footnote 3. This yields

$$\bar{R}_P = 8 + 6\frac{(\sigma_P - 3)}{3} = 2 + 2\sigma_P$$

TABLE 3-1	The Expected Return and Standard Deviation of a Portfolio of Colonel Motors and Separated Edison When ρ = +1

X_C	0	0.2	0.4	0.5	0.6	0.8	1.0
$\bar{R}_P$	8.0	9.2	10.4	11	11.6	12.8	14.0
σ_P	3.0	3.6	4.2	4.5	4.8	5.4	6.0

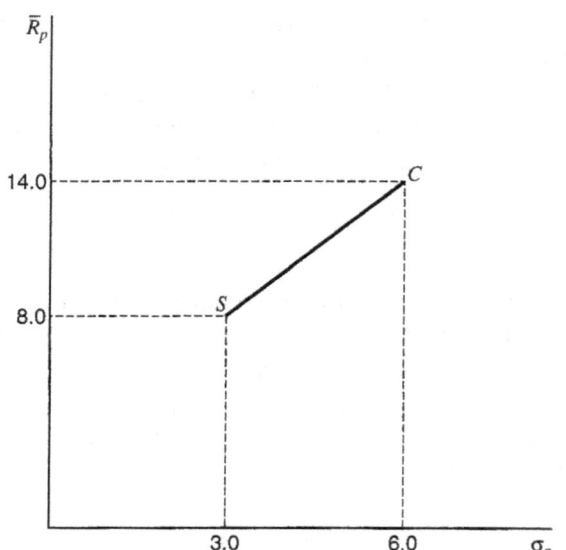

FIGURE 3-1 Relationship between expected return and standard deviation when $\rho = +1$.

Case 2—Perfect Negative Correlation ($\rho = -1.0$)

We now examine the other extreme: two assets that move perfectly together but in exactly opposite directions. In this case the standard deviation of the portfolio is [from Equation (3.4) with $\rho = -1.0$]

$$\sigma_p = [X_c^2\sigma_c^2 + (1-X_c)^2\sigma_s^2 - 2X_c(1-X_c)\sigma_c\sigma_s]^{1/2} \quad \textbf{(3.6)}$$

Once again the equation for standard deviation can be simplified. The term in the brackets is equivalent to either of the following two expressions:

$$[X_c\sigma_c - (1-X_c)\sigma_s]^2$$

or

$$[-X_c\sigma_c + (1-X_c)\sigma_s]^2 \quad \textbf{(3.7)}$$

Thus σ_p is either

$$\sigma_p = X_c\sigma_c - (1-X_c)\sigma_s$$

or

$$\sigma_p = -X_c\sigma_c + (1-X_c)\sigma_s \quad \textbf{(3.8)}$$

Since we took the square root to obtain an expression for σ_p and since the square root of a negative number is imaginary, either of the above equations holds only when its right-hand side is positive. A further examination

shows that the right-hand side of one equation is simply -1 times the other. Thus, each equation is valid only when the right-hand side is positive. Since one is always positive when the other is negative (except when both equations equal zero), there is a unique solution for the return and risk of any combination of securities C and S. These equations are very similar to the ones we obtained when we had a correlation of $+1$. Each also plots as a straight line when σ_p is plotted against X_c. Thus, one would suspect that an examination of the return on the portfolio of two assets as a function of the standard deviation would yield two straight lines, one for each expression for σ_p. As we observe in a moment, this is, in fact, the case.[5]

The value of σ_p for Equation (3.7) or (3.8) is always smaller than the value of σ_p for the case where $\rho = +1$ [Equation (3.5)] for all values of X_c between 0 and 1. Thus the risk on a portfolio of assets is always smaller when the correlation coefficient is -1 than when it is $+1$. We can go one step further. If two securities are perfectly negatively correlated (i.e., they move in exactly opposite directions), it should always be possible to find some combination of these two securities that has zero risk. By setting either Equation (3.7) or (3.8) equal to 0, we find that a portfolio with $X_c = \sigma_s/(\sigma_s + \sigma_c)$ will have zero risk. Since $\sigma_s > 0$ and $\sigma_s + \sigma_c > \sigma_s$, this implies that $0 < X_c < 1$ or that the zero-risk portfolio will always involve positive investment in both securities.

Now let us return to our example. Minimum risk occurs when $X_c = 3/(3 + 6) = \frac{1}{3}$. Furthermore, for the case of perfect negative correlation,

$$\bar{R}_p = 8 + 6X_c$$
$$\sigma_p = 6X_c - 3(1 - X_c)$$

or

$$\sigma_p = -6X_c + 3(1 - X_c)$$

there are two equations relating σ_p to X_c. Only one is appropriate for any value of X_c. The appropriate equation to define σ_p for any value of X_c is that equation for which $\sigma_p \geq 0$. Note that if $\sigma_p > 0$ from one equation, then $\sigma_p < 0$ for the other. Table 3-2 presents the return on the portfolio for

---

[5] This occurs for the same reason that the analysis for $\rho = +1$ led to one straight line, and the mathematical proof is analogous to that presented for the case of $\rho = +1$.

TABLE 3-2 The Expected Return and Standard Deviation of a Portfolio of Colonel Motors and Separated Edison When $\rho = -1$

X_C	0	0.2	0.4	0.6	0.8	1.0
$\bar{R}_P$	8.0	9.2	10.4	11.6	12.8	14.0
σ_P	3.0	1.2	0.6	2.4	4.2	6.0

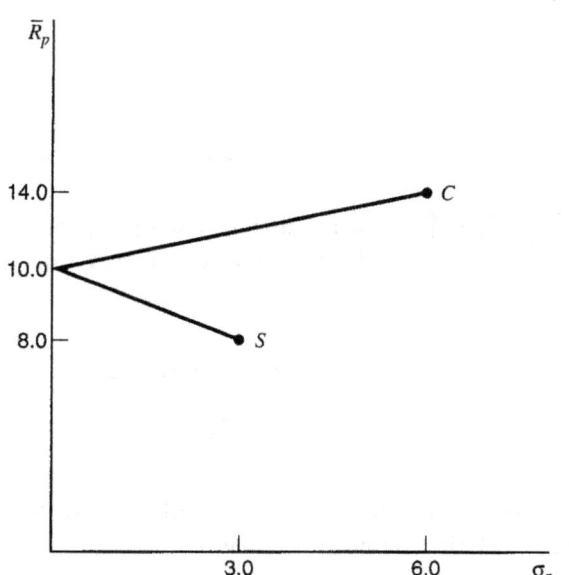

FIGURE 3-2 Relationship between expected return and standard deviation when $\rho = -1$.

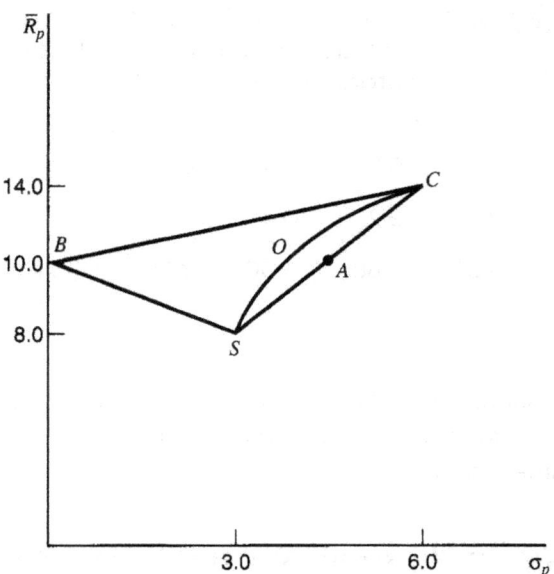

FIGURE 3-3 Relationship between expected return and standard deviation for various correlation coefficients.

selected values of X_C, and Figure 3-2 presents a graph of this relationship.[6]

Notice that a combination of the two securities exists that provides a portfolio with zero risk. Employing the formula developed before for the composition of the zero-risk portfolio, we find that X_C should equal $3/(3 + 6)$ or $\frac{1}{3}$. We

---

[6] The equation for $\bar{R}_P$ as a function of σ_P can be obtained by solving the expression relating σ_P and XC for XC and using this to eliminate X^c in the expression for $\bar{R}_P$. This yields

$$\bar{R}_P = 8 + 6\left(\frac{\sigma_P + 3}{6 + 3}\right) = 10 + \frac{2}{3}\sigma_P$$

or

$$\bar{R}_P = 8 + 6\left(\frac{\sigma_P - 3}{-6 - 3}\right) = 10 - \frac{2}{3}\sigma_P$$

can see this is correct from Figure 3-2 or by substituting $\frac{1}{3}$ for X_C in the equation for portfolio risk given previously. We have once again demonstrated the most powerful result of diversification: the ability of combinations of securities to reduce risk. In fact, it is not uncommon for combinations of two securities to have less risk than either of the assets in the combination.

We have now examined combinations of risky assets for perfect positive and perfect negative correlation. In Figure 3-3 we have plotted both of these relationships on the same graph. From this graph we should be able to see intuitively where portfolios of these two stocks should lie if correlation coefficients took on intermediate values. From the expression for the standard deviation [Equation (3.4)], we see that for any value for X_C between 0 and 1 the lower the correlation, the lower the standard deviation of the portfolio. The standard deviation reaches its lowest value for $\rho = -1$ (curve SBC) and its highest value for $\rho = +1$ (curve SAC). Therefore, these two curves should represent the limits within which all portfolios of these two securities must lie for intermediate values of the correlation coefficient. We would speculate that an intermediate correlation might produce a curve such as SOC in Figure 3-3. We demonstrate this by returning to our example and constructing

TABLE 3-3 The Expected Return and Standard Deviation for a Portfolio of Colonel Motors and Separated Edison with $\rho = 0$

X_c	0	0.2	0.4	0.6	0.8	1.0
$\bar{R}_p$	8.0	9.2	10.4	11.6	12.8	14.0
σ_p	3.00	2.68	3.00	3.79	4.84	6.0

the relationship between risk and return for portfolios of our two securities when the correlation coefficient is assumed to be 0 and +0.5.

Case 3—No Relationship between Returns on the Assets ($\rho = 0$)

The expression for return on the portfolio remains unchanged; however, because the covariance term drops out, the expression for standard deviation becomes

$$\sigma_p = [X_c^2\sigma_c^2 + (1 - X_c)^2\sigma_s^2]^{1/2}$$

For our example this yields

$$\sigma_p = [(6)^2 X_c^2 + (3)^2(1 - X_c)^2]^{1/2}$$
$$\sigma_p = [45X_c^2 - 18X_c + 9]^{1/2}$$

Table 3-3 presents the returns and standard deviation on the portfolio of Colonel Motors and Separated Edison for selected values of X_c.

A graphical presentation of the risk and return on these portfolios is shown in Figure 3-4. There is one point on this figure that is worth special attention: the portfolio that has minimum risk. This portfolio can be found in general by looking at the equation for risk:

$$\sigma_p = [X_c^2\sigma_c^2 + (1 - X_c)^2\sigma_s^2 + 2X_c(1 - X_c)\sigma_c\sigma_s\rho_{cs}]^{1/2}$$

To find the value of X_c that minimizes this equation, we take the derivative of it with respect to X_c, set the derivative equal to zero, and solve for X_c. The derivative is

$$\frac{\partial\sigma_p}{\partial X_c} = \left(\frac{1}{2}\right)\frac{[2X_c\sigma_c^2 - 2\sigma_s^2 + 2X_c\sigma_s^2 + 2\sigma_c\sigma_s\rho_{cs} - 4X_c\sigma_c\sigma_s\rho_{cs}]}{[X_c^2\sigma_c^2 + (1 - X_c)^2\sigma_s^2 + 2X_c(1 - X_c)\sigma_c\sigma_s\rho_{cs}]^{1/2}}$$

Setting this equal to zero and solving for X_c yields

$$X_c = \frac{\sigma_s^2 - \sigma_c\sigma_s\rho_{cs}}{\sigma_c^2 + \sigma_s^2 - 2\sigma_c\sigma_s\rho_{cs}} \tag{3.9}$$

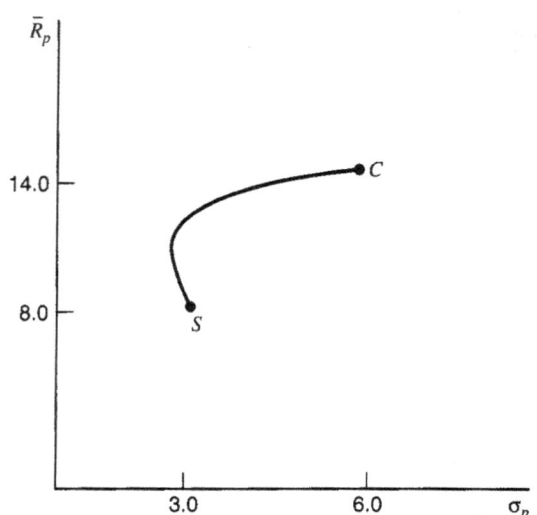

FIGURE 3-4 Relationship between expected return and standard deviation when $\rho = 0$.

In the present case ($\rho_{cs} = 0$), this reduces to

$$X_c = \frac{\sigma_s^2}{\sigma_c^2 + \sigma_s^2}$$

Continuing with the previous example, we find that the value of X_c that minimizes risk is

$$X_c = \frac{9}{9 + 36} = \frac{1}{5} = 0.20$$

This is the minimum-risk portfolio that was shown in Figure 3-4.

Case 4—Intermediate Risk ($\rho = 0.5$)

The correlation between any two actual stocks is almost always greater than 0 and considerably less than 1. To show a more typical relationship between risk and return for two stocks, we have chosen to examine the relationship when $\rho = +0.5$.

The equation for the risk of portfolios composed of Colonel Motors and Separated Edison when the correlation is 0.5 is

$$\sigma_p = [(6)^2 X_c^2 + (3)^2(1 - X_c)^2 + 2X_c(1 - X_c)(3)(6)(\tfrac{1}{2})]^{1/2}$$
$$\sigma_p = (27X_c^2 + 9)^{1/2}$$

Table 3-4 presents the returns and risks on alternative portfolios of our two stocks when the correlation between them is 0.5.

TABLE 3-4 The Expected Return and Standard Deviation for a Portfolio of Colonel Motors and Separated Edison When $\rho = 0.5$

X_C	0	0.2	0.4	0.6	0.8	1.0
$\bar{R}_P$	8.0	9.2	10.4	11.6	12.8	14.0
σ_P	3.00	3.17	3.65	4.33	5.13	6.00

This risk-return relationship is plotted in Figure 3-5 along with the risk-return relationships for other intermediate values of the correlation coefficient. Notice that in this example if $\rho = 0.5$, then the minimum risk is obtained at a value of $X_C = 0$ or where the investor has placed 100% of his funds in Separated Edison. This point could have been derived analytically from Equation (3.9). Employing this equation yields

$$X_C = \frac{9 - 18(0.5)}{9 + 36 - 2(18)(0.5)} = 0$$

In this example (i.e., $\rho_{CS} = 0.5$), there is no combination of the two securities that is less risky than the least risky asset by itself, though combinations are still less risky than they were in the case of perfect positive correlation. The particular value of the correlation coefficient for which no combination of two securities is less risky than the least risky security depends on the characteristics of the assets in question. Specifically, for all assets there is some value of ρ such that the risk of the portfolio can no longer be made less than the risk of the least risky asset in the portfolio.[7]

We have developed some insights into combinations of two securities or portfolios from the analysis performed to this point. First, we have noted that the lower (closer to −1.0) the correlation coefficient between assets, all other attributes held constant, the higher the payoff from diversification. Second, we have seen that combinations of

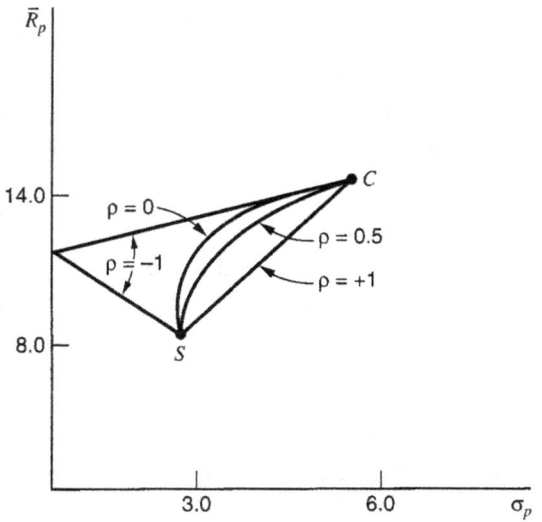

FIGURE 3-5 Relationship between expected return and standard deviation of return for various correlation coefficients.

two assets can never have more risk than that found on a straight line connecting the two assets in expected return standard deviation space. Finally, we have produced a simple expression for finding the minimum variance portfolio when two assets are combined in a portfolio. We can use this to gain more insight into the shape of the curve along which all possible combinations of assets must lie in expected return standard deviation space. This curve, which is called the portfolio possibilities curve, is the subject of the next section.

THE SHAPE OF THE PORTFOLIO POSSIBILITIES CURVE

Reexamine the earlier figures in this chapter and note that the portion of the portfolio possibility curve that lies above the minimum variance portfolio is concave while that which lies below the minimum variance portfolio is convex.[8] This is not due to the peculiarities of the examples we have chosen but rather is a general characteristic of all portfolio problems.

---

[7] The value of the correlation coefficient where this occurs is easy to determine. Equation (3.9) is the expression for the fraction of the portfolio to be held in X_C to minimize risk. Assume X_S is the least risky asset. When X_C equals zero in Equation (3.9), that means that 100% of the funds are invested in the least risky asset (i.e., $X_S = 1$) to obtain the least risky portfolio. Setting X_C equal to zero in Equation (3.9) and solving for ρ_{CS} gives $\rho_{CS} = \sigma_S/\sigma_C$. So when ρ_{CS} is equal to σ_S/σ_C, X_C will equal zero, and the least risky "combination" of assets will be 100% invested in the least risky asset alone. If ρ_{CS} is greater than σ_S/σ_C, then the least risky combination involves short selling C.

[8] A concave curve is one where a straight line connecting any two points on the curve lies entirely under the curve. If a curve is convex, a straight line connecting any two points lies totally above the curve. The only exception to this is that a straight line is both convex and concave and so can be referred to as either.

This can easily be demonstrated. Remember that the equations and diagrams we have developed are appropriate for all combinations of securities and portfolios. We now examine combinations of the minimum variance portfolio and an asset that has a higher return and risk.

Figures 3-6a, 3-6b, and 3-6c represent three hypothesized shapes for combinations of Colonel Motors and the minimum variance portfolio. The shape depicted in 3-6b cannot be possible since we have demonstrated that combinations of assets cannot have more risk than that found on a straight line connecting two assets (and that occurs only in the case of perfect positive correlation). But what about the shape presented in Figure 3-6c? Here all portfolios have less risk than the straight line connecting Colonel Motors and the minimum variance portfolio. However, this is impossible. Examine the portfolios labeled U and V. These are simply combinations of the minimum variance portfolio and Colonel Motors. Since U and V are portfolios, all combinations of U and V must lie either on a straight line connecting U and V or above such a straight line.[9] Hence 3-6c is impossible and the only legitimate shape is that shown in 3-6a, which is a concave curve. Analogous reasoning can be used to show that if we consider combinations of the minimum variance portfolio and a security or portfolio with higher variance and lower return, the curve must be convex, that is, it must look like Figure 3-7a rather than 3-7b or 3-7c.

Now that we understand the risk-return properties of combinations of two assets, we are in a position to study the attributes of combinations of all risky assets.

The Efficient Frontier with No Short Sales

In theory we could plot all conceivable risky assets and combinations of risky assets in a diagram in return standard deviation space. We used the words *in theory* not because there is a problem in calculating the risk and return on a stock or portfolio, but because there are an infinite number of possibilities that must be considered. Not only must all possible groupings of risky assets be

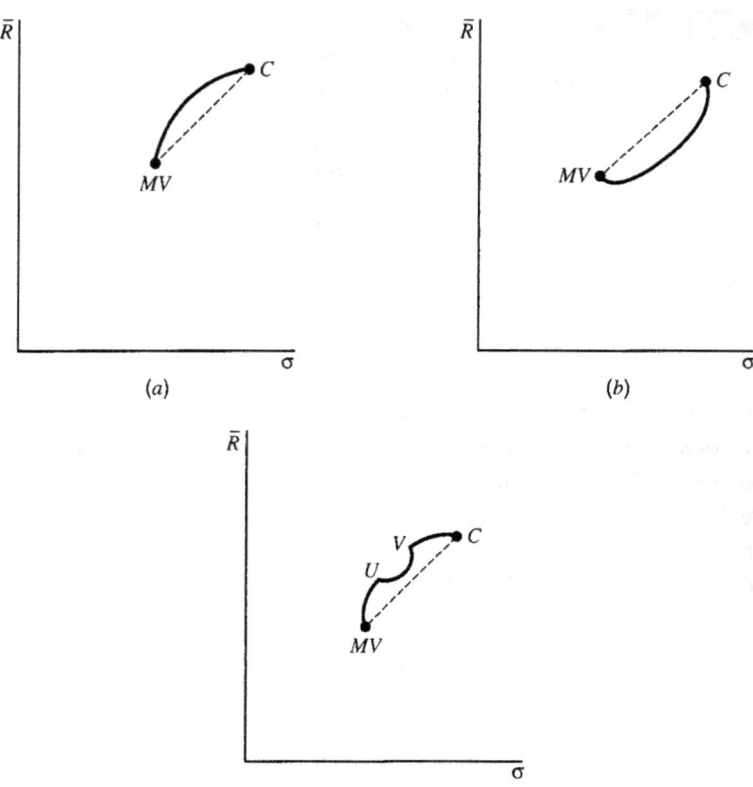

FIGURE 3-6 Various possible relationships for expected return and standard deviation when the minimum variance portfolio and Colonel Motors are combined.

considered, but all groupings must be considered in all possible percentage compositions.

If we were to plot all possibilities in risk-return space, we would get a diagram like Figure 3-8. We have taken the liberty of representing combinations as a finite number of points in constructing the diagram. Let us examine the diagram and see if we can eliminate any part of it from consideration by the investor. An investor would prefer more return to less and would prefer less risk to more. Thus, if we could find a set of portfolios that

1. offered a bigger return for the same risk, or

2. offered a lower risk for the same return,

we would have identified all portfolios an investor could consider holding. All other portfolios could be ignored.

Let us take a look at Figure 3-8. Examine portfolios A and B. Note that portfolio B would be preferred by all investors to portfolio A because it offers a higher return

---

[9] If the correlation between U and V equals +1, they will be on the straight line. If it is less than +1, the risk must be less, so combinations must be above the straight line.

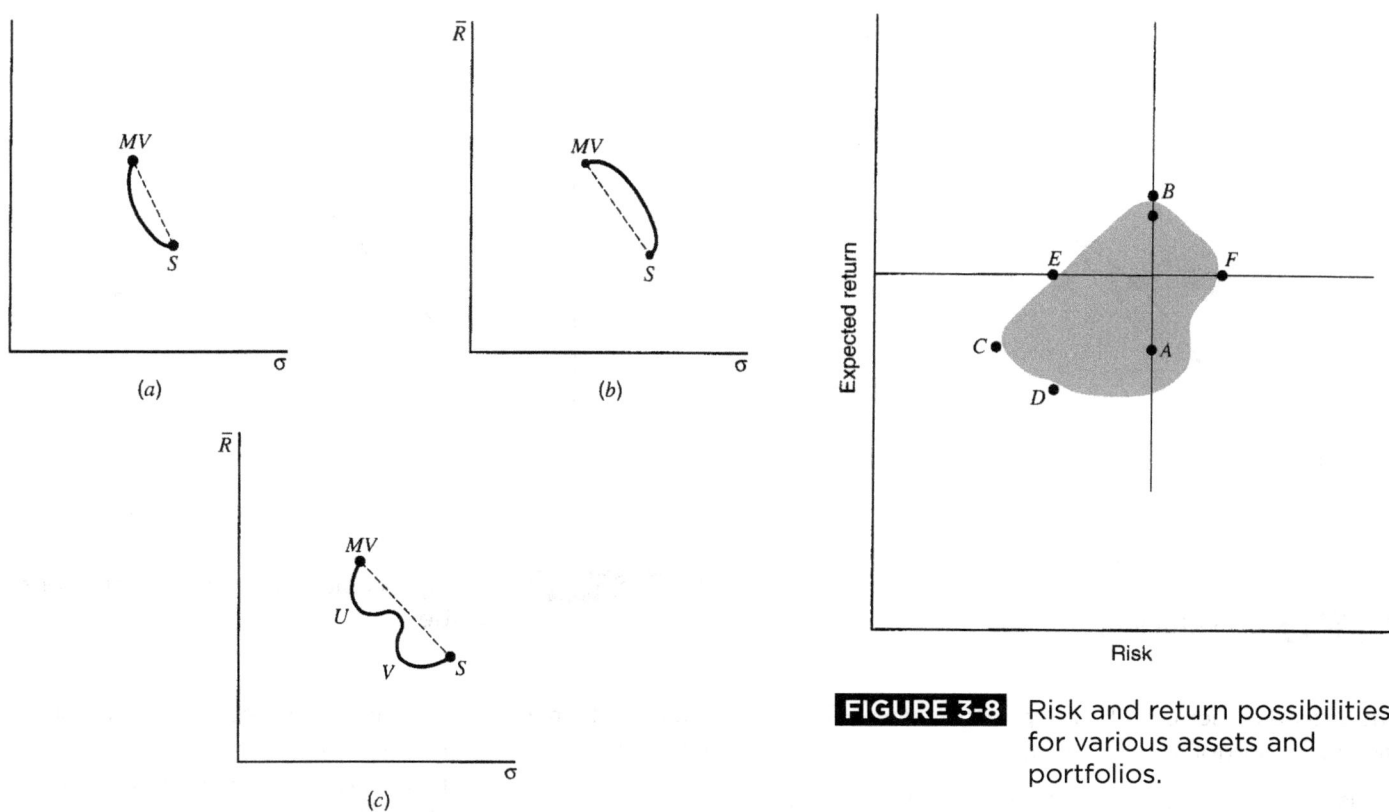

FIGURE 3-7   Various possible relationships between expected return and standard deviation of return when the minimum variance portfolio is combined with portfolio S.

FIGURE 3-8   Risk and return possibilities for various assets and portfolios.

with the same level of risk. We can also see that portfolio C would be preferable to portfolio A because it offers less risk at the same level of return. Notice that at this point in our analysis we can find no portfolio that dominates portfolio C or portfolio B. It should be obvious at this point that an efficient set of portfolios cannot include interior portfolios. We can reduce the possibility set even further. For any point in risk-return space we want to move as far as possible in the direction of increasing return and as far as possible in the direction of decreasing risk. Examine point D, which is an exterior point. We can eliminate D from further consideration given the existence of portfolio E, which has more return for the same risk. This is true for every other portfolio as we move up the outer shell from point D to point C. Point C cannot be eliminated since there is no portfolio that has less risk for the same return or more return for the same risk. But what is point C? It is the global

minimum variance portfolio.[10] Now examine point F. Point F is on the outer shell, but point E has less risk for the same return. As we move up the outer shell curve from point F, all portfolios are dominated until we come to portfolio B. Portfolio B cannot be eliminated for there is no portfolio that has the same return and less risk or the same risk and more return than point B. Point B represents that portfolio (usually a single security) that offers the highest expected return of all portfolios. Thus the efficient set consists of the envelope curve of all portfolios that lie between the global minimum variance portfolio and the maximum return portfolio. This set of portfolios is called the *efficient frontier.*

Figure 3-9 represents a graph of the efficient frontier. Notice that we have drawn the efficient frontier as a concave function. The proof that it must be concave follows logically from the earlier analysis of the combination of two securities or portfolios. The efficient frontier cannot contain a convex region such as that shown in Figure 3-10

---

[10] The global minimum variance portfolio is that portfolio that has the lowest risk of any feasible portfolio.

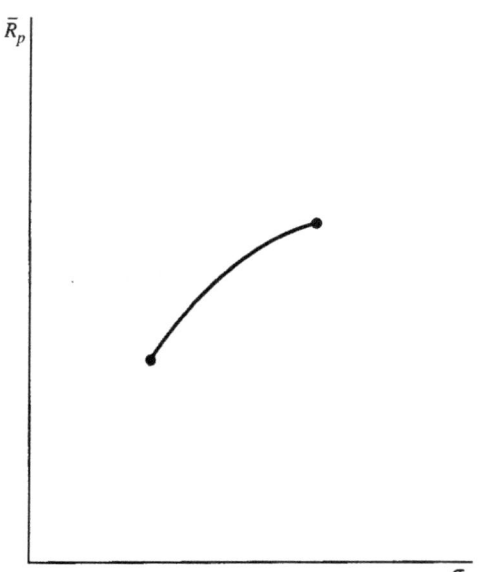

FIGURE 3-9 The efficient frontier.

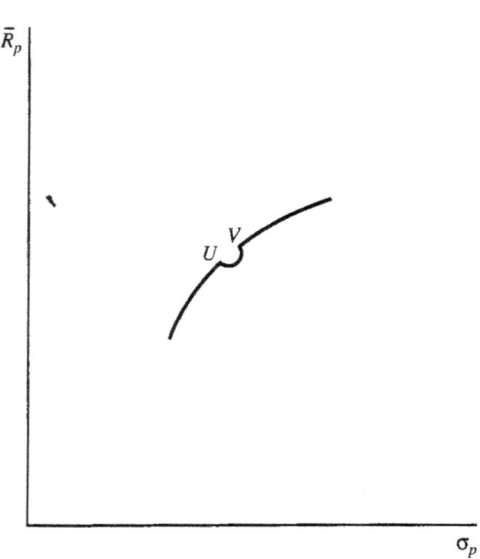

FIGURE 3-10 An impossible shape for the efficient frontier.

since as argued earlier *U* and *V* are portfolios and combinations of two portfolios must be concave.[11]

Up to this point we have seen that the efficient frontier is a concave function in expected return standard deviation space that extends from the minimum variance portfolio to the maximum return portfolio. The portfolio problem, then, is to find all portfolios along this frontier.

The Efficient Frontier with Short Sales Allowed

In the stock market (and many other capital markets), an investor can often sell a security that he or she does not own. This process is called short selling. However, the mechanics of short sales are worth repeating here. It involves in essence taking a negative position in a security. Short sales exist in sizable amounts on the New York Stock Exchange (as well as other securities markets) and the amount of short sales in New York Stock Exchange stocks is reported in the *New York Times* every Monday. In

a moment we will discuss the incorporation of short sales into our analysis. Before we do so, however, it is worthwhile pointing out that we have not been wasting our time by studying the case where short sales are disallowed. There are two reasons why this is true. The first is that most institutional investors do not short sell. Many institutions are forbidden by law from short selling, whereas still others operate under a self-imposed constraint forbidding short sales. The second is that the incorporation of short sales into our analysis involves only a minor extension of the analysis we have developed up to this point.

In this section we will employ a simplified description of the way short sales work. This has been the general description of short sales in the literature, but in footnotes we present both the deficiencies of this description and an alternative, more realistic description of short sales. Our description of short sales, which treats short sales as the ability to sell a security without owning it, assumes that there are no special transaction costs involved in this process. Let us see how this process might work.

Let us assume an investor believed that the stock of ABC company, which currently sells for $100 per share, is likely to be selling for $95 per share (expected value) at the end of the year. In addition, the investor expects ABC

---

[11] Furthermore, there can be linear segments if the two efficient portfolios are perfectly correlated. Since a linear relationship is both concave and convex, we can still refer to the efficient frontier as concave.

company to pay a $3.00 dividend at the end of the year. If the investor bought one share of ABC stock, the cash flow would be −$100.00 at time zero when the stock is purchased and +$3.00 from the dividend, plus +$95.00 from selling the stock at time 1. The cash flows are

	Time	
	0	**1**
Purchase Stock	−100	
Dividend		+ 3
Sell Stock		+95
Total Cash Flow	−100	+98

Unless this stock had very unusual correlations with other securities, it is unlikely that an investor with these expectations would want to hold any of it in his own portfolio. In fact, an investor would really like to own negative amounts of it. How might the investor do so? Assume a friend, Joelle, owned a share of ABC company and that the friend had different expectations and wished to continue holding it. The investor might borrow Joelle's stock under the promise that she will be no worse off lending him the stock. The investor could then sell the stock, receiving $100. When the company pays the $3.00 dividend, the investor must reach into his own pocket and pay Joelle $3.00. He has a cash flow of −$3.00. He has to do this because neither he nor Joelle now owns the stock and he promised that Joelle would be no worse off by lending him the stock. Now at the end of the year, the investor could purchase the stock for $95 and give it back to Joelle. The cash flows for the investor are

	Time	
	0	**1**
Sell Stock	+100	
Pay Dividend		− 3
Buy Stock		−95
Total Cash Flow	+100	−98

Notice in the example that the lender of the stock is no worse off by the process and the borrower has been able to create a security that has the opposite characteristics of buying a share of the ABC company. In the real world, Joelle might require some added compensation

for lending her stock, but we will continue to use this simplified description of short selling in analyzing portfolio possibilities.[12]

It was clear that when an investor expected the return on a security to be negative, short sales made sense. Even in the case where returns are positive, short sales can make sense, for the cash flow received at time zero from short selling one security can be used to purchase a security with a higher expected return. Return to an example employing Colonel Motors and Separated Edison. Recall that the expected return for Separated Edison was 8% while it was 14% for Colonel Motors. If we disallow short sales, the highest return an investor can get is 14% by placing 100% of the funds in Colonel Motors. With short sales, higher returns can be earned by short selling Separated Edison and placing the investor's original capital plus the initial cash flow from short sales in Colonel Motors. In doing so, however, there is a commensurate increase in risk. To see this more formally, we return to the case where the correlation coefficient between the two securities is assumed to be 0.5 and see what happens when we allow short sales. The earlier calculations in Table 3-4 and the diagram in Figure 3-5 are still valid, but now they must be extended to consider values of X greater than 1 and less than 0. Some sample calculations are shown in Table 3-5.

The new diagram with short sales is shown in Figure 3-11. The reader should note that with short sales, portfolios exist that give infinite expected rates of return. This should not be too surprising since with short sales one can sell securities with low expected returns and use the proceeds to buy securities with high expected returns. For example, suppose an investor had $100 to invest in Colonel Motors and Separated Edison. The investor could place the entire $100 in Colonel Motors and get a return of $14, or 14%. On the other hand, the investor could sell $1,000 worth of Separated Edison stock short and buy

---

[12] In the case of actual short sales, a broker plays the role of the friend and demands that funds be put up as security for the loan of the stock. These funds are in addition to the proceeds from the short sale. Since, in most cases, the amount of the funds that must be put up is quite large and the broker pays no return on these funds, the description of short sales commonly used in the literature overstates the return from short sales.

TABLE 3-5 The Expected Return and Standard Deviation When Short Sales Are Allowed

X_C	−1	−0.8	−0.6	−0.4	−0.2	+1.2	+1.4	+1.6	+1.8	+2.0
$\bar{R}$	2.0	3.2	4.4	5.6	6.8	15.2	16.4	17.6	18.8	20.0
σ	6.0	5.13	4.33	3.65	3.17	6.92	7.87	8.84	9.82	10.82

$1,100 worth of Colonel Motors. The expected earnings on the investment in Colonel Motors is $154 while the expected cost of borrowing Separated Edison is $80. Therefore, the expected return would be $74, or 74%, on the original $100 investment. Is this a preferred position? The expected return would increase from 14% to 74%, but the standard deviation would increase from 6% to 57.2%. Whether an investor should take the position offering the higher expected return would depend on the investor's preference for return relative to risk.

In Figure 3-11 we have constructed the diagram for combinations of Colonel Motors and Separated Edison, assuming a correlation coefficient of 0.5. Notice that all portfolios offering returns above the global minimum variance portfolio lie along a concave curve. The reasoning for this is directly analogous to that presented when short sales were not allowed.

When we extend this analysis to the efficient frontiers of all securities and portfolios, we get a figure such as Figure 3-12, where *MVBC* is the efficient set. Since combinations of two portfolios are concave, the efficient set is concave. The efficient set still starts with the minimum variance portfolio, but when short sales are allowed it has no finite upper bound.[13]

THE EFFICIENT FRONTIER WITH RISKLESS LENDING AND BORROWING

Up to this point we have been dealing with portfolios of risky assets. The introduction of a riskless asset into our portfolio possibility set considerably simplifies the analysis. We can consider lending at a riskless rate as investing in an asset with a certain outcome (e.g., a short-term government bill or savings account). Borrowing can be

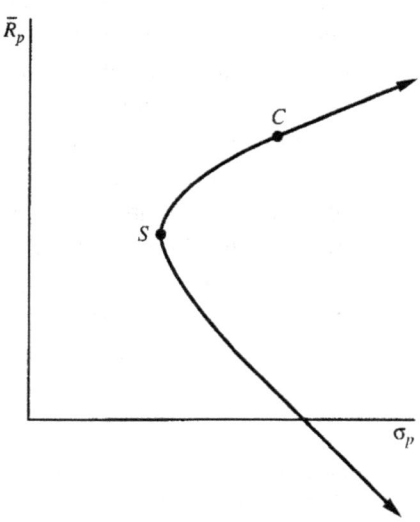

FIGURE 3-11 Expected return standard deviation combinations of Colonel Motors and Separated Edison when short sales are allowed.

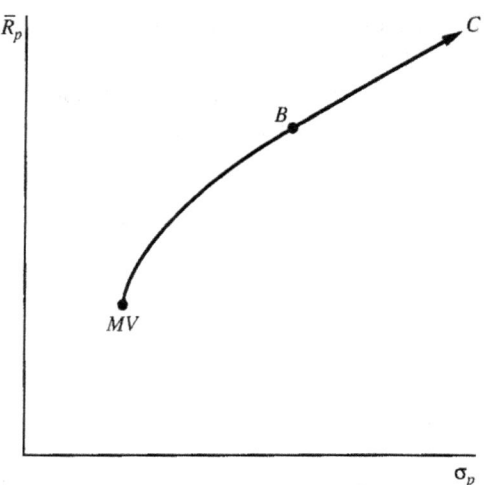

FIGURE 3-12 The efficient set when short sales are allowed.

_____
[13] Merton (1972) has shown that the efficient set is the upper half of a hyperbola.

considered as selling such a security short; thus borrowing can take place at the riskless rate.

We call the certain rate of return on the riskless asset R_F. Since the return is certain, the standard deviation of the return on the riskless asset must be zero.

We first examine the case where investors can lend and borrow unlimited amounts of funds at the riskless rate. Initially assume that the investor is interested in placing part of the funds in some portfolio A and either lending or borrowing. Under this assumption, we can easily determine the geometric pattern of all combinations of portfolio A and lending or borrowing. Call X the fraction of original funds that the investor places in portfolio A. Remember that X can be greater than 1 because we are assuming that the investor can borrow at the riskless rate and invest more than his initial funds in portfolio A. If X is the fraction of funds the investor places in portfolio A, $(1 - X)$ must be the fraction of funds that were placed in the riskless asset. The expected return on the combination of riskless asset and risky portfolio is given by

$$\bar{R}_C = (1 - X)R_F + X\bar{R}_A$$

The risk on the combination is

$$\sigma_C = [(1 - X)^2\sigma_F^2 + X^2\sigma_A^2 + 2X(1 - X)\sigma_A\sigma_F\rho_{FA}]^{1/2}$$

Since we have already argued that σ_F is zero,

$$\sigma_C = (X^2\sigma_A^2)^{1/2} = X\sigma_A$$

Solving this expression for X yields

$$X = \frac{\sigma_C}{\sigma_A}$$

Substituting this expression for X into the expression for expected return on the combination yields

$$\bar{R}_C = \left(1 - \frac{\sigma_C}{\sigma_A}\right)R_F + \frac{\sigma_C}{\sigma_A}\bar{R}_A$$

Rearranging terms,

$$\bar{R}_C = R_F + \left(\frac{\bar{R}_A - R_F}{\sigma_A}\right)\sigma_C$$

Note that this is the equation of a straight line. All combinations of riskless lending or borrowing with portfolio A lie on a straight line in expected return standard deviation space. The intercept of the line (on the return axis) is R_F, and the slope is $(\bar{R}_A - R_F)/\sigma_A$. Furthermore, the line

passes through the point $(\sigma_A, \bar{R}_A)$. This line is shown in Figure 3-13. Note that to the left of point A we have combinations of lending and portfolio A, whereas to the right of point A we have combinations of borrowing and portfolio A.

The portfolio A we selected for this analysis had no special properties. Combinations of any security or portfolio and riskless lending and borrowing lie along a straight line in expected return standard deviation of return space. Examine Figure 3-14. We could have combined portfolio B with riskless lending and borrowing and held combinations along the line R_FB rather than R_FA Combinations along R_FB are superior to combinations along R_FA since they offer greater return for the same risk. It should be obvious that what we would like to do is to rotate the straight line passing through R_F as far as we can in a counterclockwise direction. The furthest we can rotate it is through point G.[14] Point G is the tangency point between the efficient frontier and a ray passing through the point R_F on the vertical axis. The investor cannot rotate the ray

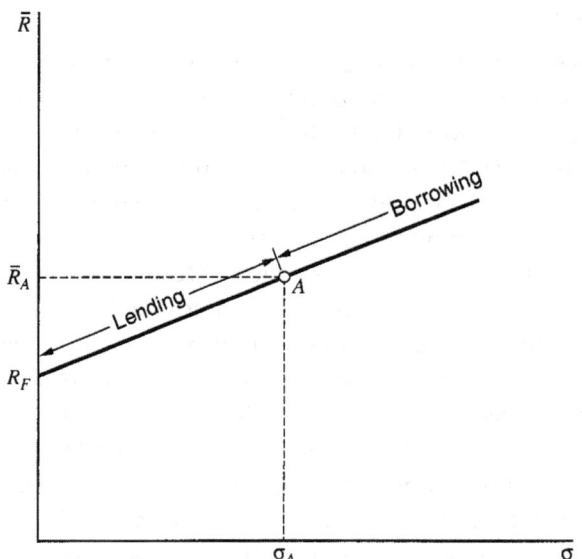

FIGURE 3-13   Expected return and risk when the risk-free rate is mixed with portfolio A.

---

[14] In this section we have drawn the efficient frontier as it would look if short sales were not allowed. However, the analysis is general and applies equally well to the case where short sales are allowed.

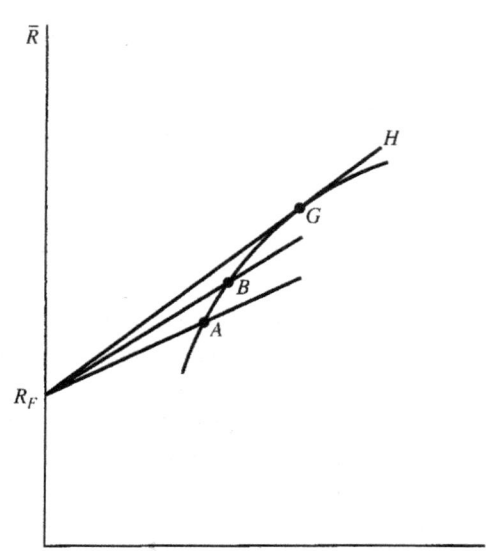

FIGURE 3-14 Combinations of the riskless asset and various risky portfolios.

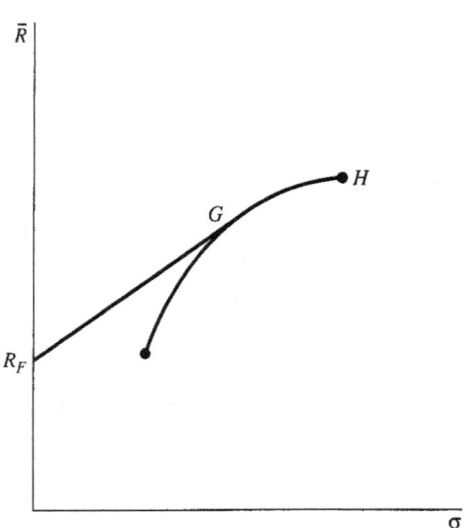

FIGURE 3-15 The efficient frontier with lending but not borrowing at the riskless rate.

further because by the definition of the efficient frontier there are no portfolios lying above the line passing through R_F and G.

All investors who believed they faced the efficient frontier and riskless lending and borrowing rates shown in Figure 3-14 would hold the same portfolio of risky assets—portfolio G. Some of these investors who were very risk-averse would select a portfolio along the segment R_F–G and place some of their money in a riskless asset and some in risky portfolio G. Others who were much more tolerant of risk would hold portfolios along the segment G–H, borrowing funds and placing their original capital plus the borrowed funds in portfolio G. Still other investors would just place the total of their original funds in risky portfolio G. All of these investors would hold risky portfolios with the exact composition of portfolio G. Thus, for the case of riskless lending and borrowing, identification of portfolio G constitutes a solution to the portfolio problem. The ability to determine the optimum portfolio of risky assets without having to know anything about the investor has a special name. It is called the separation theorem.[15]

Let us for a moment examine the shape of the efficient frontier under more restrictive assumptions about the ability of investors to lend and borrow at the risk-free rate. There is no question about the ability of investors to lend at the risk-free rate (buy government securities). If they can lend but not borrow at this rate, the efficient frontier becomes R_F–G–H in Figure 3-15. Certain investors will hold portfolios of risky assets located between G and H. However, any investor who held some riskless asset would place all remaining funds in the risky portfolio G.

Another possibility is that investors can lend at one rate but must pay a different and presumably higher rate to borrow. Calling the borrowing rate R_F', the efficient frontier would become R_F–G–H–I in Figure 3-16. Here there is a small range of risky portfolios that would be optional for investors to hold. If R_F and R_F' are not too far apart, the assumption of riskless lending and borrowing at the same rate might provide a good approximation to the optimal range G–H of risky portfolios that investors might consider holding.

EXAMPLES AND APPLICATIONS

In this section, we will discuss some considerations that affect the choice of inputs to the portfolio selection problem and provide some examples of the use of the analysis just presented.

---

[15] The words *separation theorem* has, at times, been used to describe other phenomena in finance. We continue to use it in the above sense throughout this book.

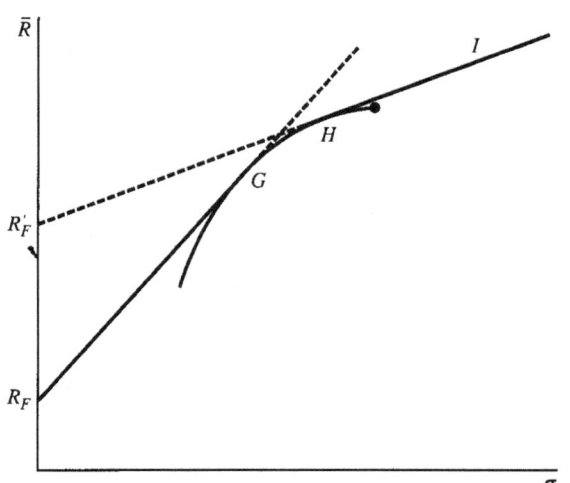

FIGURE 3-16 The efficient frontier with riskless lending and borrowing at different rates.

Considerations in Determining Inputs

Almost all asset allocation analysis starts out by estimating some of the inputs to the portfolio selection process using historical data. Analysts usually modify these historical estimates so that they better reflect beliefs about the future. However, before we do so, we will discuss some general considerations in using historical data.

Inflation-Adjusted Inputs to Optimization

The efficient frontier technology is widely used in practice to make asset allocation decisions for long-term investment, particularly for pension fund assets. When the investment horizon is measured in decades, it is important to consider how the change in the purchasing power of

currency affects investment choice. In particular, investors may care more about the future purchasing-power value of the portfolio—that is, the value after adjusting for the effects of inflation—than they care about the future nominal value of the portfolio. One approach to this problem is to apply the efficient frontier technology to *inflation-adjusted* returns. Table 3-6 compares historical statistics for U.S. stocks, government bonds, Treasury bills, and inflation. Notice that Treasury bill returns are correlated with inflation and have a larger return when inflation is higher and a lower return when inflation is less. This suggests that Treasury bills may serve as a partial inflation hedge.

Table 3-7 reports statistics for inflation-adjusted returns to stocks, bonds, and Treasury bills. The reader can use these inputs as a starting point when creating an efficient frontier for inflation-adjusted returns.

Although some securities like Treasury bills provide a partial hedge against inflation, there is no "riskless" asset in the above example—even Treasury bills have some exposure to inflation. One security recently developed in the United States and used for some time in other countries, such as the United Kingdom, provides a near-perfect inflation hedge. Since 1997, the United States has issued inflation-linked securities whose value is determined, in part, by changes in the Consumer Price Index (an inflation measure). The return of these bonds varies with inflation, making the bonds a good hedge against inflation. At times, inflation has been over 10% per year in the United States, which means that wealth invested in assets uncorrelated to changes in inflation effectively loses 10% of its purchasing power per year. Thus inflation-linked securities have the potential to protect against serious erosion of investor wealth in inflationary times.

TABLE 3-6 Returns with No Inflation Adjustment

| | Arithmetic Mean | Standard Deviation | S&P | Correlations | | |
				Bonds	T-Bills	Inflation
Stocks	10.03	15.67	1.00			
Bonds	5.73	11.14	0.22	1.00		
T-Bills	4.56	3.19	-0.15	0.24	1.00	
Inflation	4.24	3.65	-0.36	-0.20	0.38	1.00

TABLE 3-7   Returns After Adjusting for Inflation

	Arithmetic Mean	Standard Deviation	S&P	Bonds	T-Bills
S&P	5.78	17.32	1.00		
Bonds	1.49	12.39	0.37	1.00	
T-Bills	0.31	3.83	0.33	0.54	1.00

In performing investment analysis, the analyst may well want to examine inflation-adjusted returns along with or instead of nominal returns. Furthermore, inflation-linked securities are increasingly likely to be an important asset class in portfolio optimization.

Input Estimation Uncertainty

Reliable inputs are crucial to the proper use of mean-variance optimization in the asset allocation decision. It is common to use historical risk, return, and correlation as a starting point in obtaining inputs for calculating the efficient frontier. If return characteristics do not change through time, then the longer the data are available, the more accurate is the estimate of the mean. To see this, note that the formula for the standard error of the mean of a sequence of independent random variables is $\frac{\sigma^2}{N}$, where N is the sample size. For a sequence of independent returns observed through time, N is the number of time periods since the beginning of the historically observed data. Thus, under the assumption of stationary (or unchanging) expected returns and returns uncorrelated through time, more historical data will improve the estimate of expected return included in the mean-variance model, although the improvement is diminishing.

To illustrate the importance of this issue for portfolio choice, imagine that the investor is forced to choose between two investments, each with identical sample means and variances. Other things equal, the standard approach would view the two investments as equivalent. If you consider the additional information that the first sample mean was based on 1 year of data and the second on 10 years of data, common sense would suggest that the second alternative is less risky than the first. Furthermore, we can assume that the investor is mainly concerned

about next month's return, which has a mean return of $\bar{R}$ and a variance of $\sigma^2_{Pred} = \sigma^2 + \frac{\sigma^2}{T}$ where

σ^2_{Pred} is the predicted variance series

σ^2 is the variance of monthly return

T is the number of time periods

The first part of the expression captures the inherent risk in the return. The second term captures the uncertainty that comes from lack of knowledge about the true mean return. In a Bayesian analysis, the sum of the two terms on the right-hand side of this equation is referred to as the variance of the *predictive distribution* of returns. Notice that predicted variance is always greater than historical variance because of uncertainty as to the future mean.

Characteristics of security returns usually change over time. Thus, there is a trade-off between using a long time frame to improve the estimates and having potentially inaccurate estimates from the longer time period because the security characteristics have changed. Because of this conflict, most analysts modify historical estimates to reflect their beliefs about how current conditions differ from past conditions.

The choice of the time period is more complicated when a relatively new asset class is added to the mix, and the available data for the new asset is much less than for other assets. For example, consider the addition of the International Financial Corporation's (IFC) index of emerging equity markets, which is available from 1985. An analyst who wishes to use historical data as a starting point for optimization could use all available data for calculating means, standard deviations, and correlations, or use data from only the common period of observation. Applying the first approach to U.S. capital market data would mean using the entire historical data from 1926 to the present from stocks and bonds. The second

TABLE 3-8 Risk and Return over Different Horizons

	Beginning Date	Arithmetic Mean Return Starting in 1926	Arithmetic Mean Return Starting in 1985	Standard Deviation Starting in 1926	Standard Deviation Starting in 1985
S&P 500	1926	10.82	17.15	22.03	17.89
U.S. Small Stocks	1926	12.36	14.46	35.33	22.69
U.S. Government Bonds	1926	5.32	11.98	8.08	10.44
IFC Emerging Market Index	1985	11.91	11.91	26.17	26.17

Source: Courtesy of Ibbotson Associates.

TABLE 3-9 Correlation over Different Horizons

Top Triangle: All Periods	S&P 500	Small	Bonds	IFC
S&P 500	1.00	0.83	0.18	0.43
Small	0.67	1.00	0.09	0.46
Bonds	0.30	0.07	1.00	−0.15
IFC	0.43	0.46	−0.15	1.00
Bottom Triangle Common	S&P 500	Small	Bonds	IFC

Source: Courtesy of Ibbotson Associates.

approach would use only data on U.S. markets from 1985 to the present. Table 3-8 shows the inputs for the two separate approaches.

Notice that the mean return for small stocks—that is, for companies with smaller capitalization—is greater than that for large stocks over the period from 1926, but less over the period since 1985. In both periods, however, the risk of smaller stocks is substantially higher than that of large stocks. Statistics over the longer term are consistent with an equilibrium in which a higher investor risk is compensated by higher investor expected return. Statistics over the period of common observation, beginning in 1985, are inconsistent with the argument of expected reward for additional risk. Which set of inputs makes more sense as the basis for optimization? Are the differences due to poor estimation, to the small amount of data, or to changes in economic conditions? How will these different sets of inputs affect the efficient frontier? Correlations for the two different periods are provided in Tables 3-9–3-11.

The reader is urged to calculate the two different efficient frontiers and examine the differences. Even without performing the two optimizations, however, the reader will note that the highest mean portfolio on the frontier differs, depending on which set of inputs is used.

Correlations over Different Time Periods

The entries to the right of the main diagonal (1.00s) in Table 3-9 give the correlations calculated over the longest available period for both series. The entries to the left of the main diagonal (1.00s) give the correlation over the period of common observation beginning in 1985.

Does the correlation between stock and bond returns follow a predictable pattern that could help with input estimation? Li (2002) showed that the stock-bond correlation followed similar time trends across many countries. It reached a peak in 1996 of around 0.5 in most of the major industrialized countries except Japan. By 2002, the

TABLE 3-10 The Effect of Time Horizon on Risk

Time Period 1926–1991	Annualized Arithmetic Mean Return Based on Annualized 10-Year Returns	Arithmetic Mean Return Based on Annual Returns	Standard Deviation Based on Annualized 10-Year Returns	Standard Deviation Based on Annual Returns
S&P 500	9.8%	9.6%	20.7%	19.9%
U.S. Government Bonds	4.3%	4.8%	6.1%	7.7%
Treasury Bills	3.6%	3.6%	6.0%	3.2%

Source: F. Edwards and W. Goetzmann (1994).

stock-bond correlation turned negative. Why? Li found that this critical correlation changed with shifts in uncertainty about future inflation. As inflation uncertainty rises, the stock-bond correlation rises. The correlation among international equity markets changes significantly through time as well. The average correlation between major stock markets over the past 150 years has ranged from less than 10% (1880s and 1890s, and 1940 to 1980) to over 30% (1860s, 1930s, 1990s). Goetzmann, Li, and Rouwenhorst (2005) studied the relationship between globalization and market correlations over this time period. They attribute the higher correlations among equity markets to periods of greater liberalization in cross-border flows. The result of research on time variation in correlations suggests that macroeconomic conditions may have an effect on correlation forecasts, which indeed appears to be the case (Brown et al., 2009).

Short-Horizon Inputs and Long-Horizon Portfolio Choice

Another important consideration in estimating inputs to the optimization process is the effect of the investment time horizon on variance. In the previous example, we saw that under the assumption that returns were uncorrelated from one period to the next, the standard error of the mean decreased with the square root of time. This is based on a more general result that the sum of the variance of a sequence of random variables is equal to the variance of the sum. When actual returns are examined, some securities have returns that are highly correlated

over time (e.g., autocorrelated). Treasury bill returns, for example, tend to be highly autocorrelated, meaning that the return to investing in T-bills in one year does a good job at predicting the return to investing in T-bills the next year. High T-bill returns are more likely to be followed by high returns than low returns. Thus, although the standard deviation of T-bills is low over short intervals, on a percentage basis it significantly increases as the time period of observation increases from 1 to 5 to 10 years. Thus T-bills are effectively an increasingly risky asset as the investment time horizon grows. For example, research by Edwards and Goetzmann (1994) shows that the estimated annualized standard deviation for Treasury bill returns over the 10-year horizon is about 6%, compared to the 3.2% annual standard deviation measured at the one-year horizon.

Table 3-10 shows the annualized means and standard deviations for 10-year returns, derived from a simulation procedure that takes into account their autocorrelation. It also reports the means and standard deviations based on the annual returns, not accounting for autocorrelation. Notice that the mean returns are not greatly affected by the correction for autocorrelation; however, the volatility for stocks is slightly reduced at longer horizons while the volatility for bonds and T-bills is increased.

The reader can use the mean and standard deviations in Table 3-10 and the correlations provided in Table 3-11 to calculate the efficient frontier over the 1-year horizon and the 10-year horizon.

TABLE 3-11 Correlations over Different Time Horizons

Top Triangle: 10-Year	S&P	Bonds	T-Bills
S&P 500	1.00	0.06	0.19
Bonds	0.14	1.00	0.08
T-Bills	−0.03	0.22	1.00
Bottom Triangle: 1-Year			

THREE EXAMPLES

Consider first the allocation between equity and debt. The minimum variance portfolio is given by Equation (3.9). The estimated inputs for bonds and stocks are

$$\bar{R}_{S\&P} = 12.5\% \qquad \sigma_{S\&P} = 14.9\% \qquad \rho_{S\&P, B} = .45$$
$$\bar{R}_{B} = 6\% \qquad \sigma_{B} = 4.8\%$$

Plugging the values for standard deviation and correlation into Equation (3.9) gives

$$X_{S\&P} = \frac{(4.8)^2 - .45(4.8)(14.9)}{(4.8)^2 + (14.9)^2 - (2)(.45)(4.8)(14.9)}$$

$$X_{S\&P} = -.051$$

Thus the minimum variance portfolio involves short selling stock. The associated standard deviation is 4.75%, which is slightly less than the standard deviation associated with investing 100% in bonds. The dots in Figure 3-17 are plots of all combinations of the S&P index and Lehman Brothers aggregate bond index, ranging from the global minimum variance portfolio to the portfolio representing 150% in common stock and −50% in bonds. The dot next to the global minimum variance portfolio represents the expected return and standard deviation of the portfolio with 0% in common stocks. As we move to the right, each dot represents the expected return and standard deviation of a portfolio with 10% more in common stock. This is the efficient frontier with short sales allowed (although it would continue to the right). In this case, the global minimum variance portfolio is 100% in bonds.

At the time of this revision the interest rate on Treasury bills was about 5%. Using this as a riskless lending and borrowing rate, the tangency portfolio is portfolio *T* shown in Figure 3-17. The expected return and risk for

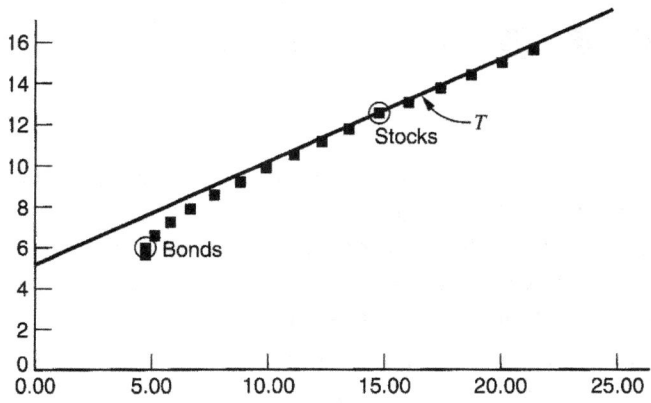

FIGURE 3-17 The efficient frontier.

portfolio *T* as read from the graph are 13.54% and 16.95%, respectively. Thus the slope of the line connecting the tangency portfolio and the efficient frontier is

$$\frac{13.54 - 5}{16.95} = 0.50$$

and the equation of the efficient frontier with riskless lending and borrowing is

$$\bar{R}_{P} = 5 + 0.50\sigma_{P}$$

Once we know the expected return of portfolio *T*, we can easily determine its composition. Simply recall that

$$\bar{R}_{P} = X_{S\&P}\bar{R}_{S\&P} + (1 - X_{S\&P})\bar{R}_{B}$$

Therefore

$$13.54 = X_{S\&P}(2.5) + (1 - X_{S\&P})6.0$$

and

$$X_{S\&P} = 116\% \qquad X_{B} = -16\%$$

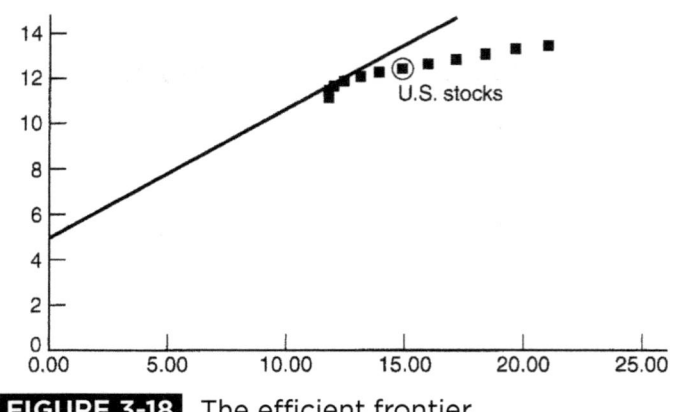

FIGURE 3-18 The efficient frontier.

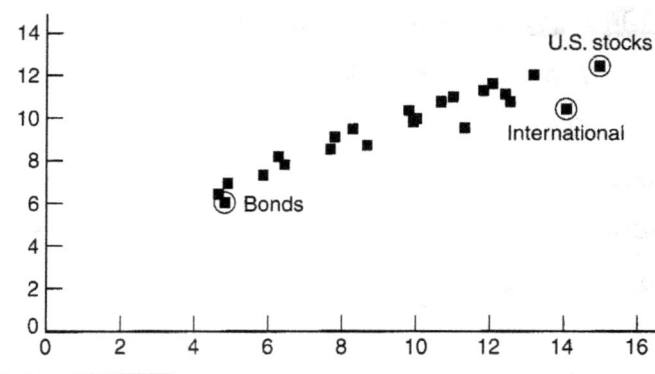

FIGURE 3-19 Combinations of bonds, domestic stocks, and international stocks.

The second example we examined was a combination of a domestic portfolio represented by the S&P index and an international portfolio represented by an average international fund. Note that part of these combinations is inefficient. The estimated inputs were

$$\bar{R}_{S\&P} = 12.5\% \qquad \sigma_{S\&P} = 14.9\% \qquad \rho_{S\&P,\ int} = 0.33$$
$$\bar{R}_{int} = 10.5\% \qquad \sigma_{int} = 14.0\%$$

Solving for the global minimum variance portfolio we have

$$X_{S\&P} = \frac{(14)^2 - 0.33(14)(14.9)}{(14.9)^2 + (14)^2 + (2)(.33)(14)(14.9)}$$

$$X_{S\&P} = 0.45$$

Thus the global minimum variance portfolio is obtained by investing 0.45 in the S&P index and 0.55 in the foreign portfolio. The resulting standard deviation is 11.76%, which is less than the standard deviation of both portfolios. This is an example of how diversification can reduce risk. Note that it is inefficient to hold the foreign portfolio by itself. An investor wishing to accept the risk of 14% on the foreign portfolio could obtain an expected return of 12.31% by putting 90.7% in the S&P index and 9.3% in the foreign portfolio. Thus at a 14% standard deviation, the increase in expected return from using the optimum combination is 1.81% with no increase in risk. The efficient frontier with no short sales is the scatter of dots in Figure 3-18 from the global minimum variance portfolio to 100% in the S&P index. The dot to the right of the global minimum variance portfolio is the expected return and standard deviation of return when there is 50% in the S&P index. Each dot as we move to the right represents the expected return and

standard deviation of return as we increase the amount in the S&P index by 10%. The efficient frontier with short sales allowed is the complete scatter of dots shown in Figure 3-18 (although it would continue to the right).

If the riskless lending and borrowing rate is 5%, then the tangency portfolio is 61% in the S&P index and 39% in the international portfolio. The associated mean return is 11.72%, and standard deviation of return is 12.04%. Thus the slope of the efficient frontier with riskless lending and borrowing is

$$\frac{11.72 - 5}{12.04} = .558$$

and the equation of the efficient frontier is

$$\bar{R}_p = 5 + .558\sigma_p$$

As a third example, consider the asset allocation problem across bonds, domestic stocks, and international stocks. We continue to use all the inputs from the prior examples. We need one additional input, the correlation coefficient between bonds and the international portfolio. Past data indicate a value of 0.05 is reasonable. Various combinations of these three assets, some of which lie on the efficient frontier and some of which do not, are plotted as dots in Figure 3-19. Note that both the international portfolio and the bond portfolio are obviously dominated by other portfolios. The figure does not include portfolios involving short sales. Thus, since the S&P has the highest expected return, it is not dominated. The efficient frontier would be the dots that have the highest mean return for a given standard deviation.

The tangency portfolio with a riskless lending and borrowing rate has the following proportions:

$$X_{S\&P} = 0.581$$

$$X_B = 0.038$$

$$X_{int} = 0.381$$

The expected return of this portfolio is 11.49%, and the standard deviation is 11.64%. Thus the slope of the efficient frontier with riskless lending and borrowing is .558 and the equation of the efficient frontier is

$$R_P = 5 + 0.558\sigma_P$$

Compare this to the efficient frontier derived with two risky assets and a riskless asset. This efficient frontier dominates the efficient frontier using only the S&P and bonds as the risky assets but to three places to the right of the decimal point is identical to the efficient frontier using only the S&P and the international portfolio as the risky assets. Thus, adding bonds to the combination of the S&P and international portfolio doesn't lead to much improvement in the efficient frontier with riskless lending and borrowing.

CONCLUSION

In this chapter we have defined the geometric properties of that set of portfolios all risk-avoiding investors would hold regardless of their specific tolerance for risk. We have defined this set—the efficient frontier—under alternative assumptions about short sales and the ability of the investor to lend and borrow at the riskless rate. Now that we understand the geometric properties of the efficient frontier, we are in a position to discuss solution techniques to the portfolio problem.

BIBLIOGRAPHY

1. Bawa, Vijay. "Admissible Portfolios for All Individuals," *Journal of Finance*, **XXXI,** No. 3 (Sept. 1976), pp. 1169–1183.
2. Ben-Horim, Moshe, and Levy, Haim. "Total Risk, Diversifiable Risk and Non-Diversifiable Risk: A Pedagogic Note," *Journal of Financial and Quantitative Analysis*, **XV,** No. 2 (June 1980), pp. 289–298.
3. Brennan, Michael J., and Kraus, Allan. "The Geometry of Separation and Myopia," *Journal of Financial and Quantitative Analysis*, **XI,** No. 2 (June 1976), pp. 171–193.
4. Brown, Stephen, and Barry, Christopher. "Differential Information and the Small Firm Effect," *Journal of Financial Economics*, **13** (1984), pp. 283–294.
5. ———. "Differential Information and Security Market Equilibrium," *Journal of Financial and Quantitative Analysis*, **20** (1985), pp. 407–422.
6. Brown, Stephen, Hiraki, Takato, Arakawa, Kiyoshi, and Ohno, Saburo, "Risk Premia in International Equity Markets Revisited, *Pacific-Basin Finance Journal* 17 (2009) (forthcoming).
7. Brumelle, Shelby. "When Does Diversification between Two Investments Pay?" *Journal of Financial and Quantitative Analysis*, **IX,** No. 3 (June 1974), pp. 473–483.
8. Buser, Stephen. "A Simplified Expression for the Efficient Frontier in Mean-Variance Portfolio Analysis," *Management Science*, **23** (April 1977), pp. 901–903.
9. Canner, Niko. "An Asset Allocation Puzzle," *American Economic Review*, Nashville, **87,** No. 1 (Mar. 1997), pp. 181–193.
10. Cass, David, and Stiglitz, Joseph. "The Structure of Investor Preferences and Asset Returns, and Separability in Portfolio Allocation: A Contribution to the Pure Theory of Mutual Funds," *Journal of Economic Theory*, **2,** No. 2 (June 1970), pp. 122–160.
11. Dalal, Ardeshir J. "On the Use of a Covariance Function in a Portfolio Model," *Journal of Financial and Quantitative Analysis*, **XVIII,** No. 2 (June 1983), pp. 223–228.
12. Edwards, Franklin, and Goetzmann, William. "Short Horizon Inputs and Long Horizon Portfolio Choice," *Journal of Portfolio Management*, **20,** No. 4 (Summer 1994), pp. 76–81.
13. Elton, Edwin J., and Gruber, Martin J. "Dynamic Programming Applications in Finance," *Journal of Finance*, **XXVI,** No. 2 (May 1971), pp. 473–505.
14. ———. "Portfolio Theory When Investment Relatives Are Lognormally Distributed," *Journal of Finance*, **XXIX,** No. 4 (Sept. 1974), pp. 1265–1273.
15. Friedman, Harris. "Real Estate Investment and Portfolio Theory," *Journal of Financial and Quantitative Analysis*, **VI,** No. 2 (March 1971), pp. 861–873.
16. Gibbons, Michael R., and Shanken, Jay. "Subperiod Aggregation and the Power of Multivariate Tests of Portfolio Efficiency," *Journal of Financial Economics*, Amsterdam, **19,** No. 2 (Dec. 1987), pp. 389–394.
17. Goetzmann, William, Li, Lingfeng, and Rouwenhorst, K. Geert, "Long-Term Global Market Correlations," *The Journal of Business*, **78,** No. 1 (2005), pp. 1–38.
18. Grauer, Robert R., and Hakansson, Nils H. "A Half Century of Returns on Levered and Unlevered Portfolios of Stocks, Bonds, and Bills, With and Without Small Stocks," *Journal of Business*, **59,** No. 2 (Apr. 1986), 287.

19. Hakansson, Nils. "Risk Disposition and the Separation Property in Portfolio Selection," *Journal of Financial and Quantitative Analysis*, **IV,** No. 4 (Dec. 1969), pp. 401–416.

20. ──. "An Induced Theory of the Firm under Risk: The Pure Mutual Fund," *Journal of Financial and Quantitative Analysis*, **V,** No. 2 (May 1970), pp. 155–178.

21. Li, Lingfeng, "Macroeconomic Factors and the Correlation of Stock and Bond Returns," Yale ICF Working Paper No. 02–46 (November 2002).

22. Merton, Robert. "An Analytic Derivation of the Efficient Portfolio Frontier," *Journal of Financial and Quantitative Analysis*, **VII,** No. 4 (Sept. 1972), pp. 1851–1872.

23. Mossin, Jan. "Optimal Multiperiod Portfolio Policies," *Journal of Business*, **41,** No. 2 (April 1968), pp. 215–229.

24. Ohlson, James. "Portfolio Selection in a Log-Stable Market," *Journal of Financial and Quantitative Analysis*, **X,** No. 2 (June 1975), pp. 285–298.

25. Ohlson, J.S., and Ziemba, W.T. "Portfolio Selection in a Lognormal Market When the Investor Has a Power Utility Function," *Journal of Financial and Quantitative Analysis*, **XI,** No. 1 (March 1976), pp. 57–71.

26. Pye, Gordon. "Lifetime Portfolio Selection in Continuous Time for a Multiplicative Class of Utility Functions," *American Economic Review*, **LXIII,** No. 5 (Dec. 1973), pp. 1013–1020.

27. Rosenberg, Barr, and Ohlson, James. "The Stationarity Distribution of Returns and Portfolio Separation in Capital Markets: A Fundamental Contradiction," *Journal of Financial and Quantitative Analysis*, **XI,** No. 3 (June 1973), pp. 393–401.

28. Shanken, Jay. "A Bayesian Approach to Testing Portfolio Efficiency," *Journal of Financial Economics*, **19,** No. 2 (Dec. 1987), pp. 195–216.

29. Smith, Keith. "Alternative Procedures for Revising Investment Portfolios," *Journal of Financial and Quantitative Analysis*, **III,** No. 4 (Dec. 1968), pp. 371–403.

30. Zhou, Guofu. "Small Sample Tests of Portfolio Efficiency," *Journal of Financial Economics*, **30,** No. 1 (Nov. 1991) pp. 165–192.

The Standard Capital Asset Pricing Model

4

Excerpt is Chapter 13 of Modern Portfolio Theory and Investment Analysis, *8th Edition, by Edwin Elton, Martin Gruber, Stephen Brown and William Goetzmann.*

Learning Objectives

After completing this reading, FRM Candidates should be able to:

- Understand the derivation and components of the CAPM.
- Describe the assumptions underlying the CAPM.

- Describe the capital market line.
- Use the CAPM to calculate the expected return on an asset.

All of the preceding chapters have been concerned with how an individual or institution, acting on a set of estimates, could select an optimum portfolio, or set of portfolios. If investors act as we have prescribed, then we should be able to draw on the analysis to determine how the aggregate of investors will behave, and how prices and returns at which markets will clear are set. The construction of general equilibrium models will allow us to determine the relevant measure of risk for any asset and the relationship between expected return and risk for any asset when markets are in equilibrium. Furthermore, though the equilibrium models are derived from models of how portfolios should be constructed, the models themselves have major implications for the characteristics of optimum portfolios.

The subject of equilibrium models is so important that we have devoted three chapters to it. In this chapter we develop the simplest form of an equilibrium model, called the standard capital asset pricing model, or the one-factor capital asset pricing model. This was the first general equilibrium model developed, and it is based on the most stringent set of assumptions. The second chapter on general equilibrium models deals with models that have been developed under more realistic sets of assumptions. The third chapter deals with a new theory of asset pricing: arbitrage pricing theory.

It is worthwhile pointing out, at this time, that the final test of a model is not how reasonable the assumptions behind it appear but how well the model describes reality. As readers proceed with this chapter they will, no doubt, find many of its assumptions objectionable. Furthermore, the final model is so simple readers may well wonder about its validity. As we will see, despite the stringent assumptions and the simplicity of the model, it does an amazingly good job of describing prices in the capital markets.

THE ASSUMPTIONS UNDERLYING THE STANDARD CAPITAL ASSET PRICING MODEL (CAPM)

The real world is sufficiently complex that to understand it and construct models of how it works, one must assume away those complexities that are thought to have only a

small (or no) effect on its behavior. As the physicist builds models of the movement of matter in a frictionless environment, the economist builds models where there are no institutional frictions to the movement of stock prices.

The first assumption we make is that there are no transaction costs. There is no cost (friction) of buying or selling any asset. If transaction costs were present, the return from any asset would be a function of whether or not the investor owned it before the decision period. Thus, to include transaction costs in the model adds a great deal of complexity. Whether it is worthwhile introducing this complexity depends on the importance of transaction costs to investors' decisions. Given the size of transaction costs, they are probably of minor importance.

The second assumption behind the CAPM is that assets are infinitely divisible. This means that investors could take any position in an investment, regardless of the size of their wealth. For example, they can buy one dollar's worth of IBM stock.

The third assumption is the absence of personal income tax.[1] This means, for example, that the individual is indifferent to the form (dividends or capital gains) in which the return on the investment is received.

The fourth assumption is that an individual cannot affect the price of a stock by his buying or selling action. This is analogous to the assumption of perfect competition. While no single investor can affect prices by an individual action, investors in total determine prices by their actions.

The fifth assumption is that investors are expected to make decisions solely in terms of expected values and standard deviations of the returns on their portfolios.

The sixth assumption is that unlimited short sales are allowed. The individual investor can sell short any amount of any shares.

The seventh assumption is unlimited lending and borrowing at the riskless rate. The investor can lend or borrow

---

[1] The major results of the model would hold if income tax and capital gains taxes were of equal size.

any amount of funds desired at a rate of interest equal to the rate for riskless securities.

The eighth and ninth assumptions deal with the homogeneity of expectations. First, investors are assumed to be concerned with the mean and variance of returns (or prices over a single period), and all investors are assumed to define the relevant period in exactly the same manner. Second, all investors are assumed to have identical expectations with respect to the necessary inputs to the portfolio decision. As we have said many times, these inputs are expected returns, the variance of returns, and the correlation matrix representing the correlation structure between all pairs of stocks.

The tenth assumption is that all assets are marketable. All assets, including human capital, can be sold and bought on the market.

Readers can now see the reason for the earlier warning that they might find many of the assumptions behind the CAPM untenable. It is clear that these assumptions do not hold in the real world just as it is clear that the physicist's frictionless environment does not really exist. The relevant questions are: How much is reality distorted by making these assumptions? What conclusions about capital markets do they lead to? Do these conclusions seem to describe the actual performance of the capital market?

THE CAPITAL ASSET PRICING MODEL

The standard form of the general equilibrium relationship for asset returns was developed independently by Sharpe, Lintner, and Mossin. Hence, it is often referred to as the Sharpe–Lintner–Mossin form of the capital asset pricing model. This model has been derived in several forms involving different degrees of rigor and mathematical complexity. There is a trade-off between these derivations. The more complex forms are more rigorous and provide a framework within which alternative sets of assumptions can be examined. However, because of their complexity, they do not convey the economic intuition behind the capital asset pricing model as readily as some of the simpler forms. Because of this, we approach the derivation of the model at two distinct levels. The first derivation consists of a simple intuitively appealing derivation of the CAPM. This is followed by a more rigorous derivation.

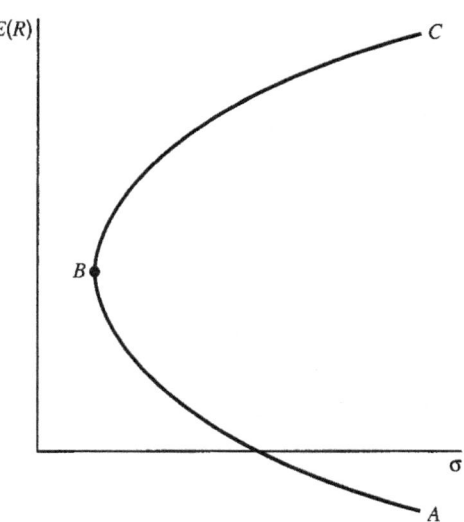

FIGURE 4-1 The efficient frontier—no lending and borrowing.

Deriving the CAPM—A Simple Approach

Recall that in the presence of short sales, but without riskless lending and borrowing, each investor faced an efficient frontier such as that shown in Figure 4-1. In this figure, *BC* represents the efficient frontier while *ABC* represents the set of minimum variance portfolios. In general the efficient frontier will differ among investors because of differences in expectations.

When we introduced riskless lending and borrowing, we showed that the portfolio of risky assets that any investor would hold could be identified without regard to the investor's risk preferences. This portfolio lies at the tangency point between the original efficient frontier of risky assets and a ray passing through the riskless return (on the vertical axis). This is depicted in Figure 4-2 where P_i denotes investor *i*'s portfolio of risky assets.[2] The investors satisfy their risk preferences by combining portfolio P_i with lending or borrowing.

If all investors have homogeneous expectations and they all face the same lending and borrowing rate, then they

---

[2] We have subscripted *P* because each individual can face a different efficient frontier and, thus select a different P_i. This is true, though the composition of P_i does not depend on investor *i*'s risk preference.

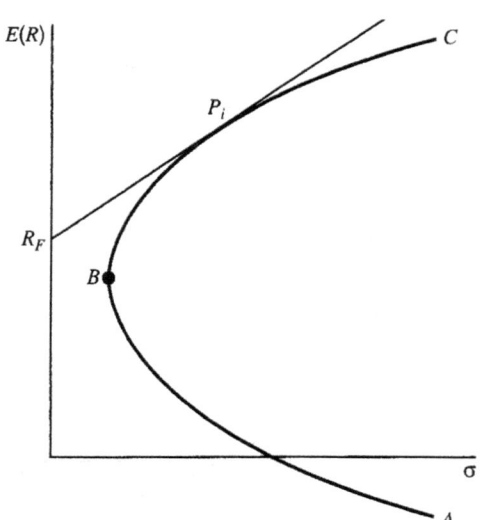

FIGURE 4-2 The efficient frontier with lending and borrowing.

will each face a diagram such as in Figure 4-2 and, furthermore, all of the diagrams will be identical. The portfolio of risky assets P_i held by any investor will be identical to the portfolio of risky assets held by any other investor. If all investors hold the same risky portfolio, then, in equilibrium, it must be the market portfolio. The market portfolio is a portfolio comprised of all risky assets. Each asset is held in the proportion that the market value of that asset represents of the total market value of all risky assets. For example, if IBM stock represents 3% of all risky assets, then the market portfolio contains 3% IBM stock and each investor will take 3% of the money that will be invested in all risky assets and place it in IBM stock.

Notice that we have already learned something important. All investors will hold combinations of only two portfolios: the market portfolio (M) and a riskless security. This is sometimes referred to as the two mutual fund theorem because all investors would be satisfied with a market fund, plus the ability to lend or borrow a riskless security.

The straight line depicted in Figure 4-2 is usually referred to as the capital market line. All investors will end up with portfolios somewhere along the capital market line and all *efficient portfolios* would lie along the capital market line. However, not all securities or portfolios lie along the capital market line. In fact, from the derivation of the efficient frontier, we know that all portfolios of risky and riskless

assets, except those that are efficient, lie below the capital market line. By looking at the capital market line, we can learn something about the market price of risk. In Chapter 3 we showed that the equation of a line connecting a riskless asset and a risky portfolio (the line we now call the capital market line) is

$$\bar{R}_e = R_F + \frac{\bar{R}_M - R_F}{\sigma_M}\sigma_e$$

where the subscript e denotes an efficient portfolio.

The term $[(\bar{R}_M - R_F)/\sigma_M]$ can be thought of as the market price of risk for all efficient portfolios.[3] It is the extra return that can be gained by increasing the level of risk (standard deviation) on an efficient portfolio by one unit. The second term on the right-hand side of this equation is simply the market price of risk times the amount of risk in a portfolio. The second term represents that element of required return that is due to risk. The first term is simply the price of time or the return that is required for delaying potential consumption, one period given perfect certainty about the future cash flow. Thus, the expected return on an efficient portfolio is

(Expected return) = (Price of time) + (Price of risk)
× (Amount of risk)

Although this equation establishes the return on an efficient portfolio, it does not describe equilibrium returns on nonefficient portfolios or on individual securities. We now turn to the development of a relationship that does so.

We argued that, for very well-diversified portfolios, Beta was the correct measure of a security's risk. For *very* well-diversified portfolios, nonsystematic risk tends to go to zero and the only relevant risk is systematic risk measured by Beta. As we have just explained, given the assumptions of homogeneous expectations and unlimited riskless lending and borrowing, all investors will hold the market portfolio. Thus the investor will hold a *very* well-diversified portfolio. Since we assume that the investor is concerned only with expected return and risk, the only dimensions of a security that need be of concern are expected return and Beta.

---

[3] The reader should be alerted to the fact that many authors have defined $(\bar{R}_M - R_F)/\sigma_M^2$ as the market price of risk. The reason we have selected $(\bar{R}_M - R_F)/\sigma_M$ will become clear as you proceed with this chapter.

Let us hypothesize two portfolios with the characteristics shown here:

Investment	Expected Return	Beta
A	10	1.0
B	12	1.4

We have already seen (Chapter 3) that the expected return from portfolio A is simply the sum of the products of the proportion invested in each stock and the expected return on each stock. We have also seen that the Beta on a portfolio is simply the sum of the product of the proportion invested in each stock times the Beta on each stock. Now consider a portfolio C made up of one half of portfolio A and one half of portfolio B. From the facts stated earlier, the expected return on this portfolio is 11 and its Beta is 1.2. These three potential investments are plotted in Figure 4-3. Notice they lie on a straight line. This is no accident. All portfolios composed of different fractions of investments A and B will lie along a straight line in expected return Beta space.[4]

Now hypothesize a new investment D that has a return of 13% and a Beta of 1.2. Such an investment cannot exist for very long. All decisions are made in terms of risk and return. This portfolio offers a higher return and the same risk as portfolio C. Hence, it would pay all investors to sell C short and buy D. Similarly, if a security were to exist with a return of 8% and a Beta of 1.2 (designated by E), it would pay arbitragers to step in and buy portfolio C while selling security E short. Such arbitrage would take place until C, D, and E all yielded the same return. This is just another illustration of the adage that two things that are equivalent cannot sell at different prices. We can demonstrate the arbitrage discussed earlier in a slightly more formal manner. Let us return to the arbitrage between

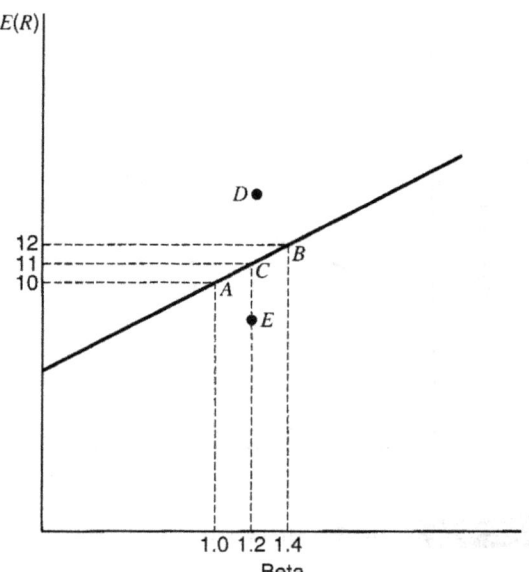

FIGURE 4-3   Combinations of portfolios.

portfolios C and D. An investor could sell $100 worth of portfolio C short and with the $100 buy portfolio D. If the investor were to do so, the characteristics of this arbitraged portfolio would be as follows:

	Cash Invested	Expected Return	Beta
Portfolio C	−$100	−$11	−1.2
Security D	+$100	$13	1.2
Arbitrage portfolio	0	$2	0

From this example it is clear that as long as a security lies above the straight line, there is a portfolio involving zero risk and zero net investment that has a positive expected profit. An investor will engage in this arbitrage as long as any security or portfolio lies above the straight line depicted in Figure 4-3. A similar arbitrage will exist if any amount lies below the straight line in Figure 4-3.

We have now established that all investments and all portfolios of investments must lie along a straight line in return-Beta space. If any investment were to lie above or below that straight line, then an opportunity would exist for riskless arbitrage. This arbitrage would continue until all investments converged to the line. There are many different ways that this straight line can be identified, for it takes only two points to identify a straight line. Since we

---

[4] If we let X stand for the fraction of funds invested in portfolio A, then the equation for return is

$$\bar{R}_P = X\bar{R}_A + (1 − X)\bar{R}_B$$

The equation for Beta is

$$\beta_P = X\beta_A + (1 − X)\beta_B$$

Solving the second equation for X and substituting in the first equation, we see that we are left with an equation of the form

$$\bar{R}_P = a + b\,\beta_P$$

or the equation of a straight line.

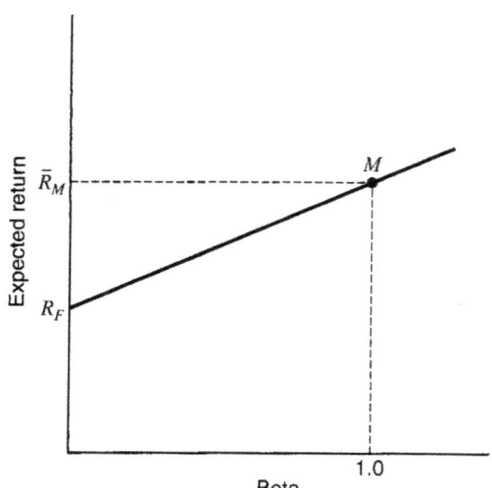

FIGURE 4-4 The security market line.

have shown that, under the assumptions of the CAPM, everybody will hold the market portfolio and since all portfolios must lie on the straight line, we will use this as one point. The market portfolio must have a Beta of 1. Thus, in Figure 4-4 the market portfolio is point M with a Beta of 1 and an expected return of $\bar{R}_M$. It is often convenient to choose the second point to identify a straight line as the intercept. The intercept occurs when Beta equals zero, or when the asset has zero systematic risk. One asset with zero systematic risk is the riskless asset. Thus, we can treat the intercept as the rate of return on a riskless asset. These two points identify the straight line shown in Figure 4-4. The equation of a straight line has the form

$$\bar{R}_i = a + b\beta i \qquad\qquad \textbf{(4.1)}$$

One point on the line is the riskless asset with a Beta of zero. Thus,

$$R_F = a + b(0)$$

or

$$R_F = a$$

A second point on the line is the market portfolio with a Beta of 1. Thus,

$$\bar{R}_M = a + b(1)$$

or

$$(\bar{R}_M - a) = b$$

Putting these together and substituting into Equation (4.1) yields

$$\bar{R}_i = R_F + \beta_i(\bar{R}_M - R_F) \qquad \textbf{(4.2)}$$

Think about this relationship for a moment. It represents one of the most important discoveries in the field of finance. Here is a simple equation, called the security market line, that describes the expected return for all assets and portfolios of assets in the economy. The expected return on any asset, or portfolio, whether it is efficient or not, can be determined from this relationship. Notice that $\bar{R}_M$ and R_F are not functions of the assets we examine. Thus, the relationship between the expected return on any two assets can be related simply to their difference in Beta. The higher Beta is for any security, the higher must be its equilibrium return. Furthermore, the relationship between Beta and expected return is linear. One of the greatest insights that comes from this equation arises from what it states is unimportant in determining return. The risk of any stock could be divided into systematic and unsystematic risk. Beta was the index of systematic risk. This equation validates the conclusion that systematic risk is the only important ingredient in determining expected returns and that nonsystematic risk plays no role.[5] Put another way, the investor gets rewarded for bearing systematic risk. It is not total variance of returns that affects expected returns, but only that part of the variance in returns that cannot be diversified away. This result has great economic intuition for, if investors can eliminate all nonsystematic risk through diversification, there is no reason they should be rewarded, in terms of higher return, for bearing it. All of these implications of the CAPM are empirically testable. Provided the tests hold, we have, with a simple model, gained great insight in the behavior of the capital markets.

We digress for a moment and point out one seeming fallacy in the potential use of the CAPM. Invariably, when a group of investors is first exposed to the CAPM, one or more investors will find a high-Beta stock that last year produced a smaller return than low-Beta stocks. The CAPM is an equilibrium relationship. High-Beta stocks are

---

[5] This result is somewhat circular for, in this proof, we assumed that Beta was the relevant risk measure. In the more rigorous proof that follows, we make no such assumption, yet we end up with the same equation for the security market line.

expected to give a higher return than low-Beta stocks because they are more risky. This does not mean that they will give a higher return over all intervals of time. In fact, if they always gave a higher return, they would be less risky, not more risky, than low-Beta stocks. Rather, because they are more risky, they will sometimes produce lower returns. However, over long periods of time, they should on the average produce higher returns.

We have written the CAPM model in the form

$$\bar{R}_i = R_F + \beta_i(\bar{R}_M - R_F)$$

This is the form in which it is most often written and the form most amenable to empirical testing. However, there are alternative forms that give added insight into its meaning. Recall that

$$\beta_i = \frac{\sigma_{iM}}{\sigma_M^2}$$

We could then write the security market line as

$$\bar{R}_i = R_F + \left(\frac{\bar{R}_M - R_F}{\sigma_M}\right)\frac{\sigma_{iM}}{\sigma_M} \qquad \textbf{(4.3)}$$

This, in fact, is the equation of a straight line located in expected return σ_{iM}/σ_M space. Recall that earlier in our discussion of the capital market, line $(\bar{R}_M - R_F)/\sigma_M$ was described as the market price of risk. Since σ_{iM}/σ_M is a definition of the risk of any security, or portfolio, we would see that the security market line, like the capital market line, states that the expected return on any security is the riskless rate of interest plus the market price of risk times the amount of risk in the security or portfolio.[6]

Many authors write the CAPM equation as

$$\bar{R}_i = R_F + \left(\frac{\bar{R}_M - R_F}{\sigma_M^2}\right)\sigma_{iM}$$

They define $(\bar{R}_M - R_F)/\sigma_M^2$ as the market price of risk and σ_{iM} as the measure of the risk of security i. We have chosen the form we used because σ_{iM}/σ_M is the measure of how the risk on a security affects the risk of the market portfolio. It seems to us that this is the appropriate way to discuss the risk of a security.

We have now completed our intuitive proof of the CAPM. We are about to present a more complex mathematical proof. There are two reasons for presenting this mathematical proof. The first is that it is more rigorous. The second, and more important, reason is that one needs

a richer framework to incorporate modifications of the assumptions of the standard CAPM. The method of proof just presented is too restrictive to allow forms of general equilibrium equations that make more realistic assumptions about the world to be derived. The framework presented subsequently can be used to derive equilibrium models under alternative assumptions and, indeed, will be used to do so in the next chapter. The reader who finds both these reasons unappealing can skip the next section and the derivations in the next chapter with no loss of continuity.

Deriving the CAPM—A More Rigorous Approach

We solved for the optimal portfolio when short sales were allowed and the investor could lend and borrow unlimited amounts of money at the riskless rate of interest. The solution involved finding the composition of the portfolio that maximized the slope of a straight line passing through the riskless rate of interest on the vertical

---

[6] Below we offer theoretical justification that σ_{iM}/σ_M is the relevant measure of the risk of any security in equilibrium. Recall that the standard deviation of the market portfolio is given by

$$\sigma_M = \left[\sum_{i=1}^{N} X_i^2\sigma_i^2 + \sum_{i=1}^{N}\sum_{\substack{j=1 \\ j \neq i}}^{N} X_i X_j \sigma_{ij}\right]^{1/2}$$

where all Xs are market proportions. Since all investors hold the market portfolio, the relevant definition of the risk of a security is the change in the risk of the market portfolio, as the holdings of that security are varied. This can be found as follows:

$$\frac{d\sigma_M}{dX_i} = \frac{d\left[\sum_{i=1}^{N} X_i^2\sigma_i^2 + \sum_{i=1}^{N}\sum_{\substack{j=1 \\ j \neq i}}^{N} X_i X_j \sigma_{ij}\right]^{1/2}}{dX_i}$$

$$= \frac{\left(\frac{1}{2}\right)\left[2X_i\sigma_i^2 + (2)\sum_{\substack{j=1 \\ j \neq i}}^{N} X_j \sigma_{ij}\right]}{\left[\sum_{i=1}^{N} X_i^2\sigma_i^2 + \sum_{i=1}^{N}\sum_{\substack{j=1 \\ j \neq i}}^{N} X_i X_j \sigma_{ij}\right]^{1/2}} = \frac{X_i^2\sigma_i^2 + \sum_{\substack{j=1 \\ j \neq i}}^{N} X_j \sigma_{ij}}{\sigma_M} = \frac{\sigma_{iM}}{\sigma_M}$$

Therefore, the relevant risk of security is equal to σ_{iM}/σ_M.

axes and the portfolio itself. This involved maximizing the function

$$\theta = \frac{\bar{R}_P - R_F}{\sigma_P}$$

When the derivative of θ was taken with respect to all securities in the portfolio and each equation was set equal to zero, a set of simultaneous equations of the following form was derived:

$$\lambda(X_1\sigma_{1k} + X_2\sigma_{2k} + \cdots + X_k\sigma_k^2 + \cdots + X_N\sigma_{Nk}) = \bar{R}_k - R_F \quad \textbf{(4.4)}$$

This equation held for each security and there is one such equation for each security in the market. If there are homogeneous expectations, then all investors must select the same optimum portfolio. If all investors select the same portfolio, then, in equilibrium, that portfolio must be a portfolio in which all securities are held in the same percentage that they represent of the market. In other words, in equilibrium, the proportion invested in security 1 must be that fraction of the total market value of all securities that security 1 represents. To get from Equation (4.4) to the CAPM involves simply recognizing that the left-hand side of Equation (4.4) is $\lambda \, \text{cov}(R_kR_M)$. To see this, first note that

$$R_M = \sum_{i=1}^{N} R_i X_i'$$

where the prime indicates market proportions. Thus

$$\text{cov}(R_kR_M) = E\left[(R_k - \bar{R}_k)\left(\sum_{i=1}^{N} R_i X_i' - \sum_{i=1}^{N} \bar{R}_i X_i'\right)\right] \quad \textbf{(4.5)}$$

Rearranging the second term

$$\text{cov}(R_kR_M) = E\left[(R_k - \bar{R}_k)\left(\sum_{i=1}^{N} X_i'(R_i - \bar{R}_i)\right)\right]$$

Multiplying out the terms

$$\begin{aligned}
\text{cov}(R_kR_M) = E[&X_1'(R_k - \bar{R}_k)(R_1 - \bar{R}_1) \\
+ &X_2'(R_k - \bar{R}_k)(R_2 - \bar{R}_2) + \cdots \\
+ &X_k'(R_k - \bar{R}_k)(R_k - \bar{R}_k) + \cdots \\
+ &X_N'(R_k - \bar{R}_k)(R_N - \bar{R}_N)]
\end{aligned}$$

Since the expected value of the sum of random variables is the sum of the expected values, factoring out the X's yields

$$\begin{aligned}
\text{cov}(R_kR_M) = &X_1'E(R_K - \bar{R}_K)(R_1 - \bar{R}_1) \\
+ &X_1'E(R_K - \bar{R}_K)(R_2 - \bar{R}_2) + \ldots \\
+ &X_K'E(R_K - \bar{R}_K)^2 + \ldots \\
+ &X_N'E(R_K - \bar{R}_K)(R_N - \bar{R}_N)
\end{aligned}$$

Earlier we argued that the Xs in Equation (4.4) were market proportions. Comparing Equation (4.5) with the left-hand side of Equation (4.4) shows that they are, indeed, equal. Thus, Equation (4.4) can be written as

$$\lambda \, \text{cov}(R_kR_M) = \bar{R}_k - R_F \quad \textbf{(4.6)}$$

Since this must hold for all securities (all possible values of k), it must hold for all portfolios of securities. One possible portfolio is the market portfolio. Writing Equation (4.6) for the market portfolio involves recognizing that $\text{cov}(R_MR_M) = \sigma_M^2$.

$$\lambda\sigma_M^2 = \bar{R}_M - R_F$$

or

$$\lambda = \frac{\bar{R}_M - R_F}{\sigma_M^2}$$

Substituting this value for λ in Equation (4.6) and rearranging yields

$$\bar{R}_k = R_F + \frac{\bar{R}_M - R_F}{\sigma_M^2}\text{cov}(R_kR_M) = R_F + \beta_k(\bar{R}_M - R_F)$$

This completes the more rigorous derivation of the security market line.

The advantages of this proof over that presented earlier are that we have not had to assume that Beta is the relevant measure of risk and we have established a framework that, as we see in the next chapter, can be used to derive general equilibrium solutions when some of the present assumptions are relaxed.

PRICES AND THE CAPM

Up to now, we have discussed equilibrium in terms of rate of return. In the introduction to this chapter, we mentioned that the CAPM could be used to describe equilibrium in terms of either return or prices. The latter is of importance in certain situations, for example, the pricing of new assets. It is very easy to move from the equilibrium relationship in terms of rates of return to one expressed in terms of prices. All that is involved is a little algebra.

Let us define

P_i as the present price of asset i.

P_M as the present price of the market portfolio (all assets).

Y_i as the dollar value of the asset one period hence. It is market value plus any dividends.

Y_M as the dollar value of the market portfolio one period hence including dividends.

$cov(Y_iY_M)$ as the covariance between Y_i and Y_M.

$var(Y_M)$ as the variance in Y_M.

r_F as $(1 + R_F)$.

The return on asset i is

$$R_i = \frac{\text{Ending value} - \text{Beginning value}}{\text{Beginning value}}$$

In symbols,

$$R_i = \frac{Y_i - P_i}{P_i} = \frac{Y_i}{P_i} - 1$$

Similarly,

$$R_M = \frac{Y_M - P_M}{P_M} = \frac{Y_M}{P_M} - 1$$

Substituting these expressions into Equation (4.3) yields

$$\frac{\bar{Y}_i}{P_i} - 1 = R_F + \left(\frac{\bar{Y}_M}{P_M} - 1 - R_F\right)\frac{cov(R_iR_M)}{\sigma_M^2} \qquad \textbf{(4.7)}$$

Now we can rewrite $cov(R_iR_M)$ as

$$cov(R_iR_M) = E\left[\left(\frac{Y_i - P_i}{P_i} - \frac{\bar{Y}_i - P_i}{P_i}\right)\left(\frac{Y_M - P_M}{P_M} - \frac{\bar{Y}_M - P_M}{P_M}\right)\right]$$

$$= E\left[\left(\frac{Y_i}{P_i} - \frac{\bar{Y}_i}{P_i}\right)\left(\frac{Y_M}{P_M} - \frac{\bar{Y}_M}{P_M}\right)\right] = \frac{1}{P_iP_M}cov(Y_iY_M)$$

Similarly,

$$\sigma_M^2 = \frac{1}{P_M^2}var(Y_M)$$

Substituting these into Equation (4.7) adding 1 to both sides of the equation and recalling that $r_F = 1 + R_F$,

$$\frac{\bar{Y}_i}{P_i} = r_F + \left(\frac{\bar{Y}_M}{P_M} - r_F\right)\frac{\dfrac{1}{P_i}\dfrac{1}{P_M}cov(Y_iY_M)}{\dfrac{1}{P_M^2}var(Y_M)}$$

Multiplying both sides of the equation by P_i and simplifying the last term on the right-hand side,

$$\bar{Y}_i = r_FP_i + (\bar{Y}_M - r_FP_M)\frac{cov(Y_iY_M)}{var(Y_M)}$$

Solving this expression for P_i,

$$P_i = \frac{1}{r_F}\left[\bar{Y}_i - (\bar{Y}_M - r_FP_M)\frac{cov(Y_iY_M)}{var(Y_M)}\right]$$

Valuation formulas of this type have often been suggested in the security analysis literature. The equation involves taking the expected dollar return next year, $(\bar{Y}_i)$, subtracting off some payment as compensation for risk taking, and then taking the present value of the net result. The term in square brackets can be thought of as the certainty equivalent of the horizon cash payment, and to find the present value of the certainty equivalent, we simply discount it at the riskless rate of interest. While this general idea is not new, the explicit definition of how to find the certainty equivalent is one of the fundamental contributions of the CAPM. It can be shown that

$$\frac{\bar{Y}_M - r_FP_M}{[var(Y_M)]^{1/2}}$$

is equal to a measure of the market price of risk and that

$$\frac{cov(Y_iY_M)}{[var(Y_M)]^{1/2}}$$

is the relevant measure of risk for any asset.

CONCLUSION

In this chapter we have discussed the Sharpe–Lintner–Mossin form of a general equilibrium relationship in the capital markets. This model, usually referred to as the capital asset pricing model or standard CAPM, is a fundamental contribution to understanding the manner in which capital markets function. It is worthwhile highlighting some of the implications of this model.

First, we have shown that, under the assumptions of the CAPM, the only portfolio of risky assets that any investor will own is the market portfolio. Recall that the market portfolio is a portfolio in which the fraction invested in any asset is equal to the market value of that asset divided by the market value of all risky assets. Each investor will adjust the risk of the market portfolio to his or her preferred risk-return combination by combining the market portfolio with lending or borrowing at the riskless rate. This leads directly to the two mutual fund theorem. The two mutual fund theorem states that all investors can construct an optimum portfolio by combining a market fund with the riskless asset. Thus, all investors will hold a

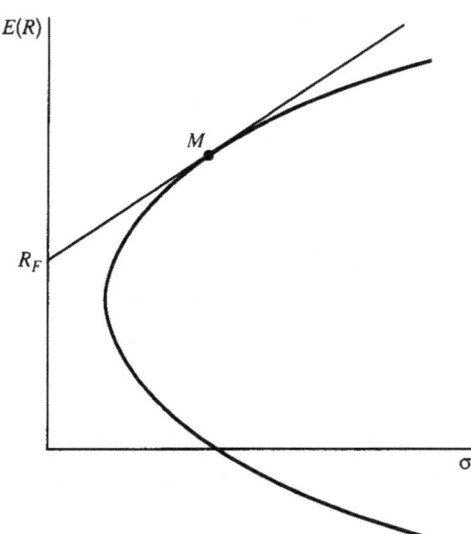

FIGURE 4-5   The efficient frontier.

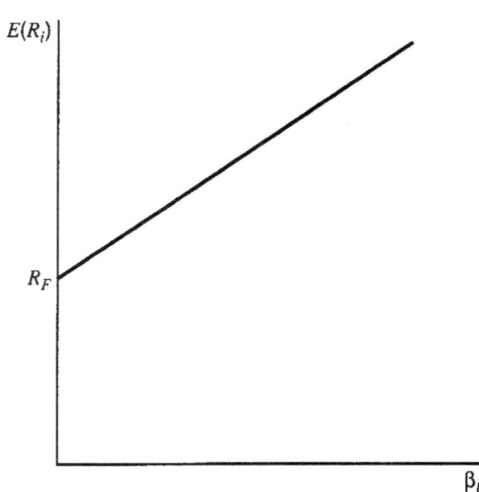

FIGURE 4-6   The security market line.

portfolio along the line connecting R_F with $\bar{R}_M$ in expected return, standard deviation of return space. See Figure 4-5.

This line, usually called the capital market line, which describes all efficient portfolios, is a pictorial representation of the equation

$$\bar{R}_e = R_F + \frac{\bar{R}_M - R_F}{\sigma_M} \sigma_e$$

Thus, we can say that the return on an efficient portfolio is given by the market price of time plus the market price of risk times the amount of risk on an efficient portfolio. Note that risk is defined as the standard deviation of return on any efficient portfolio.

From the equilibrium relationship for efficient portfolios we were able to derive the equilibrium relationship for any security or portfolio (efficient or inefficient). This relationship, presented in Figure 4-6, is given by

$$\bar{R}_i = R_F + \left(\frac{\bar{R}_M - R_F}{\sigma_M}\right)\frac{\sigma_{iM}}{\sigma_M}$$

or

$$\bar{R}_i = R_F + \beta_i(\bar{R}_M - R_F)$$

This relationship is usually called the security market line. Notice that it might have been called the security-portfolio market line for it describes the equilibrium return on all portfolios, as well as all securities.

Examination of the first form of the security market line shows that it is analogous in many ways to the capital market line. As we have shown, the impact of a security on the risk of the market portfolio is given by σ_{iM}/σ_M. Thus, we can state that the equilibrium return on any security is equal to the price of time plus the market price of risk times the relevant definition of risk for the security.

The security market line clearly shows that return is an increasing function, in fact, a linearly increasing function, of risk. Furthermore, it is only market risk that affects return. The investor receives no added return for bearing diversifiable risk.

The capital asset pricing model has been derived under a set of very restrictive assumptions. The test of a model is how well it describes reality. The key test is: Does it describe the behavior of returns in the capital markets? Before we turn to these tests, however, it is logical to examine forms of the general equilibrium relationship that exist under less restrictive assumptions. Even if the standard CAPM model explains the behavior of security returns, it obviously does not explain the behavior of individual investors. Individual investors hold nonmarket and, in fact, quite often, very small portfolios. Furthermore, by developing alternative forms of the general equilibrium relationship, we can test whether observed returns are more consistent with one of these than they are with the standard CAPM.

APPENDIX

Appropriateness of the Single-Period Asset Pricing Model

Up to now, we have assumed that all investors make investment decisions based on a single-period horizon. In fact, the portfolio an investor selects, at any point in time, is really one step in a series of portfolios that he intends to hold over time to maximize his utility of lifetime consumption. Two questions immediately become apparent:

1. What are the conditions under which the simple CAPM adequately describes market equilibrium?

2. Is there a fully general multiperiod equilibrium model?

Fama (1970) and Elton and Gruber (1974) and (1975) have explored the conditions under which the multiperiod investment consumption decision can be reduced to the problem of maximizing a one-period utility function. These conditions are:

1. The consumer's tastes for particular consumption goods and services are independent of future events (any future sets of conditions).

2. The consumer acts as if consumption opportunities in terms of goods and their prices are known at the beginning of the decision period (are not state dependent.)

3. The consumer acts as if the distribution of one-period returns on all assets are known at the beginning of the decision period (are not state dependent).

Hansen and Jagannathan (1991) have developed a very simple and elegant approach to developing a multiperiod investment consumption equilibrium model based on these assumptions, an approach that builds on earlier work by Breeden (1999) and Rubinstein (1974). The investor's problem is to allocate wealth in order to maximize the utility of consuming both now and in the future. In other words, the investor is faced with an intertemporal choice problem. Maximize the expected value of the present value of future consumption.

$$Max\ E_t\left[\sum_{j=0}^{\infty}\delta^j U(c_{t+j})\right]$$

where c_{t+j} represents future consumption, and δ^j is a subjective discount factor applied to future consumption in

period j. For a given budget constraint, the first-order conditions for this problem imply that

$$U'(c_t) = \delta^j\ E_t[(1+R_{i,t+j})U'(c_{t+j})]$$

for all assets i and periods j into the future. Dividing through by the marginal utility of consumption today, we have the important result that

$$1 = E_t[(1+R_{i,t+j})m_{t,j}]$$

where $m_{t,j} = \delta^j[U'(c_{t+j})/U'(c_t)]$ is the intertemporal marginal rate of substitution. It also has the interesting interpretation of being a *stochastic discount factor* (sometimes also referred to as a *pricing kernel*) because it takes an asset with uncertain per dollar future payoff back to the present to be valued at one dollar. If there is a riskless asset in this economy with return $R_{F,t+j}$, then $1 = E_t[(1+R_{F,t+j})m_{t,j}] = (1+R_{F,t+j})E_t[m_{t,j}]$ or $E_t[m_{t,j}] = 1/(1+R_{F,t+j})$, so that the expected value of the stochastic discount factor is equal to the discount factor used when the future payment is in fact without any risk. For the subsequent discussion, we will drop the time subscripts.

Cochrane (2001) argues that this is a straightforward way to value all financial claims. The difficulty is, however, that the stochastic discount factor m is not observable. There are three general approaches to this problem. The first is to specify m directly through assumptions made about utility and using measures of consumption. The chief difficulty associated with this approach is obtaining accurate and timely measures of aggregate consumption c. An alternative approach is to use a vector of factors, some combination of which can proxy for consumption growth. A third idea originally due to Hansen and Jagannathan (1991) is that since the stochastic discount factor prices all financial claims, we might be just as well off inferring the stochastic discount factor from the observed set of asset returns. This important insight allows us to interpret the stochastic discount factor in terms of the mean-variance efficient portfolio, an interpretation that yields the standard CAPM as a direct implication.

The relationship between the stochastic discount factor and the mean variance efficient portfolio is quite direct. Starting from the basic formula that holds for all securities i:

$$\begin{aligned}1 &= E[(1+R_i)m]\\ &= E[(1+\bar{R}_i + (R_i - \bar{R}_i)m)]\\ &= (1+\bar{R}_i)E[m] + E[(R_i - \bar{R}_i)m]\end{aligned}$$

If there is a risk-free rate $E[m] = 1/(1 + R_F)$, this implies the asset pricing relation $\bar{R}_i - R_F = -(1 + R_F) E[(R_i - \bar{R}_i)m]$, which says that the risk premium is negatively proportional to the covariance between the asset return and the stochastic discount factor. In difficult economic times, consumption is depressed and the intertemporal rate of substitution m is high. A negative covariance between asset returns and m is therefore a source of risk to investors.

As we mention above, we cannot directly observe m. However, since the same m prices all assets in the economy, we should be able to infer it from asset prices and returns. Suppose there are N assets in the economy and we infer (the unobserved) m by a hypothetical regression on the set of returns in the economy, so that

$$m = \bar{m} + \sum_{j=1}^{N}(R_j - \bar{R}_j)\gamma_j$$

where the γ_j are the hypothetical regression coefficients. The asset pricing relationship can then be written:

$$\bar{R}_i - R_F = -(1 + R_F)E[(R_i - \bar{R}_i)m]$$

$$= -(1 + R_F)\bar{m}E[(R_i - \bar{R}_i)]$$

$$-(1 + R_F)E\left[(R_i - \bar{R}_i)\sum_{j=1}^{N}(R_j - \bar{R}_j)\gamma_j\right]$$

$$= \sum_{j=1}^{N}E(R_i - \bar{R}_i)(R_j - \bar{R}_j)Z_j$$

where the coefficients $Z_j = -(1 + R_F)\gamma_j$. This equation must hold for all assets, so we have the system of equations

$$\bar{R}_i - R_F = Z_1\sigma_1^2 + Z_2\sigma_{12} + Z_3\sigma_{13} + \cdots + Z_N\sigma_{1N}$$
$$\bar{R}_2 - R_F = Z_1\sigma_{21} + Z_2\sigma_2^2 + Z_3\sigma_{23} + \cdots + Z_N\sigma_{2N}$$
$$\bar{R}_3 - R_F = Z_1\sigma_{31} + Z_2\sigma_{32} + Z_3\sigma_3^2 + \cdots + Z_N\sigma_{3N}$$
$$\vdots$$
$$\bar{R}_N - R_F = Z_1\sigma_{N1} + Z_2\sigma_{N2} + Z_3\sigma_{N3} + \cdots + Z_N\sigma_N^2$$

which the reader will recognize as the equation used to identify the mean variance efficient portfolio with riskless lending and borrowing. From this fact, we conclude immediately that the hypothetical regression coefficients γ_j are proportional to mean variance efficient portfolio weights, and hence that the best estimate of the stochastic discount factor m^* can be written as a linear function of the return on a mean variance efficient portfolio, $m^* = a + bR_{MV}$. If we further identify this portfolio as the market portfolio,

then the asset pricing relation above immediately implies the standard CAPM.

To see this, note that using this proxy for the discount factor

$$\bar{R}_i - R_F = -(1 + R_F)E[(R_i - \bar{R}_i)m^*]$$

$$= -(1 + R_F)aE[(R_i - \bar{R}_i)] - b(1 + R_F)E[(R_i - \bar{R}_i)R_{MV}]$$

$$= -b(1 + R_F)\sigma_{MV}^2\beta_i$$

which must hold for all assets, including the mean variance efficient portfolio with Beta equal to one, so that $b = -(\bar{R}_{MV} - R_F)/[(1 + R_F)/\sigma_{MV}^2]$ and $\bar{R}_i - R_F = \beta_i(\bar{R}_{MV} - R_F)$. There is an important intuition here that establishes that the particular mean variance efficient portfolio is the market portfolio. From the interpretation of the portfolio as resulting from regressing the (unknown) stochastic discount factor m on the set of observed security returns, the variability explained by the observed return portfolio, $\sigma_{m^*}^2 = b^2\sigma_{MV}^2 = [(\bar{R}_{MV} - R_F)^2/(1 + R_F)^2\sigma_{MV}^2]$ is maximized. This implies that the Sharpe ratio given as $(R_{MV} - R_F)/\sigma_{MV} = (1 + R_F)\sigma_{m^*} = (\sigma_{m^*}/\bar{m}^*)$ is also maximized, which further establishes that R_{MV} is the return on the market portfolio.

This last equation is very important because it establishes a nexus between the financial markets on the one hand and consumer preferences on the other. The fact that we can represent the maximized Sharpe ratio as the ratio of the standard deviation of the stochastic discount factor to its mean presents many financial economists with a serious problem. The average risk premium of the market measured in units of risk is far too high to be explained by any consumption-based representation of the stochastic discount factor. This is referred to as the "equity premium puzzle." As Cochrane (2001) notes, the Sharpe ratio measured in real (not nominal) terms has been about 0.5 on the basis of the past 50 years of data for the United States. Assuming the time separable power utility function, the ratio $\sigma_{m^*}/\bar{m}^*$ is approximately the risk-aversion coefficient times the standard deviation of the log of consumption. Since the rate of change in consumption is considerably less than the variance of market returns, this implies that investors are very risk averse, with a coefficient of risk aversion at least 50. A degree of risk aversion this large is difficult to motivate.

The relationship between the Sharpe ratio and the moments of the stochastic discount factor gives rise to another fascinating insight due to Hansen and Jagannathan (1991). Suppose we represent the stochastic discount factor $m^* = a + bR_{MV}$. We have shown that this choice of m^* prices all assets, $E[(1 + R)m^*] = 1$. Consider another discount factor $m = a + bR_{MV} + \varepsilon$, where ε is uncorrelated with returns R on every single asset in the economy, and has zero expectation. Then this discount factor will also price all assets $E[(1 + R)m^*] = 1$. This means that there are many possible discount factors, with $\bar{m} = \bar{m}^*$ and $\sigma^2_m = \sigma^2_{m^*} + \sigma^2_\varepsilon > \sigma^2_{m^*}$. However the choice of $m = m^*$ minimizes the volatility of the stochastic discount factor and is most preferred by investors. Hence we have the interesting bounds: $\sigma_m/\bar{m} \geq \sigma_{m^*}/\bar{m}^* = (\bar{R}_{MV} - R_F)/\sigma_{MV} \geq (\bar{R} - R_F)/\sigma_{MV}$, which are referred to as the "Hansen-Jagannathan bounds." The inequality on the left-hand side refers to the fact that consumption risk will increase if there is a source of risk ε that cannot be hedged by the set of assets represented by returns R. Imperfections in the capital markets make the world a riskier place than it needs to be. The inequality on the right-hand side reflects the reality that limits to diversification through short sale restrictions or other factors limit the opportunities available to investors. Another useful interpretation of these contrasting inequalities is that the problem of choosing a returns-based discount function by minimizing the volatility of the discount factor m is equivalent to determining a portfolio that maximizes the portfolio Sharpe ratio.

Unfortunately, this interpretation of the stochastic discount factor leads to a distinctly unattractive implication. Since $\bar{m}^* = 1/(1 + R_f) = a + b\bar{R}_{MV}$, $a = 1/(1 + R_f) + (\bar{R}_{MV} - R_F)/[(1 + R_F)\sigma^2_{MV}]\bar{R}_{MV}$ and therefore $m^* = 1/(1 + R_f) - [(\bar{R}_{MV} - R_F)/(1 + R_F)\sigma^2_{MV}](R_{MV} - \bar{R}_{MV})$, so that the implied discount rate is negative whenever the market return exceeds its mean by an amount equal to $\sigma^2_{MV}/(\bar{R}_{MV} - R_F)$ the standard deviation of the market return divided by the Sharpe ratio. Using the example given above, if the Sharpe ratio is about 0.5, the discount factor will be negative whenever the market return is two standard deviations above its mean. It is intuitive that the discount factor should fall as market return increases; after all, we are assuming that consumers have diminishing marginal utility. It is not intuitive that the discount factor should be negative, and in fact it is easy to show that there are arbitrage opportunities that arise when the representative investor is willing to throw his or her money away in this way.

As a practical matter, the empirical representation of the discount factor in terms of the return on the market

portfolio is rarely negative, and so a constraint on the discount factor to ensure that it is nonnegative should not lead to any major implications for asset prices. Hansen and Jagannathan suggest such a restriction but find it makes little difference in the case of equity markets. This assertion, however, depends strongly on the assumption that market returns are normally distributed. If returns are positively skewed, then the positive discount factor restriction may have a greater impact.

It is worth pursuing a little the implications of a positive discount factor restriction. We can represent this positive factor as $m^+ = a + b(R_{MV} - c)^-$, where $(R_{MV} - c)^-$ is the payoff of a put on the market index with exercise price $1 + c$. As before, we have

$$\bar{R}_i - R_F = -(1 + R_F)E[(R_i - \bar{R}_i)m^+]$$

$$= -(1+R_F)aE[(R_i-\bar{R}_i)] - b(1+R_F)E[(R_i-\bar{R}_i)(R_{MV}-c)^-]$$

$$= -b(1 + R_F)LPM_{MV,c}(\beta^-)_{MV,c,i}$$

where $LPM_{MV,c} = E[(R_{MV} - c)^2[R_{MV} < c]$ is referred to as the lower partial moment of the return on the mean variance efficient portfolio, a measure of downside risk, and where $\beta^-_{MV,c,i} = E[(R_i - \bar{R}_i)(R_{MV} - c)^-]/LPM_{MV,c}$ is referred to as the lower partial moment Beta, the contribution of security i to the downside risk of the market. As before, we have immediately a linear asset pricing model similar to the standard CAPM, except that the lower partial moment Beta, $\beta^-_{MV,c,i}$, replaces the more familiar Beta, β_{MV}. This generalized asset pricing model was first derived by Bawa and Lindenberg (1977) who showed that it corresponded with an equilibrium model where agents have utility functions for wealth displaying diminishing absolute risk aversion. They further show that if returns are multivariate normal or student-t, the $\beta^-_{MV,c,i}$ risk measure collapses to β_{MV} and the standard CAPM result follows.

QUESTIONS AND PROBLEMS

1. Assume that the following assets are correctly priced according to the security market line. Derive the security market line. What is the expected return on an asset with a Beta of 2?

$$\bar{R}_1 = 6\% \qquad \beta_1 = 0.5$$
$$\bar{R}_2 = 12\% \qquad \beta_2 = 1.5$$

2. Assume the security market line given below. Assume that analysts have estimated the Beta on two stocks as follows: $\beta_x = 0.5$ and $\beta_y = 2$. What must the expected return on the two securities be in order for them to be a good purchase?

$$\bar{R}_i = 0.04 + 0.08\beta_i$$

3. Assume that over some period a CAPM was estimated. The results are shown below. Assume that over the same period two mutual funds had the following results:

Fund A   Actual return = 10%   Beta = 0.8

Fund B   Actual return = 15%   Beta = 1.2

What can be said about the fund performance?

$$\bar{R}_i = 0.06 + 0.19\beta_i$$

4. Consider the CAPM line shown below. What is the excess return of the market over the risk-free rate? What is the risk-free rate?

$$\bar{R}_i = 0.04 + 0.10\beta_i$$

5. Write the CAPM shown in Problem 4 in price form.

6. Show that the standard CAPM should hold even if short sales are not allowed.

7. Assume that an asset exists with $\bar{R}_3 = 15\%$ and $\beta_3 = 1.2$. Further assume the security market line discussed in Problem 1. Design the arbitrage opportunity.

8. If the following assets are correctly priced on the security market line, what is the return of the market portfolio? What is the risk-free rate?

$$\bar{R}_1 = 9.40\% \qquad \beta_1 = 0.80$$
$$\bar{R}_2 = 13.40\% \qquad \beta_2 = 1.30$$

9. Given the following security market line

$$\bar{R}_i = 0.07 + 0.09\beta_i$$

What must be the returns for two stocks assuming their βs are 1.2 and 0.9?

BIBLIOGRAPHY

1. Aivazian, Varouj. "The Demand for Assets under Conditions of Risk: Comment," *Journal of Finance*, **XXXII,** No. 3 (June 1976), pp. 927–929.

2. Bawa, Vijay, and Lindenburg, Eric. "Capital Market Equilibrium in a Mean-Lower Partial Moment Framework," *Journal of Financial Economics*, **5** (1977), pp. 189–200.

3. Benninga, Simon, and Protopapadakis, Aris. "The Stock Market Premium, Production, and Relative Risk Aversion," *The American Economic Review*, **81,** No. 3 (June 1991), pp. 591–599.

4. Bernstein, Peter L. "What Rate of Return Can You 'Reasonably' Expect?" *Journal of Finance*, **XXVIII,** No. 2 (May 1973), pp. 273–282.

5. Breeden, Douglas. "An Intertemporal Asset Pricing Model with Stochastic Consumption and Investment Opportunities," *Journal of Financial Economics*, **7** (1999) pp. 265–296.

6. Chen, Nai-Fu, Grundy, Bruce, and Stambaugh, Robert F. "Changing Risk, Changing Risk Premiums, and Dividend Yield Effects," *The Journal of Business*, **63,** No. 1 (Jan. 1990), pp. 551–570.

7. Cochrane, John. *Asset Pricing* (New Jersey: Princeton University Press, 2001).

8. Elton, Edwin J., and Gruber, Martin J. "The Multi-period Consumption Investment Decision and Single-Period Analysis," *Oxford Economic Paper*, **26** (Sept. 1974), pp. 180–195.

9. Elton, Edwin J., and Gruber, Martin J. *Finance as a Dynamic Process* (Englewood Cliffs, NJ: Prentice Hall, 1975).

10. Fama, Eugene. "Risk, Return and Equilibrium: Some Clarifying Comments," *Journal of Finance*, **XXIII,** No. 1 (March 1968), pp. 29–40.

11. Fama, Eugene. "Multi-period Consumption Investment Decision," *American Economic Review*, **60,** (March 1970), pp. 163–174.

12. ——. "Risk, Return and Equilibrium," *Journal of Political Economy*, **79,** No. 1 (Jan./Feb. 1971), pp. 30–55.

13. ——. "Risk, Return and Portfolio Analysis: Reply to [20]," *Journal of Political Economy*, **81,** No. 3 (May/June 1973), pp. 753–755.

14. Fama, Eugene F. "Determining the Number of Priced State Variables in the ICAPM," *Journal of Financial and Quantitative Analysis*, **33,** No. 2 (June 1998), pp. 217–231.

15. Ferson, Wayne E., Harvey, C, and Campbell, R. "The Variation of Economic Risk Premiums," *The Journal of Political Economy*, **99,** No. 2 (Apr. 1991), pp. 385–416.

16. Ferson, Wayne E., Kandel, Shmuel, and Stambaugh, Robert F. "Tests of Asset Pricing with Time-Varying Expected Risk Premiums and Market Betas," *The Journal of Finance*, **42,** No. 2 (June 1987), pp. 201–220.

17. Green, Richard C. "Benchmark Portfolio Inefficiency and Deviations from the Security Market Line," *The Journal of Finance*, **41,** No. 2 (June 1986), pp. 295–312.

18. Hansen, Lars Peter, and Jagannathan, Ravi. "Implications of Security Market Data for Models of Dynamic Economics," *Journal of Political Economy*, **99** (1991), pp. 225–262.

19. Hietala, Pekka T. "Asset Pricing in Partially Segmented Markets: Evidence from the Finnish Market," *The Journal of Finance*, **44,** No. 3 (July 1989), pp. 697–718.

20. Kroll, Yoram, and Levy, Haim. "Further Tests of the Separation Theorem and the Capital Asset Pricing Model," *The American Economic Review*, **82,** No. 3 (June 1992), pp. 664–670.

21. Kroll, Yoram, Levy, Haim, and Rapoport, Amnon. "Experimental Tests of the Separation Theorem and the Capita" *The American Economic Review*, **78,** No. 3 (June 1988), pp. 500–519.

22. Levy, Haim. "The Demand for Assets under Conditions of Risk," *Journal of Finance*, **XXVIII,** No. 1 (March 1973), pp. 79–96.

23. ——. "The Demand for Assets under Conditions of Risk: Reply to [1]," *Journal of Finance*, **XXXII,** No. 3 (June 1976), pp. 930–932.

24. Lintner, John. "Security Prices, Risk, and Maximal Gains from Diversification," *Journal of Finance* (Dec. 1965), pp. 587–615.

25. ——. "The Aggregation of Investor's Diverse Judgments and Preferences in Purely Competitive Security Markets," *Journal of Financial and Quantitative Analysis*, **IV,** No. 4 (Dec. 1969), pp. 347–400.

26. ——. "The Market Price of Risk, Size of Market and Investor's Risk Aversion," *Review of Economics and Statistics*, **LII,** No. 1 (Feb. 1970), pp. 87–99.

27. Markowitz, Harry M. "Nonnegative or not Nonnegative: A Question about CAPM's," *The Journal of Finance*, **38,** No. 2 (May 1983), pp. 283–296.

28. Modigliani, Franco, and Pogue, Jerry. "An Introduction to Risk and Return," *Financial Analysts Journal*, **30,** No. 2 (Mar./Apr. 1974), pp. 68–80.

29. ——. "An Introduction to Risk and Return: Part II," *Financial Analysts Journal*, **30,** No. 3 (May/June 1974), pp. 69–86.

30. Mossin, Jan. "Equilibrium in a Capital Asset Market," Econometrica, **34** (Oct. 1996) pp. 768–783.

31. Ng, Lilian. "Tests of the CAPM with Time-Varying Covariances: A Multivariate GARCH Approach," *The Journal of Finance*, **46,** No. 4 (Sept. 1991), pp. 1507–1521.

32. Ross, Stephen. "A Simple Approach to the Valuation of Risky Streams," *Journal of Business*, **51,** No. 3 (July 1978), pp. 453–475.

33. Rubinstein, Mark. "An Aggregation Theorem for Securities Markets," *Journal of Financial Economy*, **1,** No. 3 (Sept. 1974), pp. 225–244.

34. Rubinstein, Mark E. "A Mean-Variance Synthesis of Corporate Financial Theory," *Journal of Finance*, **XXXVIII,** No. 1 (March 1973), pp. 167–181.

35. Sharpe, W. F. "Capital Asset Prices: A Theory of Market Equilibrium Under Conditions of Risk," *Journal of Finance* (Sept. 1964), pp. 425–442.

36. ——. "Bonds Versus Stocks: Some Lessons from Capital Market Theory," *Financial Analysts Journal*, **29,** No. 6 (Nov./Dec. 1973), pp. 74–80.

37. ——. "Capital Asset Prices with and Without Negative Holdings," *The Journal of Finance*, **46,** No. 2 (June 1991), pp. 489–509.

38. Stapleton, C. Richard. "Portfolio Analysis, Stock Valuation and Capital Budgeting Decision Rules for Risky Projects," *Journal of Finance*, **XXVI,** No. 1 (Mar. 1971), pp. 95–117.

39. Tinic, Seha M., and West, Richard R. "Risk, Return, and Equilibrium: A Revisit," *The Journal of Political Economy*, **94,** No. 1 (Feb. 1986), pp. 126–147.

40. Tsiang, S. C. "Risk, Return and Portfolio Analysis: Comment on [4]," *Journal of Political Economy*, **81,** No. 3 (May/June 1973), pp. 748–752.

41. Turnbull, Stuart. "Market Value and Systematic Risk," *Journal of Finance*, **XXXII,** No. 4 (Sept. 1977), pp. 1125–1142.

Nonstandard Forms of Capital Asset Pricing Models

5

Excerpt is Chapter 14 of Modern Portfolio Theory and Investment Analysis, 8th Edition, by Edwin Elton, Martin Gruber, Stephen Brown and William Goetzmann.

Learning Objectives

After completing this reading, FRM Candidates should be able to:

- Describe the impact on the CAPM of the following:
  - Short sales disallowed
  - Riskless lending and borrowing
  - Personal taxes
  - Nonmarketable assets
  - Heterogeneous expectations
  - Non-price-taking behavior

- Describe the following multiperiod versions of CAPM:
  - Consumption-oriented CAPM
  - CAPM including inflation
  - Multi-beta CAPM

The CAPM model developed in the previous chapter would provide a complete description of the behavior of capital markets if each of the assumptions set forth held. The test of the CAPM model is how well it describes reality. But even before we examine these tests, it is useful to develop equilibrium models based on more realistic assumptions. Most of the assumptions underlying the CAPM violate conditions in the real world. This does not mean that we should disregard the CAPM model, for the differences from reality may be sufficiently unimportant that they do not materially affect the explanatory power of the model. On the other hand, the incorporation of alternative, more realistic assumptions into the model has several important benefits. While the CAPM may describe equilibrium returns on the macro level, it certainly is not descriptive of micro (individual investor) behavior. For example, most individuals and many institutions hold portfolios of risky assets that do not resemble the market portfolio. We might get better insight into investor behavior by examining models developed under alternative and more realistic assumptions. Another reason for examining other equilibrium models is that it allows us to formulate and test alternative explanations of equilibrium returns. The CAPM may work well, but do other models work better and explain discrepancies from the CAPM? Finally, and perhaps most important, because the CAPM assumes several real-world influences away, it does not provide us with a mechanism for studying the impact of those influences on capital market equilibrium or on individual decision making. Only by recognizing the presence of these influences can their impact be investigated. For example, if we assume personal taxes do not exist, there is no way the equilibrium model can be used to study the effects of taxes. By constructing a model that includes taxes, we can study the impact of taxes on individual investor behavior and on equilibrium returns in the capital market.

The effects of modifying most of the assumptions of the CAPM model have been examined in the economics and finance literature. We review much of this work in this chapter. We place special emphasis on two assumptions: the ability to lend and borrow infinite sums of money at the riskless rate and the absence of personal taxes. The reason we do so is not only because there are important influences but also because they lead to the development of full-fledged general equilibrium models of a form that are amenable to testing.

In the remainder of this chapter we discuss general equilibrium models derived under more realistic assumptions about each of the following influences:

> Short sales disallowed
>
> Riskless lending and borrowing
>
> Personal taxes
>
> Nonmarketable assets
>
> Heterogeneous expectations
>
> Non-price-taking behavior
>
> Multiperiod CAPM

SHORT SALES DISALLOWED

One of the assumptions made in deriving the capital asset pricing model is that the investor can engage in unlimited short sales. Furthermore, short sales were defined in the broadest sense of the term in that the investor was allowed to sell any security (whether owned or not) and to use the proceeds to buy any other security.[1] This was a convenient assumption and it simplified the mathematics of the derivation, but it was *not* a necessary assumption. Exactly the same result would have been obtained had short sales been disallowed. The economic intuition behind this is quite simple.[2] In the CAPM framework all investors hold the market portfolio in equilibrium. Since in equilibrium no investor sells any security short, prohibiting short selling cannot change the equilibrium.[3] Thus, the same CAPM relationship would be derived irrespective of whether short sales are allowed or prohibited.

---

[1] The allowance of short sales was reflected in the constraint on our basic problem that $\Sigma X_i = 1$ while simultaneously not constraining X_i to be positive.

[2] For a formal proof, see Lintner (1971).

[3] The more mathematically inclined reader can reach this same conclusion by using the Kuhn–Tucker conditions on the basic problem outlined in the previous chapter. The derivative of the Lagrangian with respect to each security will have a Kuhn–Tucker multiplier added to it; but since each security is contained in the market portfolio, the value of each Kuhn–Tucker multiplier will be zero. Hence, the solution will be unchanged.

MODIFICATIONS OF RISKLESS LENDING AND BORROWING

A second assumption of the CAPM is that investors can lend and borrow unlimited sums of money at the riskless rate of interest. Such an assumption is clearly not descriptive of the real world. It seems much more realistic to assume that investors can lend unlimited sums of money at the riskless rate but cannot borrow at a riskless rate. The lending assumption is equivalent to investors being able to buy government securities equal in maturity to their single-period horizon. Such securities exist and they are, for all intents and purposes, riskless. Furthermore, the rate on such securities is virtually the same for all investors. On the other hand, it is not possible for investors to borrow unlimited amounts at a riskless rate. It is convenient to examine the case where investors can neither borrow nor lend at the riskless rate first, and then to extend the analysis to the case where they can lend but not borrow at the riskless rate.

No Riskless Lending or Borrowing

This model is the second most widely used general equilibrium model. The simple capital asset pricing model developed in the last chapter is the most widely used. Because of the importance of this model, we derive it twice. The first derivation stresses economic rationale, the second is more rigorous.

Simple Proof

In the last chapter we argued that systematic risk was the appropriate measure of risk and that two assets with the same systematic risk could not offer different rates of return. The essence of the argument was that the unsystematic risk of large diversified portfolios was essentially zero. Thus, even if an individual asset had a great deal of unsystematic risk, it would have little impact on portfolio risk and, therefore, unsystematic risk would not require a higher return. This was formalized in Figure 4-3, and an analogous diagram, Figure 5-1, will be used here.

Let us recall why all assets are plotted on a straight line. First, we showed that combinations of two risky portfolios

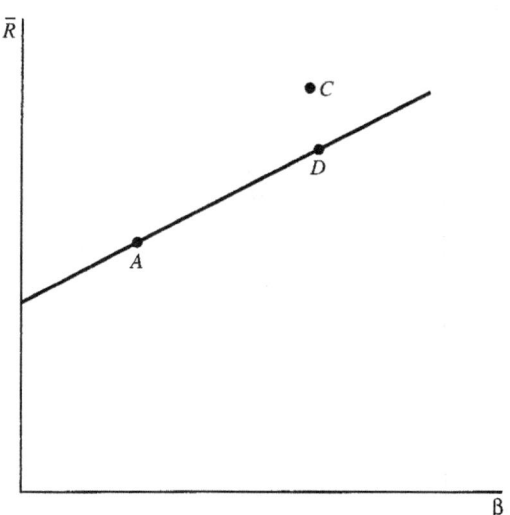

FIGURE 5-1 Portfolios in expected return Beta space.

lie on a straight line connecting them in expected return Beta space. For example, positive combinations of portfolios *A* and *D* lie on the line segment *A–D*. Thus, if securities or portfolios happened to lie on a straight line in expected return Beta space, all combinations of securities (e.g., portfolios) would lie on the same line.

Now consider securities *C* and *D* in Figure 5-1. They both have the same systematic risk, but *C* has a higher return. Clearly, an investor would purchase *C* rather than *D* until the prices adjusted so that they offered the same return. In fact, an investor could purchase *C* and sell *D* short and have an asset with positive expected return and no systematic risk. Such an opportunity cannot exist in equilibrium. In short, all portfolios and securities must plot along a straight line.

One portfolio that lies along the straight line is the market portfolio. This can be seen in either of two ways. If it did not lie along the straight line, two assets would exist with the same systematic risk and different return, and in equilibrium, equivalent assets must offer the same return. In addition, note that all combinations of securities lie on the line and the market portfolio is a weighted average of the securities.

A straight line can be described by any two points. One convenient point is the market portfolio. A second

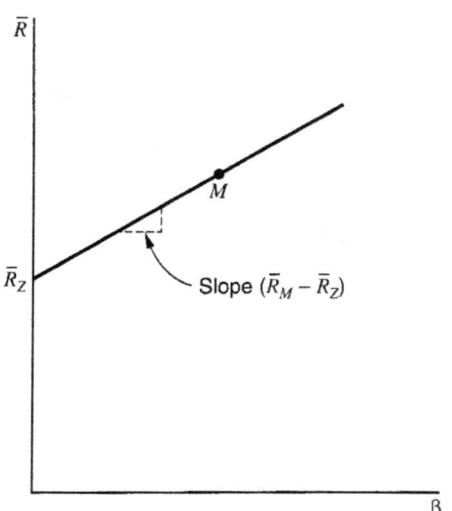

FIGURE 5-2 The zero-Beta capital asset pricing line.

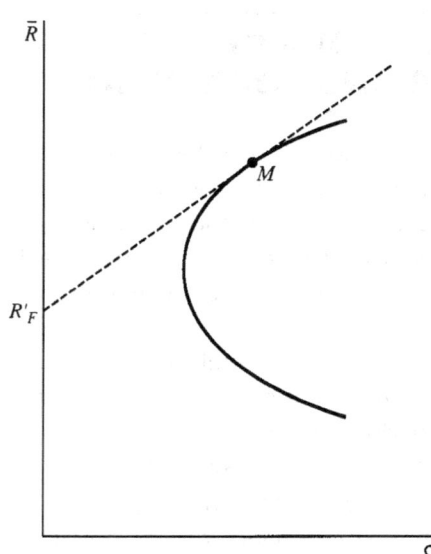

FIGURE 5-3 The opportunity set with rate R_F.

convenient portfolio is where the straight line cuts the vertical axis (where Beta equals zero).[4]

The equation of a straight line is

$$\text{Expected return} = a + b(\text{Beta})$$

This must hold for a portfolio with zero Beta. Letting $\bar{R}_Z$ be the expected return on this portfolio, we have

$$\bar{R}_Z = a + b(0) \quad \text{or} \quad a = \bar{R}_Z$$

The equation must also hold for the market portfolio. If $\bar{R}_M$ is the expected return on the market and, recalling that the Beta for the market portfolio is one, we have

$$\bar{R}_M = \bar{R}_Z + b(1) \quad \text{or} \quad b = \bar{R}_M - \bar{R}_Z$$

Putting this together and letting $\bar{R}_i$ and β_i be the expected return and Beta on an asset or portfolio, the equation for the expected return on any security or portfolio becomes

$$\bar{R}_i = \bar{R}_Z + (\bar{R}_M - \bar{R}_Z)\beta_i \qquad \textbf{(5.1)}$$

This is the so-called zero-Beta version of the capital asset pricing model and is plotted in Figure 5-2. This form of the general equilibrium relationship is often referred to alternatively as a two-factor model.

Rigorous Derivation

Assume for the moment that the market portfolio lies on the efficient frontier in expected return standard deviation space. Later in this chapter we show that it must, indeed, do so. The entire efficient frontier can be traced out by allowing the riskless rate of interest to vary and finding the tangency point between the efficient frontier and a ray passing through the riskless rate (on the vertical axis). Corresponding to every "risk-free rate," there was one point on the efficient frontier, and vice versa. There is, of course, one unique riskless rate in the market (if any). Thus, the procedure of varying the riskless rate was simply a method of obtaining the full efficient frontier. In all cases but one, what we called the riskless rate was an artificial construct we used to obtain one point on the efficient frontier. Define R'_F as the riskless rate such that if investors could lend and borrow unlimited amounts of funds at the rate R'_F, they would hold the market portfolio.

The investor who could lend and borrow at the riskless rate R'_F would face an investment opportunity set as depicted in Figure 5-3. To solve for optimal proportions, he or she would face a set of simultaneous equations directly analogous to Equation (4.4). One such equation is[5]

$$\lambda\left(X_1\sigma_{1j} + X_2\sigma_{2j} + \cdots + X_j\sigma_j^2 + \cdots + X_N\sigma_{Nj}\right) = \bar{R}_j - R'_F \quad \textbf{(5.2)}$$

---

[4] To see that such a point exists, note that the straight line must go indefinitely in both directions. All positive combinations of A and D lie on the line segment between A and D. However, if we purchase D and sell A short, we move above D, and vice versa. Thus, the line continues indefinitely and, in particular, cuts the vertical axis.

[5] These equations are first-order conditions and must hold for the tangency point of any line drawn from the vertical axis and the efficient frontier.

Note that in the equation the Xs are market proportions because R'_F is defined as that value of the riskless rate that causes investors to hold the market portfolio.

In the previous chapter we showed that the term in parentheses in the left-hand side of Equation (5.2) was simply the covariance between the return on security j and the return on the market portfolio. Thus, Equation (5.2) can be written as

$$\lambda \, \text{cov}(R_j R_M) = \bar{R}_j - R'_F$$

or

$$\bar{R}_j = R'_F + \lambda \, \text{cov}(R_j R_M) \qquad \textbf{(5.3)}$$

The expected return on the market portfolio is a weighted average of the expected return on individual securities. Since Equation (5.3) holds for each security, it must also hold for the market. Thus,

$$\bar{R}_M = R'_F + \lambda \, \text{cov}(R_M R_M)$$

But $\text{cov}(R_M R_M)$ is the variance of M so that

$$\bar{R}_M = R'_F + \lambda \sigma_M^2 \quad \text{or} \quad \lambda = \frac{\bar{R}_M - R'_F}{\sigma_M^2}$$

Substituting the expression for λ into Equation (5.3) and rearranging yields

$$\bar{R}_j = R'_F + \frac{\bar{R}_M - R'_F}{\sigma_M^2} \text{cov}(R_j R_M)$$

or

$$\bar{R}_j = R'_F + \beta_j (\bar{R}_M - R'_F) \qquad \textbf{(5.4)}$$

Note that a riskless asset with a return of R'_F does not really exist. However, there are an infinite number of assets and portfolios giving a return of R'_F. They are located along the solid portion of the line segment $R'_F - C$ shown in Figure 5-4. Examine Equation (5.4). For R_j to be equal to R'_F, the last term must be zero. Thus, any security or portfolio that has an expected return of R'_F must have a Beta (covariance with the market portfolio) equal to zero.

While equilibrium can be expressed in terms of any of the zero-Beta portfolios on the solid portion of the line segment $R'_F - C$, it makes sense to utilize the least risky zero-Beta portfolio. This is equivalent to the zero-Beta portfolio that has the least total risk. We designate the minimum variance zero-Beta portfolio as Z and its expected return as $\bar{R}_Z$.

Then, since $\bar{R}_Z = R'_F$, the security market line can be written as

$$\bar{R}_j = \bar{R}_Z + (\bar{R}_M - \bar{R}_Z)\beta_j$$

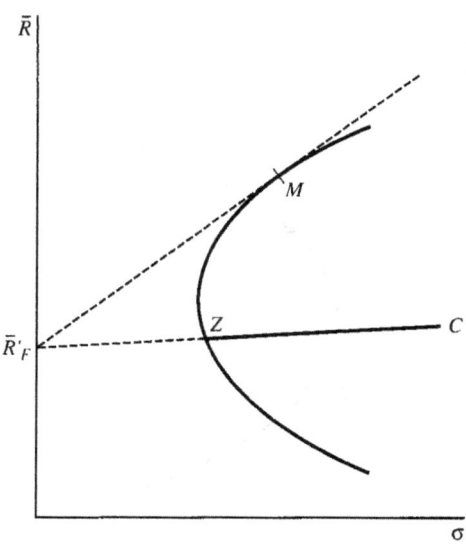

FIGURE 5-4   The location of portfolios with return R'_F

This is exactly the expression [Equation (5.1)] we found for the security market line earlier in this chapter.

Let us see if we can learn anything about the location of this minimum variance zero-Beta portfolio. First, we know that the expected return on the zero-Beta portfolio must be lower than the expected return on the market portfolio. The market portfolio is on the efficient segment of the minimum variance frontier, and the slope at this point must be positive. Thus, as we move along the line tangent to $\bar{R}_M$ toward the vertical axis, we lower return. Since $\bar{R}_Z$ is the intercept of the tangency line and the vertical axis, it has a return less than $\bar{R}_M$. Second, as we prove below, the minimum variance zero-Beta portfolio cannot be efficient.

Proof

Denote by s the portfolio that has the smallest possible variance. This portfolio can be formed as a combination of the market portfolio and the zero-Beta portfolio.

$$\sigma_s^2 = X_Z^2 \sigma_Z^2 + (1 - X_Z)^2 \sigma_M^2$$

There is no covariance term since the covariance between these two assets is zero. To find the weights in each portfolio that minimize variance, take the derivative with respect to X_Z and set it equal to zero, or

$$\frac{d\sigma_s^2}{dX_Z} = 2X_Z \sigma_Z^2 - 2\sigma_M^2 + 2X_Z \sigma_M^2 = 0$$

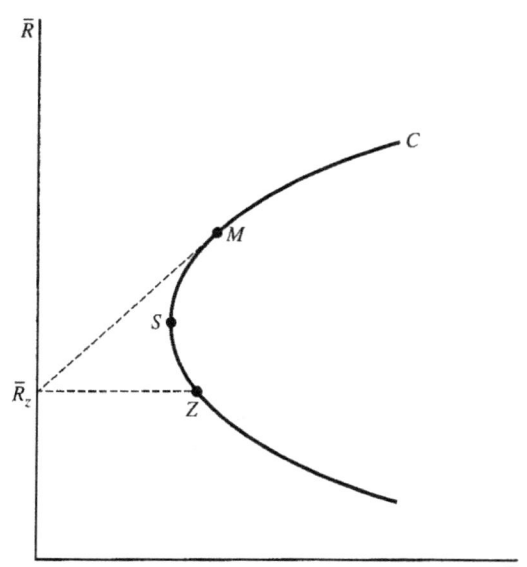

FIGURE 5-5 The minimum variance frontier.

Solving for X_z

$$X_z = \frac{\sigma_M^2}{\sigma_M^2 + \sigma_z^2}$$

Since both σ_M^2 and σ_z^2 must be positive numbers, that portfolio with the smallest possible variance must involve positive weights on both the zero-Beta and market portfolio. Since $\bar{R}_z < \bar{R}_M$, portfolios of Z and M with positive weights must have higher expected returns than Z. Since the minimum variance portfolio has higher return and smaller variance than Z, Z cannot be on the efficient portion of the minimum variance frontier.

We can locate portfolios Z, M, and s on the minimum variance frontier of all portfolios in expected return standard deviation space.[6] This is done in Figure 5-5. This figure presents the location of all efficient portfolios in expected return standard deviation space. All investors will hold some portfolio that lies along the efficient frontier (SMC). Investors who hold portfolios offering returns between s and $\bar{R}_M$ will hold combinations of the zero-Beta portfolio and the market portfolio.[7] Investors who choose to hold

portfolios to the right of M (choose returns above $\bar{R}_M$) will hold a portfolio constructed by selling portfolio Z short and buying the market portfolio. No investor will choose to hold only portfolio Z for this is an inefficient portfolio. Furthermore, since investors in the aggregate hold the market portfolio, the aggregate holding of portfolio Z (long positions minus short positions) must be exactly zero. Note also that we still have a two mutual fund theorem. All investors can be satisfied by transactions in two mutual funds: the market portfolio and the minimum variance zero-Beta portfolio.

We started out this section by assuming that the market portfolio is efficient. While we do not intend to provide a rigorous proof of its efficiency, a few comments should convince the reader of its truth. Those interested in a rigorous proof are referred to Fama (1970).

With homogeneous expectations, all investors face the same efficient frontier. Recall that with short sales allowed, all combinations of any two minimum variance portfolios are minimum variance. Thus, if we combine any two investors' portfolios, we have a minimum variance portfolio. The market portfolio is a weighted average or portfolio of each investor's portfolio where the weights are the proportion each investor owns of the total of all risky assets. Thus, it is minimum variance. Since each investor's portfolio is efficient and since the return on the market is an average of the return on the portfolios of individual investors, the return on the market portfolio is the return of a portfolio on the efficient segment of the minimum variance frontier. Thus, the market portfolio is not only minimum variance but efficient.

Riskless Lending but No Riskless Borrowing

We have gone too far in changing our assumptions. As we agreed earlier, while it is unrealistic to assume that individuals can borrow at the riskless rate, it is realistic to assume that they can lend at a rate that is riskless. Individuals can place funds in government securities that have a maturity equal to their time horizon and, thus, be guaranteed of a riskless payoff at the horizon.

If we allow riskless lending, then the investor's choice can be pictured as in Figure 5-6.[8] As we argued in earlier

---

[6] The minimum variance curve or minimum variance frontier contains the set of portfolios that offers the lowest risk at any obtainable level of return. The efficient set (frontier) is a subset of these minimum variance portfolios.

[7] Recall that the entire efficient frontier can be generated as portfolios of any two portfolios on the efficient frontier.

[8] Once again we are assuming short sales are allowed. This is a necessary assumption.

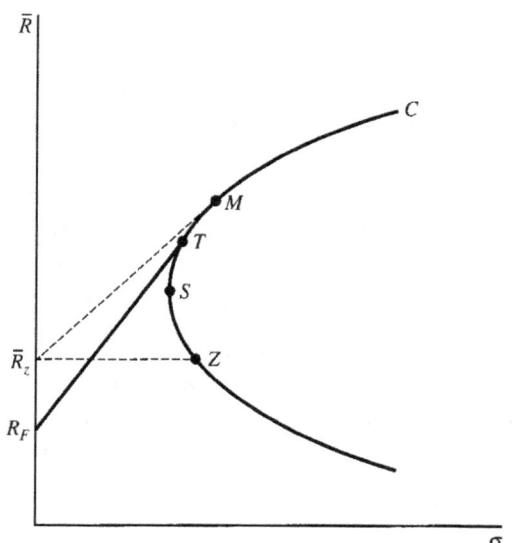

FIGURE 5-6   The opportunity set with riskless lending.

chapters, all combinations of a riskless asset and a risky portfolio lie on the straight line connecting the asset and the portfolio. The preferred combination lies on the straight line passing through the risk-free asset and tangent to the efficient frontier. This is the line $R_F T$ in Figure 5.6.

Notice that we have drawn T below and to the left of the market portfolio M and, hence, $\bar{R}_z > R_F$. This was not an accident. Let us examine why this must hold. Before we introduced the ability to lend at the riskless rate, all investors held portfolios along the efficient frontier SMC (portfolios along the line $\bar{R}_z M$ do not exist). With riskless lending, the investor can hold portfolios of riskless and risky assets along the line $R_F T$. If the investor chooses to hold an investment on the line $R_F T$, he would be placing some of his funds in the portfolio of risky assets denoted by T and some in the riskless asset. The choice to hold any portfolio of risky assets other than T would never be made. Now, why can't T and M be the same portfolio? As long as any investor has a risk-return trade-off such that he or she chooses to hold a portfolio of investments to the right of T, the market must lie to the right of T. For example, assume that all investors but one choose to lend money and hold portfolio T. Now this one investor who does not choose T must hold a portfolio to the right of T on the efficient frontier STC. If the investor did not, then he or she would be better off holding a portfolio on the line $R_F T$ and, hence, holding portfolio T. Since the market

portfolio is an average of the portfolios held by all investors, the market portfolio must be a combination of the investor's portfolio and T. Thus, it lies to the right of T. M, being to the right of T, leads directly to $\bar{R}_z$ being larger than R_F. R_F is the intersection of the vertical axis and a line tangent to the efficient frontier at T. Similarly, $\bar{R}_z$ is the intersection of the vertical axis and a line tangent at M. Since the slope of the efficient frontier at M is less than at T and since M lies above T, the line tangent at M must intersect the vertical axis above the line tangent at T.[9] Thus, $\bar{R}_z$ must be greater than R_F.

The efficient frontier is given by the straight line segment $R_F T$ and curve TMC.[10] Notice that, in the case of no lending and borrowing, combinations of all efficient portfolios were efficient. In the case where riskless lending is allowed, not all combinations of efficient portfolios are efficient. It should be obvious to the reader that combinations of a portfolio from the line segment $R_F T$ and a portfolio from the curve TMC are dominated by a portfolio lying along the curve TMC.

Portfolio T can be obtained by combining portfolios Z and M. Examining the efficient frontier we see that investors who select a portfolio along the line segment $R_F T$ are placing some of their money in portfolio T (which is constructed from the market portfolio plus portfolio Z) and some in the riskless asset. (Those that select a portfolio on the segment TM are placing some of their money in portfolio M and some in Z.) Those that select a portfolio on MC are selling portfolio Z short and investing all of the proceeds in M. (Notice that our two mutual fund theorem has been replaced with a three mutual fund theorem.) All investors can be satisfied by holding (long or short) some combination of the market portfolio, the minimum variance zero-Beta portfolio, and the riskless asset.[11]

---

[9] The property of the two slopes follows directly from the concavity of the efficient frontier proved in Chapter 3.

[10] The reader might note that portfolio T is a corner portfolio, a portfolio whose composition is different from those immediately adjacent to it. All portfolios to the right of T on the efficient frontier are made up of combinations of portfolios M and Z, while those to the left of T are made up of portfolios M and Z plus the riskless security.

[11] Note that while we continually speak of using the market portfolio and the minimum variance zero-Beta portfolio to obtain the efficient frontier, any other two minimum variance portfolios would serve equally well.

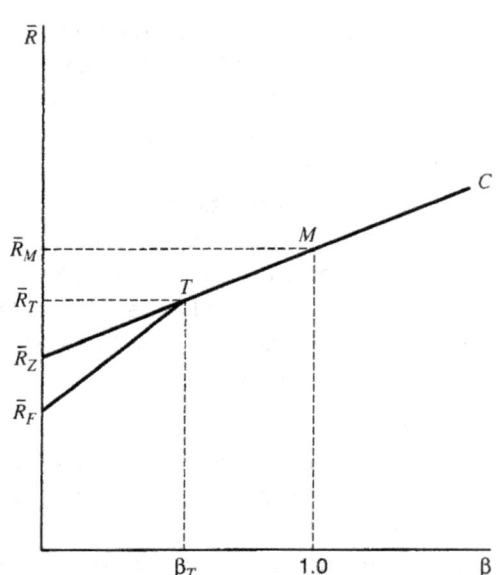

FIGURE 5-7 The location of investments in expected return Beta space.

Having examined all efficient portfolios in expected return standard deviation space, let us turn our attention to the location of securities and portfolios in expected return Beta space. Let us develop the security market line.

The market portfolio M is still an efficient portfolio. Thus, the analysis of the last section holds. All securities contained in M have an expected return given by

$$\bar{R}_j = \bar{R}_z + \beta_j(\bar{R}_M - \bar{R}_z) \qquad \textbf{(5.5)}$$

Similarly, all portfolios composed solely of risky assets have their return given by Equation (5.5). This splits as a straight line in expected return Beta space and is the line $\bar{R}_z TMC$ in Figure 5-7. This equation holds only for risky assets and for portfolios of risky assets. It does not describe the return on the riskless asset or the return on portfolios that contain the riskless asset.

In the previous chapter we examined combinations of the riskless asset and a risky portfolio and found that they lie on the straight line connecting the two points in expected return Beta space. Since investors who lend all hold risky portfolio T, the relevant line segment is $R_F T$ in Figure 5-7.

Thus, while the straight line $\bar{R}_z M$ can be thought of as the security market line for all risky assets and for all portfolios composed entirely of risk assets, it does not describe the return on portfolios (and, of particular note, on those efficient portfolios) that contain the riskless asset.

Efficient portfolios have their return given by the two line segments $R_F T$ and TC in Figure 5-7. The fact that efficient portfolios have lower return for a given level of Beta than individual assets may seem startling. But remember that securities or portfolios on $\bar{R}_z T$ have a higher standard deviation than portfolios with the same return on segment $R_F T$. (In order to understand this, remember that the return on portfolio Z is uncertain, even though it has a zero Beta, while the return on the riskless asset is certain.)

Before moving on to other models, it is well worth reviewing certain characteristics of those we have been discussing, particularly insofar as they resemble or are different from the characteristics of the simple capital asset pricing model.

First, note that, under either of these models, all investors no longer hold the same portfolio in equilibrium. This is comforting for it is more consistent with observed behavior. Of less comfort is that investors still hold most securities (either long or short) and hold many securities short. In the case where neither lending nor borrowing is allowed, we have a two mutual fund theorem. In the case where riskless lending is allowed, we have a three mutual fund theorem.

As in the case of the simple CAPM, we still get a security market line. In addition, many of the implications of this relationship are the same. For risky assets or portfolios, expected return is still a linearly increasing function of risk as measured by Beta. It is only market risk that affects the return on individual risky securities and portfolios of risky securities. On these securities the investor gains no extra return from bearing diversifiable risk. In fact, the only difference lies in the intercept and slope of the security market line.[12]

Other Lending and Borrowing Assumptions

Brennan (1971) has analyzed the situation where riskless lending and borrowing is available, but at different rates. The efficient frontier for the individual when riskless borrowing and lending at different rates is possible was analyzed in Chapter 3. If all investors face the same efficient frontier, this efficient frontier must appear as in Figure 5-8.

---

[12] In all models the efficient frontier itself is affected by diversifiable risk. Since the shape of the frontier affects the location of the tangency portfolio, diversifiable risk has some effect on security returns.

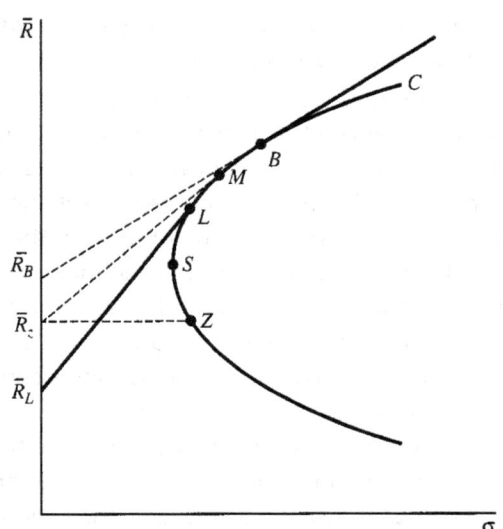

FIGURE 5-8 The opportunity set with a differential lending and borrowing rate.

In this diagram, *L* stands for the portfolio of risky securities that will be held by all investors who lend money and *B* stands for the portfolio of all securities that will be held by investors who borrow money. The market portfolio must lie on the efficient frontier and it must lie between *L* and *B*.

Let us examine why. The only portfolios of risky securities held by investors are *L* and *B* and intermediate portfolios on the curve *LB*. Earlier we showed that combinations of efficient portfolios were efficient. In the earlier section, lending and borrowing was not allowed so that the proof was that combinations of portfolios on the efficient portion of the minimum variance frontier were also on the efficient portion. The market portfolio is a weighted average of all portfolios held by individuals. Since these are efficient, we know from the earlier discussion that the market portfolio lies on the efficient portion of the minimum variance curve. But we can be even more precise. The return on the market portfolio is a weighted average of the return of portfolio *L*, portfolio *B*, and all intermediate portfolios. Thus, its return must be between *L* and *B*. Therefore, the market portfolio must lie somewhere on the efficient frontier between *L* and *B*. Having established that the market portfolio lies on the efficient frontier between *L* and B, we derive, in the same manner, the same security market line as we derived in the last section of this chapter. Equation (5.1) still holds. However, remember that this equation only describes the return on securities

and portfolios that do not have any investment in the riskless asset (long or short). Thus, the equation will not describe the return on portfolios that are combinations of a risky portfolio and a riskless asset along the straight line between $\bar{R}_L$ and *L* or with return more than $\bar{R}_B$.

Brennan (1971) has also examined the case where the borrowing rate differed from the lending rate and where these rates were different for each investor. Once again, because the market portfolio lies on the efficient frontier, an equation identical in form to Equation (5.1) describes the return on all risky assets and on all portfolios composed entirely of risky assets.

PERSONAL TAXES

The simple form of the capital asset pricing model ignores the presence of taxes in arriving at an equilibrium solution. The implication of this assumption is that investors are indifferent between receiving income in the form of capital gains or dividends and that all investors hold the same portfolio of risky assets. If we recognize the existence of taxes and, in particular, the fact that capital gains are taxed, in general, at a lower rate than dividends, the equilibrium prices should change. Investors should judge the return and risk on their portfolio after taxes. This implies that, even with homogeneous expectations about the before-tax return on a portfolio, the relevant (after-tax) efficient frontier faced by each investor will be different. However, a general equilibrium relationship should still exist since, in the aggregate, markets must clear. In the appendix at the end of this chapter we derive the general equilibrium pricing equation for all assets and portfolios, given differential taxes on income and capital gains. The return on any asset or portfolio is given by

$$E(R_i) = R_F + \beta_i[(E(R_M) - R_F) - \tau(\delta_M - R_F)] + \tau(\delta_i - R_F) \textbf{(5.6)}$$

where

> δ_M = the dividend yield (dividends divided by price) of the market portfolio
>
> δ_i = the dividend yield for stock *i*
>
> τ = a tax factor that measures the relevant market tax rates on capital gains and income. τ is a complex function of investors' tax rates and wealth. However, it should be a positive number. See the appendix for further discussion.

The equilibrium relationship for expected returns has now become very complex. When dividends are on average taxed at a higher rate than capital gains (as they are in the U.S. economy), τ is positive and expected return is an increasing function of dividend yield. This is intuitively appealing since the larger the fraction of return paid in the form of dividends, the more taxes the investor will have to pay and the larger the pretax return required. The reader may wonder why the last term contains R_F as well as the dividend yield. The reason for this is the tax treatment of interest on lending and borrowing. Since interest payments are for all intents and purposes taxed at the same rate as dividends, they enter the relationship in a parallel manner although with an opposite sign.[13] The fact that the term in square brackets has the correct form can be seen by letting security i be the market portfolio and noting that (since Beta equals 1 for the market portfolio) the equation reduces to $E(R_M) = E(R_M)$.

Examination of Equation (5.6) reveals that a security market line is no longer sufficient to describe the equilibrium relationship. In previous versions of general equilibrium relationships, the only variable associated with the individual security that affected expected return was its Beta. Now we see from Equation (5.6) that both the securities Beta and its dividend yield affect expected return. This means that equilibrium must be described in three-dimensional spaces (R_i, β_i, δ_i) rather than two-dimensional space. The resultant equilibrium relationship [Equation (5.6)] will be a plane rather than a straight line. The plane will be located such that for any value of Beta, expected return goes up as dividend yield goes up, and for any value of dividend yield, expected return goes up as Beta goes up.

If returns are determined by an equilibrium model like that presented in Equation (5.6), it should be possible to derive optimal portfolios for any investor as a function of the tax rates paid on capital gains and dividends. While the mathematics of the solution are rather complex, the economic intuition behind the results is strong.[14] All investors will hold widely diversified portfolios that resemble the market portfolio, except they will be tilted in favor of those stocks in which the investor has a competitive advantage. For example, investors whose tax bracket is below the average effective rate in the market should hold more of high-dividend stocks in their portfolio than the percentage these stocks constitute of the market portfolio, while they should hold less (and in extreme cases even short sell) stocks with very low dividends. Low-tax-bracket investors have a comparative advantage in holding high-dividend stocks for the tax disadvantage of these stocks is less disadvantageous to them than it is to the average stockholder. Individual investors in the market seem to behave as the analysis suggests they should.[15] The optimization rules described in Elton and Gruber (1978) ensure that markets will clear at the returns established in Equation (5.6).

NONMARKETABLE ASSETS

Up to now we have assumed that all assets are readily marketable so that each investor was free to adjust his or her portfolio to an optimum. In truth, every investor has nonmarketable assets or assets that he or she will not consider marketing. Human capital is an example of a non-marketable asset. People are forbidden by law from selling themselves into slavery in the United States. There is no direct way that an investor can market his or her claims to future labor income. Similarly, the investor has other future monetary claims such as social security payments or the future payments from a private retirement program that cannot be marketed. There are categories of marketable assets that, although the investor might be able to market them, he or she considers them a fixed part of the portfolio. For example, investors who own their own home can market it, but they will often not consider switching houses as part of changes in their "optimum investment

---

[13] The implications of this for investor behavior are interesting. For example, an investor could convert a dividend-paying stock into one with only a capital gains return by borrowing a sum of money such that when the sum borrowed plus the initial planned investment in a stock is invested in the stock, interest payments exactly equal the dividend payments on the stock.

[14] See Elton and Gruber (1978) for the derivation of the composition of optimal portfolios under taxation.

[15] Pettit and Stanley (1979) have found that investors tend to behave as this model suggests they should behave.

portfolio." This is due, in part, to large transaction costs but also because of nonmonetary factors.

If we divide the world up into marketable and nonmarketable assets, then a simple equation exists for the equilibrium return on all assets. Let

R_H equal the one period rate of return on nonmarketable assets

P_H equal the total value of all nonmarketable assets

P_M equal the total value of all marketable assets

All other terms are defined as before. Then, it can be shown that[16]

$$E(R_j) = R_F$$
$$+ \frac{E(R_M) - R_F}{\sigma_M^2 + P_H/P_M \, \text{cov}(R_M R_H)} \left[\text{cov}(R_j R_M) + \frac{P_H}{P_M} \text{cov}(R_j R_H) \right]$$

To contrast this with the simple capital asset pricing model we can write the simple model as

$$E(R_j) = R_F + \frac{E(R_M) - R_F}{\sigma_M^2} [\text{cov}(R_j R_M)]$$

Notice that the inclusion of nonmarketable assets leads to a general equilibrium relationship of the same form as the simple model that excluded nonmarketable assets. However, the market trade-off between return and risk is different, as is the measure of risk for any asset. Including nonmarketable assets, the market risk-return trade-off becomes

$$\frac{E(R_M) - R_F}{\sigma_M^2 + \frac{P_H}{P_M} \text{cov}(R_M R_H)}$$

rather than

$$\frac{E(R_M) - R_F}{\sigma_M^2}$$

It seems reasonable to assume that the return on the total of nonmarketable assets is positively correlated

with the return on the market, which would suggest that the market return-risk trade-off is lower than that suggested by the simple form of the model. How much lower is a function of both the covariance between the return on the nonmarketable assets and the marketable assets and the total value of nonmarketable assets relative to marketable assets. If nonmarketable assets had a very small value relative to marketable assets or if there was an extremely low correlation between the return on marketable and nonmarketable assets, there would be little harm done in using the standard CAPM. However, it seems likely that since nonmarketable assets include, at a minimum, human capital and since wage rates as well as market performance are correlated with the performance of the economy, there will be important differences between these models.

In addition, the definition of the risk of any asset has been changed. With nonmarketable assets, it is a function of the covariance of an asset with the total stock of nonmarketable assets, as well as with the total stock of marketable assets. The weight this additional term receives in determining risk depends on the total size of nonmarketable assets relative to marketable assets. The risk on any asset that is positively correlated with the total of nonmarketable assets will be higher than the risk implied by the simple form of the CAPM.

Considering the difference in both the reward-risk ratio and the size of risk itself, we can see that the equilibrium return for an asset can be either higher or lower than it is under the standard form of the CAPM. If the asset is negatively correlated with the total of nonmarketable assets, its equilibrium return will be lower for its risk and the price of risk will be lower. However, if its return is positively correlated with the return on marketable assets, its equilibrium return could be higher or lower, depending on whether the increased risk is high enough to offset the decreased market price of risk.

Mayers (1972) explores the implications of his model for the optimal portfolio holdings of individuals. As you would suspect, investors tilt their portfolio, holding a smaller percentage of those stocks (than found in the market) with which their nonmarketable securities are most highly correlated.

Brito (1977) and (1978) has examined, in more detail, the optimum portfolio holdings of individuals in equilibrium

---

[16] For a derivation see Mayers. Although this equation does not appear in Mayers (1972), it can be derived from his Equation (19) with a little algebra. The reader may be bothered by the fact that *PH* appears in our equation while the Mayers's equations make use of the income (actually income plus value) of the asset one period hence. However, there is no inconsistency as Mayers's Equation (15) allows for the determination of *PH*.

when nonmarketable assets are present. He finds that each individual can select an optimal portfolio from among three mutual funds. The first mutual fund is a portfolio that has a covariance with each marketable asset equal in magnitude but opposite in sign to the covariance between the investor's nonmarketable portfolio and each marketable asset. Note two things about this fund: First, it will have a different composition for different investors, according to the nonmarketable assets they hold. Second, the reason for its optimality has an intuitive explanation. It is that portfolio that diversifies away as much of the nonmarketable risk as it is possible to diversify away. In short, it allows the investor to "market" as much of his or her nonmarketable assets as is possible. Brito then shows that each individual will allocate the remainder of his or her wealth between the riskless security (the second fund) and a third fund that is the market portfolio minus the *aggregate* of all investments made in the first type of fund by all investors. Note that, while the second and third funds are the same for all investors, the first fund has a different composition for each investor, according to the composition of his or her nonmarketable assets.

While Mayers's analysis is important for the insight it provides into the pricing of non-marketable assets, it is at least as important for the insight it gives us into the missing asset problem. Empirical tests of general equilibrium models will always have to be conducted with the market defined as including something less than the full set of assets in the economy. The equilibrium equations described previously are perfectly valid for examining the missing asset problem, where R_M is now defined as the return on the collection of assets selected to represent the market and R_H is the return on the assets that were left out. In a manner exactly parallel to that presented, they allow us to think through the influence of missing assets on both the markets risk-return trade-off and the equilibrium return from missing assets.

HETEROGENEOUS EXPECTATIONS

Several researchers have examined the existence and characteristics of a general equilibrium solution when investors have heterogeneous expectations.[17] Although

all of these models lead to forms of an equilibrium pricing equation that have some similarity to those presented earlier in this chapter and in the last chapter, there are important differences. Equilibrium can still be expressed in terms of expected returns, covariances, and variance, but now these returns, covariances, and variances are complex weighted averages of the estimates held by different individuals. The weightings are very complex because they involve information about investor utility functions. In particular, they involve information about investors' tradeoffs (marginal rate of substitution) between expected return and variance. But this trade-off for most utility functions is a function of wealth and, hence, prices. This means that prices are required to determine the risk-return trade-offs that we need to determine prices. Thus, in general, an explicit solution to the heterogeneous expectation problem cannot be reached. The problem can be made simpler by placing additional restrictions either on investor utility functions or on the characteristics of opportunities facing the investor.

The first approach was taken by Lintner (1969). He could not derive a simple capital asset pricing model under heterogeneous expectations because the marginal rate of substitution between expected return and variances was, itself, a function of equilibrium prices. If we assume a utility function such that the marginal rate of substitution is not a function of wealth, then we will not face this problem. They were the functions exhibiting constant absolute risk aversion. Lintner assumed this type of function (to be precise, he assumed a negative exponential utility function).[18] Utilizing this function, he showed that the Sharpe-Lintner-Mossin form of the CAPM model holds and that the term $(\bar{R}_M - R_F)/\sigma_M^2$ in Equation (4.2) is proportional to the harmonic mean of the risk-avoidance coefficient, and all expected values, variances, and covariances are complicated averages of the probability beliefs and risk preferences of all individuals.

A second way to arrive at more testable models of equilibrium under heterogeneous assumptions is to place restrictions on the form that the heterogeneity can assume. Gonedes (1976) assumes that a set of basic economic activities exist such that any firm can be viewed as some combination of these basic economic activities

---

[17] See Lintner (1969), Sharpe (1970), Fama (1976), and Gonedes (1976).

[18] Lintner assumes the negative exponential utility function given by $u(w) = e^{-a_i W_i}$. The measure of risk aversion is given by a_i.

and the heterogeneous expectations arise because of disagreement about the exact combination (weighting) of those basic economic activities that represent a firm. Gonedes analyzes the case where this is the one source of heterogeneous expectations. He shows that, under this assumption, the minimum variance frontier is the same for all investors, even though they have heterogeneous expectations about the returns from different securities. Furthermore, the market portfolio is a minimum variance portfolio for each and every investor. Gonedes then proceeds to show that Beta is a sufficient measure of risk and that the equilibrium models lead to a linear relationship between expected return and Beta parallel to that found under simpler forms of the CAPM.

NON-PRICE-TAKING BEHAVIOR

Up to now we have assumed that individuals act as price takers in that they ignore the impact of their buying or selling behavior on the equilibrium price of securities and, hence, on their optimal portfolio holdings. The obvious question to ask is what happens if there are one or more investors, such as mutual funds or large pension funds, who believe that their behavior impacts price. The method of analysis used by Lindenberg (1976) and (1979) derives equilibrium conditions under all possible demands by the price affector. The price affector selects her portfolio to maximize utility given the equilibrium prices that will result from her action. Assuming that the price affector operates so as to maximize utility, we can then arrive at equilibrium conditions. Lindenberg finds that all investors, including the price taker, hold some combination of the market portfolio and the riskless asset. However, the price affector will hold less of the riskless asset (will be less of a risk avoider) than would be the case if the price affector did not recognize the fact that her actions affected price. By doing so the price affector increases utility. Because the price affector still holds a combination of the riskless asset and the market portfolio, we still get the simple form of the CAPM, but the market price of risk is lower than it would be if all investors were price takers.

Lindenberg (1979) goes on to analyze collective portfolio selection and efficient allocation among groups of investors. He finds that by colluding or merging, individuals or institutions can increase their utility. This analysis provides us with one reason for the existence of large financial institutions.

MULTIPERIOD CAPM

Up to now we have assumed that all investors make investment decisions based on a single-period horizon. In fact, the portfolio an investor selects, at any point in time, is really one step in a series of portfolios that he intends to hold over time to maximize his utility of lifetime consumption. Two questions immediately become apparent:

1. What are the conditions under which the simple CAPM adequately describes market equilibrium?
2. Is there a fully general multiperiod equilibrium model?

Fama (1970) and Elton and Gruber (1974) and (1975) have explored the conditions under which the multiperiod investment consumption decision can be reduced to the problem of maximizing a one-period utility function. These conditions are as follows:

1. The consumer's tastes for particular consumption goods and services are independent of future events (any future sets of conditions).
2. The consumer acts as if consumption opportunities in terms of goods and their prices are known at the beginning of the decision period (are not state dependent.)[19]
3. The consumer acts as if the distribution of one-period returns on all assets are known at the beginning of the decision period (are not state dependent).

Furthermore, Fama (1970) has shown that if the investor's multiperiod utility function, expressed in terms of multiperiod consumption, exhibits both a preference of more to less and risk aversion with respect to each period's consumption, then the derived one-period utility has the same properties with respect to that period's consumption.

Recall earlier that risk aversion and preferring more to less were two assumptions necessary to obtain an efficient frontier. If we make the additional assumptions of the standard CAPM, we obtain the standard CAPM even for investors with a multiperiod horizon. If we make the additional assumptions underlying the zero-Beta version of the CAPM, the zero-Beta model is appropriate for investors with a multiperiod horizon. In short, the Fama multiperiod

---

[19] A process is not state dependent if its outcomes do not depend on which one of a set of events occurs.

assumptions make single-period capital asset pricing models appropriate for investors with multiperiod horizons. The particular single-period model that results depends on the additional assumptions that are being made.

It is comforting to know that there are conditions under which the standard CAPM is appropriate when investors treat the portfolio selection problem in a multiperiod framework. However, we would expect that future utilities, returns, and prices are state dependent. For an excellent treatment of multiperiod equilibrium, under some general assumptions, the reader is referred to Stapleton and Subrahmanyam (1977). The reader should be warned that the mathematics involved are beyond any attempted in this book.

There are three cases of a multiperiod general equilibrium model that deserve special attention: the consumption CAPM, a CAPM explicitly including inflation, and the multi-Beta CAPM. The consumption CAPM is based on the assumption that in a multiperiod world an investor is concerned with the utility of lifetime consumption. It proceeds logically with a derivation under which growth in consumption, rather than the return on the market, drives security returns. A second approach, an inflation CAPM, recognizes that in a multiperiod world the investor must be concerned with inflation risk and that inflation must be recognized as a factor in an investor's preference function. The third approach is the multi-Beta model of Merton (1973). In this model, the assumptions that allow us to reduce the portfolio and equilibrium model to a single-period framework are dropped and a larger set of economic factors is found to affect security returns. We will now briefly discuss each of these models in turn.

THE CONSUMPTION-ORIENTED CAPM

A number of authors, starting with Breeden (1979) and Rubinstein (1976), have taken a different approach to defining equilibrium in the capital markets. They start with a set of assumptions: investors maximize a multiperiod utility function for lifetime consumption; have homogeneous beliefs concerning return characteristics of assets; there is an infinitely lived fixed population; there is a single consumption good; and there exists a capital market that allows investors to reach a consumption pattern such that they cannot jointly fare better by additional trades. They

are able to show, under these assumptions, that return on assets should be linearly related to the growth rate in aggregate consumption if the parameters of the linear relationship can be assumed constant over time. Furthermore, the residuals from the linear relationship are uncorrelated with the growth rate in aggregate consumption, have zero mean, and are uncorrelated with one another.

To be more explicit, define:

C_t = the growth rate in aggregate consumption per capita at time t

R_{it} = the rate of return on asset i in period t

$$R_{it} = \alpha_i + \beta_i C_t + e_{it} \qquad \textbf{(5.7)}$$

where

1. $E(e_{it}) = 0$
2. the covariance between residuals and the index is zero. $E(e_{it}, C_t) = 0$
3. $\beta_i = \dfrac{\text{Cov}(R_{it}, C_t)}{\text{Var}(C_t)}$

Having established Equation (5.7) there are a number of ways (including using the same type of arguments introduced at the start of this chapter) to show that the equilibrium condition is[20]

$$\bar{R}_i = \bar{R}_z + \gamma_1 \beta_1 \qquad \textbf{(5.8)}$$

where

1. γ_1 is the market price of the consumption Beta.
2. $\bar{R}_z$ is the expected return on a portfolio with zero consumption Beta.

This model is directly analogous to the simple form of the CAPM. The growth rate of per capita consumption has replaced the rate of return on the market portfolio as the influence affecting the time series of returns and hence equilibrium returns.

INFLATION RISK AND EQUILIBRIUM

One specific case of a multiperiod general equilibrium model that has received special attention is the case where all of Fama's assumptions are met except that

---

[20] These arguments are the no arbitrage conditions discussed more formally in Chapter 6, on Arbitrage Pricing Theory (APT).

there is uncertain inflation. Friend, Landskroner, and Losq (1976) derive a general equilibrium relationship for the expected return on any asset under uncertain inflation, assuming that all utility functions exhibit constant proportional risk aversion. Their equilibrium appears similar to the simple form of the CAPM, but both the definition of the market price of risk and the risk on an asset are modified. In particular, they show that as long as the correlation between the rate of return on the market and the rate of inflation is positive, the market price of risk is higher than that depicted in the standard CAPM. Furthermore, they show that the risk of any asset is not just a function of its covariance with the market; it is also a function of its covariance with the rate of inflation. If an asset's rate of return is positively correlated with the rate of inflation, the standard CAPM formulation overstates the risk of the asset. Finally, they show that the traditional CAPM will understate (overstate) the equilibrium rate of return on any asset if the correlation of the return on that asset with the rate of inflation is less than (greater than) the product of the correlation of the rate of return on the asset with the market return, and the correlation between the market return and the inflation rate.

THE MULTI-BETA CAPM

Although Friend, Landskroner, and Losq (1976) identified two (one new) forms of priced uncertainty in their equilibrium model, Merton (1973) has constructed a generalized intertemporal capital asset pricing model in which a number of sources of uncertainty would be priced. Merton models investors as solving lifetime consumption decisions when faced with multiple sources of uncertainty. In this multiperiod setting, uncertainty exists about not only the future value of securities, but also about such other influences as future labor income, future prices of consumption goods, future investment opportunities, and so on. Investors will form portfolios to hedge away each of these risks (to the extent possible). If sources of risk are a general concern to investors, then these sources of risk will affect the expected returns on securities. The inflation model is the simplest form of a multi-Beta CAPM where the expected return on any security can be expressed as a function of two sensitivities

$$\bar{R}_i - R_F = \beta_{iM}(\bar{R}_M - R_F) + \beta_{iI}(\bar{R}_I - R_F)$$

This expression represents the standard CAPM plus a new term. The new term is the product of a new Beta (which is the sensitivity of any security to the portfolio of securities that is held to hedge away inflation risk) and the price of inflation risk.

The multi-Beta CAPM tells us that the expected return on any security should be related to the security's sensitivity to a set of influences. The form of the expected return is

$$\bar{R}_i - R_F = \beta_{iM}(\bar{R}_M - R_F) + \beta_{iI1}(\bar{R}_{I1} - R_F) + \beta_{iI2}(\bar{R}_{I2} - R_F) + \cdots$$

In this relationship, all of the $\bar{R}_{ij}$s are expected returns on a set of portfolios that allows the investor to hedge a set of risks with which he or she is concerned. Although the theory tells us that these should be additional influences present in pricing securities and that these influences should be related to the investor's multiperiod utility functions, it does not tell us explicitly what these influences are or exactly how to form portfolios to hedge whatever risks they represent. One set of risks we might consider as potentially important is the four risks (in addition to the market): default risk, term structure risk, deflation risk, and profit risk.

We will leave this subject at this point, but will return to it in a later chapter when we discuss arbitrage pricing theory.

CONCLUSION

In this chapter we have shown that the simple form of the CAPM is remarkably robust. Modifying some of its assumptions leaves the general model unchanged, whereas modifying other assumptions leads to the appearance of new terms in the equilibrium relationship or, in some cases, to the modification of old terms. That the CAPM changes with changes in the assumptions is not unusual. What is unusual is (1) the robustness of the methodology in that it allows us to incorporate these changes, and (2) the fact that many of the conclusions of the original model hold, even with changes in assumptions.

The reader should be warned, however, that these results may seem stronger than they are. We have modified the assumptions one at a time. When assumptions are modified simultaneously, the departure from the standard CAPM may be much more serious. For example, when short sales were disallowed but lending and borrowing were allowed, the standard CAPM held. When riskless lending and borrowing were disallowed but short sales were allowed, we got a model that very much resembled the standard CAPM, except that the slope and intercept were changed. Ross (1977) has shown that when both riskless lending and borrowing and short sales are disallowed, one cannot derive a simple general equilibrium relationship.

There is no doubt that the general equilibrium models we now have are imperfect. The question is how well they describe conditions in the capital markets. We shall turn to this subject in the next chapter.

APPENDIX

DERIVATION OF THE GENERAL EQUILIBRIUM WITH TAXES

Earlier in this chapter we saw that any security or portfolio has an equilibrium return given by

$$\bar{R}_j = \bar{R}_z + \left(\bar{R}_M - \bar{R}_z\right)\frac{\sigma_{jM}}{\sigma_M^2}$$

We derived this expression by maximizing

$$\theta = \frac{\bar{R}_P - R_F'}{\sigma_P}$$

for the investor's portfolio (P) equal to the market portfolio M and the riskless rate defined as the intercept of a line tangent to point M. $\bar{R}_z$ in the foregoing solution is the return on the minimum variance portfolio that is uncorrelated with the portfolio M.

We could have repeated this analysis for any portfolio P different from M, and for assets included in portfolio P we would get the following equilibrium relationship:

$$\bar{R}_j = \bar{R}_{OP} + \left(\bar{R}_P - \bar{R}_{OP}\right)\frac{\sigma_{jP}}{\sigma_P^2}$$

where $\bar{R}_{OP}$ is the expected return on the minimum variance portfolio that is uncorrelated with portfolio P.

We will now make several changes in this expression. In a world of taxes, investors will reach equilibrium in terms of after-tax returns. The superscript A will be added to each variable to show that it holds in after-tax terms. In addition, the portfolio selected by each investor may be different because homogeneous before-tax expectations will produce heterogeneous after-tax expectations. Thus, we will use the subscript i to stand for investor i. Finally, since we are assuming unlimited lending and borrowing, an asset exists (the riskless asset) that is uncorrelated with all portfolios. Thus we can replace $\bar{R}_{OP}$ with R_F. With these changes, the equation above can be written as

$$\bar{R}_{ji}^A = R_{Fi}^A + \left(\bar{R}_{Pi}^A - R_{Fi}^A\right)\frac{\text{cov}\left(R_{ji}^A R_{Pi}^A\right)}{\left(\sigma_{Pi}^A\right)^2} \tag{A.1}$$

While expectations of after-tax returns are heterogeneous, expectations of before-tax returns are homogeneous. We can write this expression in terms of before-tax returns.

Let

δ_j = the dividend yield on stock j

t_{di} = stockholder i's marginal tax rate on interest and dividends

t_{gi} = stockholder i's marginal tax rate on capital gains

w_i = the amount of stockholder i's wealth invested in risky assets

W = the sum of all wealth invested in risky assets

$$W = \sum_i w_i$$

Then,

$$\bar{R}_{ji}^A = \left(\bar{R}_j - \delta_j\right)\left(1 - t_{gi}\right) + \delta_j\left(1 - t_{di}\right)$$

$$= \bar{R}_j\left(1 - t_{gi}\right) - \delta_j\left(t_{di} - t_{gi}\right)$$

$$\bar{R}_{Fi}^A = R_F\left(1 - t_{di}\right)$$

If we assume that next period's dividend is sufficiently predictable, then we can treat it as a certain stream and

$$\text{cov}\left(R_{ji}^A R_{Pi}^A\right) = \text{cov}\left(R_j R_{Pi}\right)\left(1 - t_{gi}\right)^2$$

$$\left(\sigma_{Pi}^A\right)^2 = \sigma_{Pi}^2\left(1 - t_{gi}\right)^2$$

Substituting in Equation (A.1),

$$\left(\bar{R}_j - \bar{R}_F\right)\left(1 - t_{gi}\right) - \left(\delta_j - R_F\right)\left(t_{di} - t_{gi}\right) = \frac{\bar{R}_{Pi}^A - R_{Fi}^A}{\sigma_{Pi}^2}\text{cov}\left(R_j R_{Pi}\right)$$

Dividing through by $1 - t_{gi}$ and multiplying through by w_i and dividing through by λ_i where λ_i is defined as

$$\frac{\bar{R}_{Pi}^A - R_{Fi}^A}{\sigma_{Pi}^2}\frac{1}{\left(1 - t_{gi}\right)}$$

we get

$$\frac{w_i}{\lambda_i}\left(\bar{R}_j - R_F\right) - \left(\delta_j - R_F\right)\frac{\left(t_{di} - t_{gi}\right)}{\left(1 - t_{gi}\right)}\frac{w_i}{\lambda_i} = w_i \operatorname{cov}\left(R_j R_{Pi}\right) \qquad \textbf{(A.2)}$$

Summing this equation across all investors and dividing by Σw_i,

$$\left(\bar{R}_j - R_F\right)\frac{\sum_i\left(w_i / \lambda_i\right)}{\sum_i w_i} - \left(\delta_j - R_F\right)$$

$$\times\left[\sum_i\frac{\left(t_{di} - t_{gi}\right)w_i}{\left(1 - t_{gi}\right)\lambda_i}\bigg/\sum_i w_i\right] = \frac{\sum_i w_i \operatorname{cov}\left(R_j R_{Pi}\right)}{\sum_i w_i}$$

But note that since

$$\frac{\sum_i w_i R_{Pi}}{\sum_i w_i} = R_M$$

the right-hand side of this equation is equal to cov($R_j R_M$). Define the following symbols:

$$H = \left(\sum_i w_i\right)\bigg/\left(\sum_i w_i / \lambda_i\right)$$

$$\tau = H\left(\sum_i\frac{\left(t_{di} - t_{gi}\right)w_i}{\left(1 - t_{gi}\right)\lambda_i}\right)\bigg/\sum_i w_i$$

We can see that the tax factor τ is a complex weighted average of the investor's tax rates where the weights on each investor's tax rate is a function of the wealth he places in risky securities and his degree of risk avoidance as expressed by the ratio of excess return to variance on the portfolio he chooses to hold. Equation (A.2) can now be written as

$$\left(\bar{R}_j - R_F\right) - \left(\delta_j - R_F\right)\tau = H\operatorname{cov}\left(R_j R_M\right) \qquad \textbf{(A.3)}$$

Since expression (A.3) must hold for any asset or portfolio, it must hold for the market portfolio. Thus,

$$\left(\bar{R}_M - R_F\right) - \left(\delta_M - R_F\right)\tau = H\sigma_M^2$$

or

$$H = \frac{\left(\bar{R}_M - R_F\right) - \left(\delta_M - R_F\right)\tau}{\sigma_M^2}$$

Substituting the expression for H into the equation and rearranging yields

$$\bar{R}_j = R_F + \frac{\left(\bar{R}_M - R_F\right) - \left(\delta_M - R_F\right)\tau}{\sigma_M^2}\operatorname{cov}\left(R_j R_M\right) + \left(\delta_j - R_F\right)\tau$$

or

$$\bar{R}_j = R_F + \beta_j\left[\left(\bar{R}_M - R_F\right) - \left(\delta_M - R_F\right)\tau\right] + \left(\delta_j - R_F\right)\tau$$

QUESTIONS AND PROBLEMS

1. Assume the equilibrium equation shown below. What is the return on the zero-Beta portfolio and the return on the market assuming the zero-Beta model holds?

   $$\bar{R}_j = 0.04 + 0.10\beta_j$$

2. In the previous chapter we showed that the standard CAPM model could be written in price form. What is the zero-Beta model in price form?

3. Given the model shown below, what is the risk-free rate if the post-tax equilibrium model describes returns?

   $$\bar{R}_j = 0.05 + 0.10\beta_j + 0.24\delta_j$$

4. Given the following situation:

   $$\bar{R}_M = 15 \qquad \sigma_M = 22$$
   $$\bar{R}_Z = 5 \qquad \sigma_Z = 8$$
   $$R_F = 3$$

   draw the minimum variance curve and efficient frontier in expected return standard deviation space. Be sure to give the coordinates of all key points. Draw the security market line.

5. You have just lectured two tax-free institutions on the necessity of including taxes in the general equilibrium relationship. One believed you and one did not. Demonstrate that if the model holds, the one that did could engage in risk-free arbitrage with the one that did not in a manner such that:

   A. Both parties believed they were making an arbitrage profit in the transaction.

   B. The one who believed in the post-tax model actually made a profit; the other institution incurred a loss.

6. Assume that returns are generated as follows

   $$R_i = \bar{R}_i + a_i\left(R_M - \bar{R}_M\right) + b_i\left(C - \bar{C}\right)$$

   where C is the rate of change in interest rates. Derive a general equilibrium relationship for security returns.

7. If $\bar{R}_M = 15\%$ and $R_F = 5\%$ and risk-free lending is allowed but riskless borrowing is not, sketch what the efficient frontier might look like in expected return standard deviation space. Sketch the security market line and the location of all portfolios in expected return Beta space. Label all points and explain why you have drawn them as you have.

8. Assume you paid a higher tax on income than on capital gains. Furthermore, assume that you believed that prices were determined by the post-tax CAPM. Now another investor comes along who believes that prices are determined by the pre-tax CAPM. Demonstrate that you can make an excess return by engaging in a two-security swap with him.

9. Most tests of the CAPM involve tests on common stock data and perform the tests using the S&P index. You have just had a revelation that bonds are also marketable assets and thus should belong in the market return. Show what effect leaving them out might have on stocks with different characteristics.

BIBLIOGRAPHY

1. Alexander, Gordon. "An Algorithmic Approach to Deriving the Minimum-Variance Zero-Beta Portfolio," *Journal of Financial Economics*, **4,** No. 2 (March 1977), pp. 231–236.

2. Arzac, Enrique, and Bawa, Vijay. "Portfolio Choice and Equilibrium in Capital Markets with Safety-First Investors," *Journal of Financial Economics*, **4,** No. 3 (May 1977), pp. 277–288.

3. Black, Fischer. "Capital Market Equilibrium with Restricted Borrowing," *Journal of Business*, **45,** No. 3 (July 1972), pp. 444–455.

4. Borch, Karl. "Equilibrium, Optimum and Prejustices in Capital Markets," *Journal of Financial and Quantitative Analysis*, **IV,** No. 1 (March 1969), pp. 4–14.

5. Breeden, D. "An Intertemporal Asset Pricing Model with Stochastic Consumption and Investment Opportunities," *Journal of Financial Economics*, **7** (1979), pp. 265–296.

6. ———. "Consumption Risk in Futures Markets," *Journal of Finance*, **35** (1980), pp. 503–520.

7. Breeden, D., and Litzenberger, R. "Prices of State-Contingent Claims Implicit in Option Prices," *Journal of Business*, **51** (1978), pp. 621–651.

8. Breeden, D., Gibbons, M., and Litzenberger, R. "Empirical Tests of the Consumption-Oriented CAPM," *Journal of Finance*, **44** (1989), pp. 231–262.

9. Brennan, Michael J. "Taxes, Market Valuation, and Corporate Financial Policy," *National Tax Journal*, **25** (1970), pp. 417–27.

10. ———. "Capital Market Equilibrium with Divergent Borrowing and Lending Rates," *Journal of Financial and Quantitative Analysis*, **VI,** No. 5 (Dec. 1971), pp. 1197–1205.

11. Brenner, Menachem, and Subrahmanyam, Marti. "Intra-Equilibrium and Inter-Equilibrium Analysis in Capital Market Theory: A Clarification," *Journal of Finance*, **XXII,** No. 4 (Sept. 1977), pp. 1313–1319.

12. Brito, O. Ney. "Marketability Restrictions and the Valuation of Capital Assets under Uncertainty," *Journal of Finance*, **XXXII,** No. 4 (Sept. 1977), pp. 1109–1123.

13. ———. "Portfolio Selection in an Economy with Marketability and Short Sales Restrictions," *Journal of Finance*, **XXXIII,** No. 2 (May 1978), pp. 589–601.

14. Chamberlain, G., and Rothschild, M. "Arbitrage, Factor Structure, and Mean-Variance Analysis on Large Asset Markets," *Econometrica*, **51** (1983), pp. 1281–1304.

15. Chen, N., Roll, R., and Ross, S. "Economic Forces and the Stock Market," *Journal of Business*, **59** (1986), pp. 386–403.

16. Connor, G. "A Unified Beta Pricing Theory," *Journal of Economic Theory*, **34** (1984), pp. 13–31.

17. Connor, G., and Korajczyk, R. "Performance Measurement with the Arbitrage Pricing Theory: A New Framework for Analysis," *Journal of Financial Economics*, **15** (1986), pp. 373–394.

18. Constantinides, George M. "Admissible Uncertainty in the Intertemporal Asset Pricing Model," *Journal of Financial Economics*, **8,** No. 1 (March 1980), pp. 71–87.

19. Cornell, B. "The Consumption Based Asset Pricing Model: A Note on Potential Tests and Applications," *Journal of Financial Economics*, **9** (1981), pp. 103–108.

20. Dhrymes, Phoebus, Friend, Irwin, and Gultekin, Bulent, "A Critical Reexamination of the Empirical Evidence on the Arbitrage Pricing Theory," *The Journal of Finance*, **39** (June 1984), pp. 323–346.

21. Dybvig, Philip H. "An Explicit Bound on Deviations from APT Pricing in a Finite Economy," *Journal of Financial Economics*, **12** (1983), pp. 483–496.

22. ———. "Distributional Analysis of Portfolio Choice," *The Journal of Business*, **61,** No. 2 (July 1988), pp. 369–393.

23. Dybvig, P., and Ross, S. "Yes, the APT Is Testable," *Journal of Finance*, **40** (1985), pp. 1173–1188.

24. Easley, David, and Jarrow, Robert A. "Consensus Beliefs Equilibrium and Market Efficiency," *The Journal of Finance*, **38,** No. 3 (June 1983), pp. 903–912.

25. Elton, Edwin J., and Gruber, Martin J. "The Multi-Period Consumption Investment Decision and Single Period Analysis," *Oxford Economic Papers*, **26** (Sept. 1974), pp. 180–195.

26. ———. *Finance as a Dynamic Process* (Englewood Cliffs, NJ: Prentice Hall, 1975).

27. ——. "Taxes and Portfolio Composition," *Journal of Financial Economics*, **6** (1978), pp. 399–410.

28. Errunza, Vihang, and Losq, Etienne. "International Asset Pricing Under Mild Segmentation: Theory and Test," *The Journal of Finance*, **40,** No. 1 (Mar. 1985), pp. 105–124.

29. Fama, Eugene. "Multi-Period Consumption-Investment Decision," *American Economic Review*, **60** (Mar. 1970), pp. 163–174.

30. ——. "Risk, Return and Equilibrium," *Journal of Political Economy*, **79,** No. 1 (Jan.-Feb. 1971), pp. 30–55.

31. ——. "A Note on the Market Model and the Two-Parameter Model," *Journal of Finance*, **XXVIII,** No. 5 (Dec. 1973), pp. 1181–1185.

32. ——. *Foundations of Finance* (New York: Basic Books, 1976).

33. Fama, E., MacBeth, J., and Schwert, G. "Asset Returns and Inflation," *Journal of Financial Economics*, **5** (1977), pp. 115–146.

34. ——. "Inflation, Interest and Relative Prices," *Journal of Business*, **52** (1979), pp. 183–209.

35. Ferson, W. "Expected Real Interest Rates and Consumption in Efficient Financial Markets: Empirical Tests," *Journal of Financial and Quantitative Analysis*, **18** (1983), pp. 477–498.

36. Figlewski, Stephen. "Information Diversity and Market Behavior," *The Journal of Finance*, **37,** No. 1 (March 1982), pp. 87–102.

37. Foster, F. Douglas. "Assessing Goodness-of-Fit of Asset Pricing Models: The Distribution the Maximal R2," *The Journal of Finance*, **52,** No. 2 (June 1997), pp. 591–607.

38. Friend, Irwin, and Westerfield, Randolph. "Co-Skewness and Capital Assets Pricing," *The Journal of Finance*, **35,** No. 4 (Sept. 1980), pp. 897–914.

39. Friend, Irwin, Landskroner, Yoram, and Losq, Etienne. "The Demand for Risky Assets and Uncertain Inflation," *Journal of Finance*, **XXXI,** No. 5 (Dec. 1976), pp. 1287–1297.

40. Gibbons, M., and Ferson, W. "Testing Asset Pricing Models with Changing Expectations and an Unobservable Market Portfolio," *Journal of Financial Economics*, **14** (1985), pp. 217–236.

41. Gonedes, Nicholas. "Capital Market Equilibrium for a Class of Heterogeneous Expectations in a Two-Parameter World," *Journal of Finance*, **XXXI,** No. 1 (March 1976), pp. 1–15.

42. Grinblatt, Mark, and Titman, Sheridan. "Factor Pricing in a Finite Economy," *Journal of Financial Economics*, **12** (1983), pp. 497–507.

43. Grossman, S., and Shiller, R. "Consumption Correlatedness and Risk Measurement in Economies with Non-Traded Assets and Heterogeneous Information," *Journal of Financial Economics*, **10** (1982), pp. 195–210.

44. Grossman, S., Melino, A., and Shiller, R. "Estimating the Continuous-Time Consumption-Based Asset-Pricing Model," *Journal of Business and Economic Statistics*, **5** (1987), pp. 315–328.

45. Guiso, Luigi, Jappelli, Tullio, and Terlizzese, Daniele. "Income Risk, Borrowing Constraints, and Portfolio Choice," *The American Economic Review*, **86,** No. 1 (Mar. 1996), pp. 158–172.

46. Hagerman, Robert, and Kim, Han. "Capital Asset Pricing with Price Level Changes," *Journal of Financial and Quantitative Analysis*, **XI,** No. 3 (Sept. 1976), pp. 381–391.

47. Hall, R. "Stochastic Implications of the Life Cycle-Permanent Income Hypothesis: Theory and Evidence," *Journal of Political Economy*, **86** (1978), pp. 971–987.

48. Hansen, L., and Singleton, K. "Generalized Instrumental Variables Estimation of Nonlinear Rational Expectations Models," *Econometrica*, **50** (1982), pp. 1269–1286.

49. ——. "Stochastic Consumption, Risk Aversion, and the Temporary Behavior of Asset Returns," *Journal of Political Economy*, **91** (1983), pp. 249–265.

50. Hart, Oliver. "On the Existence of Equilibrium in a Securities Model," *Journal of Economic Theory*, **9,** No. 3 (Nov. 1974), pp. 293–311.

51. Heckerman, Donald. "Portfolio Selection and the Structure of Capital Asset Prices When Relative Prices of Consumption Goods May Change," *Journal of Finance*, **XXVII,** No. 1 (March 1972), pp. 47–60.

52. ——. "Reply to [52]," *Journal of Finance*, **XXVIII,** No. 5 (Dec. 1973), p. 1361.

53. Hilliard, Jimmy E. "Asset Pricing under a Subset of Linear Risk Tolerance Functions and Log-Normal Market Returns," *Journal of Financial and Quantitative Analysis*, **XV,** No. 5 (Dec. 1980), pp. 1041–1062.

54. Hogan, William, and Warren, James. "Toward the Development of an Equilibrium Capital-Market Model Based on Semi-Variance," *Journal of Financial and Quantitative Analysis*, **IX,** No. 1 (Jan. 1974), pp. 1–11.

55. Hopewell, Michael. "Comment on [88]: A Model of Capital Asset Risk," *Journal of Financial and Quantitative Analysis*, **VII,** No. 2 (March 1972), pp. 1673–1677.

56. Ibbotson, Roger, and Sinquefield, Rex. *Stocks, Bonds, Bills and Inflation: The Past and the Future* (Charlottesville, VA: Financial Analysts Research Foundation, 1982).

57. Ingersoll, Jonathan E., Jr. "Some Results in the Theory of Arbitrage Pricing," *Journal of Finance*, **39** (1984), pp. 1021–1039.

58. Jarrow, Robert. "Heterogeneous Expectations, Restrictions on Short Sales, and Equilibrium Asset Prices," *The Journal of Finance*, **35,** No. 5 (Dec. 1980), pp. 1105–1114.

59. Jobson, J., and Korkie, B. "Estimation for Markowitz Efficient Portfolios," *Journal of the American Statistical Association*, **75** (1980), pp. 544–554.

60. Jobson, J., and Korkie, R. "Potential Performance Tests of Portfolio Efficiency," *Journal of Financial Economics*, **10** (1982), pp. 433–466.

61. Kamoike, Osamu. "Portfolio Selection When Future Prices of Consumption Goods May Change: Comment on [36]," *Journal of Finance*, **XXVIII,** No. 5 (Dec. 1973), pp. 1357-1360.

62. Kandel, S. "On the Exclusion of Assets from Tests of the Mean Variance Efficiency of the Market Portfolio," *Journal of Finance*, **39** (1984), pp. 63-75.

63. Kandel, S. "The Likelihood Ratio Test Statistic of Mean-Variance Efficiency without a Riskless Asset," *Journal of Financial Economics*, **13** (1984), pp. 575-592.

64. Kandel S., and Stambaugh, R. "On Correlations and the Sensitivity of Inferences about Mean-Variance Efficiency," *Journal of Financial Economics*, **18** (1987), pp. 61-90.

65. Keim, D. "Size Related Anomalies and Stock Return Seasonability: Further Empirical Evidence," *Journal of Financial Economics*, **12** (1983), pp. 13-32.

66. Korkie, Bob. "Comment: on [73]," *Journal of Financial and Quantitative Analysis*, **IX,** No. 5 (Nov. 1974), pp. 723-725.

67. Kraus, Alan, and Litzenberger, Robert. "Market Equilibrium in a Multi-Period State Preference Model with Logarithmic Utility," *Journal of Finance*, **XXX,** No. 5 (Dec. 1975), pp. 1213-1227.

68. ———. "Skewness Preference and the Valuation of Risk Assets," *Journal of Finance*, **XXXI,** No. 4 (Sept. 1976), pp. 1085-1100.

69. Kryzanowski, Lawrence, and Chau, To Hinh. "Asset Pricing Models When the Number of Securities Held Is Constrained: A Comparison and Reconciliation of the Mao and Levy Models," *Journal of Financial and Quantitative Analysis*, **XVII,** No. 1 (March 1982), pp. 63-74.

70. Kumar, Prem. "Market Equilibrium and Corporation Finance: Some Issues," *Journal of Finance*, **XXIX,** No. 4 (Sept. 1974), pp. 1175-1188.

71. Landskroner, Yoram. "Nonmarketable Assets and the Determinants of the Market Price of Risk," *Review of Economics and Statistics*, **LIX,** No. 4 (Nov. 1977), pp. 482-514.

72. ———. "Intertemporal Determination of the Market Price of Risk," *Journal of Finance*, **XXXII,** No. 5 (Dec. 1977), pp. 1671-1681.

73. Lee, Chang. "Investment Horizon and the Functional Form of the Capital Asset Pricing Model," *Review of Economics and Statistics*, **LVIII,** No. 3 (Aug. 1976), pp. 356-363.

74. Lehari, David, and Levy, Haim. "The Capital Asset Pricing Model and the Investment Horizon," *Review of Economics and Statistics*, **LIX,** No. 1 (Feb. 1977), pp. 92-104.

75. Levy, Haim. "The Capital Asset Pricing Model, Inflation, and the Investment Horizon: The Israeli Experience," *Journal of Financial and Quantitative Analysis*, **XV,** No. 3 (Sept. 1980), pp. 561-594.

76. Levy, Haim, and Levy, Azriel. "Equilibrium Under Uncertain Inflation: A Discrete Time Approach," *Journal of Financial and Quantitative Analysis*, **22,** No. 3 (Sept. 1987), pp. 285-297.

77. Lindenberg, Eric. "Imperfect Competition Among Investors in Security Markets," Ph.D. Dissertation, New York University, 1976.

78. ———. "Capital Market Equilibrium with Price Affecting Institutional Investors," in Edwin J. Elton and Martin J. Gruber (eds.), *Portfolio Theory 25 Years Later* (Amsterdam: North-Holland, 1979).

79. Lintner, John. "The Aggregation of Investors Diverse Judgments and Preferences in Purely Competitive Security Markets," *Journal of Financial and Quantitative Analysis*, **4,** No. 4 (Dec. 1969), pp. 347-100.

80. ———. "The Effect of Short Selling and Margin Requirements in Perfect Capital Markets," *Journal of Financial and Quantitative Analysis*, **VI,** No. 5 (Dec. 1971), pp. 1173-1195.

81. Litzenberger, R., and Ronn, E. "A Utility Based Model of Common Stock Returns," *Journal of Finance*, **41** (1986), pp. 67-92.

82. Long, John. "Stock Prices, Inflation, and the Term Structure of Interest Rates," *Journal of Financial Economics*, **1,** No. 2 (July 1974), pp. 131-170.

83. Losq, Etienne, and Chateau, John Peter D. "A Generalization of the CAPM Based on a Property of the Covariance Operator," *Journal of Financial and Quantitative Analysis*, **XVII,** No. 5 (Dec. 1982), pp. 783-798.

84. Lucas, R. "Asset Prices in an Exchange Economy," *Econometrica*, **46** (1978), pp. 1429-1445.

85. Mayers, D. "Nonmarketable Assets and Capital Market Equilibrium under Uncertainty," in M.C. Jensen (ed.), *Studies in Theory of Capital Markets* (New York: Praeger, 1972).

86. Mayers, David. "Nonmarketable Assets and the Determination of Capital Asset Prices in the Absence of a Riskless Asset," *Journal of Business*, **46,** No. 2 (April 1973), pp. 258-267.

87. ———. "Nonmarketable Assets: Market Segmentation and the Level of Asset Prices," *Journal of Financial and Quantitative Analysis*, **XI,** No. 1 (March 1976), pp. 1-37.

88. Merton, Robert. "An Intertemporal Capital Asset Pricing Model," *Econometrica*, **41,** No. 5 (Sept. 1973), pp. 867-888.

89. Milne, Frank, and Smith, Clifford, Jr. "Capital Asset Pricing with Proportional Transaction Cost," *Journal of Financial and Quantitative Analysis*, **XV,** No. 2 (June 1980), pp. 253-266.

90. Ohlson, James. "Equilibrium in Stable Markets," *Journal of Political Economy*, **85,** No. 4 (Aug. 1977), pp. 859-864.

91. Paxson, Christina. "Borrowing Constraints and Portfolio Choice," *The Quarterly Journal of Economics*, **105,** No. 2 (May 1990), pp. 535-543.

92. Peles, Yoram. "A Note on Risk and the Theory of Asset Value," *Journal of Financial and Quantitative Analysis*, **VI,** No. 1 (Jan. 1971), pp. 643-647.

93. Pettit, R. Richardson, and Stanley, L. "Consumption-Investment Decisions with Transaction Costs and Taxes: A Study of the Clientele Effect of Dividends," *Journal of Financial Economics*, **5,** No. 3 (1979).

94. Pettit, R. Richardson, and Westerfield, Randolph. "A Model of Capital Asset Risk," *Journal of Financial and Quantitative Analysis*, **VII,** No. 2 (March 1972), pp. 1649–1668.

95. Rabinovitch, Ramon, and Owen, Joel. "Non-Homogeneous Expectations and Information in the Capital Asset Market," *Journal of Finance*, **XXXIII,** No. 2 (May 1978), pp. 575–587.

96. Reinganum, Marc R. "A New Empirical Perspective on the CAPM," *Journal of Financial and Quantitative Analysis*, **XVI,** No. 4 (Nov. 1981), pp. 439–462.

97. Roberts, Gordon. "Endogenous Endowments and Capital Asset Prices," *Journal of Finance*, **XXX,** No. 1 (March 1975), pp. 155–162.

98. Roll, Richard, and Ross, Stephen. "An Empirical Investigation of Arbitrage Pricing Theory," *Journal of Finance* (Dec. 1980), pp. 1073–1105.

99. Rosenberg, B., and Guy, J. "Prediction of Beta from Investment Fundamentals," *Financial Analysts Journal*, **32** (1976), pp. 60–72.

100. Ross, Stephen. "Return, Risk, and Arbitrage," in I. Friend and J. Bickster (eds.), *Risks and Return in Finance* (Cambridge, MA: Ballinger, 1977).

101. ——. "The Capital Asset Pricing Model (CAPM), Short-Sale Restrictions and Related Issues," *Journal of Finance*, **XXXII,** No. 1 (March 1977), pp. 177–183.

102. ——. "Mutual Fund Separation in Financial Theory—The Separating Distributions," *Journal of Economic Theory*, **17,** No. 2 (April 1978), pp. 254–286.

103. ——. "The Current Status of the Capital Asset Pricing Model (CAPM)," *Journal of Finance*, **XXXIII,** No. 3 (June 1978), pp. 885–901.

104. Rubinstein, M. "The Valuation of Uncertain Income Streams and the Pricing of Options," *Bell Journal of Economics and Management Science*, **7** (1976), pp. 407–425.

105. Rubinstein, Mark. "The Strong Case for the Generalized Logarithmic Utility Model as the Premier Model of Financial Markets," *Journal of Finance*, **XXXI,** No. 2 (May 1976), pp. 551–571.

106. Samuelson, Paul. "Lifetime Portfolio Selection by Dynamic Stochastic Programming," *Review of Economics and Statistics*, **LI,** No. 3 (Aug. 1969), pp. 239–246.

107. Samuelson, Paul, and Merton, Robert. "Generalized Mean-Variance Tradeoffs for Best Perturbation Corrections to Approximate Portfolio Decisions," *Journal of Finance*, **XXIX,** No. 1 (March 1974), pp. 27–40.

108. Sandmo, Agnar. "Capital Risk, Consumption and Portfolio Choice," *Econometrica*, **37,** No. 4 (Oct. 1969), pp. 586–599.

109. Scholes, M., and Williams, J. "Estimating Betas from Non-synchronous Data," *Journal of Financial Economics*, **5** (1977), pp. 309–327.

110. Shanken, J. "An Asymptotic Analysis of the Traditional Risk-Return Model," Unpublished Manuscript, School of Business Administration, University of California, Berkeley, 1982.

111. ——. "Multi-Beta CAPM or Equilibrium-APT? A Reply," *Journal of Finance*, **40** (1985), pp. 1186–1189.

112. ——. "Multivariate Tests of the Zero-Beta CAPM," *Journal of Financial Economics*, **14** (Sept. 1985), pp. 327–348.

113. ——. "On Exclusion of Assets from Tests of the Mean Variance Efficiency of the Market Portfolio: An Extension," *Journal of Finance*, **41** (1986), pp. 331–337.

114. ——. "A Posterior-Odds Ratio Approach to Testing Portfolio Efficiency," Working Paper, Graduate School of Management, University of Rochester, Rochester, N.Y., 1986.

115. ——. "Testing Portfolio Efficiency when the Zero-Beta Rate Is Unknown: A Note," *Journal of Finance*, **41** (1986), pp. 269–276.

116. ——. "Multivariate Proxies and Asset Pricing Relations," *Journal of Financial Economics*, **18** (1987), pp. 91–110.

117. Shanken, Jay. "The Arbitrage Pricing Theory: Is it Testable?" *Journal of Finance*, **37** (1982), pp. 1129–1140.

118. Sharpe, William. *Portfolio Theory and Capital Markets* (New York: McGraw-Hill, 1970).

119. Siegel, Jeremy, and Warner, Jarold. "Indexation, The Risk-Free Asset, and Capital Market Equilibrium," *Journal of Finance*, **XXXII,** No. 4 (Sept. 1977), pp. 1101–1107.

120. Stapleton, Richard, and Subrahmanyam, Marti. "Multi-Period Equilibrium Asset Pricing Model," *Econometrica*, **46** (1977).

121. Stone, Bernell. "Systematic Interest-Rate Risk in a Two-Index Model of Returns," *Journal of Financial and Quantitative Analysis*, **IX,** No. 5 (Nov. 1974), pp. 709–721.

122. Viard, Alan D. "The Asset Pricing Effects of Fixed Holding Costs: An Upper Bound," *Journal of Financial and Quantitative Analysis*, **30,** No. 1 (Mar. 1995), pp. 43.

123. Williams, Joseph. "Risk, Human Capital, and the Investor's Portfolio," *Journal of Business*, **51,** No. 1 (Jan. 1978), pp. 65–89.

The Arbitrage Pricing Model APT
A New Approach to Explaining Asset Prices

6

Excerpt is Chapter 16 of Modern Portfolio Theory and Investment Analysis, *8th Edition, by Edwin Elton, Martin Gruber, Stephen Brown and William Goetzmann.*

Learning Objectives

After completing this reading, FRM Candidates should be able to:

- Describe the APT and the assumptions underlying it.
- Use the APT to calculate the expected returns on an asset.

- Explain the relationship between the CAPM and the APT.
- Describe how the APT can be used in both active and passive portfolio management.

All of the equilibrium models discussed in Chapters 4 and 5 have their basis in mean-variance analysis. All require that it is optimal for the investor to choose investments on the basis of expected return and variance. However, definitions of returns for which means and variances are calculated differ between models. For example, in the version of the capital asset pricing model (CAPM) involving taxes, investors examine means and variances of after-tax returns. As a second example, Elton and Gruber (1982) have shown that the alternative version of CAPM under conditions of uncertain inflation can be derived by assuming that investors maximize a utility function defined in terms of the mean and variance of real as compared to nominal returns. There are major obstacles to testing any of these equilibrium theories.

Ross (1976, 1977) has proposed a multifactor approach to explaining the pricing of assets. Ross had developed a mechanism that, given the process that generates security returns, derives asset prices from arbitrage arguments analogous to those used to derive CAPMs. In this chapter we first present the mechanism of arbitrage pricing theory (APT). This is the derivation of equilibrium conditions given any prespecified return-generating process.

Following this, we discuss implementation of the APT. APT theory provides interesting insight into the nature of equilibrium. However, the theory is far from easy to implement. Empirical research is still in the early stages in this area. Furthermore, alternative approaches have been advocated for implementing the theory. After discussing some of those alternatives, we present an examination of whether evidence supporting APT is necessarily inconsistent with the standard form or any alternative form of the CAPM as a model of equilibrium. We close with a discussion of both applications and advantages of APT.

APT—WHAT IS IT?

Arbitrage pricing theory is a new and different approach to determining asset prices. It is based on the law of one price: two items that are the same can't sell at different prices. The strong assumptions made about utility theory in deriving the CAPM are not necessary. In fact, the APT description of equilibrium is more general than that provided by a CAPM-type model in that pricing can

be affected by influences beyond simply means and variances. An assumption of homogeneous expectations is necessary. The assumption of investors utilizing a mean variance framework is replaced by an assumption of the process generating security returns. APT requires that the returns on any stock be linearly related to a set of indexes as shown in Equation (6.1).[1]

$$R_i = a_i + b_{i1}I_1 = b_{i2}I_2 + \cdots + b_{ij}I_j + e_i \qquad \textbf{(6.1)}$$

where

a_i = the expected level of return for stock i if all indices have a value of zero

I_j = the value of the jth index that impacts the return on stock i

b_{ij} = the sensitivity of stock i's return to the jth index

e_i = a random error term with mean equal to zero and variance equal to σ_{ei}^2

For the model to fully describe the process generating security returns,[2]

$$E(e_i e_j) = 0 \quad \text{for all } i \text{ and } j \text{ where } i \neq j$$
$$E\left[e_i(I_j - \bar{I}_j)\right] = 0 \quad \text{for all stocks and indexes}$$

If you are beginning to get the feeling that you have seen all this before, you are right. This representation is nothing more or less than the description of the multi-index model. APT is the description of the expected returns that can be derived when returns are generated by a single- or multi-index model meeting the conditions defined before. The contribution of APT is in demonstrating how (and under what conditions) one can go from a multi-index model to a description of equilibrium.

In the following pages we will demonstrate the derivation of an APT equilibrium in two different ways. The first proof stresses the economic rationale behind APT, whereas the second proof is mathematically more rigorous.

---

[1] The linearity assumption is not as restrictive as it might at first appear. Any of the indexes can be a nonlinear function of a variable. It could be a variable squared, the log of a variable, or any other nonlinear transformation that seems appropriate.

[2] It is convenient, though unnecessary, to assume the indexes are uncorrelated with each other. We show that a set of correlated indexes can always be converted to a set of uncorrelated indexes. The results remain the same with uncorrelated indexes, but the mathematics is more complex.

A Simple Proof of APT

We will demonstrate the expected returns that must arise from the APT with a two-index model. Suppose that the following two-index model describes returns:

$$R_i = a_i + b_{i1}I_1 + b_{i2}I_2 + e_i \qquad \text{(6.2)}$$

Furthermore, assume that $E(e_ie_j) \approx 0$.

If an investor holds a well-diversified portfolio, residual risk will tend to go to zero and only systematic risk will matter. The only terms in the preceding equation that affect the systematic risk in a portfolio are b_{i1} and b_{i2}. Since the investor is assumed to be concerned with expected return and risk, he or she need be concerned with only three attributes of any portfolio (p): $\bar{R}_p$, b_{p1}, and b_{p2}.

Let us hypothesize the existence of the three widely diversified portfolios shown in the following table.

Portfolio	Expected Return	b_{i1}	b_{i2}
A	15	1.0	.6
B	14	.5	1.0
C	10	.3	.2

We know from the concepts of geometry that three points determine a plane just as two points determine a line. The equation of the plane in $\bar{R}_p$, b_{p1}, and b_{p2} space defined by these three portfolios is[3]

$$\bar{R}_i = 7.75 + 5b_{i1} + 3.75b_{i2}$$

The expected return and risk measures of any portfolio of these three portfolios are given by

$$\bar{R}_p = \sum_{i=1}^{N} X_i\bar{R}_i$$

$$b_{p1} = \sum_{i=1}^{N} X_ib_{i1}$$

$$b_{p2} = \sum_{i=1}^{N} X_ib_{i2}$$

$$\sum_{i=1}^{N} X_i = 1$$

Since a weighted combination of points on a plane (where the weights sum to one) also lies on the plane, all portfolios constructed from portfolios A, B, and C lie on the lane described by portfolios A, B, and C.[4]

What happens if we consider a new portfolio not on this plane? For example, assume a portfolio E exists with an expected return of 15%, a b_{i1} of 0.6, and a b_{i2} of 0.6.

Compare this with a portfolio (call it D) constructed by placing $\frac{1}{3}$ of the funds in portfolio A, $\frac{1}{3}$ in portfolio B, and $\frac{1}{3}$ in portfolio C. The b_{pi}s on this portfolio are

$$b_{p1} = \frac{1}{3}(1.0) + \frac{1}{3}(0.5) + \frac{1}{3}(0.3) = .6$$

$$b_{p2} = \frac{1}{3}(0.6) + \frac{1}{3}(1.0) + \frac{1}{3}(0.2) = .6$$

The risk for portfolio D is identical to the risk on portfolio E. The expected return on portfolio D is

$$\frac{1}{3}(15) + \frac{1}{3}(14) + \frac{1}{3}(10) = 13$$

Alternatively, since portfolio D must lie on the plane described above, we could have obtained its expected return from the equation of the plane:

$$\bar{R}_i = 7.75 + 5(0.6) + 3.75(0.6) = 13$$

By the law of one price, two portfolios that have the same risk cannot sell at a different expected return. In this situation it would pay arbitrageurs to step in and buy portfolio E while selling an equal amount of portfolio D short. Buying portfolio E and financing it by selling D short would guarantee a riskless profit with no investment and no risk. We can see this quite easily. Assume the investor sells $100 worth of portfolio D short and buys $100 worth of portfolio E. The results are shown in the following table.

	Initial Cash Flow	End of Period Cash Flow	b_{i1}	b_{i2}
Portfolio D	+$100	−$113.0	−0.6	−0.6
Portfolio E	−$100	$115.0	0.6	0.6
Arbitrage portfolio	0	2.0	0	0

---

[3] The reader interested in verifying this can recall that the equation of a plane can be written as $R_i = \lambda_0 + \lambda_1 b_{i1} + \lambda_2 b_{i2}$. By substituting in the values of R_i, b_{i1}, and b_{i2} for portfolios A, B, and C, we obtain three equations with three unknowns: λ_0, λ_1, and λ_2. Solving the three equations gives the values of λ_0, λ_1, and λ_2 shown in the equation in the text.

[4] The reader is encouraged to form a portfolio of portfolios A, B, and C with any set of X_i summing to one. One can then see that this portfolio lies on the plane given by $\bar{R}_i = 7.75 + 5\,b_{i1} + 3.75\,b_{i2}$. One example of this is portfolio D which is analyzed shortly in the text.

The arbitrage portfolio involves zero investment, has no systematic risk (b_{i1} and b_{i2}), and earns \$2. Arbitrage would continue until portfolio E lies on the same plane as portfolios A, B, and C.

We have established that all investments and portfolios must be on a plane in expected return, b_{i1}, b_{i2} space. If an investment were to lie above or below the plane, an opportunity would exist for riskless arbitrage. The arbitrage would continue until all investments converged to a plane.

The general equation of a plane in expected return, b_{i1}, b_{i2} space is

$$\bar{R}_i = \lambda_0 + \lambda_1 b_{i1} + \lambda_2 b_{i2} \quad \text{(6.3)}$$

This is the equilibrium model produced by the APT when returns are generated by a two-index model. Notice that λ_1 is the increase in expected return for a one-unit increase in b_{i1}. Thus λ_1 and λ_2 are returns for bearing the risks associated with I_1 and I_2, respectively.

More insight can be gained into the meaning of the λs by using Equation (6.3) to examine a particular set of portfolios. Examine a portfolio with b_{i1} and b_{i2} both equal to zero. The expected return on this portfolio equals λ_0. This is a zero-b_{ij} portfolio, and we denote its return by R_F. If the riskless asset is not available, R_F is replaced with $\bar{R}_Z$ the return on a zero-Beta portfolio. Most researchers in this area assume that the intercept is in fact R_F.

Substituting $\bar{R}_F$ for λ_0 and examining a portfolio with a b_{i2} of zero and a b_{i1} of one, we see that

$$\lambda_1 = \bar{R}_1 - R_F$$

where $\bar{R}_1$ is the return on a portfolio having a b_{i1} of one and a b_{i2} of zero. In general, $\lambda_j = \bar{R}_j - R_F$ or λ_j is the expected excess return on a portfolio only subject to risk of index j and having a unit measure of this risk.

The analysis in this section can be generalized to the J index case

$$R_i = a_i + b_{i1}I_1 + b_{i2}I_2 + \cdots + b_{iJ}I_J + e_i$$

By analogous arguments it can be shown that all securities and portfolios have expected returns described by the J-dimensional hyperplane

$$\bar{R}_i = \lambda_0 + \lambda_1 b_{i1} + \lambda_2 b_{i2} + \cdots + \lambda_J b_{iJ} \quad \text{(6.4)}$$

with $\lambda_0 = R_F$ and $\lambda_j = \bar{R}_j - R_F$.

A More Rigorous Proof of APT

Once again we will derive APT assuming a two-index return-generating process. This derivation is sufficiently rich to allow generalization to any arbitrary number of indices. The two-index model we use is that presented in Equation (6.2).

Taking the expected value of Equation (6.2) and subtracting it from Equation (6.2), we have

$$R_i = \bar{R}_i + b_{i1}(I_1 - \bar{I}_1) + b_{i2}(I_2 - \bar{I}_2) + e_i \quad \text{(6.5)}$$

Now a sufficient condition for an APT proof to hold is that there are enough securities in the market so that a portfolio with the following characteristics can be formed:

$$\sum_{i=1}^{N} X_i = 0$$

$$\sum_{i=1}^{N} X_i b_{i1} = 0$$

$$\sum_{i=1}^{N} X_i b_{i2} = 0$$

$$\sum_{i=1}^{N} X_i e_i \approx 0$$

The last condition is a requirement that residual risk be approximately zero.[5] The first of these four equations states that this portfolio involves zero investment. The remaining equations imply that this portfolio has no risk. This portfolio involves no investment and no risk; therefore, it must produce an expected return of zero. In other words, the three equations plus the condition on residual risk just discussed imply that

$$\sum_{i=1}^{N} X_i \bar{R}_i = 0$$

_____

[5] The assumption of zero residual risk might seem bothersome. Original proofs of APT assumed an infinite number of securities and well-diversified arbitrage portfolios. Because with uncorrelated residuals each residual variance enters with a weight equal to the square of the fraction of money placed in that security, for well-diversified portfolios selected from an infinite or, in fact, a very large population of securities, residual risk will be very close to zero. A series of papers by Dybvig (1983), Grinblatt and Titman (1983, 1985), and Ingersoll (1984) investigate how closely the APT holds for finite economies and economies where residual risks are not uncorrelated. APT continues to hold, although it does not necessarily hold exactly the same for all securities (there can be very small errors for many securities, and there can be large pricing errors for a few securities).

Now there is another more mathematical interpretation of these equations. The equation

$$\sum_{i=1}^{N} X_i b_{i1} = 0$$

means that the vector of security proportions is orthogonal to the vector of b_{i1}s. Similarly, the first equation

$$\sum_{i=1}^{N} X_i = 0$$

means that the vector of security proportions is orthogonal to a vector of ones. We have just shown, in the previous paragraph, that if the vector of portfolio proportions is orthogonal to a vector of ones, a vector of b_{i1}s, and a vector of b_{i2}s, this implies that the vector of security proportions is orthogonal to the vector of expected returns. But there is a well-known theorem in linear algebra that states that if the fact that a vector is orthogonal to $N - 1$ vectors implies it is orthogonal to the Nth vector, then the Nth vector can be expressed as a linear combination of the $N - 1$ vectors. In this case, the vector of expected returns can be expressed as a linear combination of a vector of ones, a vector of b_{i1}s, and a vector of b_{i2}s. Thus we can write the expected value for any security as a constant times 1, plus a second constant times b_{i1}, plus a third constant times b_{i2} or

$$\bar{R}_i = \lambda_0 + \lambda_1 b_{i1} + \lambda_2 b_{i2}$$

This equation must hold for all securities and all portfolios. The λs can be evaluated by following the procedure used in the previous section of this chapter, namely, forming three portfolios with the following characteristics

1. $b_{p1} = 0$ and $b_{p2} = 0$
2. $b_{p1} = 1$ and $b_{p2} = 0$
3. $b_{p1} = 0$ and $b_{p2} = 1$

we find that

$$\bar{R}_i = R_F + b_{i1}(\bar{R}_1 - R_F) + b_{i2}(\bar{R}_2 - R_F)$$

or for the general case

$$\bar{R}_i = R_F + b_{i1}(\bar{R}_1 - R_F) + \cdots + b_{iJ}(\bar{R}_J - R_F)$$

Defining λ_0 as R_F and λ_j as $\bar{R}_j - R_F$, we can write this equation as

$$\bar{R}_i = \lambda_0 + \lambda_1 b_{i1} + \lambda_2 b_{i2} + \cdots + \lambda_J b_{iJ}$$

The principal strength of the APT approach is that it is based on the no-arbitrage condition. Because the no-arbitrage conditions should hold for any subset of securities, it is not necessary to identify all risky assets or a "market portfolio" to test the APT. It is reasonable to test it over a class of assets such as common stocks or even a smaller set such as the stocks making up the Standard & Poor's (S&P) index or all stocks on the New York Stock Exchange. One has to be somewhat careful in that the correct APT model for a larger class of securities can be different from (contain more influences than) an APT model appropriate for a smaller set of securities. Failure to find a model for a small set (type) of securities does not mean that a model does not exist across different types of securities. However, it is appropriate to use the APT to describe relative prices for a set of securities of interest to the investigator rather than deal with the whole population of risky assets. In fact, it has been argued that many tests of the CAPM were really tests of a single- or multiple-factor APT model.

An important characteristic of the APT theory is that it is extremely general. This generality is both a strength and a weakness. Although it allows us to describe equilibrium in terms of any multi-index model, it gives us no evidence as to what might be an appropriate multi-index model. Furthermore, APT tells us nothing about the size or the signs of the λs. This makes interpretation of tests difficult. We'll have more to say about this shortly.

ESTIMATING AND TESTING APT

The proof of any economic theory is how well it describes reality. Tests of APT are particularly difficult to formulate because all the theory specifies is a structure for asset pricing: the economic or firm characteristics that should affect expected return are not specified. Let us review the structure of APT that will enter any test procedure.

We can write the multifactor return-generating process as

$$R_i = a_i + \sum_{j=1}^{J} b_{ij} I_j + e_i \qquad (6.6)$$

The APT model that arises from this return-generating process can be written as

$$\bar{R}_i = R_F + \sum_{j=1}^{J} b_{ij} \lambda_j \qquad (6.7)$$

It's worth spending a little time discussing the meaning of the variables b_{ij}, I_j, and λ_j.

Notice from Equation (6.6) that each security i has a unique sensitivity to each I_j but that any I_j has a value that is the same for all securities. Any I_j affects more than one security (if it did not, it would have been compounded in the residual term e_i). These I_js have generally been given the name *factors* in the APT literature. They are identical to the influences we called *indexes* in earlier chapters. The factors affect the returns on more than one security and are the sources of covariance between securities. The b_{ij}s are unique to each security and represent an attribute of the security. This attribute may be simply the sensitivity of the security to a particular factor, or it can be a characteristic of the security such as dividend yield.

Finally, from Equation (6.7) we see that λ_j is the extra expected return required because of a security's sensitivity to the jth attribute of the security. At this point the reader might note that Equation (6.6) looks suspiciously like the type of relationship we used in first-pass regression tests of the CAPM, whereas Equation (6.7) bears a close resemblance to the type of equation used in second-pass tests. This intuition is correct. The problem is that, whereas for the CAPM the correct I_j is defined (e.g., the excess return on the market portfolio for the simple CAPM), for the multifactor model and the APT, the set of I_js is not defined by the theory. In order to test the APT one must test Equation (6.7), which means that one must have estimates of the b_{ij}s. Most tests of APT use Equation (6.6) to estimate the b_{ij}s. However, to estimate the b_{ij}s we must have definitions of the relevant I_js. The most general approach to this problem is to estimate simultaneously factors (I_js) and firm attributes (b_{ij}s) for Equation (6.7). Most of the early tests of the APT employed this methodology. It still continues to be widely used in the finance literature and in practice. We examine this type of simultaneous estimation technique shortly. Before we do so, however, let us point out two alternative methods.

One alternative method is to specify a set of attributes (firm characteristics) that might affect expected return. When using this method the b_{ij}s are directly specified. The b_{ij}s might include such characteristics as divided yield and the firm's Beta with the market. Once the b_{ij}s are specified, Equation (6.7) is used to estimate the λs and thus the APT model.

The second alternative method is to specify the factors I_js in Equation (6.6) and then to estimate the security attributes b_{ij}s and market prices of risk λ_js. Two approaches have been used to specify the factors. One approach is first to hypothesize (we hope on the basis of economic theory) a set of macroeconomic influences that might affect return and then to use Equation (6.6) to estimate the b_{ij}s. These influences might include variables such as the rate of inflation and the rate of interest.[6]

A second approach is to specify a set of portfolios as factors that the researcher believes captures the relevant influences affecting security returns. As in the previous case, Equation (6.6) is used to estimate the b_{ij}s with the return on the hypothesized portfolios used as the I_js and b_{ij}s estimated via regression analysis. For either approach, Equation (6.7) is then estimated to obtain the λ_js and the associated APT model.

If any method other than factor analysis is used to obtain the b_{ij}s for testing APT, one is really conducting a joint test of the APT and the relevancy of the factors or characteristics that have been hypothesized as determining equilibrium. Each of these general approaches will now be discussed in more detail.

Simultaneous Determination of Factors and Characteristics

A complete specification of Equation (6.6) would call for all factors (I_j) and attributes (b_{ij}) to be defined, so that the covariance between any residual return (the e_is not explained by the equation) was zero. While it is not possible to produce this exact result, there is a body of statistical methodology that is very well suited to approximating this result. These techniques are called *factor analysis*. We present a simple example of a factor analytic solution in Appendix A to provide the reader who has not worked with this technique some feel for what it accomplishes.

Factor analysis determines a specific set of I_js and b_{ij}s such that the covariance of residual returns (returns after

---

[6] BIRR has offered a commercial version of this research. A detailed description of their model can be found in Burmeister, Roll, and Ross (1994).

the influence of these indexes has been removed) is as small as possible.[7] In the terminology of factor analysis, the I_js are called *factors* and the b_{ij}s are called *factor loadings*. A specific factor analysis is performed for a specific number of hypothesized factors. By repeating this process for alternative hypotheses about the number of factors, a solution for two factors, three factors, . . . , and j factors is obtained. One can stop when the probability that the next factor explains a statistically significant portion of the covariance matrix drops below some level—for example, 50%.[8] Using this technique, it is not possible to be sure that one has captured all relevant factors. At best, statements such as the following can be made: "There is less than a 50% probability that another factor is needed." Whether one chooses to stop extracting factors when there is a 50% chance that no more are needed, or a 10% chance, or some other level is a matter of taste rather than mathematical rigor. Without a theory of how many factors should be present, the decision as to how many to extract from the data has to be made subjectively.

Factor analysis produces estimates of the factor loadings (b_{ij}) and the factors (I_j). Recall that the factor loadings b_{ij} are sensitivity measures and are like the β_js of the simple CAPM. The major difference is that one not only has identified the b_{ij}s but also has estimated how many factors (indices) there should be and has determined the definition of each I_j. Each I_j is an index consisting of a (different) weighted average of the securities on which the factor analysis is performed.

---

[7] Principal component analysis is somewhat analogous to factor analysis. Recall that principal component analysis extracts from the data a set of indexes that best explains the variance of the data. Indexes are extracted in order of importance, and as many indexes are extracted as the smaller of the number of stocks or the number of observations. Factor analysis is convariance rather than variance driven. For a specified number of indexes it finds the set of that many indexes that best explains the covariance in the original data. There are alternative ways of performing factor analysis. Most empirical work in this area uses maximum likelihood factor analysis, and the techniques developed by Joreskog (1963, 1967, 1977) are often used.

[8] See Lawley and Maxwell (1963) for a discussion of the test procedure described. The reader should be aware that these tests are based on the assumption of multivariate normality. This is the procedure applied by Roll and Ross (1980).

The next step in testing the APT is to form a set of tests directly analogous to the second-pass tests performed by Fama and MacBeth (1973) on the simple CAPM.[9] By running a cross-sectional test, estimates of λs can be computed for each time period and the average value of each λ_j and its variance over time computed. Roll and Ross (1980) were the first to perform this type of test. The mathematics of factor analysis allows this to be done more easily than with regression techniques, but the results are analogous to those that would be obtained by using the generalized least squares regression procedure. However, there are some problems with the use of factor analysis of which the reader should be aware. First, we have the same error in variables problem that we had when testing the standard CAPM. The factor loading b_{ij}s, like the Betas from the first-pass regression, are estimated with error. This means that significance tests of λs are only asymptotically correct. There are three additional problems that are unique to factor analysis. First, there is no meaning to the signs of the factors produced by factor analysis, so the signs on the b_{ij}s and on the λ_js could be reversed. Second, the scaling of the b_{ij}s and the λ_js is arbitrary. For example, all b_{ij}s could be doubled and the resultant λ_js halved. Third, there is no guarantee that factors are produced in a particular order, so when analysis is performed on separate samples, the first factor from one sample may be the third from another sample.

The procedure discussed above is that used by Roll and Ross (1980) in their classic study of APT. They applied factor analysis to 42 groups of 30 stocks using daily data for the time period July 3, 1962, to December 1972. The results of their first-pass test are rather striking. These tests show that, in over 38% of the groups, there was less than a 10% chance that a sixth factor had explanatory power and in over three-fourths of the groups there was a 50% chance that five factors were sufficient. While Roll and Ross try several different second-pass tests, their major results are that at least three factors are significant in explaining equilibrium prices but that it is unlikely that

---

[9] Alternate tests such as those advocated by Gibbons (1981), or those advocated by Burmeister et al. (1988), described later in this chapter, can be used instead of the second-pass test.

four are significant. On the surface it would appear that they find more factors significant than one would expect to find under the standard CAPM model or the zero-Beta version of the CAPM.

It is logical to question whether there is any way these results could be consistent with the CAPM or whether there seem to be additional factors at work in the market. Although we cannot answer definitely, the analysis of Cho, Elton, and Gruber (1984) would seem to indicate that there are additional influences at work. They repeat the Roll and Ross methodology for a later period and find more factors to be significant than do Roll and Ross. They then simulate a set of data using the zero-Beta form of CAPM while enforcing the same means and variances on the returns for each stock that were present in the original data. In doing so, they allow the rate on the zero-Beta portfolio and the Beta on each asset to change over time. When the Roll and Ross methodology is applied to these data, the number of factors that are found to be significant is consistent with the zero-Beta form of the CAPM. The fact that many more factors were found to be significant when actual returns were analyzed lends support to Roll and Ross's argument that additional factors beyond those embodied by the zero-Beta form of the CAPM determine equilibrium prices. While this analysis would seem to suggest that more than one or two factors are important in determining both returns and equilibrium returns, there still remain some questions about the implementation of APT through the use of factor analysis.[10]

The usefulness of an APT model cannot be differentiated from the methodology used to estimate it. The theory may well be correct, but if it cannot be implemented or estimated in a meaningful sense, then, while it remains useful as a way of thinking about the world, it cannot be used as part of the investment process. A test of the APT is a joint test of the theory and the methodology used to implement the theory.

Factor analysis is the principal methodology used to estimate simultaneously the factors that affect equilibrium return and the sensitivity of firms to these factors. One problem with employing this methodology to estimate factors is that the mathematics of factor analysis is so complex that only a limited number of securities can be analyzed at one time.[11] A set of factors and factor loadings are extracted that can best describe the behavior of a small sample of risky assets rather than all risky assets. Roll and Ross used groups of 30 assets. The reader may well ask, "So what? If the arbitrage pricing theory is correct, why don't we obtain the true factors whether we use 30 securities or 2,000 securities?" Dhrymes, Friend, and Gultekin (1984) present evidence that the number of factors that appear significant is an increasing function of the size of the group analyzed. In their samples, the number of significant factors increased from 3 for groups of 15 securities to 7 for groups of 60 securities, the largest groups studied. The authors suggest that dividing the sample into subgroups may ignore important sources of covariance between the securities in different groups and, further, that the factors identified within any subgroup may not be the same as the factor identified in a second subgroup.

While the necessity of estimating the APT for small groups provides some major problems with respect to the applicability of the result, it does provide a unique opportunity for testing the theory and methodology jointly. According to the theory,

$$\bar{R}_i = \bar{R}_z + \sum_{j=1}^{J} b_{ij}\lambda_j$$

Now if the theory is correct and if through factor analysis we have identified the correct factors in the return-generating process, and thus the b_{ij}s, then the value of the market price of all factor λ_js and the intercept should be the same for each group. Testing this is not as easy as it may seem at first. Remember that the sign of the b_{ij}s and λ_js are not uniquely determined, nor is the order in which factors appear in different groups uniquely determined.

Methodology does exist for evaluating whether the intercept is constant across groups and whether the factor prices estimated are the same across groups. The

---

[10] In the last section of this chapter we discuss an alternative way in which the zero-Beta form of the CAPM could be consistent with the Roll and Ross results.

[11] Chen (1981) has described a procedure that allows APT to be estimated and tested across large numbers of securities. However, his procedure, which involves forming a small number of portfolios of securities based on an initial factor solution for use in further tests, has been questioned by Dhrymes, Friend, and Gultekin (1984). The resolution of the adequacy of this procedure, and in particular the value of estimates for some securities versus the loss of information involved in his portfolio aggregation technique, will have to await further study.

methodology and test results have been described very well in an article by Brown and Weinstein (1983). They are able to test (1) whether the intercept term is the same for all groups, (2) whether the factor prices are the same for all groups given that the intercept is constrained to be the same, and (3) whether both the intercept and factor prices are the same for all groups, a joint hypothesis. Unfortunately their results are ambiguous. Although they cast some doubt on the use of the maximum likelihood factor analysis to explain equilibrium return successfully, as Brown and Weinstein recognize, their "results cannot be viewed as compelling evidence against the APT." Dhrymes, Friend, and Gultekin (1984) in another set of tests find that, depending on the method of grouping stocks employed, the intercept term may be significantly different or not significantly different across groups.

Other tests of the APT have failed to demonstrate its clear superiority over other models although results are mixed. Dhrymes, Friend, and Gultekin find that a multifactor model of the APT has better explanatory power than a one-factor model. This tends to support the existence of more than one factor. However, they find that the explanatory power of either model is modest and that there is some doubt about whether the risk premia (prices) of the five risk factors employed by Roll and Ross are significantly different from zero.

Other tests of the Roll and Ross–type APT have produced equally ambiguous results. For example, one test of the APT that would give us great confidence is if a stock's residual risk was not priced when added as another factor in the equilibrium pricing equation. Recall that the b_{ij}s are supposed to capture the impact of all systematic components of risk. Any other attribute of a security, and in particular its residual risk, should be unique to each security and therefore diversifiable. Roll and Ross test for the impact of residual risk and find almost no evidence that it is priced. Dhrymes, Friend, and Gultekin also test and find that both a stock's own standard deviation and skewness generally yield insignificant coefficients. However, they find that these two influences are significant at least as frequently as the factors suggested by Roll and Ross.[12]

The literature has contained a number of tests of empirically estimated factor models and APT models. Although a detailed description of the empirical methodology goes beyond the level of analysis, we wish to present here two articles that are well worth mentioning.

Lehmann and Modest (1988) implemented the idea of forming portfolios of assets that mimic factor realizations (returns). By forming a portfolio that has minimum residual risk for each factor, they can then use this set of portfolios as independent variables to estimate the sensitivities of each of a large number of securities to each influence (factor). Each portfolio is identified by finding a set of weights summing to one across stocks, so that the portfolio has minimum residual risk and a sensitivity of zero to all factors except the one under study. Lehmann and Modest are able to explain certain phenomena not explained by the standard CAPM. The standard CAPM does not satisfactorily account for extra returns associated with high dividends, the stock's own variance, small size (low capitalization), and the January effect. Lehmann and Modest show that a multi-index APT can explain away discrepancies due to dividend yield and own variance but that the extra returns on small firms and in January are only partially accounted for by the model. Nevertheless, the ability of the model to account for some influences not explained by the CAPM is in fact support for the model as an alternative to the simple CAPM. Lest we get too excited, recall that an after-tax CAPM tested by Litzenberger and Ramaswamy (1979) was also successful in accounting for returns varying with dividend yield.

Connor and Korajczyk (1986) provide a test of APT using the asymmetric principle components technique proposed by Chamberlain and Rothschild (1981). They find that with five factors, they can explain the extra return on small firms and in January better than the CAPM based on a value-weighted index.

The ability of an APT model employing a small number of factors to account for return patterns unexplained by the CAPM strongly suggests that the APT is a useful model for explaining relative prices.

[12] One other type of test has been performed on Roll and Ross–type multifactor models. In applying the standard CAPM and zero-Beta CAPM, certain anomalies have been noted. For example, small (low capitalization) firms tend consistently to produce returns in excess of those we would expect based on CAPM. This anomaly is due to either a market inefficiency or a deficiency in the CAPM as a model of equilibrium returns. If a Roll and Ross type model better explained anomalies, such as the small-firm effect, one would have added faith in such models. Reinganum (1981) has investigated this issue and finds that a Roll and Ross multifactor model could not explain the size anomaly any better than the standard CAPM.

All of the tests just described are joint tests of the APT and a particular statistical methodology used to identify both the b_{ij}s and I_js of the factor model. The results of this research are inconclusive. There is fairly strong indication that more than two factors affect returns and that more than two factors are priced. Statistical methodology has been developed and continues to be developed that allows us to better define the factors and to better form portfolios that mimic them. However, research is just beginning to explore the stability of the factor structure over time.

In Japan, APT has been tested and shows a clear superiority over the CAPM in selecting securities as well as in explaining past returns. For example, Elton and Gruber (1982, 1988) find that a five-factor APT model does a better job of explaining and predicting expected returns than does a single-factor or CAPM model. In particular, in the Japanese stock market the CAPM model appears to break down. In Japan, unlike other markets, small stocks have smaller Betas than large stocks. This should imply a lower expected return given the CAPM, and yet small stocks have significantly higher excess returns. This happens when *small* is defined as anything but the largest 100 stocks on the Tokyo Stock Exchange. These problems are not nearly as great when a multifactor model is used. Furthermore, a multifactor model does a much better job of allowing mimicking portfolios to be constructed (as both index funds and hedge portfolios for futures and option trading) than does a single-index model. The APT model is almost universally used by industry as a replacement for the CAPM model in Japan.

An Alternative Approach to Testing the APT

If we could specify a priori either the factors that affected stock returns or the characteristics of stocks that affected returns, we would then have a much easier estimation problem to solve. A debate exists among academics and practitioners about whether part of the model should be prespecified on the basis of theory or whether all of the parameters should be determined empirically. This type of debate has gone on since the dawn of modern science. The issue is discussed by Roll and Ross (1980). They state that "we do consider the basic underlying causes of the generating process of returns to be a potentially important area of research but we think it is an area that can be

investigated separately from testing asset pricing theories." The problem is that, without a theory, the empirical tools one uses are a lot weaker and the results of tests harder to interpret. For example, in the APT we have no idea of what the size or even the sign of factor prices should be. All we can say is that we expect some of them to be statistically different from zero. On the other hand, in the Sharpe-Lintner CAPM the price of Beta was supposed to be $\bar{R}_m - R_F$, a quantity that we expected to be positive and about which we have some rough idea of magnitude.

The controversy we are discussing would be easy to resolve if we had a theory of the appropriate factors or characteristics that determine security returns. Someday we hope to have one. In the absence of such a theory all we can do is examine three attempts to prespecify one set of variables in the multifactor model. One attempt hypothesized a set of firm characteristics, another hypothesized a set of macroeconomic indexes, and the third specifies a set of portfolios as the indexes.

Specifying Attributes of Securities

In the preceding section of this chapter we examined the use of maximum likelihood factor analysis to determine simultaneously the characteristics that affect return and the extra return required because of a security's sensitivity to these characteristics. If a set of characteristics that affects return could be specified a priori, then the market price of these characteristics over any period of time could be measured fairly easily.

The estimating equation would be of the form

$$\bar{R}_i = \lambda_0 + \lambda_1 b_{i1} + \lambda_2 b_{i2} + \cdots + \lambda_J b_{iJ}$$

for the case of J characteristics. In this equation the b_{ij}s would be the value each characteristic took on, and the λ_js the average extra return required because of these characteristics. The values of the λ_js would be estimated via regression analysis. This procedure is directly analogous to a second-pass test of the CAPM. In fact, we have already examined two models that could be viewed as this type of test. The first was the model tested by Fama and MacBeth (1973); although they viewed the model as a test of the CAPM, it could be viewed as a test of APT. The model they tested was

$$\bar{R}_i = \lambda_0 + \lambda_1 \beta_i + \lambda_2 \beta_i^2 + \lambda_3 S_{ei}$$

The firm characteristics examined were the Beta for each firm, the Beta for each stock squared, and the residual risk of each stock. These tests clearly show that, at least with respect to the hypothesized set of characteristics, a multifactor model did not outperform the zero-Beta form of the CAPM. None of the added characteristics were priced. Remember that tests of this type are a joint test of the APT in general and the specific characteristics that were hypothesized as explaining equilibrium returns. Fama and MacBeth tested characteristics that on the basis of economic theory should not explain equilibrium returns and concluded that they did not.

We examined a second model that hypothesized an additional firm characteristic as affecting equilibrium return. Recall that Litzenberger and Ramaswamy (1979) included dividend yield as an added variable and found that its impact was statistically significant. This should encourage the pursuit of models containing more characteristics.

One such model has been constructed and tested by Sharpe (1982). He starts with the hypothesis that equilibrium returns should be affected by the following characteristics: a stock's Beta with the S&P index, its dividend yield, the size of the firm (market value of equity), its Beta with long-term bonds, its past value of Alpha (the intercept of the regression of past excess return against excess returns on the S&P index), and eight-sector membership variables. Sharpe does not attempt an elaborate economic rationale for these variables but rather states that he has selected them more or less "ex cathedra." We would expect both Beta and dividend yield to be related positively to expected returns. Size may well be, at least in part, a proxy for liquidity. If so, size should enter the model with a negative sign. If sensitivity to interest rates is an important variable, we would expect bond Beta to play a role in determining equilibrium returns. If the past value of Alpha proves significant, it would be evidence of autocorrelation of the residuals from the CAPM. This might indicate that there are some added variables explaining cross-sectional returns that were not captured in the model. The use of sector membership as an additional set of variables implies that membership in a particular sector of the economy has an important effect on equilibrium return.

The results of applying this model to 2,197 stocks on a monthly basis for all months between 1931 and 1979 are summarized in Table 6-1, which reports the average coefficients (on an annualized basis) over the entire period and the percent of months in which the coefficients were significantly different from zero at the 5% level. Note that for those variables where we had clear expectations about the sign of the relationship and return, our expectations are borne out. Furthermore, note that while on the basis of chance we would expect any firm characteristic to be significant about 5% of the time, each characteristic was significant a much higher percentage of the time.

Another way to judge the importance of including more than one characteristic in the description of equilibrium is by examining the explanatory power (coefficient of determination) of the model as more characteristics are employed. The average coefficient of determination for monthly data when Beta is used as the only characteristic to explain cross-sectional returns is 0.037. This might seem low, but recall that monthly data are being used and portfolio grouping is not being done. This is, in fact, consistent with other studies employing similar research designs. When the security characteristics of yield, size, bond Beta, and Alpha are added, the coefficient of determination adjusting for added variables more than doubled to 0.079. When all the characteristics in Table 6-1 are used, it goes up to 0.104. The use of firm characteristics in addition to Beta has increased the explanatory power of the model. In addition, these factors seem to be significant a considerably higher percentage of the time than chance alone would explain.

Sharpe seems to have identified some additional characteristics, beyond a stock's Beta with a proxy for the market portfolio, that are useful for explaining cross-sectional returns over time. He recognizes that his model is rather ad hoc in nature, but it is an indication that increased research into significant economic characteristics of a stock should allow us to build better models of equilibrium.

A second model that is widely used in industry and that specifies a set of firm characteristics is that employed by Barra.[13] This model uses nine firm characteristics in

---

[13] See Grinold and Kahn (1994) for a description of this model. As explained in this article, the model actually makes use of a combination of firm specific characteristics and macroeconomic variables.

TABLE 6-1 Cross-sectional Data on Sharpe's Multifactor Model

Attribute	Annualized Value of Associated λ	Percent of Months in Which Associated λ Was Significantly Different from Zero
Beta	5.36	58.3
Yield	0.24	39.5
Size	-5.56	56.5
Bond Beta	-0.12	28.2
Alpha	-2.00	43.5
Sector Membership		
Basic industries	1.65	32.5
Capital goods	0.16	18.7
Construction	-1.59	15.3
Consumer goods	-0.18	39.3
Energy	6.28	36.9
Finance	-1.48	16.3
Transportation	-0.57	43.9
Utilities	-2.62	35.0

unanticipated changes in the following influences:

1. *Inflation.* Inflation impacts both the level of the discount rate and the size of the future cash flows.

2. *The term structure of interest rates.* Differences between the rate on bonds with a long maturity and a short maturity affect the value of payments far in the future relative to near-term payments.

3. *Risk premia.* Differences between the return on safe bonds (AAA) and more risky bonds (BAA) are used to measure the market's reaction to risk.

4. *Industrial production.* Changes in industrial production affect the opportunities facing investors and the real value of cash flows.

place of the five characteristics used by Sharpe. These are volatility, momentum, size, liquidity, growth, value, earnings volatility, financial leverage, and industry membership.

Specifying the Influences Affecting the Return-Generating Process

Another alternative to the joint determination of factor loadings and factors discussed in the earlier section of this chapter is the specification (one hopes on the basis of economic theory) of the set of influences or indexes (I_js) that should enter the return-generating process.

Chen, Roll, and Ross (1986) have hypothesized and tested a set of economic variables. They reason that return on stocks should be affected by any influence that affects either future cash flows from holding a security or the value of these cash flows to the investor (e.g., changes in the appropriate discount rate on future cash flows). Chen, Roll, and Ross construct sets of alternative measures of

Chen, Roll, and Ross then examined these measures or indexes

1. to see if they were correlated with the set of indexes extracted by the factor analysis used by Roll and Ross as described in a previous section of this chapter,

2. to see if they explained equilibrium returns.

When they examine the relationship between the macroeconomic variables and the factors (indexes) over the period to which the factors were formed (fit), they find a strong relationship. Furthermore, when the relationship is tested over a holdout period (a period following the fit period), the relationship continues to be strong. There appears to be a significant relationship between the hypothesized macroeconomic variables and the statistically identified systematic factors in stock market returns.

The second set of tests involves investigating whether returns are related to the sensitivity of a stock to their macroeconomic variables. The procedure is analogous to the two-step procedure used by Fama and MacBeth to investigate the CAPM. In the first stage, time-series regressions are run for each of a series of portfolios to estimate each portfolio's sensitivity to each macroeconomic variable [the b_{ij}s of Equation (6.6)]. Then the market price of risk [the λ_js of Equation (6.7)] is estimated by running a cross-sectional regression each month and looking at the average of the market price in each month. Chen, Roll, and Ross find that the macrovariables are significant explanatory influences on pricing. Furthermore, when the Beta of each portfolio with the market was introduced as an additional variable along with the sensitivity of each portfolio to the macroeconomic variables, it did not show up as significant in the second stage (cross-sectional) regression.

Chen, Roll, and Ross recognize that they cannot claim to have found the (correct) state variables for asset pricing. However, they certainly have made an important start in that direction.

Their work is continued in a series of papers by Burmeister and McElroy. Burmeister and McElroy have integrated tests of the factor models, CAPM, and APT. It is worthwhile reviewing two of their tests. The first test is constructed using the multi-index model. More specifically, returns are assumed to be generated by the following five indexes.

I_1 = Default risk as measured by the return on long-term government bonds minus the return on long-term corporate bonds plus one-half of 1%

I_2 = Time premium as measured by the return on long-term government bonds minus the one-month Treasury bill rate one month ahead

I_3 = Deflation as measured by expected inflation at the beginning of the month minus actual inflation during the month

I_4 = Change in expected sales

I_5 = The market return not captured by the first four variables

The fifth variable is a proxy for any unobserved general influences. As explained in the appendix, it is estimated by taking the residuals from a regression of a diversified portfolio (the authors use the S&P composite index) against the first four observable variables described earlier. The regression the authors found was

$$R_M - \lambda_0 = 0.00224 - 1.330 I_1 + 0.558 I_2 + 2.286 I_3 - 0.935 I_4$$

$$(0.619) \quad (-3.94) \quad (4.96) \quad (1.997) \quad (-2.27)$$

The first four factors account for about 25% ($R^2 = .24$) of the variation in the return on the S&P composite index, and each of the four coefficients is significant.

When the sensitivities (b_{ij}) are estimated for each firm, more than two-thirds of the sensitivities are statistically different from zero at the 5% level, and the five variables typically account for 30% to 50% of the variation of returns of individual firms. In general, b_{i1} appears with a significant negative coefficient, whereas b_{i2} and b_{i5} appear with significant positive coefficients. The remaining two variables have a more ambiguous impact on stock returns.

The prices (λ_i) of each of the five sensitivities implied by the model are all positive and all statistically significantly different from zero. The average value of the λs using monthly returns is contained in the following table:

	Mean λ Value	t Statistic
λ_1	0.44	4.27
λ_2	1.00	4.76
λ_3	0.04	1.83
λ_4	0.15	2.21
λ_5	0.51	3.21

Additional interesting questions can be addressed with the author's methodology. The first is whether the APT form of the return equation explains returns significantly better than the return-generating process (five-index model). The difference between these two models is that in estimating the APT form, the expected return on each stock is constrained to take on a value that does not allow arbitrage opportunities between securities. This difference is analogous to earlier tests of the CAPM where the intercept was constrained to be $R_F(1 - \beta_j)$, the no-arbitrage condition from the market model. Imposing this constraint cannot increase the explanatory power of the model; it can only decrease it. If the APT is correct, however, the decrease should be small. The fact that the decrease is not statistically significant shows that we can't reject the APT version of the return-generating process and is, at least, weak evidence in support of it.

Another test the authors perform is to restrict the coefficients to see if the market index alone explains a statistically different amount than the five-index model. The additional explanation of the four variables is statistically significant even when the APT form of the return-generating process is used.

In a later paper, Burmeister and McElroy (1988) continue their attempt to differentiate between three models: the return-generating model (the factor model), APT, and CAPM. This study differs from their previous work in two ways. They modify their definition of the observable factors, but more important, they assume there are three unobservable factors rather than one. They use three portfolios to represent these unobservable factors: the return on the S&P 500 stock index, the return on 20-year corporate bonds, and the return on 20-year government bonds.

Burmeister and McElroy conclude that at the 1% significance level the CAPM model can be rejected in favor of their APT model. Furthermore, the APT restrictions cannot be rejected at any reasonable significance level in favor of the more general factor model. This work represents the strongest evidence so far in favor of the APT model as a useful explanation of expected return.

Specifying a Set of Portfolios Affecting the Return-Generating Process

Another alternative is to specify a set of portfolios (I_js) (which may or may not include the market portfolio) that a priori are thought to capture the influences affecting security returns. These portfolios are selected on the basis of a belief about the types of securities and/or economic influences that affect security returns.[14]

An example of this type of approach is that used by Fama and French (1993) to construct a model to explain returns and expected returns on both stocks and bonds. In addition to using the returns on a market portfolio of stocks, they use the returns on other portfolios to represent the I_js in the return-generating process. These portfolios are

1. the difference in return on a portfolio of small stocks and a portfolio of large stocks (small minus large),

2. the difference in return between a portfolio of high-book-to-market stocks and a port folio of low-book-to-market stocks (high minus low),

3. the difference between the monthly long-term government bond return and the one-month Treasury bill return,

4. The difference in the monthly return on a portfolio of long-term corporate bonds and a portfolio of long-term government bonds.

Note that all variables are either the return on portfolios of assets or the difference in the return of two portfolios of assets.[15] The latter can be considered a portfolio with a set of stocks sold short. Clearly this model has elements in common with the models that have been presented earlier in this chapter. We saw that Chen, Roll, and Ross and Burmeister and McElroy use bond return variables similar to those used in this model. Whether one describes these as measures of macroeconomic variables or portfolios is largely a matter of taste. The unique aspect of this model is in the formulation of the variables representing size and book-to-market ratios. In Sharpe's model (described earlier), size enters as a firm characteristic or a b_{ij}. Size is measured in dollars (actually the natural logarithm of dollars), and a λ is associated with it via cross-sectional regression. What Fama and French have done is to convert the size component from a direct measure to a return concept by constructing a portfolio to capture this influence. The b_{ij} associated with size is not the log of size for any company i, but rather is the sensitivity of that company to the return on the size portfolio. Because size is measured by the return on a portfolio, it now enters the return-generating process as well as the pricing equation. This allows Fama and French to investigate both the time-series and cross-sectional properties of size.[16]

Fama and French test the model described above in a number of time-series tests. The cross-sectional implications are tested by examining whether the intercepts of the time series of excess returns indeed equals zero as APT would suggest.[17] They find that, in fact, the intercepts

---

[14] We should point out that this is fundamentally different from the approach of factor replicating portfolios that has been discussed by Lehmann and Modest (1988) and Huberman, Kandel, and Stambaugh (1987) among others. In these approaches, either factor analysis is used to extract factors or macroeconomic variables are hypothesized as important and then a mathematical programming problem is solved to find portfolios that mimic the underlying factors.

[15] Elton, Gruber, Das, and Hlavka (1993), Blake, Elton, and Gruber (1993), and Elton, Gruber, and Blake (1994) investigate alternative return-generating processes. In the latter paper, they develop an APT model where some or all of the indexes represent portfolios of assets.

[16] The question of which of these approaches (measuring the b_{ij} directly from firm size or estimating it from a regression on a portfolio) is better awaits further empirical investigation.

[17] This is basically a multivariable form of the Black, Jensen, and Scholes (1972) procedure.

are zero and that this portfolio model is successful in explaining expected stock returns. More specifically, they conclude that "at a minimum, our results show that five factors do a good job explaining a) common variations in bond and stock returns and b) the cross-section of average returns."

APT AND CAPM

Before continuing our examination of APT models, we should discuss the fact that the APT model—and, in fact, the existence of a multifactor model, including one where more than one factor is priced—is not necessarily inconsistent with the Sharpe–Lintner–Mossin form or one of the other forms of the CAPM.

The simplest case in which an APT model is consistent with the simple form of the CAPM is the case where the return-generating function is of the form

$$R_i = a_i + \beta_i R_m + e_i$$

If returns are generated by a single-index model, the single index is the return on the market portfolio, and a riskless rate exists, then the methodology at the beginning of the chapter can be used to show that

$$\bar{R}_i = R_F + \beta_i \left(\bar{R}_m - R_F \right)$$

If the return-generating function is more complex than this, does it imply that the simple CAPM cannot hold? The answer is no. Recall that the simple CAPM does not assume that the market is the only source of covariance between returns. Let us assume that the return-generating function is of the multi-index type

$$R_i = a_i + b_{i1} I_1 + b_{i2} I_2 + e_i \qquad \textbf{(6.8)}$$

The indexes can be industry indexes, sector indexes, or indexes of broad economic influences such as the rate of inflation. All we assume is that the set of indexes used captures all the sources of covariance between securities [e.g., $E(e_i e_j) = 0$].

The APT equilibrium model for this multifactor return-generating process with a riskless asset is

$$\bar{R}_i = R_F + b_{i1} \lambda_1 + b_{i2} \lambda_2 \qquad \textbf{(6.9)}$$

Recall that if the CAPM is the equilibrium model, it holds for all securities, as well as all portfolios of securities. Assume the indexes can be represented by portfolios

of securities. Actually, we have seen that λ_j is the excess return on a portfolio with a b_{ij} of one on one index and a b_{ij} of zero on all other indices. If the CAPM holds, the equilibrium return on each λ_j is given by the CAPM or

$$\lambda_1 = \beta_{\lambda 1} \left(\bar{R}_m - R_F \right)$$

$$\lambda_2 = \beta_{\lambda 2} \left(\bar{R}_m - R_F \right)$$

Substituting into Equation (6.9) yields

$$\bar{R}_i = R_F + b_{i1} \beta_{\lambda 1} \left(\bar{R}_m - R_F \right) + b_{i2} \beta_{\lambda 2} \left(\bar{R}_m - R_F \right)$$

$$\bar{R}_i = R_F + \left(b_{i1} \beta_{\lambda 1} + b_{i2} \beta_{\lambda 2} \right) \left(\bar{R}_m - R_F \right)$$

Defining β_i as $(b_{i1} \beta_{\lambda 1} + b_{i2} \beta_{\lambda 2})$ results in the expected return of $\bar{R}_i$ being priced by the CAPM.

$$\bar{R}_i = R_F + \beta_i \left(\bar{R}_m - R_F \right)$$

The APT solution with multiple factors appropriately priced is fully consistent with the Sharpe–Lintner–Mossin form of the CAPM.

We wish to stress this point. Employing the Roll and Ross procedure and finding that more than one λ_j is significantly different from zero is not sufficient proof to reject any CAPM. If the λs are not significantly different from $\beta_\lambda (\bar{R}_m - R_F)$, the empirical results could be fully consistent with the Sharpe–Lintner–Mossin form of the CAPM. It is perfectly possible that more than one index explains the covariance between security returns but that the CAPM holds.

While we have demonstrated this with the simple CAPM, it should be apparent to the reader that other values of λs can exist that are fully consistent with the more complex nonstandard forms of the CAPM reviewed in Chapter 5.

RECAPITULATION

The APT theory remains the newest and most promising explanation of relative returns. The theory promises to supply us with a more complete description of returns than the CAPM. Recent work, some of which employs a set of macro variables and some of which employs a set of portfolios, is quite encouraging. The fact that a number of studies have found a set of macro variables and portfolios that impact average returns and are not only priced but also priced differently than the CAPM would imply is of both practical and theoretical significance. One word of caution is in order. It is possible that these additional influences are priced not because the APT is the correct model for expected returns, but because we have not correctly identified the market in constructing our model. The residual market plus the other variable employed in the model may together simply serve as a proxy for the (true but unobserved) market. Even if this is correct, the use of these multi-index models is, on a practical level, a better explanation for returns than any of the market proxies that have been pro-posed to date.

A section on the uses of multi-index models and APT follows. Although there are many reasons for adding this section, most of which are discussed later, perhaps the key reason is that after we teach APT, so many of our students remark that it seems more complex than the CAPM and ask why we bothered with it.

Multi-index Models, APT, and Portfolio Management

The use of multi-index models and multi-index equilibrium models (APT models) in the selection of securities and the management and evaluation of portfolios is growing rapidly. Many brokerage firms, financial institutions, and financial consulting firms have developed their own multi-index models to aid in the investment process. These models have become increasingly popular because they allow risk to be more tightly controlled and they allow the investor to protect against specific types of risk to which he or she is particularly sensitive or to make specific bets on certain types of risk.

In this section we will discuss the use of APT and multi-index models to aid in passive management, active management, and portfolio evaluation. Before we do so, we will review multi-index models and APT briefly and present a simple example of an APT model that we will use to illustrate some of the phenomena we discuss in this section.

Review of Multi-index Models and APT

Earlier in this chapter we presented a return-generating process that expressed the return on any security as a linear function of a series of indexes:

$$R_i = a_i + b_{i1}I_1 + b_{i2}I_2 + b_{i3}I_3 + \cdots + e_i \quad \textbf{(6.1a)}$$

It is convenient for purposes of this section to assume that each index has been either formulated or adjusted to have a mean equal to zero. Since the indexes and residuals have a mean of zero, taking the expected value of both sides of Equation (6.1) results in

$$\bar{R}_i = a_i$$

Thus, setting the mean of each index equal to zero has the effect of ensuring that a_i is equal to the expected return on security i.

We saw that Equation (6.1a) leads to a description of expected returns given by

$$\bar{R}_i - R_F = \lambda_1 b_{i1} + \lambda_2 b_{i2} + \lambda_3 b_{i3} + \cdots \quad \textbf{(6.10)}$$

where b_{ij}s represent the sensitivity of a security's return to index j and are a measure of the risks inherent in the security under study and λs represent the reward for bearing these risks (price of risk).

Combining Equations (6.1) and (6.10) by recognizing that $a_i = \bar{R}_i$

$$R_i = R_F + \lambda_1 b_{i1} + \lambda_2 b_{i2} + \lambda_3 b_{i3} + \cdots$$
$$+ b_{i1}I_1 + b_{i2}I_2 + b_{i3}I_3 + \cdots + e_i \quad \textbf{(6.11)}$$

There are several ways of identifying the Is in Equation (6.1) and the b_{ij}s and λ_js in Equation (6.11). However, a specific model will help illustrate the use of these types of models.

Let's assume that we have identified four influences in the return-generating model (Equation 6.1) and that

I_1 = unexpected change in inflation, denoted by I_I

I_2 = unexpected change in aggregate sales, denoted by I_S

I_3 = unexpected change in oil prices, denoted by I_O

I_4 = the return in the S&P index constructed to be orthogonal to the other influences, denoted by I_M

Furthermore, assume that oil risk is not priced ($\lambda_O = 0$). Equation (6.10) becomes

$$\bar{R}_i - R_F = \lambda_I b_{iI} + \lambda_S b_{iS} + \lambda_M b_{iM}$$

while Equation (6.11) becomes

$$\bar{R}_i - R_F = \lambda_I b_{iI} + \lambda_S b_{iS} + \lambda_M b_{iM} + b_{iI}I_I + b_{iS}I_S + b_{iO}I_O + b_{iM}I_M + e_i$$

Recall that all Is have an expected value of zero.[18]

Recall that all Is have an expected value of zero.[18]

The set of λs on these factors consistent with the results reported by Burmeister, Roll, and Ross are

$$\lambda_I = -4.32$$

$$\lambda_S = 1.49$$

$$\lambda_M = 3.96$$

While the sensitivities (b) values for the S&P index were

$$b_{S\&PI} = -0.37$$

$$b_{S\&PS} = 1.71$$

$$b_{S\&PO} = 0.00$$

$$b_{S\&PM} = 1.00$$

The parameterization of the model allows us to recognize the importance of any factor in determining the expected excess return on the S&P index. To do so, simply multiply the b associated with a factor times the associated price of risk (λ).

Factor	b	λ	Contribution to S&P Expected Excess Return (%)
Inflation	−0.37	−4.32	1.59
Sales growth	1.71	1.49	2.54
Oil prices	0.00	0.00	0.00
Market	1.00	3.96	3.96
Expected excess return for S&P index			8.09

This table shows that the expected excess return (return above the riskless rate) for the S&P index is 8.09%. Sales growth contributes 2.54% to the expected return for the S&P. In other words, sensitivity to sales growth accounts for 2.54 ÷ 8.09 or 31.4% of the total expected excess return.

The same type of analysis can be used to examine the importance of the sources of risk for the expected excess return on any security or portfolio. For example, for a portfolio of growth stocks the bs, λs, and contribution to expected excess return are shown later:[19]

Factor	b	λ	Contribution to Growth Stock Portfolio Expected Excess Return (%)
Inflation	−.50	−4.32	2.16
Sales growth	2.75	1.49	4.10
Oil prices	−1.00	0.00	0.00
Market	1.30	3.96	5.15
Expected excess return for growth stock portfolio			11.41

Notice that the expected excess return for the growth stock portfolio (11.41) is higher than it was for the S&P index (8.09). This is not surprising because the growth stock portfolio has more risk, with respect to each index, than the S&P portfolio.[20]

Individual influences (indexes) have a different absolute and relative contribution to the expected excess return on a growth stock portfolio than they have on the S&P index. For example, the contribution of sales growth to expected excess return is now 4.10%. Sales growth accounts for 35.9% of the excess return on the growth stock portfolio. It is not surprising that growth stocks are more sensitive to sales growth than the typical stock. What might be surprising, though it is generally true, is that growth stocks

---

[18] The model we describe here and the values we present represent a simplified version of the model and parameters described in Burmeister, Roll, and Ross (1994). Their model contains additional influences to those cited and does not contain an oil index. We wanted to include an unpriced index to show the role of unpriced indexes in portfolio management. The Salomon Brothers risk index model also does not include an oil index for U.S. stocks though they find this index is an important influence in Japan, the United Kingdom, Germany, and France.

[19] Although estimating the cost of equity capital falls beyond the scope of this book, the preceding analysis leads naturally to estimates of cost of capital. For example, the cost of capital of any stock or portfolio can be found by adding the riskless rate to the estimate of excess return from the APT model. For growth stocks this would be R_F + 11.41. For a detailed explanation of using APT to determine cost of equity capital, see Elton, Gruber, and Mei (1994).

[20] Note that all b values, except for sensitivity to inflation, are larger for the growth stock portfolio than for the S&P portfolio. Though the b value for inflation is smaller for the growth stock portfolio, this portfolio is still less desirable with respect to inflation sensitivity because (unlike other λs) the price of inflation sensitivity (λ_I) is negative.

are more sensitive to all important indexes. So although the increase in sensitivity to sales growth causes the largest increase in expected excess returns, changes in all influences lead to greater excess return.

Let's now turn to the use of this model for investment and portfolio management. Portfolio managers can be divided into passive and active managers. Passive managers believe that mispriced securities can't be identified and thus try to hold a portfolio that mimics some set of stocks. The most common way passive management is practiced is to hold a portfolio of stocks that closely tracks a selected index. Active management involves making bets about some securities or set of securities in the sense of designing a portfolio based on a belief that one or more securities are mispriced.

Passive Management

The multi-index model can play a major role in improving passive management. It can be used to do a better job of tracking an index or to design a passive portfolio that is appropriate for a particular client.

The simplest use of a multi-index model is to create a portfolio of stocks that closely tracks an index. An obvious way to construct an index fund is to hold stocks in the same proportion they represent of the index. However, many index funds do not simply hold each stock in an index in the proportion the stock represents of the index but rather attempt to replicate the index with a smaller number of stocks. The more issues in an index, the smaller the companies represented in an index, and the less liquid the stocks in an index, the more costly it is to match the index by purchasing stocks in the same proportion they represent in the index. Clearly, once one becomes concerned with tracking an index that represents a very large segment of a market, exact matching of proportions becomes less and less appropriate. An index fund can be created using the single-index model by finding the portfolio that has a Beta of one with the desired index and that has minimum residual risks for a given portfolio size (minimum variance of the e_is in a single index form of Equation [6.1]).

Employing a multi-index model rather than a one-index model allows the creation of an index fund that more closely matches the desired index.[21] The reason for this is clear. A properly constructed multi-index model ensures

that the index has been matched in terms of all important sources of return movements (risk). On the other hand, just matching on market risk can leave the portfolio and the index with different sensitivities to the common factors affecting both, such as sensitivity to inflation. Let's consider a simple example of this. Reviewing the sensitivity coefficients, we see that both oil stocks and cyclical stocks have a sensitivity with the S&P index of 1.14. Thus, in a single-index model, except for residual risk, one would be indifferent to holding oil stocks or cyclical stocks in matching the S&P index. However, oil stocks and cyclical stocks have very different sensitivities (bs) to sales growth. Thus, a portfolio that was matched to an index on sensitivity with the S&P but was not matched on the b value with sales growth might not track the index very well in periods when unexpected changes in sales growth were large.

In general, the fewer stocks in an index-matching portfolio, the less likely that the portfolio will be matched on the common factors affecting the portfolio and the index and the greater the superiority of multi-index models over single-index models.[22] This is true because unexpected changes in the missing indices will differentially impact the residual risk in future periods if sensitivity to these missing indices is not held constant. Portfolios are often formed to serve as arbitrage portfolios in the trading of options or futures on an index. Firms typically attempt to form a small basket of stocks (25 or 50) that they can actively trade as they change their futures or options position. The number must be kept small, because the basket of stocks will be bought and sold frequently. The use of multi-index models becomes critical in these instances.

Another problem frequently encountered in passive management is the desire to match an index with a portfolio that excludes certain types of stocks. Social goals or management preferences frequently restrict the set of stocks that can be used to match an index. In the last 10 years, for example, it was not uncommon for a pension fund to declare that it would not own tobacco stocks or gambling

---

[21] See Elton and Gruber (1988) for a demonstration of the improvement in index tracking that results from using a four-index as opposed to a one-index model.

[22] See Elton and Gruber (1988) for empirical evidence on this issue.

stocks. It is likely that a sector of the market such as tobacco stocks has a sensitivity to inflation or interest rates that is different from that of the average stock. If an index fund is formed from a set of stocks that precludes tobacco stocks using the single-index model, then the sensitivity to the single-index will be matched but the sensitivity to other important influences will probably be different. Use of a multi-index model improves tracking an index.[23]

Multi-index models also help improve performance under a set of conditions that are directly opposite to those just described. An investor may decide to match an index with a portfolio that must contain certain stocks. This is very common in Japan, where stocks are often held for reasons that have their foundations in the business relationship between firms. In the United States, an investor may want to maintain (or add) certain holdings in a portfolio for business reasons or because the investor does not want to recognize certain accumulated but unrealized capital losses or gains for either tax purposes or reporting purposes.[24] The problem then is to find an overall portfolio matching as closely as possible an index but including a defined set of stocks. Because these stocks may have sensitivities to important influences that are different from the index being matched, it is important to explicitly match on each of the key risk factors.

One type of passive management that can be performed with a multi-index model, is fundamentally different from what can be done with a single-index model. The multi-index model allows one to closely match an index while purposely taking positions with respect to certain types of risk different from the positions contained in the index. For example, consider a pension fund that has cash outflows affected by inflation (COLA or cost-of-living adjustments). The payments for such a pension fund increase with inflation. Thus the overseers want a portfolio that will perform especially well when the rate of inflation increases. This can be illustrated more fully by returning to the data presented for the S&P index earlier in this chapter. The b value (sensitivity) for the S&P index with inflation was −0.37, which implies (other things held constant)

that an investment in the S&P index will tend to go down by 0.37% if the rate of inflation goes up by 1%. If a pension fund is particularly sensitive to inflation risk (because its liability payments go up with inflation), it might wish to hold a portfolio that has a zero sensitivity to inflation (or even a positive sensitivity). It could form a portfolio that had the same response to all factors affecting the S&P (except for the inflation factor) by solving a quadratic programming problem to form a portfolio that matched all S&P bs except for the b on inflation, had a zero or positive b with inflation, and had minimum residual risk.

The applications we have just discussed can be done using a multi-index model; however, assuming an APT adds additional insight into the process. It tells the investor the expected cost of changing the exposure to inflation. Observing the λ with inflation, we see that the market will accept a lower return of 4.32 for every one unit increase in sensitivity to inflation. This is because the aggregate of investors prefer stocks that offer higher return when inflation goes up. The investor who wanted zero sensitivity to inflation would expect to have a $(−4.32) \times 0.37 = −1.60$ change (decrease) in expected return to obtain the preferred position. Like most of economics, this is not a free lunch. Instead, it is a method of allowing the investor to make specified trade-offs between types of risk and expected returns.[25]

There is one variable in our model that allows the investor to take an action that is very close to a free lunch. Let's reexamine our model. One of the factors, oil price changes, had a zero λ (was given a zero price by the market). While oil prices affect returns on some stocks, changes in oil prices are not a pervasive enough influence to be priced by the market. At first glance, one might think that the sensitivity on a portfolio to oil should be set to zero. After all, why take on a risk (increased variability in returns) with no commensurate increase in expected returns? For the average investor this is correct. However, think of an investor whose cash *outflow* increases with increases in oil prices. Such an investor would want to hold a portfolio of securities that has a positive sensitivity with oil prices. Furthermore,

[23] See Elton and Gruber (1988) for empirical evidence.

[24] An example of the latter occurs in insurance companies, where the realization of gains or losses impacts the surplus account and thus the ability of the firm to write new business.

[25] Deviating from market bs to better match liabilities is different from deviating in order to take active bets on the change in one or more underlying influences. This active use of factor bets will be discussed shortly.

because oil sensitivity is not priced by the market, increasing the sensitivity to oil prices does not change expected return. Of course, if everybody wanted to hold portfolios that exhibited increased return with increases in oil prices, then the λ associated with oil prices would be positive. The fact that an investor desires, with respect to oil sensitivity, a position different from the aggregate allows the investor to improve his or her portfolio with no decrease in expected return, although there will be some increase in total risk.

Keep in mind that matching an index while making quantitative judgments on the amount of a particular type of risk to take can be done only if indexes representing these risks are contained in the multi-index model. Furthermore, the expected return (or expected cost) of these nonaverage risk positions can be determined from only an APT model.

Active Management

Most uses of multi-index models for active management parallel their use in passive management. It's easier to discuss them in reverse order to that presented previously. What a multi-index model does that cannot be done with a single-index model is allow the user to make factor bets. If you believe that unexpected inflation will accelerate at a rate above that anticipated by the market ($I_i > 0$), then you may want to place a bet by increasing your exposure (b value) with inflation. This can be done holding a portfolio with a sensitivity to inflation larger than the S&P index.[26] Obviously the more indexes included in the model, the more active bets you can make. For example, in the Salomon model described earlier in this chapter, you can take active bets on economic growth, the stage of the business cycle, long-term interest rates, short-term interest rates, inflation rates, the value of the U.S. dollar, or the state of the stock market.

Return to the simple model we have been discussing and assume that the S&P index is the appropriate benchmark and that an analyst believed that sales were going to

increase by 1% more than the market expected. The analyst might increase the b value with respect to sales on the portfolio from the 1.71 value found for the S&P index to 2.21. Under the APT model and recognizing that the λ for sales is 1.49, the increase in sales sensitivity of 0.5% would lead to a 0.5(1.49) = 0.745% increase in *expected return*, which is just sufficient to reward the investor for the additional risk. However, the additional 1% increase in sales would lead to an additional 2.21% increase in the return on the portfolio should it materialize. Of this 2.21% increase, 0.5% arose from increasing the sensitivity to sales while 1.71 would have arisen had the b been left at the level of the S&P index. The 0.5% increase is often called the excess risk adjusted return that arises from an ability to forecast factors better than the market.

Multi-index models and APT models can be used just as the single-index model and CAPM models are used to form optimal portfolios building upon estimates of the performance of individual securities. The simplest approach is that where a multi-index model is used to generate the convariance between securities while expected returns and variances are supplied by some combination of analysts' forecasts and historical data.

Another application of APT is to use APT to determine stocks that are under- or overvalued. In this procedure an analyst produces a forecast of the return on a stock. The APT is then used together with estimates of the sensitivity of the stock to the factors to calculate a required return for the stock (using an equation such as 6.10). If the estimated return is above what's required given the stock's sensitivity and the λs, the stock is purchased.

This is a generalization of the analysis that is used when the CAPM rather than the APT is used as an equilibrium model. Recall that the CAPM is a straight line in expected return Beta space (see Figure 5-2). If a firm's expected return and Beta are such that it plots above the CAPM line, it offers a higher return (given its Beta) than is required in equilibrium and is a buy. Similarly, if it plots below the line, its expected return is less than required in equilibrium and it should be sold. The analysis with APT has the same logic. Consider a two-factor APT model. In this case, the APT plots as a plane in a three-dimensional space where the axes are sensitivities to the two factors and expected return. Firms that plot above the plane

---

[26] We assume the S&P index is the relevant benchmark in this section. Actually the analysis holds with the sensitivities of any benchmark (growth stocks or the New York Stock Exchange index) substituted for sensitivities to the S&P index.

offer a higher expected return than is required given the sensitivities and λs and should be purchased.[27]

Why the APT rather than the CAPM? If the APT is the appropriate equilibrium model and the CAPM is used, then stocks with different sensitivities to the factors but the same market Beta will be incorrectly classified as equally risky. The CAPM model incorrectly implies that they have the same expected return.

To better understand this, let's return to the example we have been discussing in this chapter. Note that the lambda on growth is positive. This implies that investors require a higher expected return for stocks that have higher sensitivity to unexpected changes in growth. A stock with a high sensitivity to growth will tend (because growth has a positive price or lambda) to have a higher expected return than a stock with a lower sensitivity to growth. But this is ignored (except for the part captured in the market Beta) by the standard CAPM models. Thus the extra return investors require (as reflected in the market price of risk or lambda associated with high sensitivity to growth) will be interpreted as underpricing by the standard CAPM model. Stocks that are very sensitive to unexpected changes in growth will tend to lie above the security market line. Stocks that are sensitive to other priced influences not included in the single-index model are likely to show up as systematically underpriced or overpriced by the CAPM and to lie above or below the security market line.

One of the most common uses of the APT model is to form a portfolio of stocks that while closely tracking a target will also produce a return in excess of that index. One way to implement this type of procedure is simply to employ the index-matching procedure described earlier in this chapter but only allow selection from among a set of stocks that analysts have earmarked as superior performers. Other techniques use either numeric discrete ranking of stocks or expected return on stocks in an attempt to produce an excess return above an index while using the multi-index model to track an index as closely as possible.[28] Portfolios

designed this way have become known as *research tilted index funds.* Although some additional risk is involved (the index can't be matched as closely when selecting from a restricted set of stocks), investors who use this technique feel that an excess return can be earned with only a slight loss in the ability to track the index. The advantage of the multi-index model over the simple-index model is that the target index can be tracked more closely because the different sources of risk are explicitly taken into consideration.

The more the target being tracked differs from a diversified market portfolio, the more important it is to use a multi-index model. The extreme case and one that has received a lot of attention is the long-short investment strategy or risk-neutral strategy. If one has superior ability to identify stocks that will perform above average on an APT risk-adjusted basis and stocks that will perform below average on an APT risk-adjusted basis, then using the APT index, one can form portfolios that offer an excess return and have no risk (zero *b* risk) with respect to any factor (e.g., no risk due to change in the market level, inflation, or interest rate movements). Obviously there is also no expected return due to any factor because the Beta on each factor is set to zero. What one gets is a pure payoff from security selection with all factors including the market neutralized. We can examine this by returning to Equation (6.11). If we believe that an analyst can predict the extra return from any security over a period of time (return from security selection), Equation (6.11) can be written as

$$R_i = R_F + \alpha_i + \lambda_1 b_{i1} + \lambda_2 b_{i2} + \lambda_3 b_{i3} +$$
$$\cdots + b_{i1}I_1 + b_{i2}I_2 + b_{i3}I_3 + \cdots + e_i$$

where α_i is the extra return the security analyst predicts on security i.

Think of this equation for each of two portfolios: portfolio L is a portfolio of long positions and portfolio S is a portfolio of short positions. Furthermore, assume that the portfolios are formed so that $b_{Lj} + b_{Sj} = 0$ for all js. Then, combining the preceding equation for each of the two portfolios, we get a risk-neutral (or more specifically systematic-risk-neutral) portfolio denoted by N with a return given by

$$R_N = R_F + \alpha_L + \alpha_S$$

---

[27] The market prices of risk (λs) for the CAPM or APT models can be specified by theory or estimated using analysts' forecasts of expected return and sensitivities for a set of stocks.

[28] Many firms have their analysts place stocks into groups (often five) with group 1 being the best purchases and group 5 the stocks that should be sold.

and with a risk given by

$$e_N = e_L + e_S$$

Burmeister, Roll, and Ross (1994) examined the payoff from such a model from the period April 1991 to March 1992, assuming αs could be correctly identified. They found that over this period the S&P index had a return of 11.57% per year and a standard deviation of 18.08%. Their factor-neutral portfolio had a return of 30.04% per year and a standard deviation of 6.26% per year. While these are obviously optimistic figures, for they assume perfect foresight, they do indicate the ability of factor-neutral portfolios to lower risk and, if forecasting ability exists, increase return.

Although one can perform the same type of analysis with a single-index model rather than a multi-index model, the overall risks of the portfolio will be greater and the user likely to find he or she is undertaking factor bets (inflation, interest rate, etc.) rather than pure security selection bets.

Performance Measurement and Attribution

The last use of multi-index and APT models we should examine is in the area of portfolio performance evaluation. It is difficult to discuss the use of APT in performance measurement and evaluation without reviewing the whole literature in this area. However, consideration of the model we have discussed shows that the expected performance of any portfolio is not just a function of the portfolio's sensitivity to the market but also a function of the portfolio's sensitivity to sales growth and inflation. If influences that enter the return-generating process and APT are ignored in doing performance evaluation, not only can't the analyst's performance be attributed to the type of management decisions he or she is making, but perhaps more important, incorrect conclusions may be reached about how well managers are performing.

CONCLUSION

In this chapter, we have reviewed

1. modern concepts of arbitrage pricing,
2. alternative approaches to estimating arbitrage pricing models,
3. some uses of arbitrage pricing models.

Considerable evidence continues to be produced on the usefulness of arbitrage pricing models.

APPENDIX A

A Simple Example of Factor Analysis

In order to provide the reader who has never used any form of factor analysis with a demonstration of how it works, we include a simple example in this appendix. We choose to use principal component analysis for the example, because this leads to a solution that is easiest to interpret.[29]

We choose 10 years of monthly data on the Morgan Stanley Capital International stock indexes for each of four countries: the United States, Canada, France, and Belgium. Remember that principal components analysis extracts from this data the index that explains as much as possible of the correlation in returns between the four countries and then finds a second index that explains as much as possible of the correlation in returns not explained by the first index.[30] The indexes produced by principal components are formed by combining (weighting) the time series of return for each country with the mean return for each country extracted.

Before we perform principal component analysis, let's think about what we would expect the results to look like. We might hypothesize that the first index would be some sort of measure of how stocks in general did, that is, some general aggregation of the returns under study. In thinking about the problem, one would expect Canada and the United States to act somewhat alike and France and Belgium to act somewhat alike, whereas we would expect the differences between these paired countries to be greater. In fact, the correlations between the four countries as shown in Table 6-2 bear out this speculation.

The indexes that are the first two principal components estimated from this data are presented below. Remember that in performing principal components analysis, we do not specify the indexes we expect to find; we simply let the data determine the indexes.

---

[29] See Elton and Gruber (1994) for a detailed discussion on the use of factor analysis in multi-index models.

[30] Principal components then extract a third and fourth index. In this case, we report only the first two, since the third and fourth are not statistically significant.

TABLE 6-2 Correlation Coefficient Between
Returns in Four Countries

	Belgium	France	Canada	U.S.
Belgium	1.0			
France	0.65	1.0		
Canada	0.38	0.41	1.0	
United States	0.41	0.43	0.72	1.0

The indexes are

$$I_{1t} = 0.67\left(R_{Bt} - \bar{R}_B\right) + 0.76\left(R_{Ft} - \bar{R}_F\right)$$
$$+ 0.76\left(R_{ct} - \bar{R}_c\right) + 0.77\left(R_{ut} - \bar{R}_u\right)$$
$$I_{2t} = -0.40\left(R_{Bt} - \bar{R}_B\right) - 0.37\left(R_{Ft} - \bar{R}_F\right)$$
$$+ 0.73\left(R_{ct} - \bar{R}_c\right) + 0.41\left(R_{ut} - \bar{R}_u\right)$$

where

I_{1t} and I_{2t} are the two indexes extracted from the data.
The Rs are monthly returns, and the subscripts B, C, F, U, and t represent Belgium, Canada, France, United States, and time.

Note that the first index is very close to an equally weighted index of all four markets and thus meets our expectation that the index that would explain as much as possible of returns is the general return index. The second index is long in North America and short in Europe. It meets our expectation that the second index should capture the fact that North American and European markets are less associated with each other than with markets within their own region.

To see how well these two indexes work, we can regress the returns from each country against the two indexes. When we did so, the R^2 were 0.81 for Belgium, 0.95 for Canada, 0.84 for France, and 0.74 for the United States.

APPENDIX B

Specification of the APT with an Unobserved Market Factor

This appendix is a brief recapping of the procedures put forth in a series of articles by Burmeister, McElroy, and others. For further details see (1987, 1988, 1986) and (1988).

We can represent a return-generating process (multi-index model) with observable indices plus an unobservable index designated by index k as

$$R_{it} = \bar{R}_{it} + \sum_{j=1}^{J} b_{ij}F_{jt} + b_{ik}F_{kt} + \varepsilon_{it} \tag{B.1}$$

Making the no-arbitrage assumption of APT, expected return is approximately given by

$$\bar{R}_{it} = \lambda_{0t} + \sum_{j=1}^{J} b_{ij}\lambda_{jt} + b_{ik}\lambda_{kt} \tag{B.2}$$

We will make the assumption of McElroy and Burmeister (1988) that all λ_{ot} equal the risk-free rate and all other λs are constant over time, substituting (B.2) into (B.1).

$$R_{it} = R_{Ft} + \sum_{j=1}^{J} b_{ij}\lambda_j + \sum_{j=1}^{J} b_{ij}F_{jt} + b_{ik}\lambda_k + b_{ik}F_{kt} + \varepsilon_{it} \tag{B.3}$$

Now assume a very well-diversified portfolio called m. For this portfolio residual risk approaches zero and[31]

$$R_{mt} = \lambda_m + R_{Ft} + \sum_{i=1}^{J} b_{mj}F_{jt} + F_{kt} \tag{B.4}$$

where $\lambda_m = \sum_{j=1}^{J} b_{mj}\lambda_j + \lambda_k$

Burmeister and McElroy assume the market portfolio has no residual risk $\varepsilon_{mt} = 0$; this F_{kt} is the unobserved error term.

However, F_{kt} can be estimated by the residual of an ordinary least squares (OLS) time-series regression of R_{mt} on the observed variables as in Equation (B.4), or rearranging (B.4) yields

$$\hat{F}_{kt} = \left(R_{mt} - R_{Ft}\right) - \left[\lambda_m + \sum_{j=1}^{J} b_{mj}F_{jt}\right] \tag{B.5}$$

McElroy and Burmeister (1988) show that $\hat{F}_{kt}$ is an unbiased estimate of the common stocks F_{kt}. Thus substituting $\hat{F}_{kt}$ for F_{kt} in (B.3) and adjusting the residual yields

$$R_{it} = R_{Ft} + \sum_{j=1}^{J} b_{ij}\lambda_j + b_{ik}\lambda_k + \sum_{j=1}^{J} b_{ij}F_{jt} + b_{ik}\hat{F}_{kt} + e_{it} \tag{B.6}$$

To estimate this equation McElroy and Burmeister (1988) first use time-series analysis to estimate Equations (B.4

---

[31] The assumption is made that the unobserved variable F_{kt} is recalled to have a Beta of one with the portfolio m.

and B.5) and then nonlinear seemingly unrelated regressions to estimate (B.6).[32]

In doing so, they make one more interesting change in this model. They allow for the possibility that although APT correctly prices every security in their sample, it may not correctly price every security in the highly diversified portfolio.

QUESTIONS AND PROBLEMS

1. Assume that the following two-index model describes returns:

$$R_i = a_i + b_{i1}I_1 + b_{i2}I_2 + e_i$$

Assume that the following three portfolios are observed.

Portfolio	Expected Return	b_{i1}	b_{i2}
A	12.0	1	0.5
B	13.4	3	0.2
C	12.0	3	−0.5

Find the equation of the plane that must describe equilibrium returns.

2. Referring to the results of Problem 1, illustrate the arbitrage opportunities that would exist if a portfolio called D with the following properties were observed.

$$\bar{R}_D = 10 \quad b_{D1} = 2 \quad b_{D2} = 0$$

3. Repeat Problem 1 if the three portfolios observed have the following characteristics.

Portfolio	Expected Return	b_{i1}	b_{i2}
A	12	1.0	1
B	13	1.5	2
C	17	0.5	−3

4. Referring to the results of Problem 3, illustrate the arbitrage opportunities that would exist if a portfolio called D with the following characteristics were observed.

$$\bar{R}_D = 15 \quad b_{D1} = 1 \quad b_{D2} = 0$$

---

[32] Conditions on the relationship between e_{it} and ε_{it} are delineated in McElroy and Burmeister (1988).

5. If we accept the Sharpe model as a description of expected returns, using the data in Table 6-1 find the expected return on a stock in the construction industry with the following characteristics. Assume a riskless rate of 8%.

Beta = 1.2

Yield = 6

Size = 0.4

Bond Beta = 0.2

Alpha = 1

6. Return to Problem 1. If $(\bar{R}_M - R_F) = 4$, find the values for the following variables that would make the expected returns from Problem 1 consistent with equilibrium deter mined by the simple (Sharpe–Lintner–Mossin) CAPM.

   A. $\beta_{\lambda1}$ and $\beta_{\lambda2}$

   B. β_P for each of the three portfolios

   C. R_F

BIBLIOGRAPHY

1. Admati, Anat, and Pfleiderer, Paul. "Interpreting the Factor Risk Premia in Arbitrage Pricing Theory," *Journal of Economic Theory*, **35** (Feb. 1985), pp. 191–195.

2. Berry, Michael, Burmeister, Edwin, and McElroy, Marjorie. "Sorting Out Risks Using Known APT Factors," *Financial Analysts Journal* (March 1988), pp. 29–42.

3. Black, F. "Capital Market Equilibrium with Restricted Borrowing," *Journal of Business*, **45** (July 1972), pp. 444–454.

4. Black, Fisher, Jensen, Nick, and Scholes, Myron. "The Capital Asset Pricing Model: Some Empirical Tests," in M. Jensen (ed.), *Studies in the Theory of Capital Markets* (New York: Praeger, 1972).

5. Blake, Christopher, Elton, Edwin J., and Gruber, Martin J. "The Performance of Bond Mutual Funds," *Journal of Business*, **66,** No. 3 (July 1993), pp. 371–403.

6. Bower, Dorothy H., Bower, Richard S., and Logue, Dennis E. "Arbitrage Pricing Theory and Utility Stock Returns," *The Journal of Finance*, **39,** No. 4 (Sept. 1984), pp. 1041–1054.

7. Brennan, M. "Capital Asset Pricing and the Structure of Security Returns," Working Paper, University of British Columbia, 1971.

8. ——. "Discussion," *Journal of Finance*, **36** (May 1981), pp. 352–357.

9. Brown, S. J., and Weinstein, M. I. "A New Approach to Testing Asset Pricing Models: The Bilinear Paradigm," *Journal of Finance*, **38,** No. 3 (June 1983).

10. Burmeister, Edwin, and McElroy, Marjorie. "APT and Multifactor Asset Pricing Models with Measured and Unobserved Factors: Theoretical and Econometric Issues," Discussion Paper, Department of Economics, University of Virginia and Duke University, 1987.

11. Burmeister, Edwin, and McElroy, Marjorie. "Joint Estimation of Factor Sensitivities and Risk Premia for the Arbitrage Pricing Theory," *Journal of Finance*, **43,** No. 3 (July 1988), pp. 721–733.

12. Burmeister, Edwin, and Wall, Kent. "The Arbitrage Pricing Theory and Macroeconomic Factor Measures," *The Financial Review* (Feb. 1986).

13. Burmeister, Edwin, Roll, Richard, and Ross, Stephen, "A Practitioner's Guide to Arbitrage Pricing Theory," in *A Practitioner's Guide to Factor Models* (Charlottesville, VA: The Research Foundation of the Institute of Chartered Financial Analysts, 1994).

14. Burmeister, Edwin, Wall, Kent, and Hamilton, James. "Estimation of Unobserved Expected Monthly Inflation Using Kalman Filtering," *Journal of Business and Economic Statistics*, **4** (April 1986), pp. 147–160.

15. Chamberlain, G., and Rothschild, M. "Arbitrage, Factor Structure, and Mean-Variance Analysis on Large Asset Markets," Working Paper, University of Wisconsin at Madison, 1981.

16. Chamberlain, Gary. "Funds, Factors and Diversification in Arbitrage Pricing Models," *Econometrica*, **51** (Sept. 1983), pp. 1305–1323.

17. Chan, K. C, Chen, Nai-fu, and Hsiech, David. "An Explanatory Investigation of the Firm Size Effect," *Journal of Financial Economics*, **14** (Sept. 1985), pp. 451–471.

18. Chen, N. "The Arbitrage Pricing Theory: Estimation and Applications," Working Paper, Graduate School of Management, UCLA, 1981.

19. Chen, Nai-fu. "Some Empirical Tests of the Theory of Arbitrage Pricing," *The Journal of Finance*, **38,** No. 5 (Dec. 1983), pp. 1393–1414.

20. Chen, Nai-fu, and Ingersoll, Jonathan E., Jr. "Exact Pricing in Linear Factor Models with Finitely Many Assets: A Note," *The Journal of Finance*, **38,** No. 3 (June 1983), pp. 985–988.

21. Chen, Nai-fu, Roll, Richard, and Ross, Stephen. "Economic Forces and the Stock Market," *Journal of Business*, **59** (July 1986), pp. 386–403.

22. Cho, D. Chinhyung. "On Testing the Arbitrage Pricing Theory: Inter-Battery Factor Analysis," *The Journal of Finance*, **39,** No. 5 (Dec. 1984), pp. 1485–1502.

23. ———. "Some Fundamental Factors Effecting Asset Prices," Working Paper, University of Wisconsin, 1984.

24. Cho, D. Chinhyung, and Taylor, William. "The Seasonal Stability of the Factor Structure of Stock Returns," *Journal of Finance*, **42** (Dec. 1987), pp. 1195–1211.

25. Cho, D. Chinhyung, Elton, Edwin J., and Gruber, Martin J. "On the Robustness of the Roll and Ross Arbitrage Pricing Theory," *Journal of Financial and Quantitative Analysis*, **XIX,** No. 1 (March 1984), pp. 1–10.

26. Cho, D. Chinhyung, Eun, Cheol S., and Senbet, Lemma W. "International Arbitrage Pricing Theory: An Empirical Investigation," *The Journal of Finance*, **41,** No. 2 (June 1986), pp. 313–329.

27. Cochrane, John H. "Production-Based Asset Pricing and the Link between Stock Returns and Economic Fluctuations," *The Journal of Finance*, **46,** No. 1 (Mar. 1991), pp. 209–237.

28. Connor, G. "A Factor Pricing Theory for Capital Assets," Working Paper, Kellog Graduate School of Management, Northwestern University, 1981.

29. Connor, Gregory. "A Unified Beta Pricing Theory," *Journal of Economic Theory*, **34,** No. 3 (Oct. 1984), pp. 13–31.

30. Connor, G., and Korajczyk, R. "Performance Measurement with the Arbitrage Pricing Theory: A New Framework for Analysis," *Journal of Financial Economics*, **15,** No. 3 (1986), pp. 373–394.

31. Conway, Delores, and Reinganum, Marc. "Capital Market Factor Structure: Identification through Cross Validation," *Journal of Business and Financial Statistics*, **6,** No. 1 (Jan. 1988).

32. Dhrymes, Pheobus J., Friend, Irwin, and Gultekin, N. Bulent. "A Critical Reexamination of the Empirical Evidence on the Arbitrage Pricing Theory," *The Journal of Finance*, **39,** No. 2 (June 1984), pp. 323–346.

33. Dybvig, Phillip H. "An Explicit Bound on Deviations from APT Pricing in a Finite Economy," *Journal of Financial Economics*, **12** (1983), pp. 483–496.

34. Elton, E., and Gruber, M. "Non-Standard CAPMs and the Market Portfolio," Working Paper, New York University, Graduate School of Business, 1982.

35. Elton, Edwin J., and Gruber, Martin J. "A Multi-index Risk Model of the Japanese Stock Market," *Japan and the World Economy* **1,** No. 1 (1988).

36. Elton, Edwin J., and Gruber, Martin J. "Expectational Data and Japanese Stock Prices," *Japan and the World Economy*, **1** (1989), pp. 391–401.

37. Elton, Edwin J., and Gruber, Martin J. "Multi-Index Models Using Simultaneous Estimation of all Parameters." In *A Practitioner's Guide to Factor Models*, (The Research Foundation of the Institute of Chartered Financial Analysts, Charlottesville, Va., 1994), pp. 31–58.

38. Elton, Edwin J., Gruber, Martin J., and Blake, Christopher. "Fundamental Variables, APT, and Bond Fund Performance," Working Paper, New York University, 1994.

39. Elton, Edwin J., Gruber, Martin J., and Mei, Jianping. "Cost of Capital Using Arbitrage Pricing Theory: A Case Study of Nine New York Utilities." In *Estimating the Cost of Capital: Methods and Practice, Journal of Financial Markets, Institutions & Instruments*, **3,** No. 3, Blackwell Publishers (1994).

40. Elton, Edwin J., Gruber, Martin J., and Rentzler, Joel. "The Arbitrage Pricing Model and Returns on Assets Under Uncertain Inflation," *The Journal of Finance*, **38,** No. 2 (May 1983), pp. 525–538.

41. Elton, Edwin J., Gruber, Martin J., Das, Sanjiv, and Hlavka, Matthew. "Efficiency with Costly Information: A Reinterpretation of Evidence from Managed Portfolios," *Review of Financial Studies*, **6,** No. 1 (1993), pp. 1–22.

42. Fama, Eugene. "Stock Returns, Real Activity, Inflation and Money," *American Economic Review*, **71** (1981), pp. 545–565.

43. Fama, Eugene, and French, Kenneth. "The Cross Section of Expected Stock Returns," *The Journal of Finance*, **47,** No. 2 (June 1992), pp. 427–466.

44. Fama, Eugene, and French, Kenneth. "Common Factors in the Returns on Bonds and Stocks," Working Paper, Center for Research in Security Prices, University of Chicago, 1993.

45. Fama, Eugene, and Gibbons, Michael. "A Comparison of Inflation Forecasts," *Journal of Monetary Economics*, **13** (1984), pp. 327–348.

46. Fama, Eugene, and MacBeth, James. "Risk, Return, and Equilibrium: Empirical Tests," *Journal of Political Economy*, **38** (1973), pp. 607–636.

47. Fogler, H. Russell, John, Kose, and Tipton, James. "Three Factors Interest Rate Differentials and Stock Groups," *The Journal of Finance*, **36,** No. 2 (May 1981), pp. 323–336.

48. Garman, Mark B., and Ohlson, James A. "A Dynamic Equilibrium for the Ross Arbitrage Model." *The Journal of Finance*, **35,** No. 3 (June 1980), pp. 675–684.

49. Gehr, A., Jr. "Some Tests of the Arbitrage Pricing Theory," *Journal of the Midwest Finance Association* (1975), pp. 91–105.

50. Gibbons, M. "Multivariate Tests of Financial Models: A New Approach," *Journal of Financial Economics*, **10,** No. 1 (March 1982), pp. 3–27.

51. Gibbons, M.R. "Empirical Examination of the Return Generating Process of the Arbitrage Pricing Theory," Working Paper, Stanford University, 1981.

52. Grinblatt, Mark, and Titman, Sheridan. "Factor Pricing in a Finite Economy," *Journal of Financial Economics*, **12** (1983), pp. 497–507.

53. ——. "Approximate Factor Structures: Interpretations and Implications for Empirical Tests," *Journal of Finance*, **40** (1985), pp. 1367–1373.

54. ——. "The Relation Between Mean-Variance Efficiency and Arbitrage Pricing," *Journal of Business*, **60** (1987), pp. 97–113.

55. Grinold, Richard and Kahn, Ronald. "Multi-Factor Models for Portfolio Risk," in *A Practitioner's Guide to Factor Models*, (Charlottesville, Va.: The Research Foundation of the Institute of Chartered Financial Analysts, 1994).

56. Gultekin, Mustafa, and Gultekin, N. Bulent. "Stock Return Anomalies and Tests of the APT," *Journal of Finance*, **42** (Dec. 1987), pp. 1213–1224.

57. Hansen, Lars, and Singleton, Kenneth. "Stochastic Consumption, Risk Aversion, and the Temporal Behavior of Assets Returns," *Journal of Political Economy*, **91** (1983), pp. 249–265.

58. Harman, H. *Modern Factor Analysis*, third edition (Chicago: University of Chicago Press, 1976).

59. Huberman, Gur. "A Simple Approach to Arbitrage Pricing Theory," *Journal of Economic Theory*, **78** (1982), pp. 183–191.

60. ——. "A Review of the Arbitrage Pricing Theory," in Eatwell; John, Milgate, Murray, and Newman, Peter (eds.), *The New Palgrave: A Dictionary of Economic Theory and Doctrine* (New York: Stockton Press, 1987).

61. Huberman, Gur, and Kandel, Shmuel. "Mean-Variance Spanning," *The Journal of Finance*, **42,** No. 4 (Sept. 1987), pp. 873–888.

62. ——. "Mean-Variance Spanning," *Journal of Finance*, **42** (Sept. 1987), pp. 873–888.

63. Huberman, Gur, and Stambaugh, Robert. "Mimicking Portfolios and Exact Arbitrage Pricing," *Journal of Finance*, **42** (March 1987), pp. 1–9.

64. Huberman, Gur, Kandel, Shmuel, and Stambaugh, Robert F. "Mimicking Portfolios and Exact Arbitrage Pricing," *The Journal of Finance*, **42,** No. 1 (Mar. 1987), pp. 1–9.

65. Hughes, P. "A Test of the Arbitrage Pricing Theory," Working Paper, University of British Columbia, 1981.

66. Ibbotson, Roger, and Sinquefield, Rex. *Stocks, Bonds, Bills and Inflation: The Past and the Future* (Charlottesville, Va.: Financial Analysts Research Foundation, 1982).

67. Ikeda, Shinsuke. "Arbitrage Asset Pricing Under Exchange Risk," *The Journal of Finance*, **46,** No. 1 (Mar. 1991), pp. 447–455.

68. Ingersoll, Jonathan E., Jr. "Some Results in the Theory of Arbitrage Pricing," *Journal of Finance*, **39** (1984), pp. 1021–1039.

69. ——. *Theory of Financial Decision Making*. Totowa, N.J.: Rowman and Littlefield (1987).

70. Jobson, J.D. "A Multivariate Linear Regression Test for the Arbitrage Pricing Theory," *The Journal of Finance*, **37,** No. 4 (Sept. 1982), pp. 1037–1042.

71. Joreskog, K.G. *Statistical Estimation in Factor Analysis* (Stockholm: Almqvist & Wiksell, 1963).

72. Joreskog, K.G. "Some Contributions to Maximum Likelihood Factor Analysis," *Psychometrika*, **32,** No. 4 (Dec. 1967), pp. 443–482.

73. Joreskog, K.G. "Factor Analysis by Least Squares and Maximum Likelihood Methods," in K. Enslein, A. Ralston, and H.S. Wilf (eds.), *Statistical Methods of Digital Computers* (New York: John Wiley & Sons, 1977).

74. King, B. "Market and Industry Factors in Stock Price Behavior," *Journal of Business*, **39** (Jan. 1966), pp. 139–190.

75. Kristof, W. "Orthogonal Inter-Battery Factor Analysis," *Psychometrika*, **32,** No. 2 (June 1967), pp. 199–227.

76. Kryzanowski, L., and To, M.C. "General Factor Models and the Structure of Security Returns," *Journal of Financial and Quantitative Analysis*, **18,** No. 1 (March 1983), pp. 31–37.

77. Lawley, D.N. "The Estimation of Factor Loadings by the Method of Maximum Likelihood," *Proceedings of the Royal Society of Edinburgh, Section A*, **60** (1940), pp. 64–82.

78. Lawley, D.N., and Maxwell, M.A. *Factor Analysis as a Statistical Method* (London, U.K.: Butterworths, 1963).

79. Lehmann, Bruce, and Modest, David. "The Empirical Foundations of the Arbitrage Pricing Theory I: The Empirical Tests," *Journal of Financial Economics*, **21** (1988), pp. 213–254.

80. Levine, M.S. *Canonical Analysis and Factor Comparison* (Beverly Hills, Calif.: Sage Publications, 1977).

81. Lintner, J. "The Valuation of Risk Assets and the Selection of Risky Investments in Stock Portfolios and Capital Budgets," *Review of Economics and Statistics*, **47** (Feb. 1965), pp. 13–37.

82. Litzenberger, R. H., and Ramaswamy, K. "The Effect of Personal Taxes and Dividends on Capital Asset Prices: Theory and Empirical Evidence," *Journal of Financial Economics*, **7** (1979), pp. 163–196.

83. Lucas, Robert E., Jr. "Asset Prices in an Exchange Economy," *Econometrica*, **46** (1978), pp. 1429–1445.

84. McElroy, Marjorie, and Burmeister, Edwin. "Arbitrage Pricing Theory as a Restricted Nonlinear Multivariate Regression Model: ITNLSUR Estimates," *Journal of Business and Economic Statistics*, **VI,** No. 1 (Jan. 1988), pp. 29–42.

85. McElroy, Marjorie, and Wall, Kent. "Two Estimators for the APT Model When Factors Are Measured," *Economics Letters*, **19** (1985), pp. 271–275.

86. Merton, Robert C. "An Intertemporal Capital Asset Pricing Model," *Econometrica*, **41** (1973), pp. 867–887.

87. Morrison, D. F. *Multivariate Statistical Methods* (New York: McGraw-Hill, 1976).

88. Mossin, J. "Equilibrium in a Capital Asset Market," *Econometrika*, **34** (Oct. 1966), pp. 768–783.

89. Neyman, J., and Pearson, E.S. "On the Use and Interpretation of Certain Test Criteria for Purposes of Statistical Inferences," *Biometrika*, **20A** (1928), pp. 175–240, 263–294.

90. Ohlson, James, and Garman, Mark. "A Dynamic Equilibrium for the Ross Arbitrage Model," *Journal of Finance*, **35** (1980), pp. 675–684.

91. Oldfield, George S., Jr., and Rogalski, Richard J. "Treasury Bill Factors and Common Stock Returns," *The Journal of Finance*, **36,** No. 2 (May 1981), pp. 337–349.

92. Pallmann, Nils. "Recent Empirical Tests of the APT and the Consumption-Based CAPM," Discussion Paper, Department of Finance, New York University, 1989.

93. Pastor, Luxos. "Comparing Asset Pricing Models: An Investment Perspective," *Journal of Financial Economics*, **56,** No. 3 (June 2000), p. 335.

94. Reinganum, M. "The Arbitrage Pricing Theory: Some Empirical Results," *Journal of Finance*, **36** (May 1981), pp. 313–321.

95. Roll, R. "A Critique of the Asset Pricing Theory's Tests," *Journal of Financial Economics*, **4** (May 1977), pp. 129–176.

96. Roll, R. "Ambiguity When Performance Is Measured by the Securities Market Line," *Journal of Finance*, **33** (Sept. 1978), pp. 1051–1069.

97. Roll, R., and Ross, S. A. "An Empirical Investigation of the Arbitrage Pricing Theory," *Journal of Finance*, **35,** No. 5 (Dec. 1980), pp. 1073–1103.

98. Roll, Richard, and Ross, Stephen A. "A Critical Reexamination of the Empirical Evidence on the Arbitrage Pricing Theory: A Reply," *The Journal of Finance*, **39,** No. 2 (June 1984), pp. 347–350.

99. Ross, S.A. "The Arbitrage Theory of Capital Asset Pricing," *Journal of Economic Theory*, **13** (Dec. 1976), pp. 341–360.

100. ———. "Return Risk, and Arbitrage," in Irwin Friend and James L. Bicksler (eds.), *Risk and Return in Finance*, Vol. 1 (Cambridge, Mass.: Ballinger, 1977).

101. Rubinstein, M. "The Valuation of Uncertain Income Streams and the Pricing of Options," *Bell Journal of Economics*, 7 (1976), pp. 407–425.

102. Shanken, J. "The Arbitrage Pricing Theory: Is It Testable?" *Journal of Finance*, **37,** No. 5 (Dec. 1982), pp. 1129–1140.

103. ———. "Multi-Beta CAPM or Equilibrium-APT? A Reply," *Journal of Finance*, **40** (1985a), pp. 1186–1189.

104. ———. "Multivariate Tests of the Zero-Beta CAPM," *Journal of Financial Economics*, **14** (Sept. 1985), pp. 327–348.

105. Sharpe, W. "Capital Asset Prices: A Theory of Market Equilibrium under Conditions of Risk," *Journal of Finance*, **19** (Sept. 1964), pp. 425–442.

106. ——. "Factors in NYSE Security Returns, 1931–1979," *Journal of Portfolio Management*, **8,** No. 2 (Summer 1982), pp. 5–19.

107. Shukla, Ravi, and Trzcinka, Charles. "Sequential Tests of the Arbitrage Pricing Theory: A Comparison of Principal Components and Maximum Likelihood Factors," *The Journal of Finance*, **45,** No. 5 (Dec. 1990), pp. 1541–1564.

108. Sinclair, N.A. "Security Return Data and 'Blind' Factor Analysis," Working Paper, Australian Graduate School of Management, 1981.

109. Solnik, Bruno. "International Arbitrage Pricing Theory," *The Journal of Finance*, **38,** No. 2 (May 1983), pp. 449–458.

110. Sorensen, Eric, Mezrich, Joseph, and Thum Chee. "The Salomon Brothers U.S. Stock Risk Attribute Model." Published by The Salomon Brothers (Oct. 1989).

111. Sorensen, Eric, Salomon, R. S., Davenport, Caroline, and Fiore, Maria. Risk Analysis: The Effect of Key Macroeconomic and Market Factors on Portfolio Returns. Published by The Salomon Brothers (Nov. 1989).

112. Stambaugh, Robert. "On the Exclusion of Assets from Tests of the Two-Parameter Model," *Journal of Financial Economics*, **10** (Nov. 1982), pp. 237–268.

113. ——. "Testing the CAPM with Broader Market Indexes: A Problem of Mean Deficiency," *Journal of Banking and Finance*, **7** (March 1985), pp. 5–16.

114. Tiemann, Jonathan. "Exact Arbitrage Pricing and the Minimum-Variance Frontier," *The Journal of Finance*, **43,** No. 2 (June 1988), pp. 327–338.

115. Trzcinka, Charles. "On the Number of Factors in the Arbitrage Pricing Model," *The Journal of Finance*, **41,** No. 2 (June 1986), pp. 347–368.

Applying the CAPM to Performance Measurement

7

Excerpt is Chapter 4, Section 4.2 of Portfolio Theory and Performance Analysis, *by Noel Amenc and Veronique Le Sourd.*

Learning Objectives

After completing this reading, FRM Candidates should be able to:

- Calculate, compare, and evaluate the Treynor measure, the Sharpe measure, and Jensen's alpha.
- Compute and interpret tracking error, the information ratio, and the Sortino ratio.

- Explain the Morningstar Rating System, VaR based, and management related risk-adjusted return measures.

APPLYING THE CAPM TO PERFORMANCE MEASUREMENT: SINGLE-INDEX PERFORMANCE MEASUREMENT INDICATORS[1]

When we presented the methods for calculating the return on a portfolio or investment fund, we noted that the return value on its own was not a sufficient criterion for appreciating the performance and that it was necessary to associate a measure of the risk taken. Risk is an essential part of the investment. It can differ considerably from one portfolio to another. In addition, it is liable to evolve over time. Modern portfolio theory and the CAPM have established the link that exists between the risk and return of an investment quantitatively. More specifically, these theories highlighted the notion of rewarding risk. Therefore, we now possess the elements necessary for calculating indicators while taking both risk and return into account.

The first indicators developed came from portfolio theory and the CAPM. They are therefore more specifically related to equity portfolios. They enable a risk-adjusted performance value to be calculated. It is thus possible to compare the performance of funds with different levels of risk, while the return alone only enabled comparisons between funds with the same level of risk.

This section describes the different indicators and specifies, for each, their area of use. It again involves elementary measures because the risk is considered globally. We will see later on that the risk can be broken down into several areas, enabling a more thorough analysis.

The Treynor Measure

The Treynor (1965) ratio is defined by

$$T_P = \frac{E(R_P) - R_F}{\beta_P}$$

where

$E(R_P)$ denotes the expected return of the portfolio;

R_F denotes the return on the risk-free asset; and

β_P denotes the beta of the portfolio.

---

[1] On this subject, the interested reader could consult Broquet and van den Berg (1992), Elton and Gruber (1995), Fabozzi (1995), Grandin (1998), Jacquillat and Solnik (1997), and Gallais-Hamonno and Grandin (1999).

This indicator measures the relationship between the return on the portfolio, above the risk-free rate, and its systematic risk. This ratio is drawn directly from the CAPM. By rearranging the terms, the CAPM relationship for a portfolio is written as follows:

$$\frac{E(R_P) - R_F}{\beta_P} = E(R_M) - R_F$$

The term on the left is the Treynor ratio for the portfolio, and the term on the right can be seen as the Treynor ratio for the market portfolio, since the beta of the market portfolio is 1 by definition. Comparing the Treynor ratio for the portfolio with the Treynor ratio for the market portfolio enables us to check whether the portfolio risk is sufficiently rewarded.

The Treynor ratio is particularly appropriate for appreciating the performance of a welldiversified portfolio, since it only takes the systematic risk of the portfolio into account, i.e. the share of the risk that is not eliminated by diversification. It is also for that reason that the Treynor ratio is the most appropriate indicator for evaluating the performance of a portfolio that only constitutes a part of the investor's assets. Since the investor has diversified his investments, the systematic risk of his portfolio is all that matters.

Calculating this indicator requires a reference index to be chosen to estimate the beta of the portfolio. The results can then depend heavily on that choice, a fact that has been criticised by Roll. We shall return to this point at the end of the chapter.

The Sharpe Measure

Sharpe (1966) defined this ratio as the reward-to-variability ratio, but it was soon called the Sharpe ratio in articles that mentioned it. It is defined by

$$S_P = \frac{E(R_P) - R_F}{\sigma(R_P)}$$

where

$E(R_P)$ denotes the expected return of the portfolio;

R_F denotes the return on the risk-free asset; and

$\sigma(R_P)$ denotes the standard deviation of the portfolio returns.

This ratio measures the excess return, or risk premium, of a portfolio compared with the risk-free rate, compared, this time, with the total risk of the portfolio, measured by its standard deviation. It is drawn from the capital market line. The equation of this line, which was presented at the beginning of the chapter, can be written as follows:

$$\frac{E(R_P) - R_F}{\sigma(R_P)} = \frac{E(R_M) - R_F}{\sigma(R_M)}$$

This relationship indicates that, at equilibrium, the Sharpe ratio of the portfolio to be evaluated and the Sharpe ratio of the market portfolio are equal. The Sharpe ratio actually corresponds to the slope of the market line. If the portfolio is well diversified, then its Sharpe ratio will be close to that of the market. By comparing the Sharpe ratio of the managed portfolio and the Sharpe ratio of the market portfolio, the manager can check whether the expected return on the portfolio is sufficient to compensate for the additional share of total risk that he is taking.

Since this measure is based on the total risk, it enables the relative performance of portfolios that are not very diversified to be evaluated, because the unsystematic risk taken by the manager is included in this measure. This measure is also suitable for evaluating the performance of a portfolio that represents an individual's total investment.

The Sharpe ratio is widely used by investment firms for measuring portfolio performance. The index is drawn from portfolio theory, and not the CAPM like the Treynor and Jensen indices. It does not refer to a market index and is not therefore subject to Roll's criticism.

This ratio has also been subject to generalisations since it was initially defined. It thus offers significant possibilities for evaluating portfolio performance, while remaining simple to calculate. Sharpe (1994) sums up the variations on this measure. One of the most common involves replacing the risk-free asset with a benchmark portfolio. The measure is then called the information ratio. We will describe it in more detail later in the chapter.

The Jensen Measure

Jensen's alpha (Jensen, 1968) is defined as the differential between the return on the portfolio in excess of the risk-free rate and the return explained by the market model, or

$$E(R_P) - R_F = \alpha_P + \beta_P(E(R_M) - R_F)$$

It is calculated by carrying out the following regression:

$$R_{Pt} - R_{Ft} = \alpha_P + \beta_P(R_{Mt} - R_{Ft}) + \epsilon_{Pt}$$

The Jensen measure is based on the CAPM. The term $\beta_P(E(R_M) - R_F)$ measures the return on the portfolio

forecast by the model. α_P measures the share of additional return that is due to the manager's choices.

In order to evaluate the statistical significance of alpha, we calculate the t-statistic of the regression, which is equal to the estimated value of the alpha divided by its standard deviation. This value is obtained from the results of the regression. If the alpha values are assumed to be normally distributed, then a t-statistic greater than 2 indicates that the probability of having obtained the result through luck, and not through skill, is strictly less than 5%. In this case, the average value of alpha is significantly different from zero.

Unlike the Sharpe and Treynor measures, the Jensen measure contains the benchmark. As for the Treynor measure, only the systematic risk is taken into account. This third method, unlike the first two, does not allow portfolios with different levels of risk to be compared. The value of alpha is actually proportional to the level of risk taken, measured by the beta. To compare portfolios with different levels of risk, we can calculate the Black–Treynor ratio[2] defined by

$$\frac{\alpha_P}{\beta_P}$$

The Jensen alpha can be used to rank portfolios within peer groups. They group together portfolios that are managed in a similar manner, and that therefore have comparable levels of risk.

The Jensen measure is subject to the same criticism as the Treynor measure: the result depends on the choice of reference index. In addition, when managers practise a market timing strategy, which involves varying the beta according to anticipated movements in the market, the Jensen alpha often becomes negative, and does not then reflect the real performance of the manager. In what follows we present methods that allow this problem to be corrected by taking variations in beta into account.

Relationships Between the Different Indicators and Use of the Indicators

It is possible to formulate the relationships between the Treynor, Sharpe and Jensen indicators.

---

[2] This ratio is defined in Salvati (1997). See also Treynor and Black (1973).

Treynor and Jensen

If we take the equation defining the Jensen alpha, or

$$E(R_P) - R_F = \alpha_P + \beta_P(E(R_M) - R_F) \qquad \textbf{(7.1)}$$

and we divide on each side by β_P, then we obtain the following:

$$\frac{E(R_P) - R_F}{\beta_P} = \frac{\alpha_P}{\beta_P} + (E(R_M) - R_F)$$

We then recognise the Treynor indicator on the left-hand side of the equation. The Jensen indicator and the Treynor indicator are therefore linked by the following exact linear relationship:

$$T_P = \frac{\alpha_P}{\beta_P} + (E(R_M) - R_F)$$

Sharpe and Jensen

It is also possible to establish a relationship between the Sharpe indicator and the Jensen indicator, but this time using an approximation. To do that we replace beta with its definition, or

$$\beta_P = \frac{\rho_{PM}\sigma_P\sigma_M}{\sigma_M^2}$$

where ρ_{PM} denotes the correlation coefficient between the return on the portfolio and the return on the market index.

If the portfolio is well diversified, then the correlation coefficient ρ_{PM} is very close to 1. By replacing β_P with its approximate expression in equation (7.1) and simplifying, we obtain:

$$E(R_P) - R_F \approx \alpha_P + \frac{\sigma_P}{\sigma_M}(E(R_M) - R_F)$$

By dividing each side by σ_P, we finally obtain:

$$\frac{E(R_P) - R_F}{\sigma_P} \approx \frac{\alpha_P}{\sigma_P} + \frac{(E(R_M) - R_F)}{\sigma_M}$$

The portfolio's Sharpe indicator appears on the left-hand side, so

$$S_P \approx \frac{\alpha_P}{\sigma_P} + \frac{(E(R_M) - R_F)}{\sigma_M}$$

Treynor and Sharpe

The formulas for these two indicators are very similar. If we consider the case of a well-diversified portfolio

again, we can still use the following approximation for beta:

$$\beta_P \approx \frac{\sigma_P}{\sigma_M}$$

The Treynor indicator is then written as follows:

$$T_P \approx \frac{E(R_P) - R_F}{\sigma_P}\sigma_M$$

Hence

$$S_P \approx \frac{T_P}{\sigma_M}$$

It should be noted that only the relationship between the Treynor indicator and the Jensen indicator is exact. The other two are approximations that are only valid for a well-diversified portfolio.

Using the Different Measures

The three indicators allow us to rank portfolios for a given period. The higher the value of the indicator, the more interesting the investment. The Sharpe ratio and the Treynor ratio are based on the same principle, but use a different definition of risk. The Sharpe ratio can be used for all portfolios. The use of the Treynor ratio must be limited to well-diversified portfolios. The Jensen measure is limited to the relative study of portfolios with the same beta.

In this group of indicators the Sharpe ratio is the one that is most widely used and has the simplest interpretation: the additional return obtained is compared with a risk indicator taking into account the additional risk taken to obtain it.

These indicators are more particularly related to equity portfolios. They are calculated by using the return on the portfolio calculated for the desired period. The return on the market is approximated by the return on a representative index for the same period. The beta of the portfolio is calculated as a linear combination of the betas of the assets that make up the portfolio, with these being calculated in relation to a reference index over the study period. The value of the indicators depends on the calculation period and performance results obtained in the past are no guarantee of future performance. Sharpe wrote that the Sharpe ratio gave a better evaluation of the past and the Treynor ratio was more suitable for anticipating future performance. Table 7-1 summarises the characteristics of the three indicators.

TABLE 7-1   Characteristics of the Sharpe, Treynor and Jenson Indicators

Name	Risk Used	Source	Criticised by Roll	Usage
Sharpe	Total (sigma)	Portfolio theory	No	Ranking portfolios with different levels of risk Not very well-diversified portfolios Portfolios that constitute an individual's total personal wealth
Treynor	Systematic (beta)	CAPM	Yes	Ranking portfolios with different levels of risk Well-diversified portfolios Portfolios that constitute part of an individual's personal wealth
Jensen	Systematic (beta)	CAPM	Yes	Ranking portfolios with the same beta

Extensions to the Jensen Measure

Elton and Gruber (1995) present an additional portfolio performance measurement indicator. The principle used is the same as that of the Jensen measure, namely measuring the differential between the managed portfolio and a theoretical reference portfolio. However, the risk considered is now the total risk and the reference portfolio is no longer a portfolio located on the security market line, but a portfolio on the capital market line, with the same total risk as the portfolio to be evaluated.

More specifically, this involves evaluating a manager who has to construct a portfolio with a total risk of σ_P. He can obtain this level of risk by splitting the investment between the market portfolio and the risk-free asset. Let A be the portfolio thereby obtained. This portfolio is situated on the capital market line. Its return and risk respect the following relationship:

$$E(R_A) = R_F + \left(\frac{E(R_M) - R_F}{\sigma_M} \right) \sigma_P$$

since $\sigma_A = \sigma_P$. This portfolio is the reference portfolio.

If the manager thinks that he possesses particular stock picking skills, he can attempt to construct a portfolio with a higher return for the fixed level of risk. Let P be his portfolio. The share of performance that results from the manager's choices is then given by

$$E(R_P) - E(R_A) = E(R_P) - R_F - \left(\frac{E(R_M) - R_F}{\sigma_M} \right) \sigma_P$$

The return differential between portfolio P and portfolio A measures the manager's stock picking skills. The result can be negative if the manager does not obtain the expected result.

The idea of measuring managers' selectivity can be found in the Fama decomposition. But Fama compares the performance of the portfolio with portfolios situated on the security market line, i.e. portfolios that respect the CAPM relationship.

The Jensen measure has been the object of a certain number of generalisations, which enable the management strategy used to be included in the evaluation of the manager's value-added. Among these extensions are the models that enable a market timing strategy to be evaluated.

Finally, the modified versions of the CAPM can be used instead of the traditional CAPM to calculate the Jensen alpha. The principle remains the same: the share of the return that is not explained by the model gives the value of the Jensen alpha.

With the Black model, the alpha is characterised by

$$E(R_P) = E(R_Z) = \alpha_P + \beta_P(E(R_M) - E(R_Z))$$

With the Brennan model, the alpha is characterised by

$$E(R_P) - R_F = \alpha_P + \beta_P(E(R_M) - R_F - T(D_M - R_F)) + T(D_P - R_F)$$

where D_P is equal to the weighted sum of the dividend yields of the assets in the portfolio, or

$$D_P = \sum_{i=1}^{n} x_i D_i$$

x_i denotes the weight of asset i in the portfolio. The other notations are those that were used earlier.

We can go through all the models cited in this way. For each case, the value of α_p is estimated through regression.

The Tracking-Error

The tracking-error is a risk indicator that is used in the analysis of benchmarked funds. Benchmarked management involves constructing portfolios with the same level of risk as an index, or a portfolio chosen as a benchmark, while giving the manager the chance to deviate from the benchmark composition, with the aim of obtaining a higher return. This assumes that the manager possesses particular stock picking skills. The tracking-error then allows the risk differentials between the managed portfolio and the benchmark portfolio to be measured. It is defined by the standard deviation of the difference in return between the portfolio and the benchmark it is replicating, or

$$TE = \sigma(R_P - R_B)$$

where R_B denotes the return on the benchmark portfolio.

The lower the value, the closer the risk of the portfolio to the risk of the benchmark. Benchmarked management requires the tracking-error to remain below a certain threshold, which is fixed in advance. To respect this constraint, the portfolio must be reallocated regularly as the market evolves. It is necessary however to find the right balance between the frequency of the reallocations and the transaction costs that they incur, which have a negative impact on portfolio performance. The additional return obtained, measured by alpha, must also be sufficient to make up for the additional risk taken on by the portfolio. To check this, we use another indicator: the information ratio.

The Information Ratio

The information ratio, which is sometimes called the appraisal ratio, is defined by the residual return of the portfolio compared with its residual risk. The residual return of a portfolio corresponds to the share of the return that is not explained by the benchmark. It results from the choices made by the manager to overweight securities that he hopes will have a return greater than that of the

benchmark. The residual, or diversifiable, risk measures the residual return variations. Sharpe (1994) presents the information ratio as a generalisation of his ratio, in which the risk-free asset is replaced by a benchmark portfolio. The information ratio is defined through the following relationship:

$$IR = \frac{E(R_P) - E(R_B)}{\sigma(R_P - R_B)}$$

We recognise the tracking-error in the denominator. The ratio can also be written as follows:

$$IR = \frac{\alpha_p}{\sigma(e_p)}$$

where α_p denotes the residual portfolio return, as defined by Jensen, and $\sigma(e_p)$ denotes the standard deviation of this residual return.

As specified above, this ratio is used in the area of benchmarked management. It allows us to check that the risk taken by the manager, in deviating from the benchmark, is sufficiently rewarded. It constitutes a criterion for evaluating the manager. Managers seek to maximise its value, i.e. to reconcile a high residual return and a low tracking-error. It is important to look at the value of the information ratio and the value of the tracking-error together. For the same information ratio value, the lower the tracking-error the higher the chance that the manager's performance will persist over time.

The information ratio is therefore an indicator that allows us to evaluate the manager's level of information compared with the public information available, together with his skill in achieving a performance that is better than that of the average manager. Since this ratio does not take the systematic portfolio risk into account, it is not appropriate for comparing the performance of a well-diversified portfolio with that of a portfolio with a low degree of diversification.

The information ratio also allows us to estimate a suitable number of years for observing the performance, in order to obtain a certain confidence level for the result. To do so, we note that there is a link between the *t*-statistic of the regression, which provides the alpha value, and the information ratio. The *t*-statistic is equal to the quotient of alpha and its standard deviation, and the information ratio is equal to the same quotient, but this time using annualised values. We therefore have

$$IR \approx \frac{t_{stat}}{\sqrt{T}}$$

where T denotes the length of the period, expressed in years, during which we observed the returns. The number of years required for the result obtained to be significant, with a given level of probability, is therefore calculated by the following relationship:

$$T = \left[\frac{t_{stat}}{IR}\right]^2$$

For example, a manager who obtains an average alpha of 2.5% with a tracking-error of 4% has an information ratio equal to 0.625. If we wish the result to be significant to 95%, then the value of the t-statistic is 1.96, according to the normal distribution table, and the number of years it is necessary to observe the portfolio returns is

$$T = \left[\frac{1.96}{0.625}\right]^2 = 9.8 \text{ years}$$

This shows clearly that the results must persist over a long period to be truly significant. We should note, however, that the higher the manager's information ratio, the more the number of years decreases. The number of years also decreases if we consider a lower level of probability, by going down, for example, to 80%.

The calculation of the information ratio has been presented by assuming that the residual return came from the Jensen model. More generally, this return can come from a multi-index or multi-factor model..

The Sortino Ratio

An indicator such as the Sharpe ratio, based on the standard deviation, does not allow us to know whether the differentials compared with the mean were produced above or below the mean.

Earlier, we introduced the notion of semi-variance and its more general versions. This notion can then be used to calculate the risk-adjusted return indicators that are more specifically appropriate for asymmetrical return distributions. This allows us to evaluate the portfolios obtained through an optimisation algorithm using the semi-variance instead of the variance. The best known indicator is the Sortino ratio (cf. Sortino and Price, 1994). It is defined on

the same principle as the Sharpe ratio. However, the risk-free rate is replaced with the minimum acceptable return (MAR), i.e. the return below which the investor does not wish to drop, and the standard deviation of the returns is replaced with the standard deviation of the returns that are below the MAR, or

$$\text{Sortino ratio} = \frac{E(R_p) - MAR}{\sqrt{\frac{1}{T}\sum_{\substack{t=0 \\ R_{Pt} < MAR}}^{T} (R_{Pt} - MAR)^2}}$$

Recently Developed Risk-adjusted Return Measures

Specialised firms that study investment fund performance develop variations on the traditional measures, essentially on the Sharpe ratio. These measures are used to rank the funds and attribute management quality labels. We can cite, for example, Morningstar's rankings.

The Morningstar Rating System[3]

The Morningstar measure, which is called a risk-adjusted rating (RAR), is very widely used in the United States. This ranking system was first developed in 1985 by the firm Morningstar. In July 2002, Morningstar introduced some modifications to improve its methodology. The measure differs significantly from more traditional measures such as the Sharpe ratio and its different forms. The evaluation of funds is based on a system of stars. Sharpe (1998) presents the method used by Morningstar and describes its properties. He compares it with other types of measure and describes the limitations of the ranking system.

The principle of the Morningstar measure is to rank different funds that belong to the same peer group. The RAR for a fund is calculated as the difference between its relative return and its relative risk, or

$$RAR_{Pi} = RR_{Pi} - RRisk_{Pi}$$

where RR_{Pi} denotes the relative return for fund P_i; and $RRisk_{Pi}$ denotes the relative risk for fund P_i.

---

[3] Cf. Melnikoff (1998) and see Sharpe's web site (http://www.stanford.edu/~wfsharpe/home.htm) for a series of articles describing the calculation methods.

The relative return and the relative risk for the fund are obtained by dividing, respectively, the return and the risk of the fund by a quantity, called the base, which is common to all the funds in the peer group, or

$$RR_{Pi} = \frac{R_{Pi}}{BR_g}$$

and

$$RRisk_{Pi} = \frac{Risk_{Pi}}{BRisk_g}$$

where g denotes the peer group containing the fund P_i;

R_{Pi} denotes the return on fund P_i, in excess of the risk-free rate;

$Risk_{P_i}$ denotes the risk of fund P_i;

BR_g denotes the base used to calculate the relative returns of all the funds in the group;

$BRisk_g$ denotes the base used to calculate the relative risks of all the funds in the group.

In the first version of the methodology, the risk of a fund was measured by calculating the average of the negative values of the fund's monthly returns in excess of the short-term risk-free rate and by taking the opposite sign to obtain a positive quantity:

$$Risk_{P_i} = -\frac{1}{T}\sum_{t=1}^{T} min(R_{P_{it}}, 0)$$

where T denotes the number of months in the period being studied; and $R_{P_{it}}$ denotes the monthly return of fund P_i, in excess of the risk-free rate.

Risk calculation has been modified in the new version of the star rating. Risk is measured by monthly variations in fund returns and now takes not only downside risk but also upside volatility into account, but with more emphasis on downward volatility. Funds with highly volatile returns are penalised, whether the volatility is upside or downside. The advantages of this improvement can be understood by looking at Internet funds. These funds were not considered risky in 1999, as they only exhibited upside volatility. But their extreme gains indicated a serious potential for extreme losses, as has been demonstrated since. The new risk measure would have attributed a higher level of risk to those funds than the previous measure did. As a result, the possibility of strong short-term performance masking the inherent risk of a fund has now

been reduced and it is more difficult for high-risk funds to earn high star ratings.

The base that is used to calculate the relative return of the funds is obtained by calculating the average return of the funds in the group. If the value obtained is greater than the risk-free rate for the period, then we use the result obtained, otherwise we use the value of the risk-free rate. We therefore have

$$BR_g = max\left(\frac{1}{n}\sum_{i=1}^{n} R_{Pi}, R_F\right)$$

where n denotes the number of funds contained in the peer group; and R_F denotes the risk-free rate.

The base used to calculate the relative risk is obtained by calculating the average of the risks of the funds in the peer group, or

$$BRisk_g = \frac{1}{n}\sum_{i=1}^{n} Risk_{Pi}$$

In 1985, Morningstar defined four peer groups to establish its rankings: domestic stock funds, international stock funds, taxable bond funds and tax-exempt municipal bond funds. However, these four categories appear to be too few to make truly adequate comparisons. The improved star rating methodology[4] now uses 48 specific equity and debt peer groups. For example, equity funds are classified according to their capitalisation (large-cap, mid-cap and small-cap) and whether they are growth, value or blend. International stock funds are now subdivided into different parts of the world. By only comparing funds with funds from the same well-defined category, those that are providing superior risk-adjusted performance will be more accurately identified. For example, during periods favourable to large-cap stocks, large-cap funds received a high percentage of five-star rankings when evaluated in the broad domestic equity group. With the new system, only the best funds will receive five stars, as large-cap funds will only be compared with large-cap funds.

The ranking is then produced as follows. Each fund is attached to a single peer group. The funds in a peer group

---

[4] For more details, see Morningstar's web site www.morningstar .com, from which it is possible to visit the specific web sites for each country.

are ranked in descending order of their *RAR*. A number of stars is then attributed to each fund according to its position in the distribution of *RAR* values. The funds in the top 10% of the distribution obtain five stars; those in the following 22.5% obtain four stars; those in the following 35% obtain three stars; those in the next 22.5% obtain two stars; and, finally, those in the bottom 10% obtain one star.

The Morningstar measure is based on an investment period of one month, although funds are in fact held for longer periods, and a decrease in one month can be compensated for by an increase in the following month. This measure is not therefore very appropriate for measuring the risk of funds that are held over a long period.

Actuarial Approach

In this approach (see Melnikoff, 1998) the investor's aversion to risk is characterised by a constant, *W*, which measures his gain–shortfall equilibrium, i.e. the relationship between the expected gain desired by the investor to make up for a fixed shortfall risk. The average annual risk-adjusted return is then given by

$$RAR = R - (W - 1)S$$

where

S   denotes the average annual shortfall rate;

W   denotes the weight of the gain–shortfall aversion; and

R   denotes the average annual rate of return obtained by taking all the observed returns.

For an average individual, *W* is equal to two, which means that the individual will agree to invest if the expected amount of his gain is double the shortfall. In this case, we have simply

$$RAR = R - S$$

Analysis Based on the VaR

The VaR was defined earlier and the different methods for calculating it were briefly presented. As a reminder, the VaR measures the risk of a portfolio as the maximum amount of loss that the portfolio can sustain for a given level of confidence. We may then wish to use this definition of risk to calculate a risk-adjusted return indicator to evaluate the performance of a portfolio. In order to define a logical indicator, we divide the VaR by the initial value of the portfolio and

thus obtain a percentage loss compared with the total value of the portfolio. We then calculate a Sharpe-like type of indicator in which the standard deviation is replaced with a risk indicator based on the VaR, or

$$\frac{R_P - R_F}{\dfrac{VaR_P}{V_P^0}}$$

where

R_P denotes the return on the portfolio;

R_F denotes the return on the risk-free asset;

VaR_P denotes the VaR of the portfolio;

V_P^0 denotes the initial value of the portfolio.

This type of ratio can only be compared for different portfolios if the portfolios' VaR has been evaluated for the same confidence threshold.

Furthermore, Dowd (1999) proposes an approach based on the VaR to evaluate an investment decision. We consider the case of an investor who holds a portfolio that he is thinking of modifying, by introducing, for example, a new asset. He will study the risk and return possibilities linked to a modification of the portfolio and choose the situation for which the risk-return balance seems to be sufficiently favourable. To do that, he could decide to define the risk in terms of the increase in the portfolio's VaR. He will change the portfolio if the resulting incremental VaR (IVaR) is sufficiently low compared with the return that he can expect. This can be formalised as a decision rule based on Sharpe's decision rule.

Sharpe's rule states that the most interesting asset in a set of assets is the one that has the highest Sharpe ratio. By calculating the existing Sharpe ratio and the Sharpe ratio for the modified portfolio and comparing the results, we can then judge whether the planned modification of the portfolio is desirable.

By using the definition of the Sharpe ratio, we find that it is useful to modify the portfolio if the returns and standard deviations of the portfolio before and after the modification are linked by the following relationship:

$$\frac{R_P^{new}}{\sigma_{R_P^{new}}} \geq \frac{R_P^{old}}{\sigma_{R_P^{old}}}$$

where R_P^{old} and R_P^{new} denote, respectively, the return on the portfolio before and after the modification; and $\sigma_{R_P^{old}}$ and

$\sigma_{R_P^{new}}$ denote, respectively, the standard deviation of the portfolio before and after the modification.

We assume that part of the new portfolio is made up of the existing portfolio, in proportion $(1 - a)$, and the other part is made up of asset A in proportion a.

The return on this portfolio is written as follows:

$$R_P^{new} = aR_A + (1 - a)R_P^{old}$$

where R_A denotes the return on asset A.

By replacing R_P^{new} with its expression in the inequality between the Sharpe ratios, we obtain:

$$\frac{aR_A + (1 - a)R_P^{old}}{\sigma_{R_P^{new}}} \geq \frac{R_P^{old}}{\sigma_{R_P^{old}}}$$

which finally gives

$$R_A \geq R_P^{old} + \frac{R_P^{old}}{a}\left(\frac{\sigma_{R_P^{new}}}{\sigma_{R_P^{old}}} - 1\right)$$

This relationship indicates the inequality that the return on asset A must respect for it to be advantageous to introduce it into the portfolio. The relationship depends on proportion a. It shows that the return on asset A must be at least equal to the return on the portfolio before the modification, to which is added a factor that depends on the risk associated with the acquisition of asset A. The higher the risk, the higher the adjustment factor and the higher the return on asset A will have to be.

Under certain assumptions, this relationship can be expressed through the *VaR* instead of the standard deviation. If the portfolio returns are normally distributed, then the *VaR* of the portfolio is proportional to its standard deviation, or

$$VaR = -\alpha\sigma_{R_P}W$$

where

α denotes the confidence parameter for which the VaR is estimated;

W is a parameter that represents the size of the portfolio; and

σ_{R_P} is the standard deviation of the portfolio returns.

By using this expression of the VaR, we can calculate

$$\frac{VaR^{new}}{VaR^{old}} = \frac{W^{new}\sigma_{R_P^{new}}}{W^{old}\sigma_{R_P^{old}}}$$

which enables us to obtain the following relationship:

$$\frac{\sigma_{R_P^{new}}}{\sigma_{R_P^{old}}} = \frac{VaR^{new}}{VaR^{old}}\frac{W^{old}}{W^{new}}$$

We assume that the size of the portfolio is conserved. We therefore have $W^{old} = W^{new}$.

We therefore obtain simply, after substituting into the return on A relationship:

$$R_A \geq R_P^{old} + \frac{R_P^{old}}{a}\left(\frac{VaR^{new}}{VaR^{old}} - 1\right)$$

The incremental VaR between the new portfolio and the old portfolio, denoted by IVaR, is equal to the difference between the old and new value, or $IVaR = VaR^{new} - VaR^{old}$.

By replacing in the inequality according to the IVaR, we obtain:

$$R_A \geq R_P^{old} + \frac{R_P^{old}}{a}\left(\frac{IVaR}{VaR^{old}}\right) = R_P^{old}\left(1 + \frac{1}{a}\frac{IVaR}{VaR^{old}}\right)$$

By defining the function η_A as

$$\eta_A(VaR) = \frac{1}{a}\frac{IVaR}{VaR^{old}}$$

we can write

$$R_A \geq (1 + \eta_A(VaR))R_P^{old}$$

where $\eta A(VaR)$ denotes the percentage increase in the VaR occasioned by the acquisition of asset A, divided by the proportion invested in asset A.

Measure Taking the Management Style into Account

The risk-adjusted performance measures enable a fund to be evaluated in comparison with the market portfolio, but do not take the manager's investment style into account. The style, however, may be imposed by the management mandate constraints rather than chosen by the manager. In this case it is more useful to compare management results with a benchmark that accurately represents the manager's style, rather than comparing them with a broad benchmark representing the market (cf. Lobosco, 1999). The idea of using tailored benchmarks that are adapted to the manager's investment style comes from the work of Sharpe (1992).

Lobosco (1999) proposes a measure called *SRAP* (Style/ Risk-Adjusted Performance). This is a risk-adjusted performance measure that includes the management style as defined by Sharpe. It was inspired by the work of Modigliani and Modigliani (1997), who defined an equation that enabled the annualised risk-adjusted performance (*RAP*) of a fund to be measured in relation to the market benchmark, or

$$RAP_P = \frac{\sigma_M}{\sigma_P}(R_P - R_F) + R_F$$

where

σ_M denotes the annualised standard deviation of the market returns;

σ_P denotes the annualised standard deviation of the returns of fund *P*;

R_P denotes the annualised return of fund *P*; and

R_F denotes the risk-free rate.

This relationship is drawn directly from the capital market line. If we were at equilibrium, we would have $RAP_P = R_M$, where R_M denotes the annualised average market return.

The relationship therefore allows us to look at the performance of the fund in relation to that of the market. The most interesting funds are those with the highest *RAP* value. To obtain a relative measure, one just calculates the difference between the *RAP* for the fund and the *RAP* for the benchmark, with the benchmark's *RAP* measure being simply equal to its return.

The first step in measuring the performance of a fund, when taking the investment style into account, is to identify the combination of indices that best represents the manager's style. We then calculate the differential between the fund's *RAP* measure and the *RAP* measure of its Sharpe benchmark.

Lobosco gives the example of a fund with an annualised performance of −1.72% and a standard deviation of 17.48%. The market portfolio is represented by the Russell 3000 index, the performance of which for the same period is 16.54% with a standard deviation of 11.52%. The risk-free rate is 5.21%.

The risk-adjusted performance of this fund is therefore

$$RAP(Fund) = \frac{11.52}{17.48}(-1.72 - 5.21) + 5.21 = 0.64\%$$

Its performance in relation to the market portfolio is

$$RelativeRAP = RAP(Fund) - RAP(Market) = 0.64 - 16.54$$
$$= -15.90\%$$

If we now observe that the style of this fund corresponds to a benchmark, 61% of which is made up of the Russell 2000 index of growth stocks and 39% of the Russell 2000 index of growth stocks, the performance of this benchmark is now 2.73% with a standard deviation of 13.44%.

The risk-adjusted performance of this benchmark is given by

$$RAP(SharpeBenchmark) = \frac{11.52}{13.44}(2.73 - 5.21) + 5.21 = 3.08\%$$

and the relative performance of the portfolio compared to this benchmark is given by

$$RelativeRAP = RAP(Fund) - RAP(SharpeBenchmark)$$
$$= 0.64 - 3.08 = -2.44\%$$

The relative performance of the fund is again negative, but the differential is much lower than compared with the whole market. The management style-adjusted performance measure is therefore a useful additional measure.

Risk-adjusted Performance Measure in the Area of Multimanagement

Muralidhar (2001) has developed a new risk-adjusted performance measure that allows us to compare the performance of different managers within a group of funds with the same objectives (a peer group). This measure can be grouped with the existing information ratio, the Sharpe ratio and the Modigliani and Modigliani measure, but it does contribute new elements. It includes not only the standard deviations of each portfolio, but also the correlation of each portfolio with the benchmark and the correlations between the portfolios themselves. The method proposed by Muralidhar allows us to construct portfolios that are split optimally between a risk-free asset, a benchmark and several managers, while taking the investors' objectives into account, both in terms of risk and, above all, the relative risk compared with the benchmark.

The principle involves reducing the portfolios to those with the same risk in order to be able to compare their performance. This is the same idea as in Modigliani and Modigliani (1997) who compared the performance of a portfolio and its benchmark by defining transformations in such a way that the transformed portfolio and benchmark had the same standard deviation.

To create a correlation-adjusted performance measure, Muralidhar considers an investor who splits his portfolio between a risk-free asset, a benchmark and an investment fund. We assume that this investor accepts a certain level of annualised tracking-error compared with his benchmark, which we call the objective tracking-error. The investor wishes to obtain the highest risk-adjusted value of alpha for a given portfolio tracking-error and variance. We define as a, b and $(1 - a - b)$ the proportions invested respectively in the investment fund, the benchmark B and the risk-free asset F. The portfolio thereby obtained is said to be correlation-adjusted. It is denoted by the initials CAP (for correlation-adjusted portfolio). The return on this portfolio is given by

$$R(CAP) = aR(manager) + bR(B) + (1 - a - b)R(F)$$

The proportions to be held must be chosen in an appropriate manner so that the portfolio obtained has a tracking-error equal to the objective tracking-error and its standard deviation is equal to the standard deviation of the benchmark.

The search for the best return, in view of the constraints, leads to the calculation of optimal proportions that depend on the standard deviations and correlations of the different elements in the portfolio. The problem is considered here with a single fund, but it can be generalised to the case of several funds, to handle the case of portfolios split between several managers, and to find the optimal allocation between the different managers. The formulas that give the optimal weightings in the case of several managers have the same structure as those obtained in the case of a single manager, but they use the weightings attributed to each manager together with the correlations between the managers.

Once the optimal proportions have been calculated, the return on the CAP has been determined entirely. By carrying out the calculation for each fund being studied, we can rank the different funds.

The Muralidhar measure is certainly useful compared with the risk-adjusted performance measure that had been developed previously. We observe that the Sharpe ratio, the information ratio and the Modigliani and Modigliani measure turn out to be insufficient to allow investors to rank different funds and to construct their optimal portfolio. These risk-adjusted measures only include the standard deviations of the portfolios and the benchmark, even though it is also necessary to include the correlations between the portfolios and between the portfolios and the benchmark. The Muralidhar model therefore provides a more appropriate risk-adjusted performance measure because it takes into account both the differences in standard deviation and the differences in correlations between the portfolios. We see that it produces a ranking of funds that is different from that obtained with the other measures. In addition, neither the information ratio nor the Sharpe ratio indicates how to construct portfolios in order to produce the objective tracking-error, while the Muralidhar measure provides the composition of the portfolios that satisfy the investors' objectives.

The composition of the portfolio obtained through the Muralidhar method enables us to solve the problem of an institutional investor's optimal allocation between active and passive management, with the possible use of a leverage effect to improve the risk-adjusted performance.

All the measures described in this section enable different investment funds to be ranked based on past performance. The calculations can be carried out over several successive periods on the basis that the more stable the ranking, the easier it will be to anticipate consistent results in the future.

Overview of Enterprise Risk Management

8

Excerpt is Sections I–VI of Overview of Enterprise Risk Management *from Casualty Actuarial Society, Enterprise Risk Management Committee.*

Learning Objectives

After completing this reading, FRM Candidates should be able to:

- Describe what is meant by ERM.
- Identify and describe risks addressed by ERM.

- Describe the measures, models, and tools typically used within an ERM framework.
- Discuss practical considerations related to ERM implementation.

EXECUTIVE SUMMARY

This document is intended primarily to further the risk management education of candidates for membership in the Casualty Actuarial Society (CAS). Current members of the CAS as well as other risk management professionals should also find this material of interest.

In the first section, the evolution to and rationale for enterprise risk management (ERM) is explained. The "ERM movement" is driven by both internal (e.g., competitive advantage) and external (e.g., corporate governance) pressures—pressures that are both fundamental and enduring.

The second section defines ERM for CAS purposes, and lays out its conceptual framework. The definition makes clear that ERM is a value-creating discipline. The framework describes both the categories of risk and the types of risk management processes covered by ERM. ERM is seen to extend well beyond the hazard risks with which casualty actuaries are particularly familiar, and well beyond the quantification of risks with which they are particularly skilled—but it is clear that the casualty actuarial skill set is extremely wellsuited to the practice of ERM. ERM also extends well beyond the insurance industry, which presents a distinct opportunity for casualty actuaries to continue to expand their career horizons and take leadership roles in these varied industries.

The vocabulary of ERM is established in the third section, which also describes the measures, models and tools supporting the discipline. The close linkage between ERM and corporate performance management is made clear in this discussion. Dynamic Financial Analysis (DFA) is introduced, along with alternative approaches to capture hazard and financial risks, and their roles within an ERM context is explained. Models that treat operational and strategic risks are also discussed. Applications of these measures, models and tools to support management decision-making are outlined at the conclusion of this chapter.

With the conceptual and technical foundations of ERM thus established, the next two sections turn to the actual practice of ERM. First, relevant case studies from various industries are presented, followed by offers some practical considerations in implementing ERM.

For the reader interested in pursuing additional sources of learning on the subject, a bibliography of existing literature on ERM and its key components is continually updated, annotated and topically-organized on the CAS Web site at http://www.casact.org/research/erm/.

Enterprise risk management is a "big idea." Among other things, ERM can be viewed as the broad conceptual framework that unifies the many varied parts of the actuarial discipline. ERM provides a logical structure to link these subject areas together in a compelling way to form an integrated whole. In so doing, ERM addresses critical business issues such as growth, return, consistency and value creation. It expresses risk not just as threat, but as opportunity—the fundamental reason that business is conducted in a free enterprise system. Through ERM, the clear linkage between business fundamentals and actuarial theory and practice should engage students and professionals from various backgrounds in the study of actuarial science—a logical career strategy in a global business environment that has embraced ERM as a modern management discipline.

THE ERM EVOLUTION

Organizations have long practiced various parts of what has come to be called enterprise risk management. Identifying and prioritizing risks, either with foresight or following a disaster, has long been a standard management activity. Treating risks by transfer, through insurance or other financial products, has also been common practice, as has contingency planning and crisis management.

What has changed, beginning very near the close of the last century, is treating the vast variety of risks in a holistic manner, and elevating risk management to a senior management responsibility. Although practices have not progressed uniformly through different industries and different organizations, the general evolution toward ERM can be characterized by a number of driving forces. We discuss these characteristic forces below.

More—and More Complicated—Risks

First of all, there is a greater recognition of the variety, the increasing number, and the interaction of risks facing organizations. Hazard risks such as the threat of fire to a production facility or liability from goods and services sold have been actively managed for a long time. Financial risks have grown in importance over the past number of years. New risks emerge with the changing business environment (e.g., foreign exchange risk with growing globalization). More recently, the awareness of operational and strategic risks has increased due to a succession of high-profile cases of organizations crippled or destroyed by failure of control mechanisms (e.g., Barings Bank, Enron) or by insufficient understanding of the dynamics of their business (e.g., Long Term Capital Management, General American Insurance Company). The advance of technology, the accelerating pace of business, globalization, increasing financial sophistication and the uncertainty of irrational terrorist activity all contribute to the growing number and complexity of risks. It is reasonable to expect that this trend will continue.

Organizations have come to recognize the importance of managing *all* risks and their interactions, not just the familiar risks, or the ones that are easy to quantify. Even seemingly insignificant risks on their own have the potential, as they interact with other events and conditions, to cause great damage.

External Pressures

Motivated in part by the well-publicized catastrophic failures of corporate risk management cited above, regulators, rating agencies, stock exchanges, institutional investors and corporate governance oversight bodies have come to insist that company senior management take greater responsibility for managing risks on an enterprise-wide scale. These efforts span virtually every country in the civilized world.

In addition to these codified pressures, publicly traded companies are well aware of the increasingly vocal desire of their shareholders for stable and predictable earnings, which is one of the key objectives of ERM for many organizations.

Portfolio Point of View

Another characteristic force is the increasing tendency toward an integrated or holistic view of risks. Developments in finance (i.e., Modern Portfolio Theory) provide a framework for thinking about the collective risk of a group of financial instruments and an individual security's contribution to that collective risk. With ERM, these concepts have been generalized beyond financial risks to include

risks of all kinds, i.e., beyond a portfolio of equity investments to the entire collection of risks an organization faces. A number of principles follow from this thinking, including:

- Portfolio risk is not the simple sum of the individual risk elements.
- To understand portfolio risk, one must understand the risks of the individual elements plus their interactions.
- The portfolio risk, or risk to the entire organization, is relevant to the key risk decisions facing that organization.

The implications of these principles are having a significant impact on the practice of ERM. There is growing recognition that risks must be managed with the total organization in mind. To do otherwise (sometimes referred to as managing risk within "silos") is inefficient at best, and can be counter-productive. For example, certain risks can represent "natural hedges" against each other (if they are sufficiently negatively correlated). A classic case is that of an insurer selling both life insurance and annuity business to similarly situated customers and thereby naturally hedging away its mortality risk. To separately hedge mortality risk on these products (e.g., through reinsurance) would be cost inefficient and entirely unnecessary. Another example is that of a global conglomerate with one of its divisions long in a certain foreign currency and another short in the same currency. Separate currency hedges, while seemingly advisable from the point of view of the individual division heads, are unreasonable for the enterprise as a whole.

A holistic approach helps give organizations a true perspective on the magnitude and importance of different risks.

Quantification

A fourth characteristic force, closely tied to the third, is the growing tendency to quantify risks. Advances in technology and expertise have made quantification easier, even for the infrequent, unpredictable risks that historically have been difficult to quantify. Following a series of natural disasters, most notably hurricane Andrew in 1992, the practice of catastrophe modeling arose and is now a standard practice in insurance companies. This combination of meteorological (in the case of hurricane modeling), structural engineering, insurance and technological expertise leading to probabilistic models is a huge advancement over previous quantification attempts. By the end of the twentieth century, insurance and rein-surance companies routinely measured their exposure to hurricanes, earthquakes and other natural disasters with a greater degree of precision leading to a greater confidence in the ability to manage the exposure. More recently, such exposure-based quantification of exposure to losses has been extended to even less predictable, man-made disasters such as terrorist attacks.

The emergence of Value-at-Risk as a regulatory and man-agement standard in the financial services industry has been aided by the speed and ease in measuring certain financial risks. Data is collected constantly allowing risk profiles to be adjusted as portfolios and market conditions change. This gives financial institutions and the regula-tory bodies that oversee them a level of confidence in their ability to take actions to operate within established parameters.

Despite these advances, there will always remain risks that are not easily quantifiable. These include risks that are not well defined, unpredictable as to frequency, amount or location, risks subject to manipulation and human intervention, and newer risks. Man-made risks, operational and strategic risks are examples of these. Operational risk is a general category for a wide variety of risks, many of which are influenced by people and many of which do not have a long historical record. The tendency to quantify exposure to all these risks will cer-tainly continue.

In the same way there has been a continuing effort to better quantify individual risks, there is a growing effort to quantify portfolio risk. This effort is much more difficult because in addition to individual risks, one must quantify or explain interactions between individual risk elements. This can be extremely complex and challenging. However, there often is not the need for a great deal of precision; even a directionally correct answer may be valuable. The attempt at quantification allows the organization to ana-lyze "what if" scenarios. They are able to estimate the magnitude of risk or degree of dependency with other risks sufficiently to make informed decisions. Further, sim-ply going through the quantification process gives people a better qualitative perspective of the risk. They may gain

insight as to the likelihood or severity of the risk or to ways to prevent or mitigate the exposure.

Boundaryless Benchmarking

A fifth characteristic force pertains to scope. Common ERM practices and tools are shared across a wide variety of organizations and across the globe. The process, tools, and procedures laid out in this overview are not limited to the insurance or even financial service industries but rather are common to many organizations. Information sharing has been aided by technology but perhaps more importantly, because these practices are transferable across organizations. Organizations have become quite willing to share practices and efficiency gains with others with whom they are not direct competitors.

An example of a phenomenon common to many organi-zations and having risk management implications is real options. Many organizations face operating and strategic situations where events are uncertain, players make initial investments to get in the game and then have the oppor-tunity to make successive investments contingent on future events. The drug approval process in the pharma-ceutical industry is an example where organizations face options-like decisions. Option pricing techniques provide organizations with a means of better thinking about and managing these risks.

Different industries and organizations will continue to develop and employ variations of ERM. Different risks will be more or less important to organizations and risk man-agement practices will differ in particular ways that best suit the organization, but there will be general concepts and broad general practices and techniques that are rec-ognized and employed by organizations throughout the world.

Risk as Opportunity

A sixth characteristic force pertains to the outlook organizations have toward risk. In the past, organiza-tions tended to take a defensive posture towards risks, viewing them as situations to be minimized or avoided. Increasingly, organizations have come to recognize the opportunistic side, the value-creating potential of risk. While avoidance or minimization remain legitimate strategies for dealing with certain risks, by certain organizations at certain times, there is also the opportunity to swap, keep, and actively pursue other risks because of confidence in the organization's special ability to exploit those risks.

There are a number of reasons for this shift in attitude. Over time and with practice, organizations have become more familiar with and more capable of managing the risks they face. They develop expertise in managing those risks both because of familiarity and confidence in the organization's abilities. As a result, they may keep their own exposure and seek out opportunities to assume other organization's risks. Over time, better information about risk has become available. This has led to new markets for trading risks and more information about the cost of risks. This has allowed organizations to better evaluate risk and return trade-offs and see that the costs of transfer sometime outweigh the benefits. In addition, the existence of risk-trading markets contributes to a greater degree of confidence. Organizations can adopt a more aggressive stance if they know they can switch to a defensive stance quickly, if needed.

In some cases organizations seek out risks to increase diversification, realizing that the addition of some risks may have a minimal impact on overall risk, or in the case of hedges, may decrease enterprise risks. In essence, there is a realization that risk is not completely avoidable and, in fact, informed risk-taking is a means to competitive advantage.

Summary

It is reasonable to expect that the forces cited above will continue. Accordingly, risk management practices will become more and more sophisticated. As capabilities continue to improve, organizations will increasingly adopt ERM because they can.

> *Note:* For additional thoughts on the subject of this chapter, see Lisa K. Meulbroek, "Integrated Risk Management for the Firm: A Senior Manager's Guide," *Harvard Business School's Division of Research Working Papers 2001-2002,* http://www.hbs.edu/research/facpubs/workingpapers/papers2/0102/02-046.pdf.

ERM DEFINITION AND CONCEPTUAL FRAMEWORK

Definition

Several texts and periodicals have introduced or discussed concepts such as "strategic risk management," "integrated risk management" and "holistic risk management." These concepts are similar to, even synonymous with, ERM in that they all emphasize a comprehensive view of risk and risk management, a movement away from the "silo" approach of managing different risks within an organization separately and distinctly, and the view that risk management can be a value-creating, in addition to a risk-mitigating, process.

The CAS Committee on Enterprise Risk Management has adopted the following definition of ERM:

> "ERM is the discipline by which an organization in any industry assesses, controls, exploits, finances, and monitors risks from all sources for the purpose of increasing the organization's short- and long-term value to its stakeholders."

Several parts of this definition merit individual attention. First, ERM is a discipline. This is meant to convey that ERM is an orderly or prescribed conduct or pattern of behavior for an enterprise, that it has the full support and commitment of the management of the enterprise, that it influences corporate decision-making, and that it ultimately becomes part of the culture of that enterprise. Second, ERM, even as it is defined for CAS purposes, applies to all industries, not just the property/casualty insurance industry with which casualty actuaries are intimately familiar. Third, the specific mention of exploiting risk as a part of the risk management process (along with the stated objective of increasing short- and long-term value) demonstrates that the intention of ERM is to be value creating as well as risk mitigating. Fourth, all sources of risk are considered, not only the hazard risk with which casualty actuaries are particularly familiar, or those traditionally managed within an enterprise (such as financial risk). Lastly, ERM considers all stakeholders of the enterprise, which include shareholders and debtholders, management and officers, employees, customers, and the community within which the enterprise resides.

ERM Framework				
	Types of Risk			
Process Steps	Hazard	Financial	Operational	Strategic
Establish Context				
Identify Risks				
Analyze/Quantify Risks				
Integrate Risks				
Assess/Prioritize Risks				
Treat/Exploit Risks				
Monitor & Review				

Implicit in this definition is the recognition of ERM as a strategic decision support framework for management. It improves decision-making at all levels of the organization.

Conceptual Framework

A useful way to conceptualize ERM is along two dimensions: one spanning the *types* of risk included, and the other spanning the various risk management *process* steps, see the table above.

In discussing these risk types and process steps, we will consider an enterprise, the Coldhard Steel Company ("Coldhard Steel"), which manufactures steel products, such as roller and ball bearings, used in other industrial machinery. Coldhard Steel operates in the "rust belt" of the midwestern U.S., is family-owned, and has a unionized labor force.

Types of Risk

Coldhard Steel is exposed to a number of **hazard risks**. First-party hazard risks include the possibility of fire or tornadoes damaging its plant and equipment, and the resulting loss of revenue (i.e., business interruption). Second-party hazard risks include injury or illness to its employees, including work-related injuries that would result in workers compensation claims. Given Coldhard Steel's use of heavy machinery, as well as the benefit provisions in its principal state of operation, Coldhard Steel's workers compensation exposure is substantial. Third-party hazard risk would include the possibility of slips and falls

of visitors on its premises, products recall and/or products liability from defective products produced by Coldhard Steel.

Since Coldhard Steel has significant sales in Latin America and Europe, it is exposed to foreign exchange risk, one of many **financial risks**. Coldhard Steel is tangentially exposed to additional foreign exchange risk in that even though it buys its steel from U.S. manufacturers, these prices are influenced by imported steel. Other financial risks for Coldhard Steel to consider are commodity risk (due to possible changes in prices in the raw materials it and its suppliers use in production) and credit risk (due to its significant accounts receivables asset).

Since many employees are in the local machinists union, labor relations represents a significant **operational risk** for Coldhard Steel. Also, since the company is privately held, succession planning is critical for the time when the current owner either sells the company or passes down control to heirs. Coldhard Steel spends considerable time assessing the efficiency and reliability of its machines and processes.

Strategic risks for Coldhard Steel include fluctuations in the demand and the market price for its finished products (and substitute products), competition from suppliers of other steel products, regulatory/political issues associated with the steel industry, and technological advances in its customers' machines that could potentially render Coldhard Steel's current products obsolete.

In general, enterprises (like and unlike Coldhard Steel) are exposed to risks that can be categorized into the following four types:

- *Hazard Risks* include risks from:
  - fire and other property damage,
  - windstorm and other natural perils,
  - theft and other crime, personal injury,
  - business interruption,
  - disease and disability (including work-related injuries and diseases), and
  - liability claims.

- *Financial Risks* include risks from:
  - price (e.g. asset value, interest rate, foreign exchange, commodity),
  - liquidity (e.g. cash flow, call risk, opportunity cost),
  - credit (e.g. default, downgrade),
  - inflation/purchasing power, and
  - hedging/basis risk.
- *Operational Risks* include risks from:
  - business operations (e.g., human resources, product development, capacity, efficiency, product/service failure, channel management, supply chain management, business cyclicality),
  - empowerment (e.g., leadership, change readiness),
  - information technology (e.g., relevance, availability), and
  - information/business reporting (e.g., budgeting and planning, accounting information, pension fund, investment evaluation, taxation).
- *Strategic Risks* include risks from:
  - reputational damage (e.g., trademark/brand erosion, fraud, unfavorable publicity)
  - competition,
  - customer wants,
  - demographic and social/cultural trends,
  - technological innovation,
  - capital availability, and
  - regulatory and political trends.

The precise slotting of individual risk factors under each of these four categories is less important than the recognition that ERM covers all categories and all material risk factors that can influence the organization's value.

Process Steps

The following steps of the risk management process, which are based on those originally detailed in the Australian/New Zealand Standard in Risk Management (AS/NZS 4360), describe seven iterative elements.

- *Establish Context*—This step includes External, Internal and Risk Management Contexts.
  - The External Context starts with a definition of the relationship of the enterprise with its environment, including identification of the enterprise's strengths, weaknesses, opportunities, and threats ("SWOT analysis"). This context-setting also identifies the various stakeholders (shareholders, employees, customers, community), as well as the communication policies with these stakeholders.
  - The Internal Context starts with an understanding of the overall objectives of the enterprise, its strategies to achieve those objectives and its key performance indicators. It also includes the organization's oversight and governance structure.
  - The Risk Management Context identifies the risk categories of relevance to the enterprise and the degree of coordination throughout the organization, including the adoption of common risk metrics.

Returning to our example, Coldhard Steel has formed a Risk Management Committee that is headed by its chief financial officer, with representatives from loss control/safety, quality control, human resources, marketing, and finance. In consideration of the makeup of its labor force, a representative from the labor union is invited periodically to meetings. In terms of establishing common criteria for assessing all risks, Coldhard Steel adopted a Value at Risk approach, with an annual timeframe.

- *Identify Risks*—This step involves documenting the conditions and events (including "extreme events") that represent material threats to the enterprise's achievement of its objectives or represent areas to exploit for competitive advantage.

In our example, Coldhard Steel has used a variety of methods (e.g., surveys, internal workshops, brainstorming sessions and internal auditing) to identify the significant hazard, financial, operational and strategic risks described in the previous section.

- *Analyze/Quantify Risks*—This step involves calibrating and, wherever possible, creating probability distributions of outcomes for each material risk. This step provides necessary input for subsequent steps, such as integrating and prioritizing risks. Analysis techniques range along a spectrum from qualitative to quantitative, with sensitivity analysis, scenario analysis, and/or simulation analysis applied where appropriate.

As indicated previously, workers compensation represents a significant hazard risk for Coldhard Steel. However, it has a number of years of claims and exposure data, and, based on quantitatively extrapolating cost trends into the future, Coldhard Steel's consulting actuaries are able to determine reasonable expectations of costs and variability of these costs into the near future.

Coldhard Steel regularly monitors its account sales and accounts receivables, including performing credit analysis on its largest customers before extending additional credit. Although all sales are transacted in U.S. dollars, orders from Mexico generate 10 percent of all sales, and Coldhard Steel's financial analysts have considered hedging against devaluations in the Mexican peso.

Coldhard Steel's labor contract expires in three years, and although relations with the employees and union are considered good, senior management has asked its human resources to construct "best case," "expected" and "worst case" estimates of salary and benefit increases anticipated to be requested by labor. As part of the worst case scenario, management has asked its finance department to estimate the impacts of a prolonged labor dispute and its effects on revenue, expenses and inventories.

Coldhard Steel buys its steel from U.S. manufacturers, even though some of its competitors are taking advantage of cheaper foreign steel. Coldhard Steel is actively monitoring political discussions to gauge the likelihood that additional tariffs will be imposed on foreign steel in the near future. Coldhard Steel also monitors price levels for its finished products in relationship to the cost of its raw materials, products of its competitors, and substitute products.

- *Integrate Risks*—This step involves aggregating all risk distributions, reflecting correlations and portfolio effects, and expressing the results in terms of the impact on the enterprise's key performance indicators (i.e., the "aggregate risk profile").

Coldhard Steel's Risk Management Committee and external consultants have begun to develop a structural simulation model to integrate all risks. The various components of the model are supported by a common stochastic economic scenario generator.

- *Assess/Prioritize Risks*—This step involves determining the contribution of each risk to the aggregate risk profile, and prioritizing accordingly, so that decisions can be made as to the appropriate treatment.

Coldhard Steel has not yet quantified all risks into probability distributions, let alone integrated these risks into a complete aggregate risk profile. However, Coldhard Steel has developed judgmental assessments as to frequency and severity, and it has developed a "Risk Map", which plots all risks by these two components. Coldhard Steel has prioritized a number of risks including its workers compensation exposure (hazard), account bad debt/credit risk (financial), labor relation risk (operational), and product obsolescence risk (strategic).

- *Treat/Exploit Risks*—This step encompasses a number of different strategies, including decision as to avoid, retain (and finance), reduce, transfer, or exploit risk. For hazard risks, the prevalent transfer mechanism has been the insurance markets. Alternative risk transfer (ART) markets have developed from these with a goal of striking a balance between risk retention and risk transfer. With respect to financial risks, the capital markets have exploded over the last several decades to assist companies in dealing with commodity, interest rate, and foreign exchange risk. Until recently, companies had no mechanisms to transfer operational or strategic risks, and simply had to avoid or retain these risks.

Coldhard Steel has historically insured its workers compensation exposure. However, given its comfort in assessing its loss experience, as well as increases in insurance rates, it is considering securing coverage with a large per occurrence deductible. With respect to financial risk, Coldhard Steel is instituting new standards regarding the extension of credit to its customers. In order to avoid potential labor disputes down the road, Coldhard Steel has decided to hold early discussions with union personnel regarding wages and benefits.

Coldhard Steel believes that it is likely that additional tariffs will be imposed on foreign steel in the near future, so it is attempting to exploit this strategic risk by locking into fixed price agreements with its domestic suppliers.

- *Monitor & Review*—This step involves continual gauging of the risk environment and the performance of the risk management strategies. It also provides a context for considering risk that is scalable over a period of time (one quarter, one year, five years). The results of the ongoing reviews are fed back into the context-setting step and the cycle repeats.

Coldhard Steel's newly formed Risk Management Committee met extensively toward the end of the previous year for planning purposes, and intends to meet monthly to monitor progress on goals established.

> *Note:* The ERM Framework in this chapter was originally developed in the *Final Report of the Advisory Committee on Enterprise Risk Management* (the predecessor committee to the Enterprise Risk Management Committee). This November 2001 report is available on the CAS Web site at http://www.casact.org/research/erm/report.htm.

ERM LANGUAGE, MEASURES, MODELS AND TOOLS

As outlined in the preceding section, the first process step in the ERM framework is to establish the context (internal, external and risk management) within which the organization operates. Critical to establishing this context—and one of the worthy goals of ERM in its own right—is the creation of a common risk vernacular across all functional areas and relevant disciplines throughout the organization. This chapter summarizes the terminology in common usage among companies that practice ERM, forming a large part the emerging global "language of risk." In so doing, this chapter introduces and discusses the measures, models and tools that help organizations perform the balance of the ERM process steps.

Where appropriate, certain items are compared and contrasted; and where some items represent alternative approaches to a similar issue, relative strengths and weaknesses are discussed.

Overall Corporate Performance Measures

ERM clearly links risk management with the creation of organizational value and expresses risk in terms of impact on organizational objectives. An important aspect of ERM is therefore the strong linkage between measures of risk and measures of overall organizational performance. Thus, our discussion of ERM terminology begins with a description of key corporate performance measures. Our focus is on publicly traded corporations, and where industry-specific details are introduced, we use the financial services industry (and, more specifically, the insurance industry) for illustration.

In addition to establishing context, these performance measures have specific application in the identification of risks. Risk identification is the qualitative determination of risks that are material, i.e., that potentially can impact, for better or worse, the organization's achievement of its financial and/or strategic objectives. These objectives are usually expressed, of course, in terms of the overall corporate performance measures.

The measures defined below are fundamental to the evaluation of corporate performance. It is assumed that the reader is already familiar with the more basic accounting terms and concepts such as net income, net worth, etc.

- General Industry
  - Return on equity (ROE)—net income divided by net worth.
  - Operating earnings—net income from continuing operations, excluding realized investment gains.
  - Earnings before interest, dividends, taxes, depreciation and amortization (EBITDA)—a form of cash flow measure, useful for evaluating the operating performance of companies with high levels of debt (when the debt service costs may overwhelm other measures such as net income).
  - Cash flow return on investments (CFROI)—EBITDA divided by tangible assets.
  - Weighted average cost of capital (WACC)—the sum of the required market returns of each component of corporate capitalization, weighted by that component's share of the total capitalization.
  - Economic value added (EVA)—a corporate performance measure that stresses the ability to achieve

returns above the firm's cost of capital. It is often stated as net operating profits after tax less the product of required capital times the firm's weighted average cost of capital.

- Financial Services Industry
  - Return on risk-adjusted capital (RORAC)—a target ROE measure in which the denominator is adjusted depending on the risk associated with the instrument or project.
  - Risk-adjusted return on capital (RAROC)—a target ROE measure in which the numerator is reduced depending on the risk associated with the instrument or project.
  - Risk-adjusted return on risk-adjusted capital (RARORAC)—a combination of RAROC and RORAC in which both the numerator and denominator are adjusted (for different risks).
- Insurance Industry
  - Economic capital—market value of assets minus fair value of liabilities. Used in practice as a risk-adjusted capital measure; specifically, the amount of capital required to meet an explicit solvency constraint (e.g., a certain probability of ruin).
  - RAROC—expected net income divided by economic capital (thus, the more technically correct label is RORAC—see above—but in the insurance industry, RAROC is the term commonly used). RAROC is typically employed to evaluate the relative performance of business segments that have different levels of solvency risk; the different levels of solvency risk are reflected in the denominator. Evaluating financial performance under RAROC calls for comparison to a benchmark return; when the benchmark return is risk-adjusted (e.g., for volatility in net income), the result is similar to RARORAC (see above), though the term RAROC is still applied.
  - Embedded value—a measure of the value of business currently on the books of an insurance company; it comprises adjusted net worth (the market value of assets supporting the surplus) plus the present value of expected future profits on in force business. (Embedded value differs from appraisal value in that the latter also includes the value of future new business.) The performance measure is often expressed in terms of growth (i.e., year-on-year increase) in embedded value.

- Risk Based Capital (RBC)—a specific regulatory capital requirement promulgated by the National Association of Insurance Commissioners. It is a formula-derived minimum capital standard that sets the points at which a state insurance commissioner is authorized and expected to take regulatory action.

Risk Measures

In this section, reference is made to the term *"risk profile"* to represent the entire portfolio of risks that constitute the enterprise. Some companies represent this portfolio in terms of a cumulative probability distribution (e.g., of cumulative earnings) and use it as a base from which to determine the incremental impact (e.g., on required capital) of alternative strategies or decisions. It is in this sense that the term is used below.

Most of the measures common in the practice of ERM can be placed in one of two categories: those measures related to the degree of the organization's *solvency,* and those related to the volatility of the organization's *performance* on a "going concern" basis. The measures in these two categories are used for distinctly different purposes and focus on distinctly different areas of the organization's risk profile. Following and complementing the narrative descriptions of these measures are illustrations and formulas where appropriate.

- *Solvency-related* measures (these measures concentrate on the adverse "tail" of the probability distribution—see "risk profile" above—and are relevant for determining economic capital requirements, i.e., they relate to the risks captured in the denominator of RARORAC; they are of particular concern to customers and their proxies, e.g., regulators and rating agencies):
  - Probability of ruin—the percentile of the probability distribution corresponding to the point at which capital is exhausted. Typically, a minimum acceptable probability of ruin is specified, and economic capital is derived therefrom.
  - Shortfall risk—the probability that a random variable falls below some specified threshold level. (Probability of ruin is a special case of shortfall risk in which the threshold level is the point at which capital is exhausted.)
  - Value at risk (VaR)—the maximum loss an organization can suffer, under normal market conditions, over

a given period of time at a given probability level (technically, the inverse of the shortfall risk concept, in which the shortfall risk is specified, and the threshold level is derived therefrom). VaR is a common measure of risk in the banking sector, where it is typically calculated daily and used to monitor trading activity.

• Expected policyholder deficit (EPD) or economic cost of ruin (ECOR)—an enhancement to the probability of ruin concept (and thus shortfall risk and VaR) in which the *severity* of ruin is also reflected. Technically, it is the expected value of the shortfall. (In an analogy to bond rating, it is comparable to considering the salvage value of a bond in addition to the probability of default.) For insurance companies, the more common term is EPD, and represents the expected shortage in the funds due to policyholders in the event of liquidation.

• Tail Value at Risk (Tail VaR) or Tail Conditional Expectation (TCE)—an ECOR-like measure in the sense that both the probability and the cost of "tail events" are considered. It differs from ECOR in that it is the expected value, from first dollar, of all events beyond the tail threshold event, not just the shortfall amount.

• Tail events—unlikely but extreme events, usually from a skewed distribution. Rare outcomes, usually representing large monetary losses.

Cumulative Probability

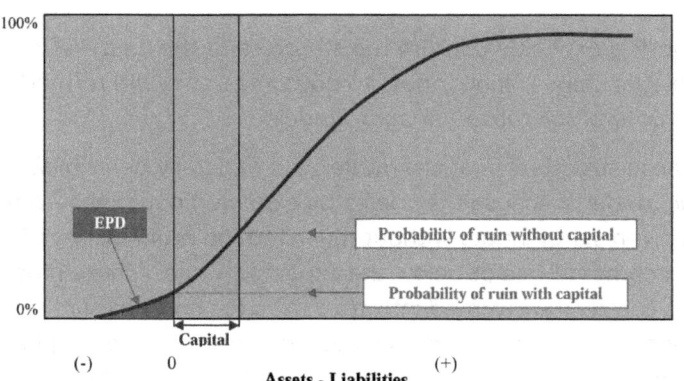

Assets - Liabilities

• *Performance-related* measures (these measures concentrate on the mid-region of the probability distribution—see "risk profile" above—i.e., the region near the mean, and are relevant for determination of the volatility around

expected results, i.e., the numerator of RARORAC; they are of particular concern to owners and their proxies, e.g., stock analysts):

• Variance—the average squared difference between a random variable and its mean.

• Standard deviation—the square root of the variance.

• Semi-variance and downside standard deviation—modifications of variance and standard deviation, respectively, in which only *unfavorable* deviations from a specified target level are considered in the calculation.

• Below-target-risk (BTR)—the expected value of unfavorable deviations of a random variable from a specified target level (such as not meeting an earnings target).

Cumulative Probability

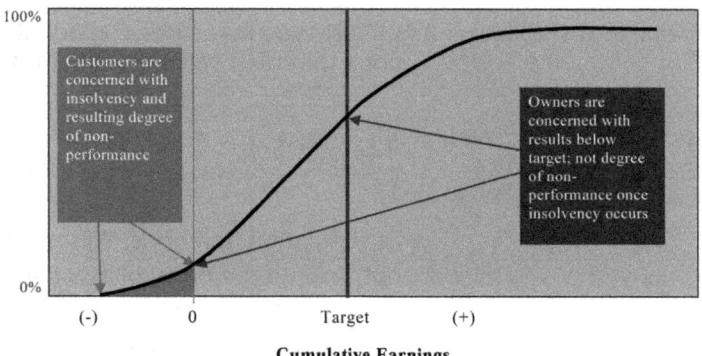

Cumulative Earnings

Risk Modeling

Risk modeling refers to the methods by which the risk and performance measures described above are determined. This chapter discusses the major classes of models used in the ERM process. It should be noted that these are general classes of models. The models used within any organization will typically be customized to accommodate the unique needs of, and the specific risks faced by, that organization. No two such models are exactly alike.

Most organizations will have at least a simple financial model of their operations that describes how various inputs (i.e., risk factors, conditions, strategies and tactics) will affect the key performance indicators (KPIs) used to manage the organization. For any given organization, these KPIs may be one or more of the overall corporate performance measures described earlier in this chapter (e.g., revenue growth, earnings growth, earnings per

Risk Measure	Formula
Standard Deviation	$\sqrt{\dfrac{\sum_{i=1}^{n}(x_i - \bar{x})^2}{n}}$ where n is the number of simulation iterations and *xbar* is the average value over all iterations. This is a commonly used measure of risk by academics and capital markets. It is interpreted as the extent to which the financial variable could deviate either above or below the expected value. Note that equal weight is given to deviations of the same magnitude regardless of whether the deviation is favorable or unfavorable. (There are different schools of thought on whether standard deviation in this context should measure total volatility or only the nondiversifiable volatility.)
Shortfall Risk	$\dfrac{\sum_{i=1}^{n}[if\,(x_i \leq T)\,then\,1, else\,0]}{n}$ * 100% where T is the target value for the financial variable and n is the number of simulation iterations. This is an improvement over standard deviation because it reflects the fact that most people are risk averse, i.e., they are more concerned with unfavorable deviations rather than favorable deviations. It is interpreted as the probability that the financial variable falls below a specified target level.
Value at Risk (VaR)	In VaR-type measures, the equation is reversed: the shortfall risk is specified first, and the corresponding value at risk (T) is solved for.
Downside Standard Deviation	$\sqrt{\dfrac{\sum_{i=1}^{n}(min[0,(x_i - T)])^2}{n}}$ where T is the target value for the financial variable and n is the number of simulation iterations. This is a further improvement over the other metrics because it focuses not only on the probability of an unfavorable deviation in a financial variable (as with shortfall risk) but also the extent to which it is unfavorable. It is interpreted as the extent to which the financial variable could deviate below a specified target level.
Below Target Risk (BTR)	BTR is similar, but the argument is not squared, and there is no square root taken of the sum.

share, growth in surplus, growth in embedded value, customer satisfaction and/or brand image). For publicly traded companies, the KPIs are often explicitly or implicitly defined by the market (i.e., they are the measures focused upon by the organization's stock analysts). These models are often used in developing strategic and operational plans. For example, insurance companies typically make assumptions regarding future trends in claim costs by business segment (e.g., by line of business, by region), which are used to determine needed rate levels by segment. These rate level projections are then combined with assumptions on volume growth and other relevant inputs to derive a pro forma estimate of overall corporate earnings (or some other KPI). Often, business decisions (e.g., rate level, volume growth) are fine-tuned in order to produce the desired expected KPI result. Because these models explicitly capture the structure of the cause/effect relationships linking inputs to outcomes, they are termed *structural (or causal) financial models.*

These structural financial models are generally *deterministic* models because they describe *expected* outcomes from a given set of inputs without regard to the probabilities of outcomes above or below the expected values. These models can be transformed into *stochastic (or probabilistic)* models by treating certain inputs as variable. For example, expected future claim cost trend might be an input to a deterministic model of corporate earnings; recognizing that there is uncertainty in this trend, a probability distribution around the expected trend would be an input to a stochastic model. The model output, corporate earnings in this case, would then also be a probability distribution.

As outlined below, the two general classes of stochastic risk models are *statistical analytic models* and *structural simulation models.* "Statistical" vs. "structural" refers to the manner in which the relationships among random variables are represented in the model; "analytic" vs. "simulation" refers to the way in which the calculations are actually carried out. These four terms are defined separately below; the way they are combined is illustrated and contrasted in the table that follows the definitions.

- Analytic methods—models whose solutions can be determined "in closed form" by solving a set of equations. These methods usually require a restrictive set of assumptions and mathematically tractable assumed probability distributions. The principal advantage over simulation methods is ease and speed of calculation.

- Simulation methods (often called Monte Carlo methods)—models that require a large number of computer-generated "trials" to approximate an answer. These methods are relatively robust and flexible, can accommodate complex relationships (e.g., so-called "path dependent" relationships commonly found in options pricing), and depend less on simplifying assumptions and standardized probability distributions. The principal advantage over analytic methods is the ability to model virtually any real-world situation to a desired degree of precision.

- Statistical methods—models that are based on observed statistical qualities of (and among) random variables without regard to cause/effect relationships. The principal advantage over structural models is ease of model parameterization from available (often public) data.
  - Mean/variance/covariance (MVC) methods—a special class of statistical methods that rely on only three parameters: mean, variance, and covariance matrix.

- Structural methods—models that are based on explicit cause/effect relationships, not simply statistical relationships such as correlations. The cause/effect linkages are typically derived from both data and expert opinion. The principal advantages over statistical methods is the ability to examine the causes driving certain outcomes (e.g., ruin scenarios), and the ability to directly model the effect of different decisions on the outcome.

- Dynamic Financial Analysis (DFA)—the name for a class of structural simulation models of insurance company operations, focusing on certain hazard and financial risks and designed to generate financial pro forma projections.

  *Note: As a practical matter and as noted above, the choice of modeling approach is typically between **statistical analytic models** and **structural simulation models**. The contrast between these modeling approaches is summarized in the table below:*

The models described above generally presuppose the existence of sufficient data with which to fully parameterize the models. This is often not the case in practice, particularly as respects operational and strategic risks.

There is a wide variety of risk modeling methods that can be applied to a specific risk. They can be thought of as lying on a continuum that is based on the extent to which they rely on historical data vs. expert input (see Figure 8-1). Along the continuum of sources of information, the methods listed on the left are ones that

Representation of Relationships	Calculation Technique	Examples	Relative Advantages
Statistical (based on observed statistical qualities without regard to cause/effect)	Analytic (closed-form formula solutions)	• RBC • Rating agency models	Speed; ease of replication; use of publicly available data (well suited for industry oversight bodies)
Structural (based on specified cause/effect linkages; statistical qualities are outputs, not inputs)	Simulation (solutions derived from repeated "draws" from the distribution)	• DFA • Many options pricing models	Flexibility; treatment of complex relationships; incorporation of decision processes; ability to examine scenario drivers (well suited for individual companies)

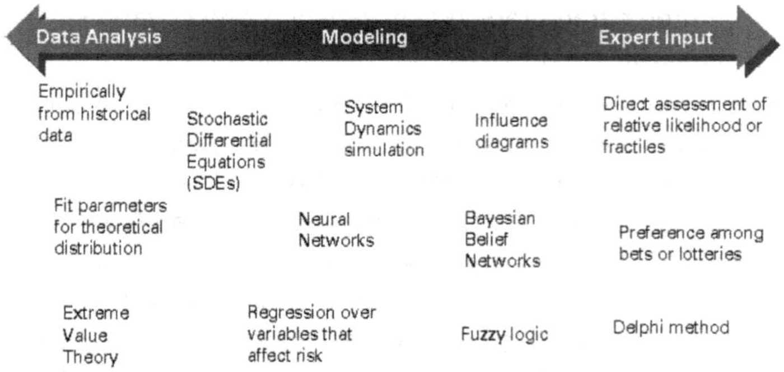

FIGURE 8-1 There is a continuum of methods for modeling risks. Each method has advantages/disadvantages over others, so it's important to select the best methods based on facts and circumstances.

rely primarily on the availability of historical data. They include, for example, empirical distributions, parametric methods to fit theoretical probability density functions, regression, stochastic differential equations and extreme value theory. These methods have been used extensively by financial institutions to model financial risks.

The methods listed on the right in Figure 8-1 rely primarily on expert input, including for example, Delphi method, preference among bets or lotteries, and influence diagrams. These have been used successfully for several decades by decision and risk analysts to model operational risks in support of management decision-making in manufacturing, particularly in the oil and gas industry, and in the medical sector. The methods listed in the middle of the continuum rely on data, to the extent that it is available, and expert judgment to supplement the missing data. In these methods, expert judgment is used to develop the model logic indicating the interactions among key variables and to quantify cause/effect relationships based on experience and ancillary or sparse data. Methods such as system dynamics simulation, Bayesian belief networks and fuzzy logic in particular are ideally suited for quantifying operational and strategic risks.

Risk Integration

Several of the risks of interest to the organization may be correlated with one another. For example, economic inflation (a driver of cost trends across multiple business segments) is highly correlated with interest rates (a driver of asset values and investment returns). It is important to capture these correlations—indeed, this is the essence of ERM. There are several ways to do this.

A direct way to express dependencies among risks is to estimate the statistical correlations between each of the individual risks. These estimates are often arrayed in a "covariance matrix."

- Covariance—a statistical measure of the degree to which two random variables are correlated. Related to correlation coefficient (correlation coefficient = covariance divided by the product of the standard deviations of the two random variables). A correlation coefficient of +1.0 indicates perfect positive correlation; −1.0 indicates perfect negative correlation (i.e., a "natural hedge"); zero indicates no correlation.

- Covariance matrix—a two-dimensional display of the covariances (or correlation coefficients) among several random variables; the covariance between any two variables is shown at their cross-section in the matrix.

The estimation of these covariances can be a practical difficulty, as the number of estimates required rises as the square of the number of risks.

An alternative way to capture risk interrelationships is through a *structural simulation model* of the enterprise, described above. In essence, a structural simulation model allows one to capture the dependencies among variable inputs in a simple, accurate and logically consistent way by virtue of the model's cause/effect linkages of these inputs to common higher-level inputs.

For example, interest rates and inflation rates are often generated stochastically by means of an economic scenario generation model, wherein these two random variables are linked to higher-level economic forces. In turn, other lower-level random variables, such as product costs, prices, asset values and investment income, are linked causally to interest rates and inflation rates within the model. Without such structural linkages, other models (such as MVC models, described above) can generate sets of random variables that are unrealistic relative to each other, regardless of how accurate the correlation estimates among them may be.

The statistical correlations among risks that are related through a structural simulation model are an emergent property (i.e., an output) of the model, not values to be separately estimated. To the extent that certain inputs are not related to a common higher-level input, yet one believes that a relationship exists between them, these correlations can be stated explicitly in terms of a covariance matrix, whose values can be determined through data analysis, expert opinion or both.

Risk Prioritization

Risk prioritization is ranking material risks on an appropriate scale, such as frequency, severity or both.

- Risk mapping—the visual representation of identified risks in a way that easily allows ranking them. This representation often takes the form of a two-dimensional grid with frequency (or likelihood of occurrence) on one axis, and severity (or degree of financial impact) on the other axis; the risks that fall in the high-frequency/ high severity quadrant are typically given highest priority risk management attention.

A more useful ranking of risks is in terms of each risk's impact on the organization's overall key performance indicators (KPIs). The marginal contribution of each individual risk factor to the overall risk profile of the organization can be determined by "turning off" that risk factor (changing that particular input from stochastic to deterministic) and examining the impact on the KPI probability distribution. This technique provides a straightforward way of isolating the impact of a particular risk factor (such as natural catastrophes) on overall capital adequacy, for example. In this way, the prioritization of risk factors, which is often done qualitatively, can be more rigorously validated.

Tool Applications for Treating/ Exploiting Risks

The techniques, models and measures above are used in various combinations to assist management decision-making in a number of areas. Several of these specific applications are discussed below, following the definitions of two generic applications ("optimization" and "candidate analysis") that are employed within some of these specific applications. Note that the following list of specific applications is not exhaustive, and is expected to grow as ERM matures as a discipline. Virtually any deci-

sion that requires evaluating risk/return trade-offs is a candidate for ERM treatment.

- Generic applications:
  - Optimization—the formal process by which decisions are made under conditions of uncertainty. Components of an optimization exercise include a statement of the range of decision options, a representation of the uncertain conditions (usually in the form of probability distributions), a statement of constraints (usually in the form of limitations on the range of decision options), and a statement of the objective to be maximized (or minimized). An example of an optimization exercise is an asset allocation study (see below under risk management applications). [See also candidate analysis, below.]
  - Candidate analysis—a restricted form of optimization analysis in which only a finite number of prespecified decision options are considered, and the best set among those options is determined through the analysis. Optimization and candidate analyses can be contrasted as follows. An optimization analysis would typically result in the derivation of an "efficient frontier" curve in risk/return space, which contains the decision options that result in maximum return for each level of risk (i.e., the optimal decision option for each level of risk). A candidate analysis would not derive the efficient frontier curve, but would simply show the finite number of decision options in comparison with each other in risk/return space (i.e., a "scatter plot"). It would not be known how close each option is to the efficient frontier of options. Conceptually, if a candidate analysis were performed on an infinite number of candidate decision options, then the "envelope" or boundary of those options would form the efficient frontier.
- Capital management:
  - Capital adequacy—the determination of the minimum amount of capital needed to satisfy a specified economic capital constraint (e.g., a certain probability of ruin), usually calculated at the enterprise level.
  - Capital structure—the determination of the optimal mix of capital by type (debt, common equity, preferred equity), given the risk profile and performance objectives of the enterprise.
  - Capital attribution—the determination of the assignment of enterprise level capital to the various

business segments (e.g., lines of business, regions, projects) that make up the enterprise, in recognition of the relative risk of each segment, for purposes of measuring segment performance on a risk-adjusted basis (e.g., to provide the denominator for a RORAC or RARORAC analysis by segment).

-Diversification credit—the recognition of the "portfolio effect," which is the fact that the economic capital required at the enterprise level will be less than the sum of the capital requirements of the business segments calculated on a stand-alone basis. The diversification credit is typically apportioned to the business segments in a manner that attempts to preserve the relative equity of the capital attribution process.

- Capital allocation—the actual deployment of capital to different business segments.
- Performance measurement—the development and implementation of appropriate risk-based metrics for evaluation of business segment performance, reflecting capital consumption, return and volatility.
- Investment strategy/asset allocation—the determination of the optimal mix of assets by asset class (usually to maximize expected return at each level of risk, i.e., according to Modern Portfolio Theory). In advanced applications, the analysis reflects the nature and structure of both assets and liabilities and is called asset/liability management (ALM).

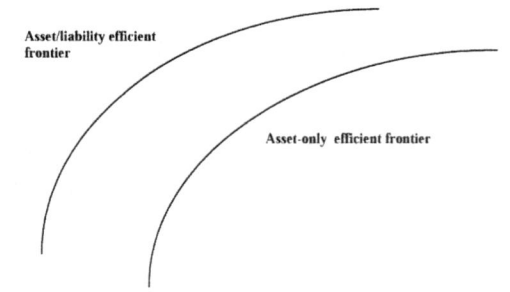

- Insurance/reinsurance/hedging strategy optimization—the determination of the optimal insurance/reinsurance/hedging program, reflecting program costs and risk reduction capability; usually conducted through candidate analysis. The risk reduction capability manifests itself in terms of both reduction in required economic capital and reduction in the cost of capital or required risk-adjusted rate of return.
- Crisis management—the proactive response of an organization to a severe event that could potentially impair its ability to meet its performance objectives.
- Contingency planning—the process of developing, and embedding in the organization, crisis management protocols in advance of crisis conditions.
- Business expansion/contraction strategy—the evaluation of merger, acquisition and divestiture options in terms of their incremental impact on the risk profile of the enterprise.
- Distribution channel strategy—the systematic evaluation of alternative channels (e.g., direct, agency, Internet), by means of simulation analysis to test impacts on growth, market share, profitability, etc. on a risk/return basis.
- Strategic planning—the use of structural simulation modeling, such as "real options" modeling, as a decision tool to assist management in selecting among alternative strategies, such as long-term research projects (see "Scientific Management at Merck", *Harvard Business Review,* 1994).

Risk Monitoring

Continual monitoring of the risk environment, and of the performance of the risk management processes, is often done by means of a senior management *risk dashboard—* the graphical presentation of the organization's key risk measures (often against their respective tolerance levels), as in the chart below.

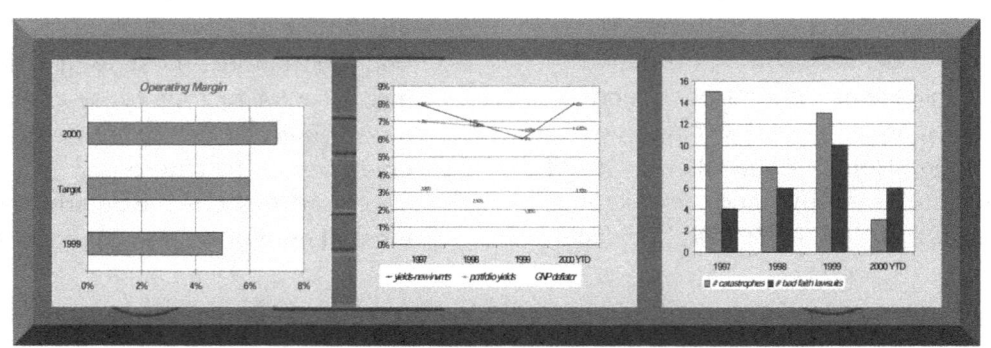

Typical measures included in the dashboard are shown in the following tables.

Marketing
■ New business sold
■ Retention of old business
■ Mix of business: new and renewal
■ Market share by customer type
■ Average premium or assets by per customer
■ % high-yield customers
■ Customer satisfaction
■ Average # of products per customer

Underwriting
■ Price achieved vs. target price
■ Exposure data (number of cars, payroll, etc.)
■ Exposure mix
■ Quotes accepted/declined
■ Variance analysis
■ Premium persistency
■ Loss ratio
■ Loss adjustment expense

Financial
■ Revenue
■ Underwriting profit
■ Investment profit
■ Pre-tax operating income
■ Net income
■ Return on equity and total capital
■ Economic value added

Sales/Distribution
■ Acquisition costs per sale
■ Sales by distribution channel
■ Growth/retention of agents

Investments
■ Cash flow
■ Yield on new investments
■ Yield on portfolio by class and duration
■ Convexity of assets
■ Duration of assets
■ Investment mix: new and portfolio
■ Credit default
■ Total return

Human Resources
■ Agency composition (number, age, service)
■ Total employment by department
▫ Number and percentage leaving the company
▫ Vacancy rates
▫ Average salary increase vs. plan
■ Employee commitment and engagement

Claims
■ Frequency and severity of claims
■ Claims department productivity

External Data
■ Audit compliance
■ Inflation rates
■ Interest rates
■ GNP
■ Competitor pricing

Note: Certain material in this chapter was drawn from the article "The Language of Enterprise Risk Management: A Practical Glossary and Discussion of Relevant Terms, Concepts, Models and Measures", by Jerry Miccolis, in the Enterprise Risk Management Expert Commentary section of the Web site of the International Risk Management Institute, http://www.irmi.com/expert/risk.asp. As noted therein, certain of these definitions were adapted from *The Dictionary of Financial Risk Management,* by Gastineau and Kritzman, 1996, Frank J. Fabozzi Associates. Certain other material was drawn from the Tillinghast—Towers Perrin monograph *RiskValueInsights™: CreatingValue Through Enterprise Risk Management,* (http://www.tillinghast.com).

ERM CASE STUDIES

This section recounts a number of success stories in which organizations made the commitment to and then benefited from ERM. Some of these benefits are explicit and measurable (e.g., increased investment returns, decreased capital requirements), others are more intangible but no less real (e.g., more enlightened strategic planning, more rigorous performance measurement/management). There should be elements from this collection of cases that will resonate with any given organization.

It also should be clear from these cases that, in terms of objectives, scope (of risks and of processes), organization, tools and techniques, there are a number of legitimate approaches to ERM and no single "correct way" that is appropriate for all entities. The proper approach to ERM for any enterprise is one that fits within the culture of that enterprise.

Risk Assessment

A large, market-leading manufacturer and distributor of consumer products with an uninterrupted 40-year history of earnings growth, embarked on ERM well before its competitors. This step followed their philosophy of "identifying and fixing things before they become problems". They were spurred by their rapid growth, increasing complexity, expansion into new areas, and the heightened scrutiny that accompanied their recent initial public offering. They conducted a comprehensive assessment of all risks that could potentially prevent the company from achieving its promised results. Views of company executives on key performance measures and risk thresholds were validated against financial models of stock analyst expectations. Multiple methodologies were used to rank order risks from all sources (hazard, financial, operational and strategic) on the basis of expected impact, and the results cross-validated. High-priority risk factors were interpreted and classified (as "strategic," "adaptation," "manageable," "business as usual") for appropriate response, and strategies for mitigation and exploitation were developed. In addition, a "Business Risk Self-assessment Toolkit" was created for ongoing use. Senior management attributes the ERM effort, and their communication of that effort to the investment community, as one of the drivers of the company's superior market valuation.

A large health plan had traditionally conducted separate and uncoordinated risk assessments through its risk management, legal and internal audit functions. It undertook an enterprise-wide risk assessment covering all functional and operational divisions. The objective was to prioritize all sources of risk against a common set of financial and customer metrics to enable senior management to focus the organization's limited resources on the proper short list of critical concerns. In addition to providing a meaningful and useful calibration of risks of varied types, this exercise surfaced critical business risks that had not been identified through any previous audit or strategic planning exercise. Senior management uses the results of this assessment to set its strategic agenda.

Distribution Strategy

A medium-sized life insurance company wanted to reconsider their distribution strategy in light of plans to demutualize the following year. The bulk of their production came from a network of career agencies, and the company wanted to investigate not only other distribution channels but also the possibility of becoming a wholesaler to other financial institutions. They decided to analyze the risk/value economics of alternative operational strategies by developing a financial model of the underlying business dynamics. The process of model development and assumption setting forced the management team to articulate the alternative strategies more clearly and with greater specificity than they had thus far. The model was used iteratively to evaluate further variations in strategy suggested by a review of the projected financials at each prior iteration. Modeling the economics provided the management team with valuable information on the risks and opportunities underlying alternative strategies. As a result, the team was able to reach consensus on a distribution strategy that was better understood and provided the best prospects of success.

Performance Measurement

A large multinational financial services group undertook an assessment of the relative levels of economic capital required by each of its life and nonlife insurance subsidiaries. This involved identifying the major sources of risk in each line of business and modeling the impact of these risk areas on the projected cash flows. The results were used to determine an appropriate level of capital at individual product level, subsidiary level, product group level (across subsidiaries) and finally at group level. An economic scenario generation model was used to allow cross-currency aggregation. The resulting attribution of capital is used as the foundation for a performance measurement system relating shareholder risk to return on capital and total shareholder return. Actual return on capital is compared to the hurdle rate implied by the shareholder risk and differences are analyzed into above- and below-the-line effects.

Asset Allocation

A property/casualty insurance company's conservative asset mix resulted in performance returns that were not competitive. They evaluated alternative asset allocation strategies, along with an integrated reinsurance program, to enhance the returns from investments and manage the risk of their business. However, the company did not want its rating from A.M. Best to be affected as a result of implementing a more aggressive investment strategy. They developed a comprehensive model of the company and evaluated multiple scenarios of economic value in relation to risk. The model allowed them to develop a strategy to alter their asset allocation. A financial integrated stop-loss reinsurance program was designed with an investment hedge to mitigate the possibility that the investment portfolio may underperform a target return. The result: enhanced expected returns of the investment portfolio and lowered downside risk on operating income. The executive team's understanding of their return opportunities in relation to the risks of the business was deepened. This insight was used to focus the work of line managers, and also used in discussions with outside parties regarding overall risk management.

Strategic Planning

A leading global manufacturer and distributor of patented pharmaceuticals has developed its ERM approach around a "real options" model. In an industry noted for very expensive, very long-term research projects, success is dependent on making the right "bets" on those research projects, both at their outset and at critical decision junctures throughout the projects' life span. The company credits its pioneering work on its Research Planning Model as a key contributor to its competitive advantage. This model captures the important medical, operational and financial risks of each project, and applies sophisticated options pricing theory to discern among alternative projects and to manage the continuing investments in projects that pass the initial screening process. This approach, by recognizing the dynamics of the *staged* research decision process, has allowed the company to pursue ultimately successful projects that would have failed a more traditional net present value screening process. (*Note:* This case study is documented in "Scientific Management at Merck: An Interview with CFO Judy Lewent," *Harvard Business Review,* January-February 1994.) Certain tools developed for this approach—most notably "decision trees"—have become routinely used in management discussions of unrelated issues throughout various organizational levels, thus contributing to the company's "common language of risk."

The board of directors at a large electric utility, motivated both by local corporate governance guidelines and the opening of their industry to competition, mandated an integrated approach to risk management throughout the organization. They piloted the process in a business unit that was manageable in size, represented a microcosm of the risks faced by the parent, and did not have entrenched risk management systems. This same unit was the focus of the parent's strategy for seeking international growth—a strategy that would take the organization into unfamiliar territory—and had no established process for managing the attendant risks in a comprehensive way. The pilot project was deemed a success and, among other things, the ERM unit is now a key participant in the organization's strategic planning process. This participation takes the form of building stochastic models around the key drivers of the strategic plan (weather conditions, customer demands, economic conditions, etc.) to assess the robustness of the plan. The board will not approve the strategic plan without such an ERM evaluation.

Product Design

A life insurer was looking to improve the product design features of its flagship universal life product; specifically, incorporating a market value adjustment to protect against having to credit high interest in times of falling asset market values. The market value adjustment could have been a serious detriment to potential policyholders and might not have received regulatory approval. Working together, senior management, an actuarial team and

the investment fund manager determined that an ALM model be developed using a set of stochastically generated interest rate scenarios. Various investment strategies were considered, covering a varying mix of mortgages, high-quality corporate bonds and CMO's. The ALM model then made projections based on the modeled relationship between the yield on these asset classes and the yield curve for treasuries as produced by the stochastic interest rate generator. Appropriate assumptions were made for defaults and prepayment risk. The yield relationships and other asset assumptions were reviewed by the fund management team, which also appraised the actuaries' assumptions underlying the model that was used to create the stochastically generated interest rate scenarios. Duration and convexity of both assets and liabilities were then analyzed, and the product design and the planned investment strategy fine-tuned to bring the assets and liabilities into balance. At this point, senior management analyzed various profit metrics for different investment strategies, looking at extreme scenarios for special review. Based on this analysis, the product appeared to hold up well even under the most extreme interest rate scenarios without any market value adjustment. The ALM analysis was effectively used to establish the product design and set the investment policy, and the product was filed without any market value adjustment.

Dividend Strategy

A medium-sized foreign life insurance company wanted to analyze the viability of their current dividend strategy for traditional business. Its market provided stable long-term dividend rates at a high level, even while market interest rates have declined, by smoothing book yields via accrual and realization of "hidden" reserves (unrealized capital gains on assets) and unallocated bonus reserves. In the prevailing low interest rate environment, the key competitive issue had become how long companies could finance their current dividend rates from existing buffers as compared to the market. In order to analyze the company's competitive position, ALM models were built for the company and a representative market company, reflecting the company's specific portfolio structure and strategies. On the basis of stochastic scenarios generation, the estimated time until ruin (until buffers had been exhausted) was determined for a range of potential ALM strategies for the company and compared to the results for the market. By varying the investment strategy, the company improved its risk/return positioning. As a result of the benchmark study, the life insurer received an indication of its current competitive position and a quantification of alternative ALM strategies, which led the company to reassess its dividend setting strategy for the entire traditional life portfolio.

Risk Financing

A very large retail company's CFO wanted to "assess the feasibility of taking a broader approach to risk management in developing the organization's future strategy." As part of this effort, they hoped to "evaluate our hazard risk and financial risk programs and strategies, to identify alternative methods of organizing and managing these exposures on a collective basis." As a first step, the company designed and built a model to provide an improved capability to evaluate its hazard and financial risks, both individually and on an aggregate portfolio basis. Criteria were developed to evaluate alternative risk financing programs based on appropriate measures of performance for risk and return. These evaluation criteria allowed the company to develop risk/return "efficient frontiers," representing a range of possible changes from their current program, on which to make informed management decisions. These decisions included:

- Choosing among competing insurance program submissions
- Determining retention levels
- Developing negotiating strategies
- Designing an overall risk financing strategy
- Prioritizing risk management activities (e.g., risk control).

The process for developing this capability included the determination of both appropriate return measures (e.g., net income, net cash flow) and appropriate risk measures (e.g., magnitude of potential loss, variance in financial measures, liquidity, compliance with bond covenants). These measures recognized and were developed from the variety of needs of key decision-makers, identified via structured interviews. Additionally, the process provided an understanding of those factors that have the greatest impact (in risk and return terms) on the performance of individual risks as well as the portfolio of all risks. To codify this process, the company developed a computer-based decision-support tool (with "senior management-friendly" graphics) that facilitated the evaluation of hazard and financial risks and allowed the decisions to be fact-based and consistent.

In addition to these examples, there are numerous others that demonstrate additional collateral benefits to undertaking an ERM process. These include:

- Improved communication and collaboration within the organization;
- Better-informed decisions at all levels in the organization by having gone through a rigorous and systematic risk identification/prioritization process; and
- Valuable change in mindset wherein risk can be a source of opportunity and not merely a threat to be avoided.

PRACTICAL CONSIDERATIONS IN IMPLEMENTING ERM

Once an enterprise decides to adopt ERM, it has to deal with a number of practical considerations in its successful implementation. These include, but are not limited to, the following:

Designating an ERM "Champion"

Given the implementation challenges, a unique individual is needed to spearhead the effort, becoming, in effect, the "champion" of the initiative. This role is often fulfilled by naming a Chief Risk Officer (CRO), who typically reports to the Chief Executive Officer or Chief Financial Officer. It is important that the organizational structure created for ERM (e.g., the CRO, the CRO's staff, the Risk Management Committee) is accountable and has the authority to be a change agent. Senior sponsorship needs to be high enough in the organization to have a top-level view of all the risks facing the enterprise, see across all organizational "silos," and have sufficient authority to effect changes in business practice.

Making ERM Part of the Enterprise Culture ("Tearing Down the Silos")

Under the historical, fragmented approach to risk management, numerous personnel are involved in various aspects of risk management. Typical of such approaches, the risk management department is responsible for hazard risks; the treasury department is responsible for financial risks; the human resources department is responsible for workers compensation, health, and employee risks; information technology is responsible for many operational risks; and the marketing department is responsible for many strategic risks. More than likely, these departments report to different managers within the organization, use different risk assessment procedures and terminology, calibrate risk on different scales, and have different timeframes in mind. Instituting such a sweeping change as implementing ERM may invoke defensive postures as these departments try to protect "their turf." The successful ERM approach would be one that coordinates all these different departments, recognizes the need for education, but allows for individual department initiative, flexibility, and autonomy.

Determining All Possible Risks of the Organization

As the list of risks included in the ERM Framework demonstrates, there is a multitude of risks facing every enterprise. Often the greatest risks are those not contemplated. Who in the property and casualty insurance industry could have conceived the magnitude of environmental risks assumed in insurance policies prior to the mid-1980's, or the terrorism exposure in the early 2000's? Who in the pharmaceutical industry could have conceived of effect of criminal tampering with products on store shelves? How can these risks be quantified, integrated or treated, if they cannot be identified? Some organizations have used their risk management committees to conduct and participate in periodic, structured "disaster scenario" brainstorming exercises specifically to contemplate and, as appropriate, plan for such "unthinkable" events.

Quantifying Operational and Strategic Risks

Although a great body of literature exists in the quantification of hazard and financial risks, not all enterprises are able to quantify intangible risks such as operational and strategic risk. It is difficult to determine point estimates of likelihoods (i.e., frequency) and consequences (i.e., severity) of these risks, let alone determine probability distributions around these estimates. Not only do models

generally not exist, but historical data that are the input to these models often do not exist either. Even if attempted, the cost of quantifying these risks needs to be considered in relationship to its benefit.

Enterprises can overcome these difficulties by starting with qualitative analysis of operational and strategic risk to determine those that are material and to prioritize them. In addition, some have advocated the use of causal models, as opposed to parametric models, to quantify these risks. These causal models often already exist (e.g., in strategic planning, in logistics) in some form within the organization and may simply need to be "stochasticized."

Integrating Risks (Determining Dependencies, Etc.)

Actuaries and financial analysts know of the difficulty in determining appropriate relationships or correlations for risks just within their respective areas of expertise, hazard and financial risks. These difficulties include:

- Past causal relationships are often not indicative of future relationships.
- There are differences in time frames (short-term, medium-term, long-term) to consider.
- Selecting correlation factors becomes cumbersome as the number of risks to review increases.

These difficulties are compounded when considering operational and strategic risks, both within these risk categories and among other risk categories.

Building structural models in modular form, which allows enhancement in manageable successive stages over time, is one practical approach some companies have employed.

Lack of Appropriate Risk Transfer Mechanisms

Although risk transfer mechanisms for hazard and financial risks exist via the insurance, reinsurance and capital markets, these markets are not complete in the sense of being able to provide all products and services that enterprises may need. These markets need to continue to evolve over time (such as the development of the alternative risk market for hazard risks) in order to provide products that will meet the risk transfer needs of enterprises.

Risk transfer mechanisms for operational and strategic risks are even less mature.

Monitoring the Process

Ideally, ERM is not a one-time "project," but a discipline that evolves over time as risks and opportunities within an enterprise change. The successful ERM process will include regular progress reports and comparisons to previous risk assessments so changes and refinements can be made as appropriate. Changes in the risk environment, based on new information, may result in changing strategies employed to treat and exploit risk. Regularly monitoring results can, and should, be tied to the time scales identified for the risks actively managed.

Start Slowly—Build Upon Successes

Because of the traditional, fragmented approach to risk management described earlier and the complexity of many businesses, enterprises often find it useful to start their ERM initiative slowly, tackling smaller projects first, so tangible results can be achieved early. The CRO or Risk Management Committee or both also may have limited resources initially, so they have to think on a smaller scale until successful projects are completed. However, the early successes can help to generate momentum and enthusiasm (and perhaps funding) for future ERM initiatives.

The case studies in the preceding chapter include examples of how different companies in various industries started small in terms of any or all of the following:

- Risk type (e.g., combining hazard and financial risks first, then planning to layer in strategic and operational risks);
- Process step (e.g., starting with a qualitative enterprise-wide risk assessment, then proceeding to risk quantification);
- Organizational component (e.g., piloting ERM within a single corporate division).

Just as there is no one correct approach to overall ERM design, there is no one correct path to incrementally building toward ERM. Both are dependent on the unique business imperatives and culture of each organization.

Financial Disasters 9

Excerpt is Chapter 4 of Financial Risk Management: A Practitioner's Guide to Managing Market and Credit Risk *by Steve Allen.*

Learning Objectives

After completing this reading, FRM Candidates should be able to:

- Describe the key factors that led to and the lessons learned from the following risk management case studies:
  - Chase Manhattan and their involvement with Drysdale Securities
  - Kidder Peabody
  - Barings
  - Allied Irish Bank
  - Union Bank of Switzerland (UBS)
  - Long Term Capital Management (LTCM)
  - Metallgesellschaft
  - Bankers Trust

One of the fundamental goals of financial risk management is to avoid the type of disasters that can threaten the viability of a firm. So we should expect that a study of such events that have occurred in the past will prove instructive. A complete catalog of all such incidents is beyond the scope of this book, but I have tried to include the most enlightening examples that relate to the operation of financial markets, as this is the primary focus of this manuscript.

A broad categorization of financial disasters would involve a three-part division:

- Cases in which the firm or its investors and lenders were seriously misled about the size and nature of the positions it had

- Cases in which the firm and its investors and lenders had reasonable knowledge of its positions, but had losses result from unexpectedly large market moves

- Cases in which losses did not result from positions held by the firm, but instead resulted from fiduciary or reputational exposure to positions held by the firm's customers

DISASTERS DUE TO MISLEADING REPORTING

A striking feature of all the financial disasters we will study involving cases in which a firm or its investors and lenders have been misled about the size and nature of its positions is that they all involve a significant degree of deliberation on the part of some individuals to create or exploit incorrect information. This is not to say situations do not exist in which firms are misled without any deliberation on the part of any individual. Everyone who has been in the financial industry for some time knows of many instances when everyone at the firm was misled about the nature of positions because a ticket was entered into a system incorrectly. Most typically, this will represent a purchase entered as a sale, or vice versa. However, although the size of such errors and the time it takes to detect them can sometimes lead to substantial losses, I am not aware of any such incident that has resulted in losses that were large enough to threaten the viability of a firm.

An error in legal interpretation can also seriously mislead a firm about its positions without any deliberate exploitation of the situation. However, such cases, although they can result in large losses, tend to be spread across many firms rather than concentrated at a single firm, perhaps because lawyers tend to check potentially controversial legal opinions with one another. The best known case of this type was when derivatives contracted by British municipalities were voided.

If we accept that all cases of financial disaster due to firms being misled about their positions involve some degree of complicity on the part of some individuals, we cannot regard them completely as cases of incorrectly reported positions. Some of the individuals involved know the correct positions, at least approximately, whereas others are thoroughly misinformed. Understanding such cases therefore requires examining two different questions:

- Why does the first group persist in taking large positions they know can lead to large losses for the firm despite their knowledge of the positions?

- How do they succeed in keeping this knowledge from the second group, who we can presume would put a stop to the position taking if they were fully informed?

I will suggest that the answer to the first question tends to be fairly uniform across disasters, while the answer to the second question varies.

The willingness to take large risky positions is driven by moral hazard. Moral hazard represents an asymmetry in reward structure and asymmetry in information—in other words, the group with the best information on the nature of the risk of a position has a greater participation in potential upside than potential downside. This often leads insiders to desire large risky positions that offer them commensurately large potential gains. The idea is that a trader owns an option on his profits; therefore, the trader will gain from increasing volatility. The normal counterweights against this are the attempts to place controls on the amount of risk taken by representatives of senior management, stockholders, creditors, and government regulators, who all own a larger share of the potential downside than the traders. However, when those who could exercise this control substantially lack knowledge of the positions, the temptation exists for traders to exploit the control weakness to run inflated positions. This action often leads to another motivation spurring the growth of risky positions—the Ponzi scheme.

Some traders who take risky positions that are unauthorized but disguised by a control weakness will make profits on these positions. These positions are then possibly closed down without anyone being the wiser. However, some unauthorized positions will lead to losses and traders will be strongly tempted to take on even larger, riskier positions in an attempt to cover up unauthorized losses. This is where the Ponzi scheme comes in. I think it helps to explain how losses from unauthorized positions can grow to be so overwhelmingly large. Stigum (1989) quotes an "astute trader" with regard to the losses in the Chase/Drysdale financial disaster: "I find it puzzling that Drysdale could lose so much so fast. If you charged me to lose one-fourth of a billion, I think it would be hard to do; I would probably end up making money some of the time because I would buy something going down and it would go up. They must have been extraordinarily good at losing money." I would suggest that the reason traders whose positions are unauthorized can be so "extraordinarily good at losing money" is that normal constraints that force them to justify positions to outsiders are lacking and small unauthorized losses already put a trader at risk of her job and reputation. With no significant downside left, truly reckless positions are undertaken in an attempt to make enough money to cover the previous losses. This is closely related to double-or-nothing betting strategies, which can start with very small stakes and quickly mushroom to extraordinary levels in an effort to get back to even.

This snowballing pattern can be seen in many financial disasters. Nick Leeson's losses on behalf of Barings were just $21 million in 1993, $185 million in 1994, and $619 million in just the first 2 months of 1995 (Chew [1996], Table 10.2). John Rusnak's unauthorized trading at Allied Irish Bank (AIB) accumulated losses of $90 million in its first 5 years through 1999, $210 million in 2000, and $374 million in 2001 (Ludwig [2002], Section H). Joseph Jett's phantom trades at Kidder Peabody started off small and ended with booked trades in excess of the quantity of all bonds the U.S. Treasury had issued.

The key to preventing financial disasters based on misrepresented positions is therefore the ability to spot unauthorized position taking in a timely enough fashion to prevent this explosive growth in position size. The lessons we can learn from these cases primarily center on why it took so long for knowledge of the misreported positions to spread

from an insider group to the firm's management. We will examine each case by providing a brief summary of how the unauthorized position arose, how it failed to come to management's attention, and what lessons can be learned. In each instance, I will provide references for those seeking more detailed knowledge of the case.

Chase Manhattan Bank/Drysdale Securities

Incident

In 3 months of 1976, Drysdale Government Securities, a newly founded subsidiary of an established firm, succeeded in obtaining unsecured borrowing of about $300 million by exploiting a flaw in the market practices for computing the value of U.S. government bond collateral. This unsecured borrowing exceeded any amount they would have been approved for, given that the firm had only $20 million in capital. Drysdale used the borrowed money to take outright positions in bond markets. When they lost money on the positions they put on, they lacked cash with which to pay back their borrowings. Drysdale went bankrupt, losing virtually all of the $300 million in unsecured borrowings. Chase Manhattan absorbed almost all of these losses because they had brokered most of Drysdale's securities borrowings. Although Chase employees believed they were only acting as agents on these transactions and were not taking any direct risk on behalf of Chase, the legal documentation of the securities borrowings did not support their claim.

Result

Chase's financial viability was not threatened by losses of this size, but they were large enough to severely damage its reputation and stock valuation for several years.

How the Unauthorized Positions Arose

Misrepresentation in obtaining loans is unfortunately not that uncommon in bank lending. A classic example would be Anthony De Angelis, "The Salad Oil King," who, in 1963, obtained $175 million in loans supposedly secured by large salad oil holdings, which turned out to be vast drums filled with water with a thin layer of salad oil floating on top. Lending officers who came to check on their collateral were bamboozled into only looking at a sample from the top of each tank.

The following are some reasons for featuring the Drysdale shenanigans in this section rather than any number of other cases of misrepresentation:

- Drysdale utilized a weakness in trading markets to obtain its funds.
- Drysdale lost the borrowed money in the financial markets.
- It is highly unusual for a single firm to bear this large a proportion of this large a borrowing sting.

There is not much question as to how Drysdale managed to obtain the unsecured funds. They took systematic advantage of a computational shortcut in determining the value of borrowed securities. To save time and effort, borrowed securities were routinely valued as collateral without accounting for accrued coupon interest. By seeking to borrow large amounts of securities with high coupons and a short time left until the next coupon date, Drysdale could take maximum advantage of the difference in the amount of cash the borrowed security could be sold for (which included accrued interest) and the amount of cash collateral that needed to be posted against the borrowed security (which did not include accrued interest).

How the Unauthorized Positions Failed to Be Detected

Chase Manhattan allowed such a sizable position to be built up largely because they believed that the firm's capital was not at risk. The relatively inexperienced managers running the securities borrowing and lending operation were convinced they were simply acting as middlemen between Drysdale and a large group of bond lenders. Through their inexperience, they both failed to realize that the wording in the borrowing agreements would most likely be found by a court to indicate that Chase was taking full responsibility for payments due against the securities borrowings or to realize the need for experienced legal counsel to review the contracts.

How the Unauthorized Positions Were Eventually Detected

There was some limit to the size of bond positions Drysdale could borrow, even given the assumption that the borrowings were fully collateralized. At some point, the size of their losses exceeded the amount of unauthorized borrowings they could raise and they had to declare bankruptcy.

Lessons Learned

The securities industry as a whole learned that it needed to make its methods for computing collateral value on bond borrowings more precise. Chase, and other firms who may have had similar control deficiencies, learned the need for a process that forced areas contemplating new product offerings to receive prior approval from representatives of the principal risk control functions within the firm.

Further Reading

Chapter 14 of Stigum (1989) gives a detailed description of the Chase/Drysdale incident, some prior misadventures in bond borrowing collateralization, and the subsequent market reforms.

Kidder Peabody

Incident

Between 1992 and 1994, Joseph Jett, head of the government bond trading desk, entered into a series of trades that were incorrectly reported in the firm's accounting system, artificially inflating reported profits. When this was ultimately corrected in April 1994, $350 million in previously reported gains had to be reversed.

Result

Although Jett's trades had not resulted in any actual loss of cash for Kidder, the announcement of such a massive misreporting of earnings triggered a substantial loss of confidence in the competence of the firm's management by customers and General Electric, which owned Kidder. In October 1994, General Electric sold Kidder to Paine Webber, which dismantled the firm.

How the Unauthorized Positions Arose

A flaw in accounting for forward transactions in the computer system for government bond trading failed to take into account the present valuing of the forward. This enabled a trader purchasing a cash bond and delivering it at a forward price to book an instant profit. Over the period between booking and delivery, the profit would inevitably dissipate, since the cash position had a financing cost that was unmatched by any financing gain on the forward position.

Had the computer system been used as it was originally intended (for a handful of forward trades with only a few days to forward delivery), the size of error would have been small. However, the system permitted entry not only of contracted forward trades, but also of intended forward delivery of bonds to the U.S. Treasury, which did not actually need to be acted on, but could be rolled forward into further intentions to deliver in the future. Both the size of the forward positions and the length of the forward delivery period were constantly increased to magnify the accounting error. This permitted a classic Ponzi scheme of ever mounting hypothetical profits covering the fact that previously promised profits never materialized.

Although it has never been completely clear how thoroughly Jett understood the full mechanics of the illusion, he had certainly worked out the link between his entry of forward trades and the recording of profit, and increasingly exploited the opportunity.

How the Unauthorized Positions Failed to Be Detected

Suspicions regarding the source of Jett's extraordinary profit performance were widespread throughout the episode. It was broadly perceived that no plausible account was being offered of a successful trading strategy that would explain the size of reported earnings. On several occasions, accusations were made that spelled out exactly the mechanism behind the inflated reporting. Jett seemed to have had a talent for developing explanations that succeeded in totally confusing everyone (including, perhaps, himself) as to what was going on. However, he was clearly aided and abetted by a management satisfied enough not to take too close a look at what seemed like a magical source of profits.

How the Unauthorized Positions Were Eventually Detected

Large increases in the size of his reported positions and earnings eventually triggered a more thorough investigation of Jett's operation.

Lessons to Be Learned

Two lessons can be drawn from this: Always investigate a stream of large unexpected profits thoroughly and make sure you completely understand the source. Periodically review models and systems to see if changes in the way they are being used require changes in simplifying assumptions.

Further Reading

Jett has written a detailed account of the whole affair (see Jett [1999]). However, his talent for obscurity remains and it is not possible to tell from his account just what he believes generated either his large profits or subsequent losses. For an account of the mechanics of the deception, one must rely on the investigation conducted by Gary Lynch on behalf of Kidder. Summaries of this investigation can be found in Hansell (1997), Mayer (1995), and Weiss (1994).

Barings

Incident

The incident involved the loss of roughly $1.25 billion due to the unauthorized trading activities during 1993 to 1995 of a single, relatively junior trader named Nick Leeson.

Result

The size of the losses relative to Barings' capital along with potential additional losses on outstanding trades forced Barings into bankruptcy in February 1995.

How the Unauthorized Positions Arose

Leeson, who was supposed to be running a low-risk, limited return arbitrage business for Barings in Singapore, was actually taking increasingly large speculative positions in Japanese stocks and interest rate futures and options. He disguised his speculative position taking by reporting that he was taking the positions on behalf of fictitious customers. By booking the losses to these nonexistent customer accounts, he was able to manufacture fairly substantial reported profits for his own accounts, enabling him to earn a $720,000 bonus in 1994.

How the Unauthorized Positions Failed to Be Detected

A certain amount of credit must be given to Leeson's industriousness in perpetrating a deliberate fraud. He worked hard at creating false accounts and was able to exploit his knowledge of weaknesses in the firm's controls. However, anyone reading an account of the incident will have to give primary credit to the stupendous incompetence on the part of Barings' management, which ignored every known control rule and failed to act on myriad obvious indications of something being wrong. What is particularly amazing is that all those trades were carried out in exchange-traded markets that require immediate cash settlement of all positions, thereby severely limiting the ability to hide positions (although Leeson did even manage to get some false reporting past the futures exchange to reduce the amount of cash required).

The most blatant of management failures was an attempt to save money by allowing Leeson to function as head of trading and the back office at an isolated branch. Even when auditors' reports warned about the danger of allowing Leeson to settle his own trades, thereby depriving the firm of an independent check on his activities, Barings' management persisted in their folly. Equally damning was management's failure to inquire how a low-risk trading strategy was supposedly generating such a large profit. Even when covering these supposed customer losses on the exchanges required Barings to send massive amounts of cash to the Singapore branch, no inquires were launched as to the cause. A large part of this failure can be attributed to the very poor structuring of management information so that different risk control areas could be looking at reports that did not tie together. The funding area would see a report indicating that cash was required to cover losses of a customer, not the firm, thereby avoiding alarm bells about the trading losses. A logical consequence is that credit exposure to customers must be large since the supposed covering of customer losses would entail a loan from Barings to the customer. However, information provided to the credit risk area was not integrated with information provided to funding and showed no such credit extension.

How the Unauthorized Positions Were Eventually Detected

The size of losses Leeson was trying to cover up eventually got too overwhelming and he took flight, leaving behind an admission of irregularities.

Lessons to Be Learned

One might be tempted to say that the primary lesson is that there are limits to how incompetent you can be and still hope to manage a major financial firm. However, to try to take away something positive, the major lessons would be the absolute necessity of an independent trading back office, the need to make thorough inquiries about unexpected sources of profit (or loss), and the need to make thorough inquiries about any large unanticipated movement of cash.

Further Readings

A concise and excellent summary of the Barings case constitutes Chapter 10 of Chew (1996). Chapter 11 of Mayer (1997) contains less insight on the causes, but is strong on the financial and political maneuvers required to avoid serious damage to the financial system from the Barings failure. Leeson has written a full-length book that appears to be reasonably honest as to how he evaded detection (Leeson 1996). Fay (1996) and Rawnsley (1995) are also full-length accounts.

Allied Irish Bank (AIB)

Incident John Rusnak, a currency option trader in charge of a very small trading book in AIB's Allfirst First Maryland Bancorp subsidiary, entered into massive unauthorized trades during the period 1997 through 2002, ultimately resulting in $691 million in losses.

Result

This resulted in a major blow to AIB's reputation and stock price.

How the Unauthorized Positions Arose

Rusnak was supposed to be running a small arbitrage between foreign exchange (FX) options and FX spot and forward markets. He was actually running large outright positions and disguising them from management.

How the Unauthorized Positions Failed to Be Detected

To quote the investigating report, "Mr. Rusnak was unusually clever and devious." He invented imaginary trades that offset his real trades, making his trading positions appear small. He persuaded back-office personnel not to check these bogus trades. He obtained cash to cover his losses by selling deep-in-the-money options, which provided cash up front in exchange for a high probability of needing to pay out even more cash at a later date, and covered up his position by offsetting these real trades with further imaginary trades. He entered false positions into the firm's system for calculating value at risk (VaR) to mislead managers about the size of his positions.

In many ways, Rusnak's pattern of behavior was a close copy of Nick Leeson's at Barings, using similar imaginary transactions to cover up real ones. Rusnak operated without Leeson's advantage of running his own back office, but had the offsetting advantage that he was operating in an over-the-counter market in which there was not an immediate need to put up cash against losses. He also was extremely modest in the amount of false profit he claimed so he did not set off the warning flags of large unexplained profits from small operations, which Leeson and Jett at Kidder Peabody triggered in their desire to collect large bonuses.

Like Barings, AIB's management and risk control units demonstrated a fairly startling level of incompetence in failing to figure out that something was amiss. AIB at least has the excuse that Rusnak's business continued to look small and insignificant, so it never drew much management attention. However, the scope and length of time over which Rusnak's deception continued provided ample opportunity for even the most minimal level of controls to catch up with him.

The most egregious was the back office's failure to confirm all trades. Rusnak succeeded in convincing back-office personnel that not all of these trades needed to be confirmed. He relied partly on an argument that trades whose initial payments offset one another didn't really need to be checked since they did not give rise to net immediate cash flow, ignoring the fact that the purported trades had different terms and hence significant impact on future cash flows. He relied partly on booking imaginary trades with counterparties in the Asian time zone, making confirmation for U.S.-based back-office staff a potentially unpleasant task involving middle-of-the-night phone calls, perhaps making it easier to persuade them that this work was not really necessary. He also relied on arguments that costs should be cut by weakening or eliminating key controls.

Once this outside control was missing, the way was opened for the ongoing manipulation of trading records. Auditors could have caught this, but the spot audits performed used far too small a sample. Suspicious movements in cash balances, daily trading profit and loss (P&L), sizes of gross positions, and levels of daily turnover were all ignored by Rusnak's managers

through a combination of inexperience in FX options and over-reliance on trust in Rusnak's supposedly excellent character as a substitute for vigilant supervision. His management was too willing to withhold information from control functions and too compliant with Rusnak's bullying of operations personnel as part of a general culture of hostility toward control staff. This is precisely the sort of front-office pressure that reduces support staff independence.

How the Unauthorized Positions Were Eventually Detected

In December 2001, a back-office supervisor noticed trade tickets that did not have confirmations attached. When informed that the back-office personnel did not believe all trades required confirmations, he insisted that confirmation be sought for existing unconfirmed trades. Although it took some time for the instructions to be carried out, when they finally were carried out in early February 2002, despite some efforts by Rusnak to forge written confirmations and bully the back office into not seeking verbal confirmations, his fraud was bought to light within a few days.

Lessons to Be Learned

This incident does not provide many new lessons beyond the lessons that should already have been learned from Barings. This case does emphasize the need to avoid engaging in small ventures in which the firm lacks any depth of expertise—there is simply too much reliance on the knowledge and probity of a single individual.

On the positive side, the investigative report on this fraud has provided risk control units throughout the financial industry with a set of delicious quotes that are sure to be trotted out anytime they feel threatened by cost-cutting measures or front-office bullying and lack of cooperation. The following are a few choice samples from Ludwig (2002):

- When one risk control analyst questioned why a risk measurement system was taking market inputs from a front-office-controlled system rather than from an independent source, she was told that AIB "would not pay for a $10,000 data feed from Reuters to the back office."

- When questioned about confirmations, "Mr. Rusnak became angry. He said he was making money for the bank, and that if the back office continued to question everything he did, they would drive him to quit . . . Mr. Rusnak's supervisor warned that if Mr. Rusnak left the bank, the loss of his profitable trading would force job cuts in the back office."

- "When required, Mr. Rusnak was able to use a strong personality to bully those who questioned him, particularly in Operations." His supervisors "tolerated numerous instances of severe friction between Mr. Rusnak and the back-office staff."

- Rusnak's supervisor "discouraged outside control groups from gaining access to information in his area and reflexively supported Mr. Rusnak whenever questions about his trading arose."

- " . . . in response to general efforts to reduce expense and increase revenues, the Allfirst treasurer permitted the weakening or elimination of key controls for which he was responsible . . . Mr. Rusnak was able to manipulate this concern for additional cost cutting into his fraud."

Further Reading

Since this is the newest of the disasters, not much has been written on it yet. I have relied heavily on the very prompt and thorough report issued by Ludwig (2002).

Union Bank of Switzerland (UBS)

Incident

This incident involves losses of between $400 million and $700 million in equity derivatives during 1997, which appear to have been exacerbated by lack of internal controls. A loss of $700 million during 1998 was due to a large position in Long Term Capital Management (LTCM).

Result

The 1997 losses forced UBS into a merger on unfavorable terms with Swiss Bank Corporation (SBC) at the end of 1997. The 1998 losses came after that merger.

Were the Positions Unauthorized?

Less is known about the UBS disaster than the other incidents discussed in this chapter. Even the size of the losses has never been fully disclosed. Considerable controversy exists about whether the 1997 losses just reflected poor decision making or unlucky outcomes or whether an

improper control structure led to positions that management would not have authorized. The 1998 losses were the result of a position that certainly had been approved by the UBS management, but evidence suggests that it failed to receive adequate scrutiny from the firm's risk controllers and that it was not adequately disclosed to the SBC management that took over the firm.

What seems uncontroversial is that the equity derivatives business was being run without the degree of management oversight that would be normally expected in a firm of the size and sophistication of UBS, but there is disagreement about how much this situation contributed to the losses. The equity derivatives department was given an unusual degree of independence within the firm with little oversight by, or sharing of information with, the corporate risk managers. The person with senior risk management authority for the department doubled as head of quantitative analytics. As head of analytics, he was both a contributor to the business decisions he was responsible for reviewing and had his compensation tied to trading results, which are both violations of the fundamental principles of independent oversight.

The equity derivative losses appear to have been primarily due to four factors:

- A change in British tax laws, which impacted the value of some long-dated stock options

- A large position in Japanese bank warrants, which was inadequately hedged against a significant drop in the underlying stocks

- An overly aggressive valuation of long-dated options on equity baskets, utilizing correlation assumptions that were out of line with those used by competitors

- Losses on other long-dated basket options, which may have been due to modelling deficiencies

The first two transactions were ones where UBS had similar positions to many of its competitors so it would be difficult to accuse the firm of excessive risk taking, although its Japanese warrant positions appear to have been unreasonably large relative to competitors. The last two problems appear to have been more unique to UBS. Many competitors made accusations that their prices for trades were off the market.

The losses related to LTCM came as the result of a position personally approved by Mathis Cabiallavetta, the UBS

CEO, so they were certainly authorized in one sense. However, accusations have been made that the trades were approved without adequate review by risk control areas and were never properly represented in the firm's risk management systems. Although about 40 percent of the exposure represented a direct investment in LTCM that had large potential profits to weigh against the risk, about 60 percent of the exposure was an option written on the value of LTCM shares. However, there was no effective way in which such an option could be risk managed given the illiquidity of LTCM shares and restrictions that LTCM placed on UBS delta hedging the position.

The imbalance in risk/reward trade-off for an option that was that difficult to risk manage had caused other investment banks to reject the proposed trade. UBS appears to have entered into the option because of its desire for a direct investment in LTCM, which LTCM tied to agreement to the option. Agreeing to this type of bundled transaction can certainly be a legitimate business decision, but it is unclear whether the full risk of the option had been analyzed by UBS or whether stress tests of the two positions taken together had been performed.

Lessons Learned

This incident emphasizes the need for independent risk oversight.

Further Reading

The fullest account of the equity derivative losses is contained in a book by Schutz (2000), which contains many lurid accusations about improper dealings between the equity derivatives department and senior management of the firm. Schutz has been accused of inaccuracy in some of these charges—see the October 1998 issue of *Derivatives Strategy* for details. There is also a good summary in the January 31, 1998 issue of the *Economist*.

A good account of the LTCM transaction is Shirreff (1998). Lowenstein (2000), an account of the LTCM collapse, also covers the UBS story in some detail.

Other Cases

Other disasters involving unauthorized positions will be covered more briefly, because they had less of an impact on the firm involved, because it is harder to uncover details on what occurred, or because they do not have any lessons to teach beyond those of the cases already discussed:

- Toshihida Iguchi of Daiwa Bank's New York office lost $1.1 billion trading Treasury bonds between 1984 and 1995. He hid his losses and made his operation appear to be quite profitable by forging trading slips, which enabled him to sell without authorization bonds held in customer accounts to produce funds he could claim were part of his trading profit. His fraud was aided by a situation similar to Nick Leeson's at Barings—Iguchi was head of trading and the back-office support function. In addition to the losses, Daiwa lost its license to trade in the United States, but this was primarily due to its failure to promptly disclose the fraud once senior executives of the firm learned of it. A more detailed account of this by Rob Jamesson of ERisk can be found on their Web site, www.erisk.com.

- The Sumitomo Corporation of Japan lost $2.6 billion in a failed attempt by Yasuo Hamanaka, a senior trader, to corner the world's copper market—that is, to drive up prices by controlling a large portion of the available supply. Sumitomo management claimed that Hamanaka had employed fraudulent means in hiding the size of his positions from them. Hamanaka claimed that he had disclosed the positions to senior management. Hamanaka was sent to jail for his actions. The available details are sketchy, but some can be found in Dwyer (1996), *Asiaweek* (1996), Kooi (1996), and McKay (1999).

- Askin Capital Management and Granite Capital, hedge funds that invested in mortgage securities, went bankrupt in 1994 with losses of $600 million. It was revealed that David Askin, the manager of the funds, was valuing positions with his own marks substituted for dealer quotes and using these position values in reports to investors in the funds and in marketing materials to attract new clients. For a brief discussion, see Mayer (1997).

- Merrill Lynch reportedly lost $350 million in trading mortgage securities in 1987, due to risk reporting that used a 13-year duration for all securities created from a pool of 30-year mortgages. Although this duration is roughly correct for an undivided pool of 30-year mortgages, when the interest-only (IO) part is sold and the principal-only (PO) part is kept, as Merrill was doing, the correct duration is 30 years. See Crouhy, Galai, and Mark (2001).

- National Westminster Bank in 1997 reported a loss on interest rate caps and swaptions of about $140 million. The losses were attributed to trades dating back to 1994 and had been masked by deliberate use by traders of incorrect volatility inputs for less liquid maturities. The loss of confidence in management caused by this incident may have contributed to NatWest's sale to the Royal Bank of Scotland. I have heard from market sources that the traders were taking advantage of the middle-office saving costs by checking only a sample of volatility marks against market sources, although it is unclear how the traders were able to determine in advance which quotes would be checked. A more detailed account by Eric Wolfe can be obtained on ERisk's Web site, www.erisk.com.

DISASTERS DUE TO LARGE MARKET MOVES

We will now look at financial disasters that were not caused by incorrect position information, but were caused by unanticipated market moves. The first question that should be asked is how is a disaster possible if positions are known. No matter what strategy is chosen, as losses start to mount beyond acceptable bounds, why aren't the positions closed out? The answer is lack of liquidity. We will focus on this aspect of these disasters.

Long Term Capital Management (LTCM)

The case we will consider at greatest length is that of the large hedge fund managed by LTCM, which came close to bankruptcy in 1998. In many ways, it represents an ideal example for this type of case since all of its positions were marked to a market value daily, the market values were supplied by the dealers on the other end of each trade, no accusations have been made of anyone at LTCM providing misleading information about positions taken, and the near failure came in the midst of some of the largest market moves in recent memory.

To review the facts, LTCM had been formed in 1994 by about a dozen partners. Many of these partners had previously worked together at Salomon Brothers in a highly successful proprietary trading group. Over the period

from 1994 until early 1998, the LTCM fund produced quite spectacular returns for its investors. From the beginning, the partners made clear that they would be highly secretive about the particulars of their investment portfolio, even by the standard of other hedge funds. (Since hedge funds are only open to wealthy investors and cannot be publicly offered the way mutual funds are, they are not subject to legal requirements to disclose their holdings.)

Within the firm, however, the management style favored sharing information openly, and essentially every investment decision was made by all the partners acting together, an approach that virtually eliminates the possibility of a rogue trader making decisions based on information concealed from other members of the firm. Although it is true that outside investors in the fund did not have access to much information beyond the month-end valuation of its assets and the track record of its performance, it is equally true that the investors knew these rules prior to their decision to invest. Since the partners who managed the fund were such strong believers in the fund that they had invested most of their net worth in it (several even borrowed to invest more than their net worth), their incentives were closely aligned with investors (in other words, there was little room for moral hazard). If anything, the concentration of partner assets in the fund should have led to more risk-averse decision making than might have been optimal for outside investors, who invested only a small portion of their wealth in the fund, with the exception of UBS.

In fact, even if investors had been given access to more information, there is little they could have done with it, since they were locked into their investments for extended time periods (generally, 3 years). This reflected the basic investment philosophy of LTCM, which was to locate trading opportunities that represented what they believed were temporary disruptions in price relationships due to short-term market pressures, which were almost certain to be reversed over longer time periods. To take advantage of such opportunities, they needed to know they had access to patient capital that would not be withdrawn if markets seemed to be temporarily going against them. This also helped to explain why LTCM was so secretive about its holdings. These were not quick in-and-out trades, but long-term holdings, and they needed to prevent other firms from learning the positions and trading against them.

The following are two examples of the type of positions the LTCM fund was taking:

- LTCM was long U.S. interest rate swaps and short U.S. government bonds at a time when these spreads were at historically high levels. Over the life of the trade, this position will make money as long as the average spread between the London Interbank Offering Rates (LIBORs) at which swaps are reset and the RP rates at which government bonds are funded is not higher than the spread at which the trade was entered into. Over longer time periods, the range for the average of LIBOR-RP spreads is not that wide, but in the short run, swap spreads can show large swings based on relative investor demand for the safety of governments versus the higher yield of corporate bonds (with corporate bond issuers then demanding interest rate swaps to convert fixed debt to floating debt).

- LTCM sold equity options at historically high implied volatilities. Over the life of the trade, this position will make money if the actual volatility is lower than the implied, but in the short run, investor demand for protection against stock market crashes can raise implied volatilities to very high levels. Perold (1999A) presents further analysis of why LTCM viewed these trades as excellent long-term investments and presents several other examples of positions they entered into.

One additional element was needed to obtain the potential returns LTCM was looking for. They needed to be able to finance positions for longer terms in order to be able to ensure there was no pressure on them to sell positions before they reached the price relationships LTCM was waiting for. However, the banks and investment banks who financed hedge fund positions were the very competitors that they least wanted to share information on holdings with. How were they to persuade firms to take credit risk without knowing much about the trading positions of the hedge fund?

To understand why the lenders were comfortable in doing this, we need to digress a moment into how credit works in a futures exchange. A futures exchange represents the extreme of being willing to lend without knowledge of the borrower. Someone who purchases, for example, a bond for future delivery, needs to deposit only a small percentage of the agreed purchase price as margin and does not need to disclose anything about her financial condition.

The futures exchange is counting on the nature of the transaction itself to provide confidence that money will not be lost in the transaction. This is because any time the value of the bond falls, the purchaser is required to immediately provide added margin to fully cover the decline in value. If the purchaser does not do so, her position is closed out without delay. Loss is only possible if the price has declined so much since the last time the price fell and margin was added that the incremental price drop exceeds the amount of initial margin or if closing out the option results in a large price move. The probability of this occurring is kept low by setting initial margins high enough, restricting the size of position that can be taken by any one investor, and designing futures contract to cover sufficiently standardized products to ensure enough liquidity that the close-out of a trade will not cause a big price jump.

LTCM wanted to deal in over-the-counter markets as well as on futures exchanges partly because they wanted to deal in some contracts more individually tailored than those available on futures exchanges and partly because of the position size restrictions of exchanges. However, the mechanism used to assure lenders in over-the-counter markets is similar—the requirement to cover declines in market value by immediately putting up cash. If a firm fails to put up the cash, then positions are closed out. LTCM almost always negotiated terms that avoided posting the initial margin. Lenders were satisfied with the lack of initial margin based on the size of the LTCM fund's equity, the track record of their excellent returns, and their recognized investment management skills. Lenders retained the option of demanding initial margin if fund equity fell too much.

This dependence on short-term swings in valuation represented a potential Achilles' heel for LTCM's long-term focused investment strategy. Because they were seeking opportunities where market pressures were causing deviation from long-run relationships, a strong possibility always existed that these same market pressures would push the deviation even further. LTCM would then immediately need to come up with cash to fund the change in market valuation. This would not be a problem if some of their trades were moving in their favor at the same time as others were moving against them, since LTCM would receive cash on upswings in value to balance putting up cash on downswings (again, the same structure as exchange-traded futures). However, if many of their trades were to move against them in tandem, LTCM would need to raise cash quickly, either from investors or by cutting positions.

In the actual events of August and September 1998, this is exactly what led to LTCM's rapid downfall. The initial trigger was a combination of the Russian debt default of August, which unsettled the markets, and the June 1998 decision by Salomon Brothers to liquidate proprietary positions it was holding, which were similar to many of those held by LTCM. The LTCM fund's equity began to decline precipitously, from $4.1 billion as of the end of July 1998, and it was very reluctant to cut positions in a turbulent market in which any large position sale could easily move the valuations even further against them. This left the option of seeking new equity from investors. LTCM pursued this path vigorously, but the very act of their doing so created two perverse effects. First, rumors of their predicament caused competitors to drive market prices even further against what they guessed were LTCM's positions, in anticipation of LTCM being forced to unload the positions at distressed prices. Second, to persuade potential investors to provide new money in the midst of volatile markets, LTCM was forced to disclose information about the actual positions they held. As competitors learned more about the actual positions, their pressure on market prices in the direction unfavorable to LTCM intensified.

As market valuations continued to move against LTCM and the lack of liquidity made it even more unlikely that reducing positions would be a viable plan, it became increasingly probable that in the absence of a truly large infusion of new equity, the LTCM fund would be bankrupt. Its creditors started to prepare to close out LTCM's positions, but quickly came to fear that they were so large and the markets were so illiquid that the creditors would suffer serious losses in the course of doing so. The lenders were also concerned that the impact of closing out these positions would depress values in the already fragile markets and thereby cause considerable damage to other positions held by the creditors and other investment firms they were financing.

Ultimately, 14 of the largest creditors, all major investment banks or commercial banks with large investment banking operations, contributed a fresh $3.65 billion in equity investment in the LTCM fund to permit the firm to keep operating and allow for a substantial time period in which to close out positions. In return, the creditors received substantial control over fund management. The existing investors had their investment valued at the then current market value of $400 million so they had only a 10 percent share in the positions of the fund. Although some of the partners remained employed to help wind down investments, it was the consortium of 14 creditors who now exercised control and insisted on winding down all positions.

As a result, the markets calmed down. By 2000, the fund had been wound down with the 14 creditors having recovered all of the equity they invested and avoided any losses on the LTCM positions they had held at the time of the bailout. This outcome lends support to two propositions: LTCM was largely right about the long-term values underlying its positions, and the creditors were right to see the primary problem as one of liquidity, which required patience to ride out.

Please note that the bailout was not primarily a rescue of LTCM's investors or management, but a rescue of LTCM's creditors by a concerted action of these creditors. Even recently, I continue to encounter the view that the bailout involved the use of U.S. government funds, helped the LTCM investors and management avoid the consequences of their mistakes, and therefore contributed to an attitude that some firms are "too big to fail" and so can afford to take extra risks because they can count on the government absorbing some of their losses.

I do not think evidence is available to support any of these claims. (An interested reader can form her own conclusions by looking at the detailed account of the negotiations on the rescue package in Lowenstein [2000]. An opposing viewpoint can be found in Shirreff [2000].) The only government involvement was some coordination by the Federal Reserve, acting out of legitimate concern for the potential impact on the financial markets. The LTCM creditors took a risk by investing money in the fund, but did so in their own self-interest, believing (correctly, as it turns out) that they were thereby lowering their total risk of loss. LTCM's investors and managers had little left to lose at the point of the bailout since they could not lose more than their initial investment. It is true that, without a rescue, the fund would have been liquidated, which would have almost certainly wiped out the remaining $400 million market value of the investors. However, in exchange for this rescue, they were able to retain only a 10 percent interest in the fund's positions, since the $3.65 billion in new investment was explicitly not being used to enable new trades, but only to wind down the existing positions.

LTCM management was certainly aware of the potential for short-term market movements to disrupt their fundamental trading strategy of focusing on longer-term relationships. They tried to limit this risk by insisting that their positions pass value at risk (VaR) tests based on whether potential losses over 1 month due to adverse market moves would reduce equity to unacceptable levels. Where they seem to have fallen short of best practices was a failure to supplement VaR measures with a full set of stress test scenarios. They did run stress versions of VaR based on a higher than historical level of correlations, but it is doubtful that this offers the same degree of conservatism as a set of fully worked through scenarios.

A lesson that all market participants have learned from the LTCM incident is that a stress scenario is needed to look at the impact of a competitor holding similar positions exiting the market, as when Salomon decided to cut back on proprietary trading. However, even by best practice standards of the time, LTCM should have constructed a stress test based on common economic factors that could cause impacts across their positions, such as a flight to quality by investors, which would widen all credit spreads, including swap spreads, and increase premiums on buying protection against stock market crashes, hence increasing option volatility.

Another point on which LTCM's risk management could be criticized is a failure to account for the illiquidity of its largest positions in its VaR or stress runs. LTCM knew that the position valuations it was receiving from dealers did not reflect the concentration of some of LTCM's positions, either because dealers were not taking liquidity into account in their marks or because each dealer only knew a small part of LTCM's total size in its largest positions.

Two other criticisms have been made of LTCM's management of risk with which I disagree. One is that a simple computation of leverage would have shown that LTCM's positions were too risky. However, leverage by itself is not an adequate measure of risk of default. It must be multiplied by volatility of the firm's assets. But this just gets us back to testing through VaR or stress scenarios. The second criticism is that LTCM showed unreasonable faith in the outcome of models. I see no evidence to support this claim. Major positions LTCM entered into—U.S. swap spreads to narrow, equity volatilities to decline—were ones that many proprietary position takers had entered into. For example, the bias in equity implied volatilities due to demand for downside protection by shareholders had long been widely recognized as a fairly certain profit opportunity for investors with long enough time horizons. That some firms made more use of models to inform their trading judgement while others relied more on trader experience tells me nothing about the relative quality of their decision making.

Most of the focus of LTCM studies has been on the decision making of LTCM management and the losses of the investors. I believe this emphasis is misplaced. It is a fairly common occurrence, and to be expected, that investment funds will have severe drops in valuation. The bankruptcy of an investment fund does not ordinarily threaten the stability of the financial system the way the bankruptcy of a firm that makes markets or is a critical part of the payments system would. It just represents the losses of a small number of investors. Nor is there a major difference in consequences between bankruptcy and a large loss short of bankruptcy for an investment fund. It shouldn't matter to an investor whether a fund in which she has invested $10 million goes bankrupt or if a fund in which she has invested $30 million loses a third of its value. By contrast, losses short of bankruptcy only hurt the stockholders of a bank, while bankruptcy could hurt depositors and lead to loss of confidence in the banking system.

The reason that an LTCM failure came close to disrupting the financial markets and required a major rescue operation was its potential impact on the creditors to LTCM so we need to take a closer look at their role in the story. In retrospect, the creditors to LTCM believed they had been too lax in their credit standards and the incident triggered a major industry study of credit practices relating to trading counterparties (Counterparty Risk Management Policy Group [1999]).

Some suggestions for improved practices, many of which are extensively addressed in this study, have been:

- **A greater reluctance to allow trading without initial margin for counterparties whose principal business is investing and trading.** A counterparty that has other substantial business lines, for example, auto manufacturing or retail banking, is unlikely to have all of their economic resources threatened by a large move in financial markets. However, a firm that is primarily engaged in these markets is vulnerable to illiquidity spreading from one market to another as firms close out positions in one market to meet margin calls in another market. For such firms, initial margin is needed as a cushion against market volatility.

- **Factoring the potential costs of liquidating positions in an adverse market environment into estimates of the price at which trades can be unwound.** These estimates should be based on the size of positions as well as the general liquidity of the market. These potential liquidation costs should impact estimates of the amount of credit being extended and requirements for initial margin.

- **A push for greater disclosure by counterparties of their trading strategies and positions.** Reliance on historical records of return as an indicator of the volatility of a portfolio can be very misleading because it cannot capture the impact of changes in trading style. Increased allowance for liquidation costs of positions will be very inexact if the creditor only knows the positions that a counterparty holds with the creditor without knowing the impact of other positions held. To try to deal with counterparties' legitimate fears that disclosure of their positions will lead to taking advantage of this knowledge, creditors are implementing more stringent internal policies against the sharing of information between the firm's credit officers and the firm's traders.

- **Better use of stress tests in assessing credit risk.** To some extent, this involves using more extreme stresses than were previously used in measuring risk to reflect the increased market volatility that has been experienced in recent years. However, a major emphasis is also on more integration of market risk and credit risk stress testing to take into account overlap in risks. In the LTCM case, this would have required recognition by a creditor to LTCM that many of the largest positions being held by LTCM were also being held by other investment funds to which the firm had counterparty credit exposure, as well as by the firm's own proprietary traders. A full stress test would then look at the losses that would be incurred by a large market move and subsequent decrease in liquidity across all of these similar positions.

A complete account of the LTCM case covering all aspects of the history of the fund and its managers, the involvement of creditors, and the negotiations over its rescue can be found in Lowenstein (2000). The Harvard Business School case studies of Perold (1999A) and Perold (1999B) are a detailed but concise analysis of the fund's investment strategy and the dilemma that it faced in August 1998.

Metallgesellschaft (MG)

The disaster at Metallgesellschaft (MG) reveals another aspect of liquidity management. In 1992, an American subsidiary of MG, Metallgesellschaft Refining and Marketing (MGRM), began a program of entering into long-term contracts to supply customers with gas and oil products at fixed costs and hedge these contracts with short-term gas and oil futures. Although some controversy exists about how effective this hedging strategy was from a P&L standpoint, as we'll discuss in just a moment, the fundamental consequence of this strategy for liquidity management is certain. The futures being used to hedge were exchange-traded instruments requiring daily cash settlement. The long-term contracts with customers involved no such cash settlement. So no matter how effective the hedging strategy was, the consequence of a large downward move in gas and oil prices would be to require MGRM to pay cash against its futures positions that would be offset by money owed to MGRM by customers who would be paid in the future.

A properly designed hedge will reflect both the cash paid and the financing cost of that cash during the period until the customer payment is due and hence will be effective from a P&L standpoint. However, the funding must still be obtained, which can lead to funding liquidity risk. Such cash needs must be planned in advance. Limits need to be set on positions based on the amount of cash shortfall that can be funded.

It appears that MGRM did not communicate to its parent company the possible need for such funding. In 1993, when a large decrease in gas and oil prices had resulted in funding needs of around $900 million, the MG parent responded by closing down the future positions, leaving unhedged exposure to gas and oil price increases through the customer contracts. Faced with this open exposure, MG negotiated unwinds of these contracts at unfavorable terms. It may be that MG, with lack of advance warning as to possible cash needs, responded to the demand for cash as a sign that the trading strategy was deeply flawed—if only Barings' management had reacted similarly.

As mentioned earlier, the MG incident spurred considerable debate as to whether MGRM's trading strategy was reasonable or fundamentally flawed. Most notably, Culp and Miller (1995A) wrote an article defending the reasonableness of the strategy, and Mello and Parsons (1995) wrote an article attacking the Culp and Miller conclusions, which were then defended by Culp and Miller (1995B). Although it is difficult to settle the factual arguments about the particular events in the MG case, I believe the following lessons can be drawn:

- It is often a key component of a market maker's business strategy to extend available liquidity in a market. This requires the use of shorter-term hedges against longer-term contracts. Experience shows that this can be successfully carried out when proper risk controls are applied.

- The uncertainty of roll cost is a key risk for strategies involving shorter-term hedges against longer-term risk. This requires the use of valuation reserves based on conservative assumptions of future roll cost. MGRM does not appear to have utilized valuation reserves; it just based its valuation on the historical averages of roll costs.

- A firm running short-term hedges against longer-term risk requires the flexibility to choose the shorter-term hedge that offers the best trade-off between risk and reward. It may legitimately choose to follow a hedging strategy other than a theoretical minimum variance hedge, or choose not to hedge with the longest future available, based on liquidity considerations, or take into account the expectation of positive roll cost as part of potential return. It is not reasonable to conclude, as Mello and Parsons do, that these choices indicate that the firm is engaged in pure speculation rather than hedging. At the same time, regardless of a firm's conclusions about probable return, its assessment of risk should include valuation reserves, as in the previous point, and volume limits based on reasonable stress testing of assumptions.

DISASTERS DUE TO THE CONDUCT OF CUSTOMER BUSINESS

In this section, we focus on disasters that did not involve any direct financial loss to the firm, but were completely a matter of reputational risk due to the conduct of customer business.

Banker's Trust (BT)

The classic case of this type is the Banker's Trust (BT) incident of 1994, when BT was sued by Procter & Gamble (P&G) and Gibson Greetings. Both P&G and Gibson claimed that they had suffered large losses in derivatives trades they had entered into with BT due to being misled by BT as to the nature of the positions. These were trades on which BT had little market or credit risk, since they had hedged the market risk on them with other derivatives and there was no credit issue of P&G or Gibson being unable to pay the amount they owed. However, the evidence uncovered in the course of legal discovery for these lawsuits was severely damaging to BT's reputation for fair business dealing, led to the resignation of the firm's CEO, and ultimately had such negative consequences for their ability to do business that they were forced into an acquisition by Deutschebank, which essentially amounted to a dismemberment of the firm.

The exact terms of these derivative trades were quite complex and are not essential to understanding the incident. Interested readers are referred to Chew (1996, Chapter 2) for details. The key point is that the trades offered P&G and Gibson a reasonably probable but small reduction in funding expenses in exchange for a potentially large loss under some less probable circumstances. P&G and Gibson had been entering into such trades for several years prior to 1994 with good results. The derivatives were not tailored to any particular needs of P&G or Gibson in the sense that the circumstances under which the derivatives would lose them money were not designed to coincide with cases in which other P&G or Gibson positions would be making money. Their objective was just to reduce expected funding costs. Since the only way to reduce costs in some cases is to raise them in others, P&G and Gibson can be presumed to have understood that they could lose money under some economic circumstances. On what basis could they claim that BT had misled them?

One element that established some prima facie suspicion of BT was the sheer complexity of the structures. It was hard to believe that BT's clients started out with any particular belief about whether there was a small enough probability of loss of a structure to be comfortable entering into it. BT would have had to carefully explain all the intricacies of the payoffs to the clients for them to be fully informed.

Since it was quite clear that the exact nature of the structures hadn't been tailored to meet client needs, why had BT utilized so complex a design? The most probable reason was that they were designed to be complex enough to make it difficult for clients to comparison shop the pricing to competitor firms. However, this also made the clients highly dependent on BT on an ongoing basis. If they wanted to unwind the position, they couldn't count on getting a competitive quote from another firm.

BT claimed that they had adequately explained all the payoffs and risks to P&G and Gibson. But then came the discovery phase of the lawsuit. BT, like all trading firms, taped all phone lines of traders and marketers as a means of resolving disputes about verbal contracts. However, this taping also picked up internal conversations between BT personnel. When subpoenaed, they produced evidence of BT staff boasting of how thoroughly they had fooled the clients as to the true value of the trades and how little the clients understood the true risks. Further, the internal BT tapes showed that price quotes to P&G and Gibson were being manipulated to mislead them. At first, they were given valuations of the trades that were much too high to mask the degree of profit BT was able to book up front. Later, they were given valuations that were too low because this was BT's bid at which to buy back the trade or swap it into a new trade offering even more profit to BT. For more details on what was revealed in the tapes, see Holland and Himelstein (1995).

The BT scandal caused all financial firms to tighten up their procedures for dealing with customers, both in better controls on matching the degree of complexity of trades to the degree of financial sophistication of customers and in providing for customers to obtain price quotes from an area independent of the front office.

Another lesson that you would think would be learned is to be cautious about how you use any form of communication that can later be made public. BT's reputation was certainly hurt by the objective facts about their conduct, but it was even further damaged by the arrogant and insulting tone some of their employees used in referring to clients, which could be documented through recorded conversations. However, even with such an instructive example, we have seen Merrill Lynch's reputation being damaged in 2002 by remarks their stock analysts made in emails and tape-recorded conversations (see the article "Value of Trust" in the June 6, 2002 *Economist*) along with a number of similar incidents surrounding Wall Street's relations with Enron (see the article "Banks on Trial" in the July 25, 2002 *Economist*).

Other Cases

The following are some examples of other cases in which firms damaged their reputation by the manner in which they dealt with customers:

- Prudential-Bache Securities was found to have seriously misled thousands of customers concerning the risk of proposed investments in limited partnerships. In addition to damaging their reputation, Prudential-Bache had to pay more than $1 billion in fines and settlements. An account of this incident can be found in Eichenwald (1995).

- In 1995, a fund manager at Morgan Grenfell Asset Management directed mutual fund investments into highly speculative stocks, utilizing shell companies to evade legal restrictions on the percentage of a firm's stock that could be owned by a single fund. In addition to damage to their reputation, Morgan Grenfell had to pay roughly $600 million to compensate investors for resulting losses. A brief case study can be found on ERisk's Web site, www.erisk.com.

- JPMorgan's reputation was damaged by allegations that it misled a group of Korean corporate investors as to the risk in derivative trades that lost hundreds of millions of dollars based on the precipitous decline in the Thai bhat exchange rate against the dollar in 1997. An account of these trades and the ensuing lawsuits can be found in Gillen, Lee, and Austin (1999).

Risk Management Failures
What Are They and When Do They Happen?

Excerpt is Risk Management Failures: What Are They and When Do They Happen? *by René Stulz, Fisher College of Business Custom Editioning Paper Series.*

Learning Objectives

After completing this reading, FRM Candidates should be able to:

- Define the role of risk management and explain why a large financial loss is not necessarily a failure of risk management.
- Describe how risk management can fail.
- Describe how risk can be mismeasured.
- Explain how a firm can fail to take known and unknown risks into account in making strategic decisions.

- Explain the importance of communication in effective risk management.
- Describe how firms can fail to correctly monitor and manage risk on an ongoing basis.
- Explain the role of risk metrics and discuss the shortcomings of existing risk metrics.

Abstract

A large loss is not evidence of a risk management failure because a large loss can happen even if risk management is flawless. I provide a typology of risk management failures and show how various types of risk management failures occur. Because of the limitations of past data in assessing the probability and the implications of a financial crisis, I conclude that financial institutions should use scenarios for credible financial crisis threats even if they perceive the probability of such events to be extremely small.

In commentaries on the financial crisis that started during the summer of 2007, a constant refrain is that somehow risk management failed and that there were risk management failures at financial institutions across the world. For instance, an article in the Financial Times states that "it is obvious that there has been a massive failure of risk management across most of Wall Street."[1] In this article, I want to examine what it means for risk management to fail. I show that the fact that an institution makes an extremely large loss does not imply that risk management failed or that the institution made a mistake. This article does not examine the subprime financial crisis or problems of financial institutions during that crisis directly. Rather, it is an attempt to make sure that if risk management is blamed, it is for the right reasons. Otherwise, changes in risk management that take place in response to the crisis might be counterproductive and top executives and investors could keep expecting more from risk management than what it can actually deliver. I therefore show when bad outcomes can be blamed on risk management and when they cannot. In the process of doing so, I provide a typology of risk management failures.

To examine risk management failures more concretely, I go back to the problems experienced by the hedge fund LTCM in 1998 to analyze how one might conclude that the failure of LTCM was a risk management failure or not. I then generalize from that example to describe what constitutes a risk management failure and what does not. I will show that some events considered in the financial press to be risk management failures actually are not risk

management failures, but at the same time I will analyze many different ways in which risk management can fail. I then address the question of whether lessons from risk management failures can be used to help improve the practice of risk management. In the last part of this article, I discuss an approach to risk management that might enable institutions to better manage risks such as those that threatened them during the subprime financial crisis.

WAS THE COLLAPSE OF LONG-TERM CAPITAL MANAGEMENT A RISK MANAGEMENT FAILURE?

The story of Long-Term Capital Management (LTCM) is well-known.[2] In 1994, ex-Salomon Brothers traders and two future Nobel Prize winners started a hedge fund, the Long-Term Capital Fund. LTCM was the company that managed the fund. The fund performed superbly for most of its life: Investors earned 20% for ten months in 1994, 43% in 1995, 41% in 1996, and 17% in 1997. In August and September 1998, following the default of Russia on its ruble denominated debt, world capital markets were in crisis and the hedge fund LTCM lost most of its capital. Before its collapse, LTCM had capital close to $5 billion, assets in excess of $100 billion, and derivatives for a notional amount in excess of $1 trillion. By mid-September, LTCM's capital had fallen by more than $3.5 billion and the Federal Reserve Bank of New York coordinated a rescue by private financial institutions that injected $3.65 billion in the fund.

Does a loss of more than 70% of capital represent a risk management failure? Does a loss that requires a rescue by banks involving an injection of $3.65 billion of new capital show that risk management failed? It turns out that it is not easy to answer these questions. To define a risk management failure, one must first define the role of risk management.

In a typical firm, the role of risk management is first to assess the risks faced by the firm, communicate these

---

[1] "Wall Street dispatch: Imagination and common sense brew a safer culture," by David Wighton, Nov. 26, 2007, FT.com.

[2] The best public source for data on LTCM is a collection of four case studies by André Perold published in 1999, Long-Term Capital Management (A)—(D), available from Harvard Business School Publishing. Many books have been written on LTCM. Some of the numbers used in this article come from Roger Lowenstein, When genius failed: The rise and fall of Long-Term Capital Management, Random House, 2000.

risks to those who make risk-taking decisions for the firm, and finally manage and monitor those risks to make sure that the firm only bears the risks its management and board of directors want it to bear. In general, a firm will specify a risk measure that it focuses on together with additional risk metrics. When that risk measure exceeds the firm's tolerance for risk, risk is reduced. Alternatively, when the risk measure is too low for the firm's risk tolerance, the firm increases its risk. Because firms are generally more concerned about unexpected losses, a frequently used risk measure is Value-at-Risk or VaR, a measure of downside risk. VaR is the maximum loss at a given confidence level over a given period of time. Hence, if the 95% confidence level is used and a firm has a one-day VaR of $150 million, the firm has a 5% chance of making a loss in excess of $150 million over the next day if the VaR is correctly estimated. This measure might be estimated daily or over longer periods of time.

Even with our definition of the role of risk management, the returns of LTCM do not tell us anything about whether its risk management failed. To understand why, it is helpful to consider a very simple hypothetical example. Suppose that you stood in the shoes of the managers of LTCM in January 1998 and had the opportunity to invest in trades that, overall, had a 99% chance of producing a return for the fund before fees of 25% and a 1% chance of making a loss of 70% over the coming year. Though this example is hypothetical, it is plausible in light of the returns of LTCM and what LTCM was telling its investors. First, in its two best years the fund earned more than 50% before fees, so that a return of 25% does not sound implausible. Second, LTCM wrote to its investors to tell them that it expected that the fund would experience a loss in excess of 20% only in one year out of 50—here, instead, one year out of 100 can be expected to have a loss of 70%.[3] Let's assume that whether the fund had the high return or not depended on the flip of a weighted coin, so that the risk of the fund would have been completely diversifiable for its investors. With this hypothetical example, the expected return on the fund would then have been 24.05%. Such an expected return would have been a great expected return for a hedge fund or for any investment as this would have been the expected return for bearing diversifiable risk, given my assumptions. Had the managers had the

opportunity to keep repeating this investment, 99 years out of 100 they would have earned 25% before fees and would have been stars.

In my hypothetical example, when the managers of the funds (the partners) made their choice, they knew the true distribution of possible outcomes of the fund. Hence, they knew the distribution of gains and losses perfectly—the risk managers should have earned a gold medal for their work. Suppose, however, that the bad outcome occurs. In this case, the fund would have made headlines for having lost $3.5 billion. Some would argue that the risk of the fund was poorly managed. However, by construction, risk management could not have been improved in this case. The managers knew exactly the risks they faced—and they decided to take them. Therefore, there is no sense in which risk management failed. Ex post, the only argument one could make is that the managers took risks they should not have, but that is not a risk management issue as long as the risks were properly understood. Rather, it is an issue of assessing the costs of losses versus the gains from making large profits.

Deciding whether to take a known risk is not a decision for risk managers. The decision depends on the risk appetite of an institution. However, defining the risk appetite is a decision for the board and top management. That decision is at the heart of the firm's strategy and of how it creates value for its shareholders. A decision to take a known risk may turn out poorly even though, at the time it was made, the expectation was that taking the risk increased shareholder wealth and hence was in the best interest of the shareholders.

In the case of LTCM, it could be argued that the cost of losing $3.5 billion for the investors in LTCM was just that—namely, there were no additional costs beyond the direct monetary loss. For most firms, however, large losses have deadweight costs. These deadweight costs are at the foundation of financial theories of why risk management creates shareholder wealth.[4] If a financial institution makes a large loss, the institution may, for instance, have to scale back its investments because of being financially constrained, have to sell assets in unfavorable markets, lose valuable employees who become concerned for their bonuses, lose customers who are concerned about

---

[3] See Lowenstein, p. 63.

[4] See René M. Stulz, Risk Management and Derivatives, Thompson Publishing, 2003.

the institution being distracted or not having sufficient resources to help them, and face increased scrutiny from regulators. In any institution, the board and top management have to take into account these deadweight costs of large losses when making decisions that create the risk of large losses.

Risk managers can estimate whether an action is profitable for the firm given its risk appetite because they can evaluate how much capital is required to support that action.[5] However, an action that is not profitable for a given level of risk appetite can become profitable if the firm's risk appetite increases because less capital is required to support that action. Whether taking large risks is worthwhile for an institution ultimately depends on the firm's strategy. Risk managers do not set strategy. Suppose that a firm sets its risk appetite by choosing a target credit rating. Such an approach is well-established. Once the credit rating is chosen, there are multiple combinations of risk and capital that achieve the target rating. For a given choice of leverage, the firm does not have much choice in choosing its risk level if it wants to achieve its target rating. However, faced with good opportunities, the firm could choose to have less leverage so that it can bear more risk or it could choose to depart from its credit rating target.

LTCM provides a good example of such tradeoffs. In the fall of 1997, the managers of LTCM concluded that they did not want to manage a business earning 17% for its investors, which is what their investors had earned for the year. Instead, they wanted the higher returns achieved in 1995 and 1996. At the end of 1997, LTCM had capital of $7.4 billion but decided to return roughly 36% of the capital to its investors. With less capital, LTCM could still execute the same trades. However, now, to implement them it had to borrow more and hence had to increase its leverage. By increasing its leverage, it could boost the return to its shareholders if things went well at the expense of making more losses if things went poorly. Was increasing leverage a poor risk management decision? In my example, the partners of LTCM knew the risks and the rewards from

doing so. In the well-worn language of financial economics, increasing leverage was a positive NPV decision when it was made, but obviously ex post it was a costly decision as it meant that when assets fell in value, the fund's equity fell in value faster than it would have with less leverage.

There has been much discussion of incentives of top management during the credit crisis, with various commentators arguing that part of the problem has been that top management had incentives to take too much risk. This may well be so, but before reaching conclusions one should not forget that financial economists have argued for decades that incentives of management become better aligned with those of shareholders when management has a large stake in the firm's equity. Top management owned hundreds of millions of dollars of equity in Bear Stearns and Lehman at the peak of the valuation of these firms. Similarly, the partners of LTCM collectively had almost $2 billion invested in the fund at the beginning of 1998. If such equity stakes do not incentivize managers to make the right decisions for their shareholders, what would?

In summary, risk management does not prevent losses. With good risk management, large losses can occur when those making the risk-taking decisions conclude that taking large, well-understood risks creates value for their organization.

A TYPOLOGY OF RISK MANAGEMENT FAILURES

How can risk management go wrong? The way we describe the role of risk management suggests important ways in which risk management can go wrong. We started by saying that the first step in risk management is to measure risk. Let's assume, for now, that the right risk measure is used given the situation of the firm. This measure could be VaR or could be some other measure. Two types of mistakes can be made in measuring risk. Known risks can be mismeasured and some risks can be ignored, either because they are unknown or viewed as not material. Once risks are measured, they have to be communicated to the firm's leadership. A failure in communicating risk to management is a risk management failure as well. After management decides what kind of risks to take, risk management has to make sure that the firm takes these risks. In other words, risk managers must then manage the

---

[5] My article with Brian Nocco, Enterprise Risk Management: Theory and Practice, Journal of Applied Corporate Finance, Fall 2006, v18(8), 8–20, describes the key principles of enterprise risk management, issues that arise in its implementation, and the role of capital allocation.

firm's risk, a task that may involve identifying appropriate risk mitigating actions, hedging some risks, and rejecting some proposed trades or projects. Lastly, a firm's risk managers may fail to use appropriate risk metrics.

With this perspective, there are six types of risk management failures:

1. Mismeasurement of known risks.
2. Failure to take risks into account.
3. Failure in communicating the risks to top management.
4. Failure in monitoring risks.
5. Failure in managing risks.
6. Failure to use appropriate risk metrics.

We discuss each one of these types of failures in turn.

Mismeasurement of Known Risks

In the LTCM example, risk mismeasurement could have taken a number of different forms. When measuring risk, risk managers attempt to understand the distribution of possible returns. With our simple example, the distribution was a binomial distribution—the outcome of the toss of a weighted coin. Risk managers could make a mistake in assessing the probability of a large loss or the size of the large loss if it occurs. However, in addition, they could use the wrong distribution altogether. Further, financial institutions have many positions, each position has a return from a given distribution, but these returns are related across positions, and that relation may be assessed incorrectly—a simple way to put this is that correlations may be mismeasured. Correlations are extremely important in risk management because the benefit of diversification falls as correlations increase.

With the LTCM example, it could be that the true probability of a loss of 70% was higher than 1%, say 25%. In this case, the expected return of LTCM in my hypothetical example would have been a paltry 1.25%. At the time, investors could have earned a higher expected return by investing in T-bills. In this case, the risk management mistake—assessing the probability of the bad outcome at 1% instead of 25%—would have had disastrous consequences for the fund because it would have led it to make trades that would have destroyed value.

Suppose that LTCM had made the mistake we just discussed. How would we know? We cannot identify such a mistake ex post because LTCM lost 70% only once. Having lost 70%, it could have done so whether the true probability of that loss was 1% or 25%. In fact, under the hypothetical conditions of my example, we can learn nothing from the fact that LTCM lost 70% about whether it made a risk management mistake of that type. It could have been that, as of January 1998, the probability of such a loss was infinitesimal or extremely large. It could have been a one in one hundred year event or a one in four year event for the portfolio of trades they had assembled.

Another risk management mistake would occur if the distribution is not binomial, but a different distribution altogether. For instance, it could be, keeping with the hypothetical example, that there was a 1% chance of a 70% loss and additionally a 9% chance of a 100% loss. In this case, the expected return would have been 12.8%, but there would also have been a nontrivial probability of a total wipeout.

When an institution has many positions or projects, the risk of the institution depends on how the risks of the different positions or projects are related. If the correlation between the positions or projects is high, it is more likely that all the firm's activities perform poorly at the same time, which leads to a higher probability of a large loss. These correlations can be difficult to assess and they change over time, at times abruptly. A partner of LTCM described the problem they faced in August and September as being one where correlations that they thought were extremely small suddenly became large. With this perspective, correlations would have been misestimated. It is well-known in finance that correlations increase in periods of crisis. Failure to assess correlations correctly would lead to the wrong assessment of the risk of a portfolio or of a firm. The problem of mismeasurement of correlations is more subtle, however, if correlations are random and sometimes turn out to be unexpectedly large ex post. In this case, risk managers could not be expected to know what correlations will be, but their assessment of the risk of a portfolio or of the firm would depend on their estimates of the distribution of the correlations. In this case, it would be possible for realized correlations to be different from their expected value and yet there would be no risk management failure.

When risks are known, statistical techniques are generally brought to bear to estimate the distribution of risks.

Such approaches work well when there is a lot of data and when it is reasonable to believe that the returns will have the same statistical distribution in the future as they had in the past. For instance, suppose that a risk manager wants to estimate the volatility of the return of a liquid stock. She will have hundreds of data points to fit a model. In most cases, the risk manager will have a model of the volatility of the stock that will perform reasonably well.

Historical data is at times of little use, because a known risk has not manifested itself in the past. For instance, with the subprime crisis, there was no historical data of a downturn in the real estate market during which a large amount of securitized subprime mortgages was outstanding. In such a situation, risk measurement cannot be done by simply using historical data since there is a risk of a decrease in real estate prices that has not manifested itself in a comparable historical period. With such a case, statistical risk measurement reaches its limits and risk management goes from science to art. Proper understanding of risks involves an assessment of the likelihood of a decrease in real estate prices and of the economic impact of such a decrease on the prices of securities. Such probability assessments have a significant element of subjectivity. Different risk managers can reach very different conclusions.

There is a fundamental problem with the performance of risk measurement when assessments become subjective. Suppose that all parties agree that an established statistical model works well. There is then little room for people to disagree. However, subjective forecasts are easily questioned. Why would a risk manager have a better understanding of the probability of a drop in real estate prices than experts in real estate? If experts in real estate conclude that a sharp drop in prices is unlikely, why would an organization then listen to a risk manager who wants to spend a large amount of money on a stress test to figure out the impact of such a large drop? As risk management moves away from established quantitative models, it becomes easily embroiled in intra-firm politics. At that point, the outcome for the firm depends much more on the firm's risk appetite and on its culture than on its risk management models.

Mismeasurement Due to Ignored Risks

Ignored risks can take three different forms that have different implications for a firm. First, a firm may ignore a risk even though that risk is known. Second, somebody in the firm knows about a risk, but that risk is not captured by the risk models. Third, there is a realization of a truly unknown risk. We examine these possibilities in turn.

Ignored Known Risks

Consider again the case of LTCM. LTCM could have failed to take into account a risk that, if realized, would have led to a large loss. A good example of this possibility is as follows. Before Russia defaulted on its domestic debt in August 1998, many hedge funds took positions where they bought high-yielding Russian debt, hedged the debt against default risk, and finally hedged the debt against exchange rate risk. It was easy to believe that the resulting position had no risk. However, to hedge the currency risk, the funds had to sell rubles forward against dollars. The banks willing to stand on the other side of those trades were often Russian banks. When Russia defaulted, it imposed a moratorium on these banks and many collapsed, as a result, the hedge funds ended up having exchange rate risk because their counterparties did not honor the hedges. Had they taken into account counterparty risk properly, they would have understood that their positions had substantial risk in the event of an adverse shock to the Russian banking system.

I have no reason to believe that LTCM behaved like these other hedge funds. Further, LTCM's Russian exposures were relatively small. However, suppose that it made losses because it did not correctly account for the risks of counterparties. Ex post, just knowing that LTCM lost 70% would not be sufficient to conclude that LTCM missed the counterparty risk in its risk models because it could have made a similar loss without missing that risk. Consequently, to assess whether LTCM made mistakes, one would have to look at the information it had when it made decisions, whether that information was flawed, and whether its use of that information was wrong.

Mistakes in Information Collection

The consequences of a risk management mistake are the same whether the risk was ignored because nobody in the firm knew about it or because somebody knew about it but it did not enter the relevant risk models. One of the benefits of implementing properly firm-wide risk management is that all risks are accounted for. If some risks are not accounted for when risk is measured for a firm, the risks left out are not adequately monitored and they can become large because organizations have a tendency to expand unmonitored risks. For instance, consider a trader whose risks are only partly monitored. Typically, traders have a compensation formula that involves an option payoff—they receive a significant share of the profits they generate, but they do not have to give back the losses. If only some of the risks of a trader are monitored, he can increase his expected compensation by increasing the risks that are not monitored, without suffering any of the consequences.

It is common practice in risk management to divide risks into market, credit, and operational risks. This distinction is partly artificial and driven by regulatory considerations. Typically, firms have trading books that are marked to market, while the credit book uses accrual accounting. However, this division of risk may be implemented in a way that ignores large chunks of risk. For instance, a firm has funding risks. Funding may become more expensive and/or less available precisely when the firm experiences bad market outcomes. To wit, an important factor contributing to the failure of Bear Stearns was the limitations it faced in accessing the repo market in its last week. Similarly, while Basle II rules have a rather restricted view of operational risk, business risks are often of critical importance and have to be carefully assessed as part of the evaluation of a firm's risk even though they are not part of the regulatory definition of operational risk. These risks may be highly correlated with both credit and market risks for financial institutions. For instance, for many banks, the loss of income from securitizations was the realization of a business risk that was correlated with a market risk, namely the loss in value of securities issued through securitizations, and with credit risks, namely the inability to use securitization to lay off the risks associated with loans.

Accounting for all the risks in risk measurement is a difficult and costly task. However, not performing that task for an organization means that the firm's top executives are managing the company with blinders on—they see only part of the big picture they have to understand to manage effectively. There are well-known examples of incomplete risk aggregation leading to large losses from risks that were not accounted for. Perhaps one of the best examples is the one of a bank that no longer exists, the Union Bank of Switzerland. In the second half of the 1990s, the bank was putting together risk management systems that

would aggregate risks within its trading operations. One group of traders that focused on equity derivatives was extremely successful. However, this group of traders was using different computers from the rest of the bank, so that integrating their systems into the bank's systems would have required them to change computers. Eventually, the bank decided, at the top level, that it was more important to let the traders make money than disrupt what they were doing through changes of computers. Soon thereafter, this group of traders lost a large amount of money for the bank. The loss was partly responsible for the bank having to merge with another Swiss bank.[6]

Problems of aggregation were important at various stages of the subprime crisis as well. In particular, the management of UBS sent a report to its shareholders explaining why the bank had such large write-downs. In this report, UBS explains that "Efforts were made to capture Subprime holdings by mid-February 2007, however, materials did not effectively include the Super Senior and Negative Basis positions." (p. 39). It is interesting to note that, according to the report, the Super Senior positions were not included because they were hedged and hence were assigned no risk by the risk models—an evaluation which was consistent with past data used by many risk managers.

Unknown Risks

Most unknown risks do not create risk management problems. To see this, we can go back to the statistical model of risk measurement for a stock. Suppose that a risk manager models the return of a stock using the normal distribution and that he has no reason to believe that future returns will come from a different distribution than the one that held in the past. With this model, each period, the stock return will be random. It will come from a known distribution. The risk manager does not need to know why the return of the stock in one period is 10% and in another period is –15%. He has captured the relevant risk characteristics of the stock through his estimation of the statistical distribution of the returns of the stock. With his work, he knows that the volatility is 20% and that there is a 5%

---

[6] See Dirk Schütz, La Chute de l'UBS: Les raisons du déclin de l'Union de Banques Suisses, Bilan, 1998.

chance of a loss of say 30% or higher over a period. He does not need to be in a position to explain what events are associated with various losses.

Other unknown risks may not matter simply because they have a trivially low probability. There is some probability that a building will be hit by an asteroid. That risk does not affect any management decisions. Ignoring that risk has no implications for risk management.

The unknown risks that represent risk management failures are risks that, had the firm's managers known about them, their actions would have been different. Risk managers have to look out for unknown risks, but once everything is said and done, some risks will remain unknown. Because of this, they have to conclude that they do not capture all risks in their models and, therefore, some capital has to be made available to cope with unknown risks.

Communication Failures

Risk management is not an activity undertaken by risk managers for risk managers. Rather, it is an activity undertaken to enable the firm to maximize shareholder value by taking optimal decisions across the firm. In particular, the firm has to choose the level of risk it is exposed to and has to make sure that risks taken throughout the organization are valuable for shareholders. Therefore, risk management has to provide timely information to the board and top management that enables them to make decisions concerning the firm's risk and to factor the firm's risk in their decisions. In order for the board and the top management to understand the risk situation of the firm, this situation has to be communicated to them in a way that they can understand properly. If a firm has perfect risk systems, but the board and the top management cannot understand the output of these systems because the risk manager cannot communicate this output properly, the firm's systems may do more harm than good by inspiring false confidence in the performance of risk management. Even worse, information can arrive to top management too late or too distorted by intermediaries.

Communication failures seem to have played a role in the most recent crisis. For example, the UBS report to its shareholders explains that "A number of attempts were made to present Subprime or housing related exposures. The reports did not, however, communicate an effective

message for a number of reasons, in particular because the reports were overly complex, presented outdated data or were not made available to the right audience." (p. 39). An industry commission that drew lessons from the crisis emphasized communication issues as well. It concluded that "risk monitoring and management reduces to the basis of getting the right information, at the right time, to the right people, such that those people can make the most informed judgments possible."[7] Finally, a report from the Senior Supervisors Group, which includes top regulators from the U.S., England, and Germany as well as other countries, also emphasized communication issues, stating for instance that "In some cases, hierarchical structures tended to serve as filters when information was sent up the management chain, leading to delays or distortions in sharing important data with senior management."[8]

Failures in Monitoring and Managing Risks

Risk management is responsible for making sure that the firm takes the risks that it wants to take and not others. As a result, risk managers must constantly monitor the risks the firm is taking. Further, they have to hedge and mitigate known risks to meet the objectives of top management.

We have already discussed the problem that a firm may be taking risks that it does not know about. When we discussed that problem, we focused on it as an inventory issue. However, there is a different perspective on this problem which is particularly relevant in financial firms. For the typical non-financial firm, risks often change slowly. Not so for financial firms. For a financial firm, risks can change sharply even if the firm does not take new positions. The problem arises from the fact that financial firms have many derivatives positions and positions with embedded derivatives. Over time, these positions have become more complex.

---

[7] "Containing systemic risk: The road to reform," The Report of the CRMPG III, August 6, 2008.

[8] Senior Supervisors Group, "Observations on Risk Management Practices during the Recent Market Turbulence," March 6, 2008, p. 9.

The risk properties of portfolios of derivatives can change very rapidly with no trading whatsoever. This is because complex derivatives often have exposures to risk factors that are extremely sensitive to market conditions. Strikingly, it is perfectly possible with some products to see changes such that, during the same day, a security could have an exposure to interest rates so that it gains substantially if interest rates increase and later in the day have an exposure such that it loses substantially if interest rates increase. For such a product, hedges adjusted daily could end up creating large losses because the hedge that is optimal at the start of the day could end up aggravating the risk exposure at the end of the day.

One of the most obvious demonstrations of how risk exposures can change is the pricing of subprime derivatives. The ABX indices have been the most readily available data on the value of securities issued against subprime mortgage collateral. The indices are equally-weighted averages of credit-default swaps on securitization tranches. New indices were created every six months, reflecting new securitizations. Initially, the AAA indices, which represent the pricing of credit default swaps on AAA-rated tranches of securitizations, exhibited almost no variation, so that reasonable assessments of the risk of the AAA-rated tranches of securitizations using historical data would have been that they had little risk. Yet, suddenly, the value of these securities fell off a cliff as shown on Figure 10-1. Holders of AAA-rated tranches of subprime securities made sudden large losses if they chose to use the ABX indices as proxies for the value of their holdings.

When the risk characteristics of securities can change very rapidly, it is challenging for risk monitors to capture these changes and for risk managers to adjust hedges appropriately. This challenge is especially great when risk characteristics can change dramatically for small changes

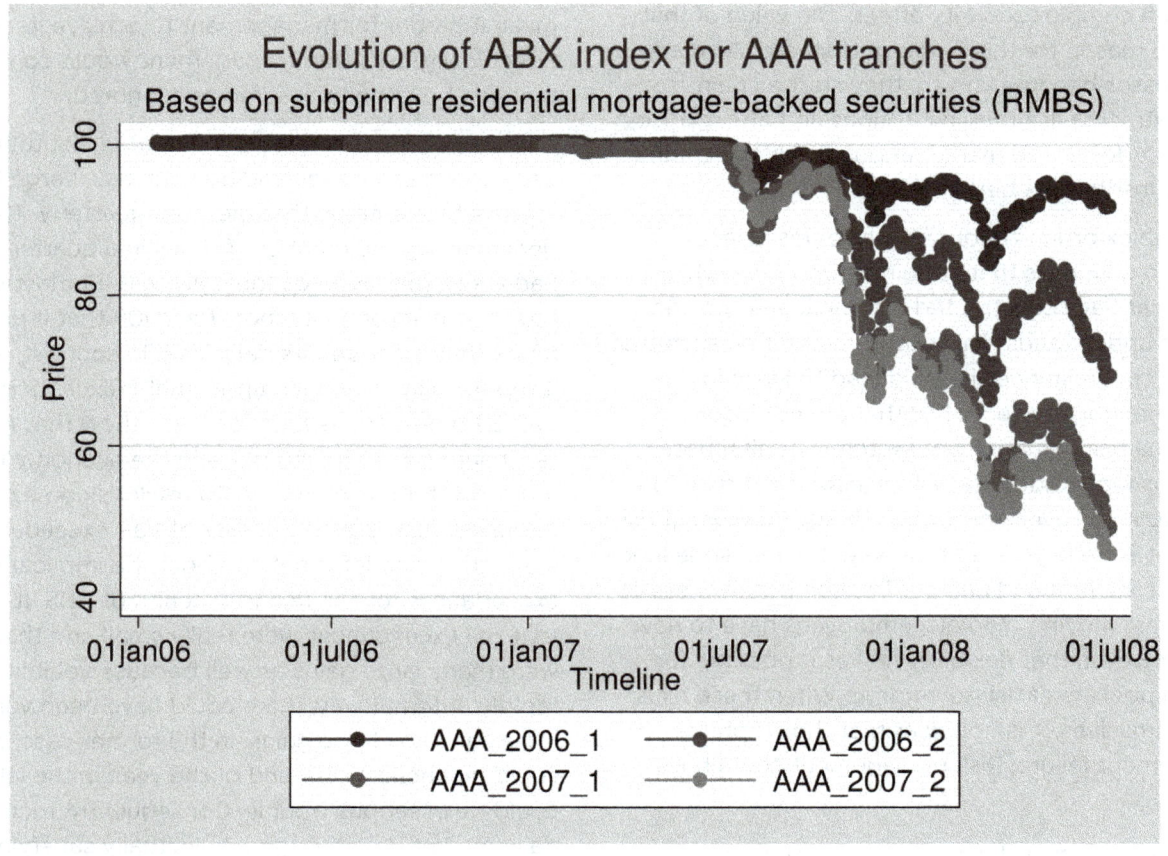

FIGURE 10-1

in the determinants of security prices. As a result, risk managers may fail to adequately measure risks or hedge risks simply because risk characteristics of securities may change too quickly to enable these managers to assess these characteristics properly or to put on correct hedges.

An important component of risk management is to identify possible solutions that can be implemented quickly if a firm has to reduce its risk over a short period of time. Contingency hedging plans are therefore critical. Lack of such plans could make it impossible for a firm to cope with unexpected difficulties. At the same time, however, when liquidity dries up in the markets, many risk-mitigating options that can be used easily outside of crisis periods can no longer be used.

Paradoxically, the introduction of mark-to-market accounting makes it even harder for risk managers to estimate risk and put on adequate hedges.[9] In many ways, mark-to-market has introduced the Heisenberg Principle into financial markets: For large organizations, observing the value of a complex security affects the value of that security. The reason for this is straightforward: As mark-to-market losses become known, they start a chain reaction of adjustments at other institutions and affect prices of possible trades as the market understands the capital positions of institutions better.

In large complex organizations, it is also possible for individuals to take risks that remain hidden for a while. A trader might have constructed a complicated position that only he understands. This position might be such that under some circumstances it could lead to large losses. The position might use securities that are not incorporated in the risk management systems. At all times, organizations face tradeoffs. Risk management might be structured to know everything at all times. However, if risk management were organized that way, it would stifle innovation within the firm and hamper the competitiveness of the firm. In fast moving markets, employees have to have flexibility. However, that flexibility makes it possible for unobserved pockets of risk to emerge. When these risks manifest themselves, it is not clear that they represent a risk management failure. Risk management could have

made sure that these risks were not taken, but ex ante shareholders would have been worse off. Besides eliminating flexibility within the firm, risk monitoring is costly so that at some point, tighter risk monitoring is not efficient.

The effectiveness of risk monitoring and control depends crucially on an institution's culture and incentives. If risk is everybody's business in an organization, it is harder for pockets of risk to be left unobserved. If employees' compensation is affected by how they take risks, they will take risk more judiciously. The best risk models in a firm with poor culture and poor incentives will be much less effective than in a firm where the incentives of employees are better aligned with the risk-taking objectives of the firm.

Risk Measures and Risk Management Failures

So far, we have taken the risk metrics as given. We now show that focusing on metrics that are too narrow may make it harder for management to achieve its objectives. Specifically, risks that management would consider important can be left unmeasured and ignored.

A widely used risk measure in financial institutions is a daily VaR measure for trading activities. Large banks usually disclose data on that measure quarterly. They will generally say the number of times in a quarter the P&L had a loss that exceeds the daily VaR. For instance, UBS reported in its annual report for 2006 that it never had a loss that exceeded its daily VaR. In contrast, in 2007, it reported in its annual report that it exceeded its daily VaR 29 times. The results for 2007 show that fundamental changes were taking place in the economy that made it difficult for risk managers to track risk on a daily basis. However, such a large number of VaR exceedances provide little or no information about the implication of these exceedances for the financial health of UBS. It could be that the exceedances were really small and that there were many large gains as well because volatility increased rapidly. Alternatively, there could have been very large losses and few large gains. In the former case, the firm could be ahead at the end of the year. In the latter case, it could be in serious trouble. Consequently, focusing on the daily market VaR, though intellectually satisfying for risk managers because the most up-to-date quantitative techniques can be brought to bear on the problem, can only be one part of risk management and not the one that top

---

[9] For a discussion of some of the issues concerning mark-to-market accounting that accounts for possible feedback effects, see Guillaume Plantin, Haresh Sapra, and Hyun Song Shin, Marking to Market: Panacea or Pandora's Box?, 2008, Journal of Accounting Research 46, 435–460.

management should focus on. Top management has to focus on the longer-run implications of risk.

Short-run VaR measures can be low and the firm can appear to do an extremely good job with them, yet it can fail. I have not seen monthly VaR estimates from LTCM. However, from March 1994 to December 1997, LTCM had only eight months with losses and the worst monthly loss was 2.9%. In contrast, it had 37 months with gains.[10] As a result, one would have a hard time using historical monthly returns to conclude that its risk management was flawed. Consider a firm that has a one-day VaR of $100 million for its trading book at the 1% probability level. This means that the firm has a one percent chance of losing more than $100 million. If this firm exceeded its VaR once over 100 trading days and lost $10 billion, all existing statistical tests of risk management performance based on VaR exceedances would indicate that the firm has excellent risk management. VaR does not capture catastrophic losses that have a small probability of occurring.

Daily VaR measures assume that assets can be sold quickly or hedged, so that a firm can limit its losses essentially within a day. However, both in 1998 and over the last year, we have seen that markets can become suddenly less liquid, so that daily VaR measures lose their meaning. If a firm sits on a portfolio that cannot be traded, a daily VaR measure is not a measure of the risk of the portfolio because the firm is stuck with the portfolio for a much longer period of time.

To assess risk, firms have to look at longer horizons and have to take a comprehensive view of their risks. A one-year horizon is widely used in enterprise risk management for measures of firm-wide risk. Generally, financial institutions that focus on firm-wide risk at a one-year horizon aim for credit ratings that imply an extremely small probability of default. Such approaches are useful in assessing a firm's risk, in estimating the optimal amount of capital for a firm, and estimating the profitability of projects and lines of business through a careful evaluation of the cost of the capital required to bear their risks. However, at the same time, such approaches are not sufficient.

A high target credit rating effectively means that the firm tries to avoid default in all but the most extreme circumstances. If a firm aims for an AA credit rating, it effectively chooses a probability of default which is such that it would default less frequently than one year out of a thousand. Crises occur much more often than that, so that the firm has to have a strategy which allows it to survive crises. Further, the probability of a crisis is difficult to estimate precisely, so that even if the estimate of the probability is very small, estimation error could be such that the true, unknown, probability is much higher. Consequently, the firm has to focus on crisis events in its risk measurement and management.

Existing risk models are generally not designed to capture risks associated with crises and to help firms manage them. These models use historical data and are most precise for short horizons—like days. With short horizons, crises are extremely rare events. Yet, when we consider years, crises are not extremely rare events. Months and years are a better horizon to evaluate risk when it comes to crises for at least two reasons. First, as evidenced since the summer of 2007, crises involve a dramatic withdrawal of liquidity from the markets. The withdrawal of liquidity means that firms are stuck with positions that they never expected to hold for a long time because price pressure costs involved in trading out of these positions are extremely high. Positions whose risk was evaluated over one day because the firm thought it could trade out of these positions suddenly became positions that had to be held for weeks or months. Second, during crisis periods, firms will make multiple losses that exceed their daily VaRs and these losses can be large enough to substantially weaken them. As a result, risk measures have to contemplate the distribution of large losses over time rather than over one day.

Crises involve complicated interactions across risks and across institutions. Statistical risk models typically take returns to be exogenous to the firm and ignore risk concentrations across institutions. Such an approach is appropriate for many institutions, but it is insufficient for institutions that, for whatever reasons, are important in specific markets and whose actions affect security prices. For instance, it is well-known that LTCM had extremely large positions in the index option market where it was short. During the crisis, it had little ability to change these positions because it was so large in that market. Further, a large institution can be exposed to predatory trading—i.e., of trades made by others designed to exploit its problems. An example of predatory trading is a situation where traders from other institutions benefit from pushing a

---

[10] These monthly returns are for Long-Term Capital Management, L.P. (B), prepared by André Perold, Harvard Business School, 1999.

price down if they can because it might force a fire sale. Typical risk management models would not account for this. They would not account for the fact that if the institution is large in a market, its losses can lead to more losses. As a firm makes a loss, it may drag down prices for other institutions and make funding more costly across institutions, which can have feedback effects for the institution. Ignoring these potential feedback effects may lead to an understatement of the risk of positions in the event of a crisis.

There is little hope for statistical risk models relying on historical data to capture such complicated situations. Rather, a firm has to augment these models with scenario analysis that investigates how crises can unfold and how they will affect it under various assumptions about how it reacts to the crisis. With such scenarios in hand, top management can then understand how crises can endanger the franchise of their institution and how to manage risks before they occur so that they can survive them. Such a scenario approach requires economic and financial analysis. It cannot be done by risk management departments populated by physicists and mathematicians. Such an approach also cannot be successful unless top management believes that the scenarios considered represent legitimate threats to the institution and that the institution has to protect itself against such threats.

SUMMARY

Risk management has made considerable progress since 1998. The difficulties of the last year have convinced many observers that somehow there are deep flaws in risk management and that the problems of the last year are partly explained by risk management failures. In this paper, I show that one ought to distinguish carefully between risk-taking decisions that unexpectedly lead to losses and risk management assessments of risk. There are many ways that risk management failures can occur, but not every loss reflects a risk management failure. However, risk management practice can be improved by taking into account the lessons from financial crises.

These crises happen often enough that they have to be carefully modeled and institutions have to focus on scenario analyses that assess the implications of crises for their financial health and survival. Such scenario analyses cannot be built from quantitative models using past data, but instead they must use economic analysis to evaluate the impact of the withdrawal of liquidity and the feedback effects that are common in financial crises. To successfully impact firm strategy, such analyses have to be deeply rooted in a firm's culture and in the strategic thinking of top management.

GARP Code of Conduct

11

Excerpt is GARP Code of Conduct *by GARP.*

Learning Objectives

After completing this reading, FRM Candidates should be able to:

- Describe the responsibility of each GARP member with respect to professional integrity, ethical conduct, conflicts of interest, confidentiality of information and adherence to generally accepted practices in risk management.
- Describe the potential consequences of violating the GARP Code of Conduct.

INTRODUCTION

The GARP Code of Conduct ("Code") sets forth principles of professional conduct for Global Association of Risk Professional ("GARP") Financial Risk Management program (FRM®) certification and other GARP certification and diploma holders and candidates, GARP's Board of Trustees, its Regional Directors, GARP Committee Members and GARP's staff (hereinafter collectively referred to as "GARP Members") in support of the advancement of the financial risk management profession. These principles promote the highest levels of ethical conduct and disclosure and provide direction and support for both the individual practitioner and the risk management profession.

The pursuit of high ethical standards goes beyond following the letter of applicable rules and regulations and behaving in accordance with the intentions of those laws and regulations, it is about pursuing a universal ethical culture.

All individuals, firms and associations have an ethical character. Some of the biggest risks faced by firms today do not involve legal or compliance violations but rest on decisions involving ethical considerations and the application of appropriate standards of conduct to business decision making.

There is no single prescriptive ethical standard that can be globally applied. We can only expect that GARP Members will continuously consider ethical issues and adjust their conduct accordingly as they engage in their daily activities.

This document makes references to professional standards and generally accepted risk management practices. Risk practitioners should understand these as concepts that reflect an evolving shared body of professional standards and practices. In considering the issues this raises ethical behavior must weigh the circumstances and the culture of the applicable global community in which the practitioner resides.

CODE OF CONDUCT

The Code is comprised of the following Principles, Professional Standards and Rules of Conduct which GARP Members agree to uphold and implement.

Principles

Professional Integrity and Ethical Conduct

GARP Members shall act with honesty, integrity, and competence to fulfill the risk professional's responsibilities and to uphold the reputation of the risk management profession. GARP Members must avoid disguised contrivances in assessments, measurements and processes that are intended to provide business advantage at the expense of honesty and truthfulness.

Conflicts of Interest

GARP Members have a responsibility to promote the interests of all relevant constituencies and will not knowingly perform risk management services directly or indirectly involving an actual or potential conflict of interest unless full disclosure has been provided to all affected parties of any actual or apparent conflict of interest. Where conflicts are unavoidable GARP Members commit to their full disclosure and management

Confidentiality

GARP Members will take all reasonable precautionary measures to prevent intentional and unintentional disclosure of confidential information.

Professional Standards

Fundamental Responsibilities

- GARP Members must endeavor, and encourage others, to operate at the highest level of professional skill.

- GARP Members should always continue to perfect their expertise.

- GARP Members have a personal ethical responsibility and cannot out-source or delegate that responsibility to others.

Best Practices

- GARP Members will promote and adhere to applicable 'best practice standards', and will ensure that risk management activities performed under his/her direct supervision or management satisfies these applicable standards.

- GARP Members recognize that risk management does not exist in a vacuum.

- GARP Members commit to considering the wider impact of their assessments and actions on their colleagues and the wider community and environment in which they work.

Communication and Disclosure

GARP Members issuing any communications on behalf of their firm will ensure that the communications are clear, appropriate to the circumstances and their intended audience, and satisfy applicable standards of conduct.

RULES OF CONDUCT

Professional Integrity and Ethical Conduct

GARP Members

1. Shall act professionally, ethically and with integrity in all dealings with employers, existing or potential clients, the public, and other practitioners in the financial services industry.

2. Shall exercise reasonable judgment in the provision of risk services while maintaining independence of thought and direction. GARP Members must not offer, solicit, or accept any gift, benefit, compensation, or consideration that could be reasonably expected to compromise their own or another's independence and objectivity.

3. Must take reasonable precautions to ensure that the Member's services are not used for improper, fraudulent or illegal purposes.

4. Shall not knowingly misrepresent details relating to analysis, recommendations, actions, or other professional activities.

5. Shall not engage in any professional conduct involving dishonesty or deception or engage in any act that reflects negatively on their integrity, character, trustworthiness, or professional ability or on the risk management profession.

6. Shall not engage in any conduct or commit any act that compromises the integrity of the GARP, the (Financial Risk Manager) FRM® designation or the integrity or validity of the examinations leading to the award of the right to use the FRM designation or any other credentials that may be offered by GARP.

7. Shall endeavor to be mindful of cultural differences regarding ethical behavior and customs, and to avoid any actions that are, or may have the appearance of being unethical according to local customs. If there appears to be a conflict or overlap of standards, the GARP member should always seek to apply the higher standard.

Conflict of Interest

GARP Members Shall

1. Act fairly in all situations and must fully disclose any actual or potential conflict to all affected parties.

2. Make full and fair disclosure of all matters that could reasonably be expected to impair their independence and objectivity or interfere with their respective duties to their employer, clients, and prospective clients.

Confidentiality

GARP Members

1. Shall not make use of confidential information for inappropriate purposes and unless having received prior consent shall maintain the confidentiality of their work, their employer or client.

2. Must not use confidential information to benefit personally.

Fundamental Responsibilities

GARP Members Shall

1. Comply with all applicable laws, rules, and regulations (including this Code) governing the GARP Members' professional activities and shall not knowingly participate or assist in any violation of such laws, rules, or regulations.

2. Have ethical responsibilities and cannot out-source or delegate those responsibilities to others.

3. Understand the needs and complexity of their employer or client, and should provide appropriate and suitable risk management services and advice.

4. Be diligent about not overstating the accuracy or certainty of results or conclusions.

5. Clearly disclose the relevant limits of their specific knowledge and expertise concerning risk assessment, industry practices and applicable laws and regulations.

General Accepted Practices

GARP Members Shall

1. Execute all services with diligence and perform all work in a manner that is independent from interested parties. GARP Members should collect, analyze and distribute risk information with the highest level of professional objectivity.

2. Shall be familiar with current generally accepted risk management practices and shall clearly indicate any departure from their use.

3. Shall ensure that communications include factual data and do not contain false information.

4. Shall make a distinction between fact and opinion in the presentation of analysis and recommendations.

APPLICABILITY AND ENFORCEMENT

Every GARP Member should know and abide by this Code. Local laws and regulations may also impose obligations on GARP Members. Where local requirements conflict with the Code, such requirements will have precedence.

Violation(s) of this Code may result in, among other things, the temporary suspension or permanent removal of the GARP Member from GARP's Membership roles, and may also include temporarily or permanently removing from the violator the right to use or refer to having earned the FRM designation or any other GARP granted designation, following a formal determination that such a violation has occurred.

Sample Exam Questions—Foundations of Risk Management

1. The efficient frontier is defined by the set of portfolios that, for each volatility level, maximizes the expected return. According to the capital asset pricing model (CAPM), which of the following statements are correct with respect to the efficient frontier?

   i. The capital market line is the straight line connecting the risk-free asset with the zero beta minimum variance portfolio.

   ii. The capital market line always has a positive slope and its steepness depends on the market risk premium and the volatility of the market portfolio.

   iii. The complete efficient frontier without a risk-free asset can be obtained by combining the minimum variance portfolio and the market portfolio.

   iv. The efficient frontier allows different individuals to have different portfolios of risky assets based upon their own risk aversion and forecast for asset returns.

   v. The efficient frontier assumes no transaction costs, no taxes, a common investment horizon for all investors, and that the return distribution has no skewness.

   A. ii, iii and v

   B. i, ii and iii

   C. i, iv and v

   D. ii, iii and iv

2. A high net worth investor is monitoring the performance of an index tracking fund in which she has invested. The performance figures of the fund and the benchmark portfolio are summarized in the table below:

Year	Benchmark Return	Fund Return
2005	9.00%	1.00%
2006	7.00%	3.00%
2007	7.00%	5.00%
2008	5.00%	4.00%
2009	2.00%	1.50%

What is the tracking error of the fund over this period?

   A. 0.09%

   B. 1.10%

   C. 3.05%

   D. 4.09%

3. Roy Thomson, a global investment risk manager of FBN Bank, is assessing Markets A and B using a two-factor model:

$$R_i = \acute{\alpha}_i + \beta_{i,1} F_1 + \beta_{i,2} F_2 + \acute{\epsilon}_i,$$

where R_i is the return for asset 'i'; β is the factor sensitivity; and 'F' is the factor. The random error $\acute{\epsilon}_i$ has a mean of zero and is uncorrelated with the factors and with the random error of the other asset returns. In order to determine the covariance between Markets A and B, Thomson developed the following factor covariance matrix for global assets:

Factor Covariance Matrix for Global Assets		
	Global Equity Factor	**Global Bond Factor**
Global Equity Factor	0.3424	0.0122
Global Bond Factor	0.0122	0.0079

Suppose the factor sensitivities to the global equity factor are 0.70 for market A and 0.85 for Market B, and the factor sensitivities to the global bond factors are 0.30 for market A and 0.55 for Market B. The covariance between Market A and Market B is closest to:

A. 0.213

B. 0.461

C. 0.205

D. 0.453

4. To benefit shareholders, a firm with a debt overhang that has exhausted its sources of internal financing will:

A. raise additional equity capital.

B. issue more debt.

C. replace riskier projects with lower risk projects.

D. replace low risk projects with higher risk projects and/or not take on additional projects.

5. There are both *absolute risk* (measured without reference to a benchmark) and *relative risk* (measured against a benchmark) measures of market risk. Which of the following is an *absolute* measure of market risk?

A. Tracking error

B. Volatility of total returns

C. Correlation with a benchmark portfolio

D. Deviations from a benchmark index

6. Which of the following is not considered a failure of risk management?

A. Incorrect measurement of known risks

B. Failure in communicating risk issues to top management

C. Failure to minimize losses on credit portfolios

D. Failure to use appropriate risk metrics

7. Which of the following is a common attribute of the collapse at both Metallgesellschaft and Long-Term Capital Management (LTCM)?

   A. Cash flow problems caused by large mark to market losses

   B. High leverage

   C. Fraud

   D. There are no similarities between the causes of the collapse at Metallgesellschaft and LTCM.

8. For a firm that has both debt and equity outstanding, the existence of which of the following typically would not be a sufficient incentive to implement costly risk management practices by itself?

   A. Graduated corporate tax rates

   B. Bankruptcy costs

   C. Financial distress costs

   D. Cash flow volatility

9. According to the Capital Asset Pricing Model (CAPM), over a single time period, investors seek to maximize their:

   A. wealth and are concerned about the tails of return distributions.

   B. wealth and are not concerned about the tails of return distributions.

   C. expected utility and are concerned about the tails of return distributions.

   D. expected utility and are not concerned about the tails of return distributions.

10. Gregory is analyzing the historical performance of two commodity funds tracking the Reuters/Jefferies-CRB® Index (CRB) as benchmark. He collated the data on the monthly returns and decided to use the information ratio (IR) to assess which fund achieved higher returns more efficiently and presented his findings.

	Fund I	Fund II	Benchmark returns
Average monthly returns	1.488%	1.468%	1.415%
Average excess return	0.073%	0.053%	0.000%
Standard deviation of returns	0.294%	0.237%	0.238%
Tracking error	0.344%	0.341%	0.000%

What is the information ratio for each fund and what conclusion can be drawn?

   A. IR for Fund I = 0.212, IR for Fund II = 0.155; Fund II performed better as it has a lower IR.

   B. IR for Fund I = 0.212, IR for Fund II = 0.155; Fund I performed better as it has a higher IR.

   C. IR for Fund I = 0.248, IR for Fund II = 0.224; Fund I performed better as it has a higher IR.

   D. IR for Fund I = 0.248, IR for Fund II = 0.224; Fund II performed better as it has a lower IR.

Sample Exam Questions Answers & Explanations— Foundations of Risk Management

1. **Answer: A**

   Explanation: Within modern portfolio theory (MPT), the efficient frontier is a combination of assets that has the best possible expected level of return for its level of risk. The efficient frontier is the positively sloped portion of the opportunity set that offers the highest expected return for a given risk level. The efficient frontier is at the top of the feasible set of portfolio combinations. ii, iii and v are correct statements.

   The capital market line connects the risk-free asset and the market portfolio. The efficient frontier does allow investors to have different risk aversions, but assumes that they all have the same forecast for asset returns.

2. **Answer: C**

   Explanation: Relative risk measures risk relative to a benchmark index, and measures it in terms of tracking error or deviation from the index.

   We need to calculate the standard deviation (square root of the variance) of the series:

   $$\{0.08,\ 0.04,\ 0.02,\ 0.01,\ 0.005\}.$$

   Perform the calculation by computing the difference of each data point from the mean, square the result of each, take the average of those values, and then take the square root. This is equal to 3.04%.

3. **Answer: A**

   Explanation:

   Covariance is a measure of how the variables move together.

   $\text{Cov}(A, B) = \beta_{A,1}\,\beta_{B,1}\,\sigma_{F1}^2 + \beta_{A,2}\,\beta_{B,2}\,\sigma_{F2}^2 + (\beta_{A,1}\,\beta_{B,2} + \beta_{A,2}\,\beta_{B,1})\,\text{Cov}(F_1, F_2)$

   $= (0.70)(0.85)(0.3424) + (0.30)(0.55)(0.0079) + [(0.70)(0.55) + (0.30)(0.85)](0.0122)$

   $= 0.213$

4. **Answer: D**

   Explanation: When a firm has a large amount of debt, it can make investment decisions that benefit shareholders but negatively affect the firm's total value. This is debt overhang. Shareholders that face debt overhang would prefer high risk projects since a loss tends not to affect them, but they would benefit from the upside, or large profit.

5. **Answer: B**

   Explanation: Market risk is the risk of losses from movements in market prices. Absolute risk measures these changes in terms of the volatility of total returns. Tracking error is a relative measure of market risk defined as the deviation from a benchmark index. Correlation refers to a benchmark. Deviation from the benchmark index is a consideration in measuring *relative* risk.

6. **Answer: C**

   Explanation: If the firm's management chooses to ignore the advice of risk management and follow a risky strategy, this is not necessarily a failure of risk management.

7. **Answer: A**

   Explanation: Metallgesellschaft and Long Term Capital Management (LTCM) dealt in the derivatives market in huge quantities and both experienced a cash flow crisis due to the change in economic conditions. This led to huge mark-to-market losses and margin calls.

8. **Answer: D**

   Explanation: Shareholders are diversified; they have no reason to care about diversifiable risks. Therefore, they are not willing to discount expected cash flow at a lower rate if the firm makes cash flow less risky by eliminating diversifiable risk. The tax argument for risk management is straight forward: If it moves a dollar away from a possible outcome in which the taxpayer is subject to a high tax rate and shifts it to a possible outcome where the taxpayer incurs a low tax rate, a firm or investor reduces the present value of taxes to be paid. The tax rationale for risk management applies whenever income is taxed at different levels. Both bankruptcy and financial distress costs reduce firm value and cannot be eliminated by homemade risk management and for which the risk management irrelevance theorem does not hold.

9. **Answer: D**

   Explanation: CAPM assumes investors seek to maximize the expected utility of their wealth at the end of the period, and that when choosing their portfolios, investors only consider the first two moments of return distribution: the expected return and the variance. Hence, investors are not concerned with the tails of the return distribution.

10. **Answer: B**

    Explanation: The information ratio may be calculated by either a comparison of the residual return to residual risk, or the excess return to tracking error. The higher the IR, the better 'informed' the manager is at picking assets to invest in. Since neither residual return nor risk is given, only the latter is an option.

    $IR = E(R_p - R_b)/\text{Tracking Error}$

    For Fund I: IR = 0.00073/0.00344 = 0.212; For Fund II: IR = 0.00053/0.00341 = 0.155

Index